PROJECTIVE TECHNIQUES
FOR ADOLESCENTS AND CHILDREN

Albert I. Rabin, Ph.D, is professor emeritus of psychology at Michigan State University and adjunct professor in the School of Human Behavior at U.S. International University. He is founder and former director of the psychological clinic at Michigan State University. Dr. Rabin also served as lecturer at Boston University Graduate School and professor at the City University of New York. In addition, he was visiting professor at the Hebrew and Bar-Ilan Universities (Israel) and at the University of Aarhus (Denmark).

Dr. Rabin has published more than 150 articles and reviews in different professional and scientific journals and has contributed chapters to more than 30 edited books. In addition, he has authored, co-authored, edited, or co-edited 13 books in the areas of assessment, personality development, and kibbutz child rearing. Some of the more recent volumes include *Assessment with Projective Techniques* (1981), *Twenty Years Later: Kibbutz Children Grown Up* (1982), *Patterns of Supplementary Parenting* (1982), and *Personality and the Prediction of Behavior* (1984).

From 1965 to 1973, Dr. Rabin served on the Board of Consulting Editors of the *Journal of Consulting and Clinical Psychology*, and since 1969 has served as consulting editor of the *Journal of Personality Assessment*. He received the Distinguished Contribution Award of the Society for Personality Assessment and the Distinguished Faculty Award of Michigan State University.

Projective Techniques for Adolescents and Children

A. I. Rabin, Ph.D.

Editor

SPRINGER PUBLISHING COMPANY
New York

Springer Publishing Company, Inc.
536 Broadway
New York, New York 10012

86 87 88 89 90 / 5 4 3 2 1

Library of Congress Cataloging-in-Publication Data
Main entry under title:

Projective techniques for adolescents and children.

    Bibliography: p.
    Includes indexes.
    1. Projective techniques for youth. 2. Projective
techniques for children. I. Rabin, Albert I.
BF698.7.P76 1986   155.4'18   85-27897
ISBN 0-8261-4920-0

Printed in the United States of America

Contents

Contributors

Hagit Benziman
Assistant Professor of Psychology
Hebrew University
Jerusalem

Melvin Berg
Staff Psychologist
Colmery-O'Neil Veterans
    Administration Medical Center
Topeka, Kansas

Richard H. Dana
Professor of Psychology
University of Arkansas

Stuart L. Doneson
Adjunct Instructor
Department of Psychiatry
Michigan State University

Emanuel F. Hammer
Clinical Professor
Postdoctoral Psychotherapy and
    Psychoanalysis Program
Institute for Advanced Psychological
    Studies
Adelphi University

Henry G. Hansburg
Private Practice
Visiting Professor
California School of Professional
    Psychology
Los Angeles

Mary R. Haworth
Clinical Associate Professor
Department of Psychiatry
Georgetown University

Wayne H. Holtzman
President
Hogg Foundation for Mental
    Health
University of Texas

Max L. Hutt
Independent Practice
Formerly Professor of Psychology
    and Director
Clinical Training Program
University of Michigan

Martha A. Karson
Adjunct Clinical Professor
Department of Psychology
Michigan State University

Vita Krall
Chief Child Psychologist and
    Director of Training in Clinical
    Psychology
Michael Reese Hospital and Medical
    Center
Chicago

Janice Levine
Associate Consultant
Clinical Training Program
Department of Psychology
University of Wisconsin

Richard Levine
Clinical Assistant Professor
Department of Psychiatry
University of Wisconsin

Nina Rausch de Traubenberg
Professor of Clinical Psychology
Rene Descartes University
Paris

Edwin E. Wagner
Professor of Psychology
University of Akron

Edythe Wiggs
Lecturer
George Mason University

Zoli Zlotogorski
Assistant Professor
Hebrew University
Jerusalem

Preface

During the heyday of the projective techniques, more than a quarter of a century ago, their use extended to the personality assessment of children and adolescents as well as adults. The standard methods and specially devised techniques for younger clients have been widely used in a variety of clinical settings; over the years, however, there have been changes in the field. Some of the methods have not stood the test of time, while accumulated data and research with others have fortified their position in the standard battery of instruments employed in diagnosis and personality assessment.

The present volume updates the field and deals with the use of projectives with adolescents as well as children. Several of the chapter authors have originated the techniques to which their respective chapters are devoted. Furthermore, the contributors to this volume do not represent a unitary theoretical orientation. The book's eclecticism ranges from modern dynamic theory and object relations to rather "tough-minded" psychometric empiricism.

The book is subdivided into six sections. Following the brief introductory chapter that constitutes the first part, there are four chapters devoted to pictorial and thematic methods, which comprise Part II. The third part, also containing four chapters, deals with inkblot techniques for children and adolescents. Part IV contains two chapters on verbal methods, while Part V includes four chapters that are not readily categorized under a particular rubric, describing various graphic and play techniques as well as some other, innovative ones. Finally, Part VI presents two chapters in which clinical applications of the previously described methods are illustrated.

Overall, this is a rather practical book in which the student and practitioner are introduced to a wide array of assessment methods that may be useful in cross-sectional evaluations and in longitudinal studies of developmental change and progress following intervention. A number of chapters stress, and illustrate, the continuity between assessment and intervention. Clinical psychologists, school psychologists, and others engaged in the assessment and diagnosis of children and adolescents will find this a useful handbook for their purposes. Researchers in human personality and behavior also will find it helpful to consult this volume in their quest for an in-depth exploration and understanding of the human psyche.

A. I. Rabin, Ph.D.

Acknowledgments

The editor wishes to acknowledge, with thanks, the expertise, cooperativeness, and patience of the contributors to this volume. Thanks are also due to the various authors and publishers who graciously gave us permission to quote from their works; they are acknowledged individually in the text itself.

I am also indebted to Dr. Mary R. Haworth for her generous help in the early stages of the book. Wendy Sabbath's helpful comments and numerous services in the preparation of the final manuscript are also, hereby, gratefully acknowledged.

I
Introduction

1
Concerning Projective Techniques

A. I. Rabin

Two major trends may be noted in the century-old psychological testing movement. These are broad patterns that are different from each other along a number of dimensions. The references here are to the so-called objective testing tradition and to the projective movement. A fundamental difference between the two lies in the tasks of the examinee. The "objective" test or the structured test limits rather drastically the range of the responses of the person being tested. Respondents to personality questionnaires, for example, may be confined to the circling of yes or no responses or to placing marks along three-, five-, or seven-point (or more) scales representing a range or continuum between extremes.

In the case of projective techniques, respondents are much more free; hence these methods are sometimes also described as "response free." Stimulus demands are not as structured as in the case of questionnaires or intelligence tests. Responses expected are not yes or no. Freedom to respond is considerable; it may vary from the almost limitless possibilities when responding to an unstructured inkblot ("What might this be?") to the relatively more circumscribed range of responses possible in a sentence-completion test, where the respondent completes a sentence stem ("My father and I . . ."). In the latter instance there is still a great number of possible responses, but it is clear that they have to be relevant to the relationship between the respondent and his father. Arithmetic or information questions—such as "Who is the President of the United States?"—that are included in intelligence tests are clearly more limiting and restrictive in the response demands.

A somewhat different perspective on the two testing trends is presented by McClelland in his essay on "motive dispositions" (1980). In referring to his obtained Thematic Apperception Test (TAT) material, he states:

> The fact is that we were obtaining a sample of a person's behavior or thought in a standardized situation. I favor referring to these thought samples as operant because in Skinner's sense, it is not possible to identify the exact stimulus that elicits them. More generally speaking they are responses that the subject generates spontaneously. Not the stimulus nor the response or the instructional set is strictly controlled by the experiments. (p. 12)

The author goes on to describe the different structured methods as follows:

> By way of contrast, respondent measures often specify the stimulus, the response and instructional set. . . . Personality test subjects are presented with a specific stimulus (e.g., "I work like a slave"); they are limited to agreeing or disagreeing with it to a greater or lesser degree; and they are set to give an overall evaluation of this behavior in a specified area. (p. 12)

McClelland feels that the term *operant* is broader than the term *projective* because it stresses the spontaneity involved in responding without retaining the theoretical aspect relating to projection to be discussed in the following pages.

REGARDING THE TERM *PROJECTION*

The term *projective techniques* has its origins in the well-known Freudian term *projection*. This term generally is understood and used in its narrower and more limited sense—that of one of the defense mechanisms. As a defense mechanism, projection is defined as "the powers by which specific impulses, wishes, aspects of the self, or internal objects are imagined to be located in some object external to oneself" (Rycroft, 1968, p. 125-b). However, in psychoanalytic theory, projection also is employed in a much broader and encompassing fashion. To quote from *Totem and Taboo* (Freud, 1919):

> But projection is not especially created for the purpose of defense, it also comes into being where there are no conflicts. The projection of inner perception to the outside is a primitive mechanism which, for instance, also influences our sense perceptions, so that it normally has the greatest share in shaping our outer world. Under conditions that have not yet been sufficiently determined even inner perceptions of ideational and emotional pro-

cesses are projected outwardly, like sense perceptions, and are used to shape the outer world. (pp. 107–108)

Thus, the process of projection is an aspect of our normal, everyday mode of thinking and perceiving; it is the general tendency to *externalize* in our responding to the environment and interpreting it. It is in this broader sense that the term *projection* is being employed in the context of projective technique testing and personality evaluation. A recent experimental study of children's emotional attributions is supportive of this theoretical stance (Brody & Carter, 1982).

Other theoretical orientations may view the response process in projective techniques somewhat differently (Holzberg, 1968), and Fulkerson (1965) stresses decision theory without evoking complex dynamics or unconscious processes.

PROJECTIVE TECHNIQUES

Projective techniques are assessment methods that are based on the principle of projection, broadly conceived. In a sense, people are projecting all the time; when perceiving and responding to the environment they are expressing their personal needs, motivations, and unique characteristics. When a person faces a particular stimulus or situation she responds in her own terms to the evocation, that is, in her own idiomatic or particular manner. It is from this personal mode that the inferences concerning the personality processes are made. Frank (1948), who was among the first to utilize the term *projective methods*, states that "the essential feature of a projective technique is that it evokes from the subject what is in various ways expressive of his private world and personality process" (p. 47). He further points out that the personality referred to is "a dynamic process, the conformal activity of the individual who is engaged in creating, maintaining and defending that private world" (p. 8).

A more comprehensive definition of projective techniques, which takes account of the complexity of the methods in evoking personality expressions as well as the nature of the stimulus and the process of interpretation, is offered by Garner Lindzey in his well-known monograph, *Projective Techniques and Cross-Cultural Research* (1961). He states that

a projective technique is an instrument that is considered especially sensitive to covert or unconscious aspects of behavior, it permits or encourages a wide variety of subject responses, is highly multidimensional, and it evokes unusually rich and profuse response data with a minimum of subject awareness concerning the purpose of the test. . . . The stimulus material presented by the projective test is ambiguous, interpreters of the test depend on holistic analysis, the test evokes fantasy responses, and there are no correct or incorrect responses to the test. (p. 45)

Several of the points stressed in this broad and comprehensive definition reiterate those mentioned earlier, while others will be discussed in the more complete elaboration of the meaning of projective methods. We emphasize the fact that projective techniques tap, or are sensitive to, "unconscious aspects of behavior." Questionnaires or other self-report instruments do not tell us much about unconscious needs and motives that shape a person's behavior. "It is astonishing how often this simple truism has been ignored by psychometrically-oriented personality theorists wedded to their questionnaires" (McClelland, 1981, p. 92). One may add that even many clinical psychologists could be readily subjected to the same criticism. Furthermore, McClelland notes that "the fact is that American personality psychologists have never really accepted the notion of the unconscious" (p. 93).

We mentioned earlier that projectives are operant instruments that allow the subject–client to express a rich and wide variety of response material while being unaware of the relationship between his productions and the interpretations that might be imposed upon them or inferences drawn from them. This, of course, can be a great advantage. On the one hand it offers a reduction or possible elimination of defensiveness; but, on the other hand, there may be an increase of anxiety when the person is faced with a relatively ambiguous and unstructured situation. The anxiety of the respondent may be somewhat mitigated, however, by the knowledge that there are no right or wrong responses.

Projective tests are not simply tests of perception. The task of the examinee is not to merely describe the inkblot, that is, to say what is there; rather, it is to give information as to what this might be. The subject–client is invited to speculate, imagine, examine possibilities, and make decisions regarding the response to be made. Similarly, in the case of a TAT or CAT card, a mere description is not what is called for. What is expected is a *story* about the figures, with a beginning and an end and including the thinking and feeling of the persons represented in the photograph. Here, too, the test must evoke fantasy responses. Thus, the resulting response to the projective test material is an amalgam of the perceptual and the imaginative. There is a mutual impact between the two. On the one hand, the reality of the stimulus governs the outer limits of the fantasy; on the other hand, the response of what is perceived, what is "there," is enriched by the fantasy, by the provisional display of primary process thinking.

Finally, Lindzey states that interpreters of projective techniques "depend on holistic analysis." The reference here is to the notion that the final interpretation arrived at is of a total, integrated, and dynamic personality picture. Using the concept of "bandwidth," borrowed from information theory, it may be stated that most projective methods are "wide-band" methods. Bandwidth refers to the scope of information that the test is designed to obtain (Levine, 1981). Projective techniques, especially the major ones such as the Rorschach and TAT, offer a great deal of information upon which the "total personality" description is based (e.g., Blatt, 1975). They are clearly different from such specific methods as achievement tests or mechanical aptitude tests, which are narrow-band methods designed to obtain information on rather limited, circumscribed areas of competence.

It will be noted in the several chapters of this volume that projective methods vary in their bandwidth. As indicated above, the scope and range of information of the TAT and Rorschach are quite broad and extensive; similarly, the scope and breadth of personality interpretation is considerable. On the other hand, some of the methods are more focused and may be viewed as more narrow in their range. The very names "Separation Anxiety Test" or "Picture Frustration Test," for example, indicate more focused and perhaps more circumscribed missions.

It may be remarked, parenthetically, that the narrow-band methods are not ordinarily expanded to deal with many personality parameters. On the other hand, demands upon wide-band methods may be more circumscribed in specific clinical or research situations, and only a few, selected personality dimensions or rather specific predictions may be elicited. A perfect example may be the employment of the TAT for the study of the achievement motive. Existing methods may be adapted or newly devised methods invented for the purpose of study and diagnosis of specific variables or problems (Rabin, 1968).

PROJECTIVE METHODS WITH ADOLESCENTS AND CHILDREN

The original studies with the major projective methods (Rorschach, TAT) involved primarily adult subjects; however, very soon the methods were adapted to and employed with children and adolescents. Age norms for the older methods became available, and a variety of techniques especially devised for different age groups published, as will be seen from the descriptions in the present volume.

Generally, greater flexibility in the test administration procedures with children is recommended. Although on the surface a projective technique (without right and wrong answers) may be less threatening to the child than the more structured instruments, anxiety about the performance is not eliminated. The uncertainty about the situation, involving decision-making regarding alternate possibilities of responses, may be particularly disturbing to some children. The importance of creating an appropriately secure and trusting atmosphere before the "games" are introduced cannot be overstressed.

As to interpretation, the backdrop of published (and private) norms is most important in evaluating the level of maturity and development. The relevant specific details appear in the several chapters that follow.

PAST, PRESENT, AND FUTURE OF PSYCHOLOGICAL ASSESSMENT

Psychological assessment of personality, or psychodiagnosis, has been a major concern of psychologists for several decades. Clinical psychologists, as well as personologists, have devised methods and researched and applied them in order to attain a credible and reliable description of the unique human personality. For a time, the skills and knowledge of assessment were the primary contributions of clinical psychologists in the field of mental health. Assessment was, and remains, the unique contribution of psychologists among the professionals in the field. However, during the past two or three decades there has been a drop in psychologists' involvement with assessment; a variety of other interests have captured their time and attention: individual and group psychotherapy, behavior modification, prevention, and a wide range of community-oriented activities. Perhaps the involvement of many clinical psychologists in private practice has made the often long and arduous task of formal assessment much less cost-effective than other activities.

An additional aspect that is not to be overlooked is the frequent disappointment and disaffection with the adequacy, reliability, and validity of the several assessment methods. The psychologist, reared in the atmosphere of respect for science and for the psychometric purity of his instruments, often finds them wanting. However, despite the reservations, he employs these instruments as a check upon, and as support for, his frequently subjective clinical judgment. Korchin and Schuldberg (1981) have listed a number of reasons for the decline of psychological testing: the availability of new roles for clinical psychologists, the opposition of some ideologies to testing, the overselling of psychodiagnosis, reduced emphasis on the part of younger faculty in universities, the fact that assessment is hard work, concern of civil libertarians about possible abuse, and the expense involved. Nevertheless, the evidence supports the continuing vitality of assessment in clinical settings (Korchin & Schuldberg, 1981; Lubin et al., 1984; Piotrowski & Keller, 1978; Weiner, 1983).

As part of the general trend in the employment of assessment methods, a decline in the use of projective techniques has occurred as well. Here one may see a notable discrepancy between the attitudes of clinicians in the field and the attitudes of the clinical faculty in graduate training programs. Assessment in hospitals and clinics (Lubin, Larsen, & Matarazzo, 1984; Piotrowski & Keller, 1978) is very much alive, including the use of projective techniques. As a matter of fact, as of 1982, five projective methods (Rorschach, TAT, Sentence Completion, House-Tree-Person Test, and the Draw-a-Person Test) were among the top 10 most frequently used tests (Lubin et al., 1984). Yet views of clinical teaching faculty in a sizable sample of APA-approved clinical training programs are at variance with this reality (Piotrowski & Keller, 1984). Many of them are critical of projective techniques and feel that there has been a rise in interest and application of nonprojective methods. More than half of the respondents to the Piotrowski and Keller questionnaire, however, have pointed out the importance of the Rorschach, TAT, and Sentence Completion method in the training of clinical psychologists. Nearly half of the respondents also reported at least one course in projectives is required in their training programs.

It is interesting to relay the following quotation, obtained by Piotrowski and Keller (1984) from one of the respondents to their questionnaire:

> Much of the projective test misuse has been due to inadequate basic training in the universities. People who do not really know testing, nor who have had extensive clinical experience are often assigned to teach these courses. They cannot extract the rich clinical information contained in a test battery, cannot do blind analyses, and as a result cannot teach or lead students adequately in this area. Consequently, the validity of these tests has been underestimated since they are often used improperly or superficially without the extensive and intensive training and experience needed for their appropriate application. (pp. 453–454)

Perhaps the state of affairs just described reflects the "two cultures" in psychology (Kimble, 1984); that is, there may be a conflict between the "tough-minded" and "tender-minded," the scientific and clinical, which remains unresolved at the university level.

There has been a lot of "gloom and doom" and pronouncements of bankruptcy for the assessment enterprise in general and for projective techniques in particular. However, the present state of affairs and recent developments in the field of human services and clinical psychology contradict the dire predictions regarding the future of personality assessment and psychodiagnosis. The new domains of personality disorders (borderline personality, narcissistic personality), psychological health, coping and stress, and other recent concerns in the field increase the demands for psychological assessment and evaluation (Dana, 1984; Lerner, 1984; Millon, 1984). Furthermore, as Weiner (1983) points out with respect to the new professional areas such as pediatric psychology, geropsychology, and neuropsychology:

> A common feature of these newly emerging areas of professional emphasis in clinical psychology is that providing necessary interventions is often a less challenging and prestigious activity than *being able to determine what kind of intervention is indicated*—which is a question of differential diagnosis frequently referable to some form of personality or behavioral assessment. (p. 456)

Thus, the future of personality description, assessment, and diagnosis with the aid of our present testing armamentarium appears much brighter than predicted. However, continuous attention to the improvement of our tools, via careful research on these methods, will assure their continuing viability and utility in the field of applied psychology.

REFERENCES

Blatt, S. J. (1975). The validity of projective techniques and their research and clinical contribution. *Journal of Personality Assessment, 39*(4), 327-343.

Brody, L. R., & Carter, A. S. (1982). Children's emotional attributions to self versus others: An explanation of an assumption underlying projective techniques. *Journal of Consulting and Clinical Psychology, 50,* 665-671.

Dana, R. H. (1984). Personality assessment: Practice and teaching for the next decade. *Journal of Personality Assessment, 48,* 46-57.

Frank, L. (1948). *Projective methods.* Springfield, IL: Charles C. Thomas.

Freud, S. (1919). *Totem and taboo.* New York: Moffatt, Yard & Co.

Fulkerson, S. C. (1965). Some implications of the new cognitive theory for projective techniques. *Journal of Consulting Psychology, 29,* 191-197.

Holzberg, J. D. (1968). Psychological theory and projective techniques. In A. I. Rabin (Ed.), *Projective techniques in personality assessment* (pp. 18-63). New York: Springer.

Kimble, G. (1984). Psychology's two cultures. *American Psychologist, 39,* 833-839.

Korchin, S. J., & Schuldberg, D. (1981). The future of clinical assessment. *American Psychologist, 36,* 1147-1158.

Lerner, P. (1984). Projective techniques and personality assessment. In N. S.

Erdler & J. M. Hunt (Eds), *Personality and the behavior disorders* (2nd ed.) (Vol. 1) (pp. 283-309). New York: John Wiley.

Levine, D. (1981). Why and when to test: The social context of psychological testing. In A. I. Rabin (Ed.), *Assessment with projective techniques* (pp. 553-580). New York: Springer.

Lindzey, G. (1961). *Projective techniques and cross-cultural research.* New York: Appleton-Century-Crofts.

Lubin, B., Larsen, R. M., & Matarazzo, I. D. (1984). Patterns of psychological test usage in the United States: 1932-1982. *American Psychologist, 39,* 451-453.

McClelland, D. C. (1980). Motive dispositions: The merits of operant and respondent measures. *Review of Personality and Social Psychology, 1,* 10-41.

McClelland, D. C. (1981). Is personality consistent? In A. I. Rabin, J. Aronoff, A. M. Barclay, & R. A. Zucker (Eds.), *Further explorations in personality* (pp. 87-113). New York: John Wiley.

Millon, T. (1984). On the rennaissance of personality assessment and personality theory. *Journal of Personality Assessment, 48,* 450-466.

Piotrowski, C., & Keller, J. W. (1978). Psychological test usage in southeastern outpatient mental health facilities in 1975. *Professional Psychology, 9*(1), 63-67.

Piotrowski, C., & Keller, J. W. (1984). Psychodiagnostic testing in APA approved clinical psychology programs. *Professional Psychology: Research and Practice, 15*(3), 450-456.

Rabin, A. I. (1968). Adapting and devising projective methods for special purposes. In A. I. Rabin (Ed.), *Projective techniques in personality assessment* (pp. 611-626). New York: Springer.

Rycroft, C. (1968). *A critical dictionary of psychoanalysis.* New York: Basic Books.

Weiner, I. B. (1983). The future of psychodiagnosis revisited. *Journal of Personality Assessment, 48*(5), 451-461.

II
Picture
Techniques

2
Thematic Apperception Test Used with Adolescents*

Richard H. Dana

Henry Murray (1938) developed the Thematic Apperception Test (TAT) in the 1930s as a vehicle for application of his personality theory to college students. Through the TAT, past experience and present needs could be mobilized by ambiguous pictures for which the viewer was instructed to "tell a story." Projection was the mechanism that fused fantasy with these ambiguous stimuli to enable these stories to be used for a description of psychological organization. The TAT differed from the Rorschach by using picture stimuli that were relatively more recognizable to assessees, who, as a result, could exercise more voluntary control over the story content by excluding, omitting, or minimizing story characteristics in a manner not feasible with the Rorschach.

For many years the TAT was used clinically in a manner similar to the Rorschach, but without benefit of a consensually acceptable analogous scoring system. Story content was compared with subjective norms based upon the experience of the assessor, or with fragmentary norms from small, unrepresentative samples reported in the literature. Inferences were made from content using one or more of several generalized formats for clinical interpretation (e.g., Henry, 1956; Stein, 1955; Tomkins, 1947).

*Acknowledgment is made to Dr. Virginia R. Krauft, Director of School Services and Clinical Projects and to Joan H. Gibson, Psychological Examiner, for the TAT stories used herein.

While there are several scoring systems that have competed for research attention, these systems were never incorporated into routine TAT practice. In fact, Vane (1981), in a review of the major standardization attempts by Arnold, Dana, Eron, McClelland/Atkinson, and Murstein, concluded that these objective approaches were inadequate to the task. In her survey of 91 accredited doctoral programs, Vane found that dynamic, psychoanalytic, and need-press approaches were taught by 44, 25, and 20 programs, respectively, although several of these approaches often were taught in the same program. Projective techniques were not taught in 18 programs, while 11 programs omitted the TAT altogether from their instruction in projective techniques.

Lubin, Larsen, and Matarazzo (1984) report survey results for 30 psychological instruments from 1948, 1959, 1969, and 1982 that document a recent reduction in TAT usage to a ranking of 5. This ranking does not necessarily indicate that the TAT is less frequently used but only that other competing tests (Wechsler Adult Intelligence Scale, Minnesota Multiphasic Personality Inventory, Bender-Gestalt, and Rorschach) have now become more popular. The TAT has been first or second in frequency of recommendations for students by clinical psychology programs (Piotrowski & Keller, 1984; Wade, Baker, Morton, & Baker, 1978). However, neither Klopfer and Taulbee (1976) nor Dana (1972) found any cohesive body of knowledge about the technique or its applications, and Lanyon (1984) devoted only three annual review paragraphs under "other projectives" to the TAT.

The TAT is a projective technique for adults, but it may be used with children and adolescents. Approximately 10 percent of the over 2,000 TAT references appearing in the most recent *Mental Measurements Yearbook* (Buros, 1978) pertain to children and adolescents. However, over time other sets of cards for children, especially the Children's Apperception Test (CAT and CAT-H), have been deemed preferable for younger children (Myer, Rosenkrantz, & Holmes, 1972) while the revised Michigan Picture Test (Hutt, 1980) may be used for children and adolescents aged from 7½ years through 15 years. A recent set of cards for children (McArthur & Roberts, 1982) provides norms for 13 content and three validity scales. For adolescents, the Symonds Picture Story Test (Symonds, 1948) and a newcomer for males (Cooper, 1981) are available. This proliferation of special TAT sets may be dated from Sherwood's (1957) review of stimulus characteristics and now includes cards for black children (Dlepu & Kimbrough, 1982; Triplett & Brunson, 1982) and Native American children (Henry, 1947).

As a result of competing sets of pictures, a lack of acceptable objective scores, and recent decline of TAT research productivity, any singular usefulness of the Murray TAT cards for children and adolescents has diminished. In fact, Vukovich (1983) found that practicing school psychologists, for example, used the TAT less than 5 percent of the time. This chapter will attempt to refurbish the TAT image by incorporating research and protocol examples into a format for interpretation of child and adolescent records.

DESCRIPTION OF MATERIALS

The Murray TAT contains 31 pictures, 11 of which are for persons over 14 years of age (numbers 1, 2, 4, 5, 10, 11, 13, 14, 15, 19, 20). There are seven "parallel" pictures for adults and children from 7 to 14 years (numbers 3, 6, 7, 8, 9, 17, 18) using BM (boy/male) card designations for males and GF (girl/female) card designations for females. These paired cards do not constitute equivalent stimuli. There are two additional adult cards (12M, 12F), one card for children of either sex (12BG), one for male children (13B), one card for female children (13G), and a blank card (16) for all assessees. Murray intended his pictures to be a comprehensive array of life settings, although no systematic card selection procedures were used. Cards 1 through 10 compose an "everyday" series with relatively less ambiguity, and cards 11 through 20 are designed to be more "unusual, dramatic, and bizarre." Table 2.1 presents the card descriptions.

ADMINISTRATION

Because the TAT is not a psychometric instrument, any simple administration is complicated by the verbal instructions for storytelling; by recording procedures other than verbatim, handwritten stories by the assessor; and by the adequacy of protocol data as evidenced by the number of cards used, the length of stories, and card rejections.

Murray (1943) used directions emphasizing that the TAT was a test of imagination, one form of intelligence. These directions may have been effective with Harvard undergraduates, but other persons often are intimidated by them. Typical contemporary directions request a story that includes seven parts: description of the card, what the character(s) are doing, what may have happened in the past, what might occur in the future, feelings and thoughts of the characters, and an outcome. Nonstandard TAT directions will affect stories, especially whenever the request is made for particular kinds of content. Enhanced directions may produce stress effects in the stories suggestive of upset, tension, and dysphoria.

Assessors typically write down the stories verbatim. Any deviation from

TABLE 2.1 TAT Cards: Description and Stimulus Demand

Card No.	Description	Stimulus Demand
1	A young boy is contemplating a violin, which rests on a table in front of him.	Achievement; family dynamics
2	Country scene: In the foreground is a young woman with books in her hand; in the background a man is working in the fields and an older woman is looking on.	Independence/dependence; family relationships
3BM	On the floor against a couch is the huddled form of a boy with his head bowed on his right arm. Beside him on the floor is a revolver.	Central value
3GF	A young woman is standing with downcast head, her face covered with her right hand. Her left arm is stretched forward against a wooden door.	Central value
4	A woman is clutching the shoulders of a man whose face and body are averted as if he were trying to pull away from her.	Balance of power in heterosexual relationship
5	A middle-aged woman is standing on the threshold of a half-opened door looking into a room.	Mother–adolescent child relationship
6BM	A short, elderly woman stands with her back turned to a tall young man. The latter is looking downward with a perplexed expression.	Mother–son relationship
6GF	A young woman sitting on the edge of a sofa looks back over her shoulder at an older man with a pipe in his mouth who seems to be addressing her.	Father–daughter relationship
7BM	A gray-haired man is looking at a younger man who is sullenly staring into space.	Father–son relationship
7GF	An older woman is sitting on a sofa close beside a girl, speaking or reading to her. The girl, who holds a doll in her lap, is looking away.	Mother–daughter relationship
8BM	An adolescent boy looks straight out of the picture. The barrel of a rifle is visible at one side, and in the background is the dim scene of a surgical operation, like a reverie image.	Father–son relationship

TABLE 2.1 (*Continued*)

Card No.	Description	Stimulus Demand
8GF	A young woman sits with her chin in her hand looking off into space.	Fantasy
9BM	Four men in overalls are lying on the grass taking it easy.	Social attitudes
9GF	A young woman with a magazine and a purse in her hand looks from behind a tree at another young woman in party dress running along a beach.	Sibling relationship
10	A young woman leans her head against a man's shoulder.	Quality of heterosexual relationship: intimacy
11	A road skirts a deep chasm between high cliffs. On the road in the distance are obscure figures. Protruding from the rocky wall on one side is the long head and neck of a dragon.	Symbolization of current problem
12M	A young man is lying on a couch with his eyes closed. Leaning over him is the gaunt form of an elderly man, his hand stretched out above the face of the reclining figure.	Attitudes toward receiving help
12F	In this portrait of a young woman, a weird old woman with a shawl over her head is grimacing in the background.	Mother–daughter relationship
12BG	A rowboat is drawn up on the bank of a woodland stream. There are no human figures in the picture.	Isolation
13MF	A young man is standing with downcast head buried in his arm. Behind him is the figure of a woman lying in bed.	Heterosexual relationship
13B	A little boy is sitting on the doorstep of a log cabin.	Fantasy
13G	A little girl is climbing a winding flight of stairs.	
14	The silhouette of a man (or woman) is shown against a bright window. The rest of the picture is totally black.	Fantasy: achievement/depression
15	A gaunt man with clenched hands is standing among gravestones.	Depression
16	Blank card.	Ideal life situation; symbolized current problem

TABLE 2.1   (*Continued*)

Card No.	Description	Stimulus Demand
17BM	A naked man is clinging to a rope. He is in the act of climbing up or down.	Achievement; narcissism
17GF	A bridge over water is shown. A female figure leans over the railing. In the background are tall buildings and small figures of men.	Depression/suicide
18BM	A man is clutched from behind by three hands. The figures of his antagonists are invisible.	Locus of control
18GF	A woman has her hands squeezed around the throat of another woman whom she appears to be pushing backward across the banister of a stairway.	Attitudes toward mother
19	This is a weird picture of cloud formations overhanging a snow-covered cabin in the country.	Family dynamics
20	Shown here is the dimly illuminated figure of a man (or woman) in the dead of night leaning against a lamp post.	Alienation/fantasy

Source: The descriptions given here are adapted from and reprinted by permission of the publisher from Henry A. Murray, *Thematic Apperception Test,* Cambridge, MA: Harvard University Press, 1943 by the President and Fellows of Harvard College, © 1971 by Henry A. Murray. The stimulus demand column is adapted from *A Human Science Model for Personality Assessment with Projective Techniques,* Richard H. Dana, Springfield, IL: C. C. Thomas, 1982.

verbatim recording may result in stories that are less useful for interpretation, since they will contain an interlarding of assessor and assessee content. It is permissible to tape-record the stories whenever the assessee is unable or unwilling to control the rate of storytelling or the length of the protocol. There are two caveats to such recording: (1) the assessor needs to have a verbatim, typed transcription of the stories to use for interpretation and (2) the assessor should be physically present and attentive whenever the stories are dictated, since assessor-absent conditions result in more negative story content and thus can introduce a pathology bias. However, comparisons of tape recordings, assessee-written stories, and assessor-written stories from the same college-student assessees have produced no difference in "personality revealingness" measured by frequencies of needs, pressures, inner states, and defense mechanisms (Baty & Dreger, 1975).

Although Murray used a series of 20 cards that were administered in two separate sessions, it is now conventional to use a smaller number of selected cards, often 2, 3, 4, 6 (BM or GF), and 7 (BM or GF), supplemented by several others, including 16. While the cards in this short form are suitable for adolescents, cards 1, 8BM, 12BG, 13B, 13G, and 19 are especially appropriate for younger children. Gerver (1946; also reported in Rotter, 1946) found that five- to 10-year-old children were most responsive to cards 7GF, 18GF, 3GF, and 8GF, in that order, and least responsive to 19, 18BM, 11, and 12BG. Whenever fewer than 20 cards are administered as a short form, it is still preferable to present them in their original sequence, rather than in a random order, although position effects per se may be of less importance than the stimulus properties of the cards themselves (Murstein, 1963).

Murray (1943) indicated that stories of 300 words or more were to be anticipated from college students. Other normative data suggest that less than 150 words may be typical for well-functioning adults as well as 10-year-old children. Children in the first three grades may produce 60- to 75-word stories (Armstrong, 1954), although Friedman (1972) has provided data for Iowa Pediatrics assessees from a random sample taken during a six-year period for age ranges of 5 to 7, 8 to 11, and 12 to 15. The youngest groups, 5 to 7 years, produced stories that ranged from 12 words (18BM) to 52 words (12GF) with a mean of 29 words and no sex differences. The 8-11 and 12-15 age 'groups had no sex differences, a mean of 63 words, and a range from 55 words (3BM) to 112 words (17GF). Significant sex differences in story length occurred only for the 8-11 age group, with girls producing longer stories. Length of story, however, is confounded by strong achievement needs. Adolescents who have high need for achievement produce not only longer stories but will have greater verbal fluency as well (Schaible, 1975).

Whenever children reject specific cards, it is tempting to consider specific card hypotheses, as is done routinely with the Rorschach. No general conclusions about card rejection by children are justified, however, since card rejection is multiply determined by low intellectual level, lack of creativity, inability to respond to the pictorial stimulus, maladjustment, and other reasons that are even more difficult to label. Data from 1,201 6- to 11-year-old children on cards 1, 2, 5, 8BM, and 16 indicated that these variables accounted for only 25 percent of the variance in card rejection (Orloff, 1973).

Administration of the TAT to adolescents and children should be informal and adhere to consensual directions for inclusion of specific story components. However, stories may be tape-recorded whenever this facilitates the data gathering and the assessor can have accurately transcribed stories as the basis for subsequent interpretation. Selection of a smaller number of cards from the entire set usually will be necessary. To provide maximal personality data, assessee-relevant cards may be chosen in preparing a tailored set using the less ambiguous pictures. The standard card order should be used because order effects are unknown, and assessors also should be aware that there will be additional problems in using selected TAT cards as a basis for expert testimony unless a scoring system based upon a particular short form also is employed. Assessors should provide a context of support, helpfulness, and interest for the storytelling, ask questions about the stories either during or after the administration proper (but note in the recording where these questions have been asked), and be assured that very short stories do provide usable information.

UNDERLYING HYPOTHESES AND INTERPRETATION

We still have no consensual approach to TAT interpretation that is derived from research. There are a number of interpretive schemata which vary in detail and complexity, and there are literally dozens of objective scoring systems that have generated a modest research literature, including validation studies. This lack of any consensual interpretive format presents one major obstacle to continuation of the high frequency of TAT usage in the immediate future. Exner and Weiner's (1982) comprehensive Rorschach system for children and adolescents has been widely accepted because it provides a synthesis of Rorschach scores and a normative basis for practice. Lacks (1984) has made a similar contribution to the continued vitality of the Bender-Gestalt.

Two recent expositions of guidelines for interpretation of the TAT (Dana, 1982) have been distilled from accumulated clinical experience. These guidelines include a variety of story characteristics: congruence with pictorial stimuli, conformity with directions, distance, conflict, and literal content used in conjunction with available implicit thematic norms. However, such guidelines have two defects. First, they are applicable only to persons of college age and older. Second, they do not explicitly acknowledge or incorporate the empirical research literature. In this chapter these guidelines will be supplemented to provide a set of hypotheses to be used for TAT interpretation with adolescents. At present these hypotheses should be considered as one possible frame of reference for interpretation and not as a scoring system, due to lack of explicit directions, reliability data, and norms that reflect age, sex, and setting or pathology.

Table 2.2 presents five major hypotheses that represent both structural and content dimensions of the TAT protocol. These hypotheses provide a

TABLE 2.2 Underlying Hypotheses and Specific Personality/Psychopathology Areas for Interpretation of Adolescent TAT Stories

Hypothesis	Interpretation Area
Well functioning persons comply with stimulus demands, including directions and identification of relatively well-structured picture contents	Ego strength/ego sufficiency
Motives or needs can be used to describe salient personality characteristics, and certain needs are stable over time	Self-assertion for males; prosocial behavior for females
Girls often provide stories in which deprivation is followed by enhancement, while boys use a reverse order	Sex-role development and identity
Specific kinds of content may be identified and their frequencies used to describe current functioning and/or indicate organization of personality	Psychopathology
Assessees may exercise voluntary or involuntary control over the contents of stories and/or style of storytelling	Control; defenses

format for interpretation that includes the issues of ego strength and sufficiency, needs that pertain to self-assertion and prosocial behavior, sex-role development and identity, content dimensions that are relevant for clinical diagnosis and personality organization, and the kind of control exercised by assessees over content of stories. These control issues are germane to literalness of interpretation and fantasy-behavior relationships. Each hypothesis will be described separately, and examples of TAT stories will be used for illustration.

Ego Strength : Compliance with Stimulus Demands

Compliance with stimulus demands is a complex requirement, although some specific stimulus components may be delineated. First, most of the TAT pictures have a negative emotional tone and evoke sad stories with unhappy outcomes (Eron, 1950). Second, assessors must be alert for stories that are not congruent with either the pictorial representations or the affect components of the card. For example, if card 3BM does not yield a story involving loss, grief, or dysphoria and card 10 does not result in an innocuous story, there should be awareness of denial and/or conflict in the area represented by the stimulus demand of the card (see Table 2.1). Third, compliance with the seven components of the usual directions is significantly related to psychopathology (Dana, 1959) and ego strength/ego sufficiency (Dana & Cunningham, 1983; Nawas, 1971). Fourth, Rapaport (1943) noted that adequate perception of parts is of almost equal importance as the ability to follow directions. Stimulus properties used by most persons have been identified for some cards (2, 3BM, 4, 6BM/GF, 7BM/GF) (Dana, 1959), and frequencies of particular themes have been catalogued (Eron, 1950, 1953). However, only Murstein (1972) has provided normative expectations for each of the 31 cards that are applicable for age 17 and above. These card descriptions include *Who* (sex, age, relationship), *What* is going on, *Why* it is happening, and *End*, all for large samples.

Wyatt (1947) has described such deviations from characteristic performance as omissions, distortions, and exacerbation of reality. Silverman (1964) has enumerated TAT variables related to ego disturbance in adolescence. These variables include the following:

1. *Disturbances in thinking*: peculiar verbalizations, slips of the tongue, verbal incoherence/confusion, bizarre/absurd ideas, verbal condensation, self-reference, inappropriate symbolism, logical or affective contradiction, memory loosening, autistic logic, disturbance of frame of reference, break in story continuity, arbitrary turn of events, non sequitur, vague/cryptic/literal response to question, and overgeneralization
2. *Disturbances in perception*: distortion, omission, fluidity, and arbitrariness
3. *Behavioral controls*: inappropriate concurrent behavior or affect during assessment and withholding ideas

The cards that were rated highest in likelihood of arousing thoughts of physical aggression (18GF, 8BM, 18BM, 13MF, 12M, 4, 3BM) elicited more ego disturbance.

Needs

Murray (1938) scored 19 needs as they appeared in each story, using ratings from 1 to 5 that were determined by criteria of intensity, duration, frequency, and importance. Descriptive statistical data for college students were based on stories of at least 300 words. There is a large literature that provides unequivocal demonstration that needs can be scored reliably (Dana, 1968).

There has been controversy regarding the relationship of TAT fantasy to overt behavior. When needs are aroused experimentally, they may appear directly in TAT stories. However, TAT stories may be playful reverie (primary process) or problem-solving exercises (secondary process). In fact, Lazarus (1966) has suggested that needs appear in TAT stories whenever they are not expressed behaviorally, but it may be more accurate to state that either language, fantasy, or action may be the outlet (Santostefano, 1970).

The data most relevant to this controversy have come from the Oakland Growth Study (Skolnick, 1966). Skolnick found that needs reflecting prosocial fantasy for women (Affiliation and Achievement) and needs indicative of self-assertive fantasy for men (Power and Aggression) were stable from ages 17 to 37. Stability in male aggressive behavior and female passivity/dependency from preschool to adulthood also has been reported by others (Kagan & Moss, 1962). TAT needs in adolescents for both sexes are less clearly related to concurrent behaviors than in adults. However, these needs appear to be less stable for women than for men. The sex-related nature of prosocial and self-assertive dimensions may be culture-specific, and related to the time of data collection.

The TAT cards elicit needs differentially. Campus (1976) documents that card ambiguity affects the expression of needs in college students and has listed the relevant cards for each of 17 needs. Table 2.3 uses Campus' data to indicate TAT cards that elicit prosocial needs (Achievement, Affiliation, Nurturance) and self-assertive needs (Aggression, Autonomy, Dominance). These stimulus-value data are highly congruent with Stein's (1955) common themes. Anxiety/conflict concerning arousal of needs can be evaluated directly for cards (Table 2.3) that are unambiguous in eliciting particular needs (Kagan, 1959).

Sex-role Development

May (1966) has offered a psychoanalytic rationale for sex differences in fantasy patterns. Archetypal male experience, epitomized by Murray's (1955) Icarus theme, emphasizes ascension in everyday experience accompanied by feats of inherent fallibility and ultimate loss of conscious control. Women are more in touch with psychic experience, more able to adapt to painful life events, and prone to believe in potential recoverability from lapses in conscious control. In applying this rationale to TAT stories, May (1966, 1969, 1975) discovered that girls typically relate stories containing negative experience (deprivation) followed by positive emotion or recovery (enhancement), while boys typically tell stories with this pattern reversed. This pattern appears by age 6 and is established by age 9 or 10, with an increasingly clear sex differentiation in fantasy patterns thereafter (Cramer & Bryson, 1973; May, 1971). Failure to expose this pattern in adolescent TAT stories has implications not only for psychopathology but also for the adequacy of sex-role development and sexual identity.

TABLE 2.3 TAT Cards that Elicit Prosocial Needs for Achievement (Ach), Affiliation (Aff), and Nurturance (Nur); and Self-Assertive Needs for Aggression (Agg), Autonomy (Aut), and Dominance (Dom), in Sex-appropriate Cards for College Males (M) and Females (F)

Card	Need
2	Ach, Aut, Dom (M), Nur (F)
3	Agg
4	Ach (F), Aff (F), Agg (M), Dom, Nur (F)
8	Ach (F), Aff (F), Nur (F)
9	Aff (M)
10	Aff, Nur
11	Aut (F)
14	Ach (M)
15	Agg (F)
17	Ach (M), Aff, Dom (M)
18	Agg (M)

Source: Adapted from N. Campus, A measure of needs to assess the stimulus characteristics of TAT cards. *Journal of Personality Assessment, 40,* 1976, 248–258. Used with permission.

Content Dimensions

This section relates to identification of TAT content characteristics within a developmental frame of reference. There are several studies that provide some expectations for TAT developmental content that are helpful. TAT characteristics of late- and early-maturing 17-year-old girls and boys are available using Murray scores (Jones & Mussen, 1958; Mussen & Jones, 1957). The TAT stories for late-maturing girls and boys contained more negative self-evaluations, prolonged dependency, feelings of rejection, rebellion, and strong affiliation needs. TAT stories for early-maturing girls and boys showed better overall psychological functioning, with self-perceptions of maturity and competence.

Harrison (1951) used 12 cards from the Murray series, including numbers 2, 3BM, 5, 6GF, 7GF, and 8GF, with 300 girls from 10 to 19 years old, in order to provide a qualitative TAT picture of adolescence. No uniform prepuberty personality pattern was found for 12-year-old girls, although interest was focused on relationships with parents, particularly mothers. Ambivalence was expressed toward mother through dependency and revolt. Conflicts between parents or between parents and children provide a picture of tempest at home. Psychosexual immaturity is the norm. There were more daydreams and autistic thinking and evidence of emotional distress among older girls, although rates of actual distress were equivalent in all three groups. Unhappy, morbid, violent, and bloody stories with disturbed family relations were common. While stories were affect laden, loose, and uncontrolled, they displayed very little creative imagination. Stories were typically brief, with unlikely themes that suggested minimal reality testing.

Pubertal girls averaged 13.2 years old, and there were no gross differences between their stories and those from the prepubescents. There were more psychosexual themes, but sex misidentification of TAT characters was common. There was an increase in nurturant themes and considerable empathy for mother figures.

Late adolescent girls thought like young women (18.4 years average). Heterosexual relations were more salient than familial situations. Stories frequently involved siblings and fathers as well as mothers, and conflict with father was typical. Feminine role orientation was characteristically present, with some romanticism and idealism. Acceptance of their femininity was related to good adjustment. Disturbed marital relations were very common among parental figures in TAT stories. There was a greater diversity of themes, and affect was moderated and less diffuse. Their outlook on life was predominantly realistic, practical, and matter-of-fact.

Assessee Control over Story Content

As was suggested previously, whatever is present in assessee behavior and/or potentially available in personality organization may or may not appear in TAT stories. One of the difficulties in extrapolating from TAT stories to overt behavior lies in the control that the assessee may exert over story content and/or affect expression. Assessees can consciously introduce false needs into their stories or withhold true needs (Holmes, 1974). When this is done involuntarily, the control is related to defensive style. Heilbrun (1977) has isolated defensive styles of projection and repression in TAT stories. Projectors attribute their own unfavorable traits to other persons, including their TAT story characters, while repressors avoid threatening content. Males more frequently use projection, females use more repression, and some assessees use neither defensive style (Heilbrun, 1978). Projection results in TAT stories that reveal needs that are more congruent with overt behavior.

Lefcourt (1966) found that college-student projectors (sensitizers) not only used more words but had more feeling or thinking in their TAT stories. Normal (1969) used MMPI criteria for anxiety and repression to discover that anxiety results in extreme TAT responses while repression results in neutral stories. Jones (1956) described an intriguing method for eliciting more revealing stories from repressors. He asked hospital patients with bland stories to retake a five-card TAT by providing "the most unlikely story."

Tomkins (1947) and Piotrowski (1950) believe that remoteness of unacceptable motives from conscious awareness is indicated by distance of persons in stories from the assessee. Story characters may differ in age, sex, race, occupation, social status, condition, activity, geography, time, and so forth. Using cards 1, 4, 6GF, 7 (BM or GF), and 13F, motives that were self-evaluated as being less acceptable to hospitalized assessees (adults) were distanced in TAT stories (Pile, Mischel, & Bernstein, 1959).

Another aspect of control has to do with the energy required to bind or contain a particular conflict. Tomkins (1947) believes that the percentage of stories containing similar conflictual themes, feelings, or behaviors is an index of the amount of total energy used in this manner. The likelihood of overt expression is related not only to the amount of energy consumed but to the remoteness of the conflict.

Whenever specific needs are conscious and/or conflictual, the TAT may offer a vehicle for expression. For example, young women who are aware of aggressive needs tend to expose these needs directly in their stories (Kagan & Moss, 1961). Moreover, affiliation needs in TAT stories were associated with affiliative behavior in males who report being self-revealing (Sherwood, 1966). These fragmentary findings do support the long-standing clinical belief that assessees who render their TAT characters aware and insightful concerning their own and others' motives also will have these qualities themselves.

Example for Application of Interpretive Guidelines

The following seven stories were told by a 12-year-old boy who had been referred to a school psychologist. This format uses the hypotheses described earlier in order to generate specific questions that were applied to these TAT stories. These questions are shown in Table 2.4 and should be referred to after examination of the stories, as a guide to the sequence and content of interpretation. Table 2.1 may be referred to for descriptions of the content of the cards used for these stories.

> **Card 1.** I don't know nothing about musical instruments. I can't think of a story right now. I can tell you he doesn't like his musical instrument, though. [Feeling?] Probably a little aggravated about it. [Happen?] If he's like me, he'd bust it so he wouldn't have to play it.

> **Card 2.** Looks like they're at the grape orchard. What are these row things? [Q] He's getting ready to catch the horse. She's watching him and she's getting ready to go home and study. [Happen?] He's gonna chase off that horse. She's gonna go home and study for a test. He doesn't look too happy about his job.

> **Card 3BM.** She's mad because someone got her mad. [Happened?] She probably just got a divorce. [Q] And she doesn't get to have any kids, poor

TABLE 2.4   Summary of TAT Literature: Format for Application of Hypotheses

Hypothesis	Application
Ego strength/weakness	Are directions followed? Is each story congruent with stimulus and affective card pull? Do neutral and blatant cards elicit neutral and blatant stories? Are the major parts of each picture incorporated into a story? Are there any ego disturbance characteristics?
Needs	Which stories appear as playful reverie and problem solving? Are needs elicited by appropriate cards (by sex)? Is conflict/anxiety present in stories for need-specific cards? What is the balance of prosocial and self-assertive needs? Which needs are exaggerated? Which needs are omitted?
Sex role	Do girls have themes of negative experience followed by positive emotion? Do boys have themes of positive experience followed by negative emotion?
Content	Are stories congruent with age-specific expectations?
Assessee control	Can defensive style be ascertained? Projection = longer stories, more feeling/thinking words; negative description of TAT characters. For projectors TAT needs may correspond to overt behavior. Repression = bland stories. Ask for "most unlikely story." Conflict: % stories with similar themes, feelings, behaviors? Tally of remoteness indicators: % of stories, kind, number? Are characters in TAT stories aware of their own motives or motives of others?

woman. [S. laughs.] [Happen?] She's gonna marry someone else. [Q] Not unless she's gonna shoot herself first.

Card 6BM. These two were just in an argument. That or he's the guy like on "My Favorite Martian" who stops by at the worst possible moment. And she's the one that causes the worst possible moment. [Q] Got into an argument. [About what?] What planet he came from. [Happen?] They're both gonna leave the room.

Card 13B. Looks like he's sitting up in a barn thinking about something. About what he's gonna tell his mom about why he got bad grades. He's like my sister. Looking for an excuse to tell Mom about her bad grades. [Happen?] He's not going to be able to think of one and going to get a whipping when he gets home.

Card 17BM. He's playing Tarzan, in the movie where he's going to kill the elephant. No, that's where the guy is going to kill him because he has that woman with him. He's swinging from tree to tree. [Happen?] The man's gonna shoot him like in the movie. The elephant carries him off and drops him in the river and he comes back to life.

Card 8BM. They're gonna have an operation on him. Because he knows something he's not going to tell. Have an operation and kill him. [Feeling? Boy] Worried about if he's going to get caught and thinking about if he's going to tell on them. He [man on table] probably cut off this man's arm. He doesn't have an arm. Probably trying to get even with him. [Happen?] He's gonna die and he's going to get put in prison. And he decided he's gonna report them. He grabbed the gun and shot this one and this one.

These stories indicate minimal to moderate ability to follow directions, with three or four of the seven parts of the directions being incorporated into most stories, with the exception of the first card in which there is only feeling and present behavior. However, it required questioning to elicit conformity to directions, as these parts were not included spontaneously. Stories are congruent with picture stimuli except for cards 1 and 17BM. In card 1 either the novelty of the situation, the implied achievement theme, or even a conspicuous lack of musical talent disrupts expectations. In card 17BM the introduction of an elephant and a woman with a theme of violence is atypical for this stimulus, although consistent with a Tarzan motif. The assessee does reasonably well at incorporating major parts of each stimulus into stories.

However, there are some mild signs of ego disturbance. In card 2 the horse is being "caught" and "chased off." The sequence of events goes from character to character rather than from activity to activity. In card 17BM there is confusion regarding who is doing the killing as well as in the sequence of actions. In 8BM there is confusion and disturbed perception (e.g., "He doesn't have an arm"). This distress is largely restricted to cards 2, 17BM, and 8BM. It is feasible to infer that this boy has relatively low ego strength. Moreover, there are ego deficits in areas of achievement/work and in fantasized anticipation (distortion?) of gross punishment for noncompliance.

Five of the seven stories contain themes of aggression, while anger/ unhappiness occurs in four stories. The stories for cards 6BM and 13B appear as problem-solving attempts while 1, 2, and 3BM depict blockage/inertia. Cards 17BM and 8BM are sheer reveries in which the assessee is both victim and aggressor.

These stories do not display the sex-typed positive experience followed by negative emotion. The feeling/tone is predominantly negative, and only in his most ebullient fantasy can there be a positive outcome. As a result these stories are silent on sex role, probably because of this boy's preoccupation with anger and hurt rather than any sexual identity issues per se. Moreover, his stories are not age consistent. They suggest a much younger child, one who is television bound, fantasy ridden, and still exclusively oriented toward parental displeasure and negative sanctions for his behavior.

This assessee does appear to project in a literal fashion the ingredients of his current life. Conflict occurs in all stories except for card 2, in which there is a lack of interaction, possible perceptual distortion, and confusion regarding what happens at home. Card 6BM displays some blame, but awareness is limited to anticipation of punishment (card 13B).

In summary, these stories portray a 12-year-old boy whose social functioning is approximately at an 8-year-old's level. His control is very poor and although he expects retribution for misdeeds he is unable to avoid consequences. While he is of average intelligence as indicated by adequate use of stimulus features and directions, he probably does not involve himself constructively in schoolwork. He has too much inner distress and too little control or regard for means–ends sequences of behavior to focus on achievement. While he is afraid of displeasing parents and wants to avoid violent punishment, he sees no feasible way to comply with their demands. He is seldom positively rewarded for compliance and has not developed the usual age-specific interests, controls, or behavioral sequences that could result in acceptance by parents and peers.

CLINICAL AND RESEARCH APPLICATIONS

The TAT is a powerful projective technique for use with adolescents whose potential for personality assessment has been underutilized. The TAT has demonstrated high reliability over a wide range of scoring systems. This chapter provides evidence for use of the standard Murray TAT cards with adolescents who are at least 12 years of age. There is currently no sound basis for using the TAT in the absence of other concurrent assessment data. Once representative norms for adolescents on relevant structural and content scoring dimensions are available, however, the TAT could have status as an independent assessment device comparable to the Rorschach.

As early as 1951, Shneidman analyzed the concepts present in 16 interpretations of one set of adult stories and found 85.5 percent of the content to represent personality description while the remainder suggested symptoms, diagnoses, and etiology. Personality contents included affects (13%), defenses (12%), interpersonal data (12%), sexuality (9%), and attitudes (8%). More specifically for adolescents, Henry and Farley (1959) found that predictive validities were better for peer relations, emotional adjustment, and intrapsychic problems than for family relations and mental functioning.

The feasibility of objective scoring and the failure of extant scoring systems has been described elsewhere (Vane, 1981). This chapter argues for normative data on particular objective scores that tap the structure and content of TAT stories with fidelity and completeness. Five major areas were suggested for further development: (1) ego strength/weakness, (2) needs, (3) sex-role/identity, (4) assessee control, and (5) content. Most of these areas are represented by the six factors from 31 TAT scores that emerged from application of structural and thematic manuals to a national probability subsample of 1,398 adolescents (Neuman, Neuman, & Sells, 1974). Neuman et al. used five cards with 12-to-17-year-old adolescents and made comparisons with criterion measures for school adjustment, health, intellectual development, social adjustment, and emotional adjustment. There were no substantive relationships between TAT scores and these criterion measures.

TAT scores that are derived to provide population norms may need to be validated in a manner that takes into account those scores that have demonstrated behavioral correlates by sex as well as the defensive styles that conceal/reveal content that is a literal rendition of overt behavior. The use of moderator variables is crucial to the demonstration of nomothetic TAT fantasy–behavior relationships. Nonetheless, the Neuman et al. (1974) study established the feasibility of a normative basis for interpretation, indicated that significant aspects of language development occur by age 12, and showed that TAT scales can have cross-cultural relevance.

The unique applicability of the TAT for cross-cultural assessment has been recognized for many years, particularly with cards designed for specific populations. Cross-cultural assessment (Dana, 1984) and an example of TAT usage (Dana, in press) have been described elsewhere. Assessors are responsible and ethically obligated to provide themselves with information and the special skills necessary for application of the TAT to minority adolescents, since most clinical programs do not provide adequate training in this area.

Some genuine basis for assessee acceptance of the assessor as a person must precede assessment. Minority assessees, including adolescents, often expect the worst possible outcomes for any interaction with professional persons and bring with them implicit residues of historical issues (e.g., genocide for Native Americans, slavery for blacks, economic exploitation for Hispanics). In addition, minority persons have different styles of social interaction that markedly affect their test behavior. Differences in eye contact, response time, and an absence of middle-class, white expectations for achievement in the form of providing appropriate story content often result in meager stories. The behavioral etiquette of assessment is culture specific, and ignorance of this etiquette results in descriptive protocols that may not be amenable to any interpretation whatsoever. Assessors are urged to be familiar with cultural differences in relationship (e.g., Gibbs, 1982, for blacks) as well as lifestyle and culturally unique practices of their clients (e.g., Everett, Proctor, & Cartmell, 1983, for Native Americans). General reference also should be made to the Sundberg and Gonzales (1981) review.

The TAT remains a conspicuously useful instrument for idiographic personality study with adolescents; however, its continued vitality necessitates that interpretation be based on the available research literature. Ultimately, this literature should provide a normative basis for individual interpretations. This chapter has presented one set of guidelines for TAT interpretation with adolescents that emerges from the research history.

REFERENCES

Armstrong, M. (1954). Children's responses to animal and human features in thematic pictures. *Journal of Consulting Psychology, 18*, 67–70.

Baty, M. A., & Dreger, R. M. (1975). A comparison of three methods to record TAT protocols. *Journal of Clinical Psychology, 31*, 348.

Buros, O. K. (1978). *The eighth mental measurements yearbook* (Vol. 1). Highland Park, NJ: Gryphon.

Campus, N. (1976). A measure of needs to assess the stimulus characteristics of TAT cards. *Journal of Personality Assessment, 40*, 248–258.

Cooper, A. (1981). A basic TAT set for adolescent males. *Journal of Clinical Psychology, 37*, 411–414.

Cramer, P., & Bryson, J. (1973). The development of sex-related fantasy patterns. *Developmental Psychology, 8*, 131–134.

Dana, R. H. (1959). Proposal for objective scoring of the TAT. *Perceptual and Motor Skills, 10* (Supp. 1), 27–43.

Dana, R. H. (1968). Thematic techniques and clinical practice. *Journal of Projective Techniques and Personality Assessment, 32*, 204–214.

Dana, R. H. (1972). The Thematic Apperception Test. In O. K. Buros (Ed.), *The seventh mental measurements yearbook* (pp. 457–460). Highland Park, NJ: Gryphon.

Dana, R. H. (1982). *A human science model for personality assessment with projective techniques.* Springfield, IL: Charles C. Thomas.

Dana, R. H. (1984). Personality assessment: Practice and teaching for the next decade. *Journal of Personality Assessment, 48,* 46–57.

Dana, R. H. (in press). The Thematic Apperception Test (TAT). In C. S. Newmark (Ed.), *Major psychological assessment instruments.* Newton, MA: Allyn & Bacon.

Dana, R. H., & Cunningham, K. M. (1983). Convergent validity of Rorschach and Thematic Apperception Test ego strength measures. *Perceptual and Motor Skills, 57,* 1101–1102.

Dlepu, O., & Kimbrough, C. (1982). Feeling-tone and card preferences of black elementary children for the TCB and TAT. *Journal of Non-White Concerns in Personnel and Guidance, 10*(2), 50–56.

Eron, L. D. (1950). A normative study of the Thematic Apperception Test. *Psychological Monographs, 64*(9, Whole No. 315).

Eron, L. D. (1953). Responses of women to the Thematic Apperception Test. *Journal of Consulting Psychology, 17,* 269–272.

Everett, F., Proctor, N., & Cartmell, B. (1983). Providing psychological services to American Indian children and families. *Professional Psychology: Research and Practice, 14,* 588–603.

Exner, J. E., & Weiner, I. B. (1982). *The Rorschach: A comprehensive system. Assessment of Children and Adolescents* (Vol. 3). New York: John Wiley.

Friedman, R. J. (1972). TAT story length in children. *Psychology in the Schools, 9,* 413–414.

Gerver, J. M. (1946). *Level of interpretation of children on the Thematic Apperception Test.* Unpublished M.A. thesis, Ohio State University.

Gibbs, J. T. (1982, November). Establishing a treatment relationship with black clients: Interpersonal vs. instrumental strategies. Paper presented at the National Association of Social Work Conference on Clinical Practice, Washington, DC.

Harrison, R. (1951). The Thematic Apperception Test. In L. K. Frank, R. Harrison, E. Hellersberg, K. Machover, & M. Steiner (Eds.), Personality development in adolescent girls. *Monographs of the Society for Research in Child Development, 16*(Serial No. 53).

Heilbrun, A. B., Jr. (1977). The influence of defensive styles upon the predictive validity of the Thematic Apperception Test. *Journal of Personality Assessment, 41,* 486–491.

Heilbrun, A. B., Jr. (1978). Projective and repressive styles of processing aversive information. *Journal of Consulting and Clinical Psychology, 46,* 156–164.

Henry, W. E. (1956). *The analysis of fantasy.* New York: John Wiley.

Henry, W. E., & Farley, J. (1959). The validity of the Thematic Apperception Test in the study of adolescent personality. *Psychological Monographs, 73*(17, Whole No. 487).

Henry, W. W. (1947). The Thematic Apperception Test in the study of culture-personality relations. *Genetic Psychology Monographs, 35,* 3–135.

Holmes, D. S. (1974). The conscious control of thematic projection. *Journal of Consulting and Clinical Psychology, 42,* 323–329.

Hutt, M. L. (1980). *The Michigan Picture Test—Revised.* New York: Grune & Stratton.

Jones, M. C., & Mussen, P. H. (1958). Self-conceptions, motivations, and interpersonal attitudes of early- and late-maturing girls. *Child Development, 29,* 491–501.

Jones, R. M. (1956). The negation TAT: A projective method for eliciting repressed thought content. *Journal of Projective Techniques, 20,* 297–302.

Kagan, J. (1959). The stability of TAT fantasy and stimulus ambiguity. *Journal of Consulting Psychology, 23,* 266–271.

Kagan, J., & Moss, H. A. (1961). The availability of conflictual ideas: A neglected parameter in assessing projective test responses. *Journal of Personality, 29,* 217–234.

Kagan, J., & Moss, H. (1962). *Birth to maturity: A study in psychological development.* New York: John Wiley.

Klopfer, W. G., & Taulbee, E. S. (1976). Projective tests. *Annual Review of Psychology, 27,* 543–567.

Lacks, P. (1984). *Bender Gestalt screening for brain dysfunction.* New York: John Wiley.

Lanyon, R. I. (1984). Personality assessment. *Annual Review of Psychology, 35,* 667–701.

Lazarus, R. S. (1966). Story telling and the measurement of motivation: The direct versus substitutive controversy. *Journal of Consulting Psychology, 30,* 483–487.

Lefcourt, H. M. (1966). Repression-sensitization: A measure of the evaluation of emotional responses. *Journal of Consulting Psychology, 30,* 444–449.

Lubin, B., Larsen, R. M., & Matarazzo, J. D. (1984). Patterns of psychological test usage in the United States: 1935–1982. *American Psychologist, 39,* 451–454.

May, R. (1966). Sex differences in fantasy pattern. *Journal of Projective Techniques and Personality Assessment, 30,* 576–586.

May, R. (1969). Deprivation/enhancement fantasy patterns in men and women. *Journal of Projective Techniques and Personality Assessment, 33,* 464–469.

May, R. (1971). A method for studying the development of gender identity. *Developmental Psychology, 5,* 484–487.

May, R. (1975). Further studies on deprivation/enhancement patterns. *Journal of Personality Assessment, 39,* 116–122.

McArthur, D. S., & Roberts, G. E. (1982). *Roberts Apperception Test for Children manual.* Los Angeles: Western Psychological Services.

Murray, H. A. (1938). *Explorations in personality.* New York: Oxford.

Murray, H. A. (1943). *Thematic Apperception Test manual.* Cambridge, MA: Harvard University Press.

Murray, H. A. (1955). American Icarus. In A. Burton & R. E. Harris (Eds.), *Clinical studies of personality* (pp. 615–641). New York: Harper.

Murstein, B. I. (1963). *Theory and research in projective techniques.* New York: John Wiley.

Murstein, B. I. (1972). Normative written TAT responses for a college sample. *Journal of Personality Assessment, 36,* 109–147.

Mussen, P. H., & Jones, M. C. (1957). Self-conceptions, motivations, and interpersonal attitudes of late- and early-maturing boys. *Child Development, 28,* 243–256.

Myer, B., Rosenkrantz, A., & Holmes, G. (1972). A comparison of the TAT, CAT, and CAT-H among second grade girls. *Journal of Personality Assessment, 36,* 440–444.

Nawas, M. M. (1971). Change in complexity of ego functioning and complexity from adolescent to young adulthood. *Developmental Psychology, 6,* 412–415.

Neuman, R. S., Neuman, J. F., & Sells, S. B. (1974). *Language and adjustment scales for the Thematic Apperception Test for youths 12-17 years* (DHEW Publication No. HRA 75-1336). Rockville, MD: National Center for Health Statistics.

Normal, R. P. (1969). Extreme response tendency as a function of emotional adjustment and stimulus ambiguity. *Journal of Consulting and Clinical Psychology, 33,* 406–410.

Orloff, H. (1973). Thematic Apperception Test card rejection in a large sample of normal children. *Multivariate Behavioral Research, 8,* 63–70.

Pile, E., Mischel, W., & Bernstein, L. (1959). A note on remoteness of TAT figures as an interpretive concept. *Journal of Consulting Psychology, 23,* 252–255.

Piotrowski, C., & Keller, J. W. (1984). Psychodiagnostic testing in APA-approved clinical psychology programs. *Professional Psychology: Research and Practice, 15,* 450–456.

Piotrowski, Z. A. (1950). A new evaluation of the Thematic Apperception Test. *Psychoanalytic Review, 37,* 101–127.

Rapaport, D. (1943). The clinical application of the Thematic Apperception Test. *Bulletin of the Menninger Clinic, 7,* 106–113.

Rotter, J. B. (1946). Thematic Apperception Tests: Suggestions for administration and interpretation. *Journal of Personality, 15,* 70–92.

Santostefano, S. (1970). Assessment of motives in children. *Psychological Reports, 26,* 639–649.

Schaible, M. (1975). An analysis of noncontent TAT variables in a longitudinal sample. *Journal of Personality Assessment, 39,* 480–485.

Sherwood, E. T. (1957). On the designing of TAT pictures, with special reference to a set for an African people assimilating western culture. *Journal of Social Psychology, 45,* 161–190.

Sherwood, J. J. (1966). Self-report and projective measures of achievement and affiliation. *Journal of Consulting and Clinical Psychology, 30,* 329–337.

Shneidman, E. S. (Ed.). (1951). *Thematic Apperception Test analysis.* New York: Grune & Stratton.

Silverman, L. B. (1964). Ego disturbance in TAT stories as a function of aggression-arousing stimulus properties. *Journal of Nervous and Mental Disease, 138,* 248–254.

Skolnick, A. (1966). Stability and interrelations of thematic test imagery over 20 years. *Child Development, 37,* 389–396.

Stein, M. (1955). *The Thematic Apperception Test.* Cambridge, MA: Addison-Wesley.

Sundberg, N. D., & Gonzales, L. R. (1981). Cross-cultural and cross-ethnic assessment: Overview and issues. In P. McReynolds (Ed.), *Advances in Psychological Assessment* (Vol. 5) (pp. 460–541). San Francisco: Jossey-Bass.

Symonds, P. M. (1948). *Manual for the Symonds Picture-Story Test.* New York: Bureau of Publications, Teachers College, Columbia University.

Tomkins, S. S. (1947). *The Thematic Apperception Test.* New York: Grune & Stratton.

Triplett, S., & Brunson, P. (1982). TCB and TAT response characteristics in black males and females: A replication. *Journal of Non-White Concerns in Personnel and Guidance, 10*(2), 73–77.

Vane, J. R. (1981). The Thematic Apperception Test: A review. *Clinical Psychology Review, 1,* 319–336.

Vukovich, D. H. (1983). The use of projective assessment by school psychologists. *School Psychology Review, 12,* 358–364.

Wade, T. C., Baker, T. B., Morton, T. L., & Baker, L. (1978). The status of psychological testing in clinical psychology: Relationships between test use and professional activities and orientations. *Journal of Personality Assessment, 42,* 3–10.

Wyatt, F. (1947). The scoring and analysis of the Thematic Apperception Test. *Journal of Psychology, 24,* 319–330.

3
Children's Apperception Test

Mary R. Haworth

The initial Children's Apperception Test (CAT), using animal figures, was published by Leopold and Sonya Bellak in 1949 as a thematic apperception test for young children (ages 3 to 10 years) that would serve purposes similar to those of the Thematic Apperception Test (TAT) already in use with older children, adolescents, and adults. The 10 plates comprising the test are shown in Figures 3.1 and 3.2.* The appearance of an "animal" test for children immediately stimulated research on, as well as debate over, the relative merits of animal versus human figures as projective stimuli. This research has been extensively reviewed by Haworth (1966) and Bellak (1971).

In 1965 the Bellaks published the Children's Apperception Test—Human (CAT-H), which shows human figures in situations as analogous as possible to those pictured in the animal version. Earlier, in 1952, the CAT Supplement (CAT-S) appeared. This set, designed for the very young child, employs heavy cardboard cutout animal figures shown against restricted backgrounds depicting family and peer activities.

Although the use of animal figures on the original CAT was thought to produce a more culture-free stimulus than would human characters, some of the settings proved to be unsuited for use in countries where toilet fixtures, beds, tricycles, chairs, and sofas differ considerably from those typical of Western cultures. Consequently, Samiko Marui developed a Japanese adaptation and Uma Chowdury produced a form for India. Both of these sets are reproduced in Haworth's *The CAT: Facts about Fantasy* (1966). More recently a Philippine version (the PACT) has

---

*The card numbers have been inserted on the plates but do not appear on the actual test cards.

FIGURE 3.1 Plates 1 through 5 of the Children's Apperception Test—Animal (CAT).

Source: Reproduced with the permission of Leopold Bellak and C.P.S., Inc., P.O. Box 83, Larchmont, NY 10538.

FIGURE 3.2 Plates 6 through 10 of the Children's Apperception Test—Animal (CAT).

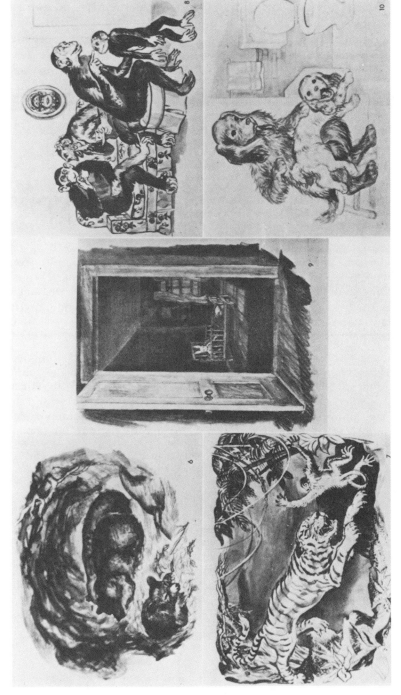

Source: Reproduced with the permission of Leopold Bellak and C.P.S., Inc., P.O. Box 83, Larchmont, NY 10538.

appeared (Langmay, 1975a, 1975b), which is described as portraying situations similar to those of the CAT but using human figures in more ambiguous pictures, as well as being less psychoanalytically oriented. In Czechoslovakia, Strnadová and Bös (1977) developed the CATO for the assessment of a child's interpersonal relations within the family and the wider social environment. Finally, the original CAT manual has been published in French, Italian, German, Spanish, and Portugese.

DESCRIPTION OF THE CAT TEST CARDS

The manual for the CAT (Bellak & Bellak, 1961, pp. 3–4) gives a brief description of each card and of the most typical responses to each of the pictures, as follows:*

> *Picture #1: Chicks seated around a table on which is a large bowl of food. Off to one side is a large chicken, dimly outlined.* Responses revolve around eating, being or not being sufficiently fed by either parent. Themes of sibling rivalry enter in around who gets more, who is well behaved and not, etc. Food may be seen as a reward or, inversely, its withholding seen as punishment; general problems of orality are dealt with: satisfaction or frustration, feeding problems per se.
>
> *Picture #2: One bear pulling a rope on one side while another bear and a baby bear pull on the other side.* It is interesting to observe whether the baby here identifies the figure with whom he cooperates (if at all) as the father or the mother. It may be seen as a serious fight with accompanying fear of aggression, fulfillment of the child's own aggression or autonomy. More benignly, this picture may be seen as a game (tug-of-war, for example). Sometimes the rope itself may be a source of concern, i.e., breakage of the rope as a toy and fear of subsequent punishment; or again, purely as a symbol concerning masturbation with the rope-breaking representing castration fears.
>
> *Picture #3: A lion with pipe and cane, sitting in a chair; in the lower right corner a little mouse appears in a hole.* This is usually seen as a father figure equipped with such symbols as pipe and cane. The latter may be seen either as an instrument of aggression or may be used to turn this paternal figure into an old, helpless one of whom one need not be afraid. This is usually a defensive process. If the lion is seen as a strong paternal figure, it will be important to note whether he is a benign or a dangerous power.
> The mouse is seen by the great majority of children, and often taken as the identification figure. In such a case—by tricks and circumstance—the mouse may be turned into the more powerful one. On the other hand, it may

---

*Reproduced from the manual with permission of the authors, Leopold and Sonya S. Bellak, and the publisher, C.P.S., Inc., P.O. Box 83, Larchmont, NY 10538.

be totally in the power of the lion. Some children identify themselves with the lion and there will be subjects who will switch identification one or more times, giving evidence of confusion about role, conflict between compliance and autonomy, etc.

Picture #4: A kangaroo with a bonnet on her head, carrying a basket with a milk bottle; in her pouch is a baby kangaroo with a balloon; on a bicycle, a larger kangaroo child. This usually elicits themes of sibling rivalry, or some concern with the origin of babies. In both cases, the relation to the mother is often an important feature. Sometimes a child who is an older sibling will identify himself with the pouch baby, thus indicating a wish to regress in order to be nearer to the mother. On the other hand, a child who is in reality the younger one, may identify himself with the older one, thus signifying his wish for independence and mastery. The basket may give rise to themes of feeding. A theme of flight from danger may also occasionally be introduced. Our experience thus far suggests that this can be related to unconscious fear in the area of father–mother relationship, sex, pregnancy, etc.

Picture #5: A darkened room with a large bed in the background; a crib in the foreground in which are two baby bears. Productions concerning primal scene in all variations are common here; the child is concerned with what goes on between the parents in bed. These stories reflect a good deal of conjecture, observation, confusion, and emotional involvement on the part of the children. The two children in the crib lend themselves to themes of mutual manipulation and exploration between children.

Picture #6: A darkened cave with two dimly outlined bear figures in the background; a baby bear lying in the foreground. This again is a picture eliciting primarily stories concerning the primal scene. It is used in addition to #5 since practical experience has shown that #6 will enlarge frequently and greatly upon whatever was held back in response to the previous picture. Plain jealousy in this triangle situation will at times be reflected. Problems of masturbation at bedtime may appear in response to either #5 or #6.

Picture #7: A tiger with bared fangs and claws, leaping at a monkey which is also leaping through the air. Fears of aggression and manners of dealing with them are here exposed. The degree of anxiety in the child often becomes apparent. It may be so great as to lead to rejection of the picture, or, the defenses may be good enough (or unrealistic enough) to turn it into an innocuous story. The monkey may even outsmart the tiger. The tails of the animals lend themselves easily to the projection of fears or wishes of castration.

Picture #8: Two adult monkeys sitting on a sofa drinking from tea cups. One adult monkey in foreground sitting on a hassock talking to a baby monkey. Here one often sees the role in which the child places himself within the family constellation. His interpretation of the dominant (foreground) monkey as either a father or mother figure becomes significant in relation to his perception of it as a benign monkey or as an admonishing, inhibiting one. The tea cups will, on occasion, give rise to themes of orality again.

Picture #9: A darkened room seen through an open door from a lighted room. In the darkened one there is a child's bed in which a rabbit sits up looking through the door. Themes of fear of darkness, of being left alone, desertion by parents, significant curiosity as to what goes on in the next room, are all common responses to this picture.

Picture #10: A baby dog lying across the knees of an adult dog; both figures with a minimum of expressive features. The figures are set in the foreground of a bathroom. This leads to stories of "crime and punishment," revealing something about the child's moral conceptions. There are frequent stories about toilet training as well as masturbation. Regressive trends will be more clearly revealed in this picture than in some others.

TEST ADMINISTRATION

As in all testing of young children, the clinician's approach must be adapted to the child's age, type of behavioral activity, and degree of distractibility. It is essential that the examiner's verbalizations, instructions, and explanations be appropriate to the child's developmental and cognitive level.

The cards are presented one at a time with all but the current card being kept face down or out of sight. The numbered order of the cards should be followed whenever possible since certain cards were designed for sequential impact. The child is asked to tell a story to each picture; if it seems necessary, assurance can be given that there are no right or wrong answers. The child should be encouraged to tell what is going on in the picture, what happened before, and what will happen next. Younger children will need more prompting in these areas, while older children very quickly realize what is expected.

Insofar as possible all remarks of the child should be recorded, including false starts, slips of the tongue, personal references, and other asides. Word-finding problems and other signs suggestive of aphasic difficulties often can be picked up from the story reports and add an additional diagnostic dimension to the test situation.

INTERPRETATION

Scoring Schedules

As an aid in the evaluation and interpretation of CAT protocols, Bellak (1955) and Haworth (1965) have each developed record forms for use in summarizing responses in terms of anxieties, defenses, superego and ego manifestations, identifications, and regressions. Bellak's *Short Form TAT and CAT Blank* (1955), for use with either the CAT or TAT, provides columns for recording the highlights of each story with respect to each of the following dimensions: unconscious structure and drives (based on the main themes, views, and needs of story heroes), conception of the world, relationships to others, significant conflicts, nature of anxieties, main defenses, superego structure, integration, and strength of the ego. One final column is used to present a composite summary of all 10 stories on each of the dimensions.

Haworth's *Schedule of Adaptive Mechanisms in CAT Responses* (1965) is a means of evaluating the relative use of various defense mechanisms: reaction formation, ambivalence and undoing, isolation, repression and denial, deception, symbolization, projection, and/or introjection. Immature or disorganized responses are assessed through evidence of fears and anxieties, regression, and weak or absent controls. An additional measure evaluates same-sex versus opposite-sex identification. Each of the above categories contains from 6 to 10 specific types of responses to be checked if they appear in any of the stories. For example, for Projection/Introjection, some of the seven items include "attacker is attacked," "child is active aggressor," and "characters blame others or have secrets."

While the schedule was designed as an aid in making a qualitative analysis of the stories, it is also possible to use it as a rough, quantitative measure for making comparisons between subjects and groups. A specified number of checks are required in each category to constitute a "critical score" for that dimension. The highest possible number of critical scores would be 10, one for each category. Research has demonstrated that five or more critical scores should be regarded as serious enough to warrant further study and possible clinical intervention (Haworth, 1963).

Recurrent and Sequential Themes

There are other aspects of the interpretive process that need to be considered but cannot be encompassed in any formal schedule. One needs to watch for recurrent themes throughout the protocol. These may take the form of a persistent repetition of phrases, characters, or events (e.g., ghosts or storms) in several stories. The same affect, attitude, or situation may appear frequently (e.g., a rebellious child or a punishing or absent parent). It is also important to note any sequence of themes that may reveal information about the child's ways of coping, such as a story dealing with rebellion followed by one of obedience, or aggression toward a father figure followed by restitution toward the father in a subsequent story.

Two instances of sequential patterns with respect to specific cards have been noted in the literature. Bellak and Bellak (1961), when discussing the importance of maintaining the predetermined order of administration, noted that a response to card 6 often will be an elaboration on the previous response to card 5, especially if the child repressed or omitted content (parental, sexual) on card 5. Haworth (1966) has pointed to sequential reactions from card 6 to card 9 suggestive of phobic or panic reactions when attack themes are given to *both* cards. The attack taking place on card 9 usually is a fulfillment of the specific fear of attack expressed on card 6. In contrast, a more realistic adjustment to stress can be inferred when there is an attack theme on only one of these two cards, and especially if that attack is either feared or dreamed of, but is not described as actually taking place.

Identification Clues

The determination of identification figures unquestionably involves some degree of subjectivity and guesswork, but a few guidelines have proved helpful. These are based not only on the labeling of boy or girl, father or mother, but also on the roles played by the identified parental figures. In terms of the specification of the sex of child characters, the situation is more clear-cut for boys than for girls, due to the still persistent cultural stereotype of assigning the male gender to animals. For a girl to speak of the child figures as boys probably has little or no significance, while there would be the strong suggestion of a feminine orientation if a boy persistently sees the child characters as girls.

With parental figures, oedipal theory can be used in evaluating the responses of both boys and girls, but in terms of the *actual* sex of the child respondent (rather than the sex assigned to the child character in the story). Normal identification processes can be assumed to be operating if the child describes the opposite-sex parent figure as loving, nurturant, and sympathetic, while the same-sex parent is the one who scolds, ignores, or punishes (as well as occasionally also being helpful and understanding). Conversely, confused or overtly cross-sex identification becomes more likely when the normally loved, opposite-sex parent is seen as the one who is rejecting, domineering, or punishing, while the same-sex parent is seen as passive or weak.

To summarize identification issues, one should consider (1) the sex ascribed to the parent figures; (2) the sex of the storyteller in relation to the sex of the parent figures; (3) the parental role functions, affects, and behaviors described in the stories; and (4) for boys, the sex attributed to the child characters.

Family and Case History Information

Finally, when interpreting CAT data it is important to consider any possible references to incidents in the child's past or present situation, including family constellation (e.g., divorce, stepparents, adoption, and sex and names of siblings) and critical events and life crises (e.g., operations, injuries, assaults, sexual abuse, and death of a family member). This should be done with the view of using the CAT to assess the impact of these experiences on the child. Attention to the affect displayed in telling the stories, the extent to which allusions to the known situations are stressed, or the obvious omission of any reference to significant events or problems would facilitate the assessment of the degree to which the child has adjusted to and accepted the situation, or is still protesting and grieving, or has resorted to denial and repression.

Illustrative Example: Child whose Parents Have Separated

The following protocol is presented as an example of the extent to which a young child's reactions to the break-up of the family can be revealed in the CAT responses. Tommy was 6 years of age, of average intelligence but inattentive in first grade, and making very little academic progress. His parents divorced when he was 4 years old, and his mother, with whom he was living, had remarried six months before he was referred. His responses to the 10 CAT cards were as follows:

Card 1. The mother got out the big bowls for the little babies, and her own. The babies have napkins around their heads, only one don't. [Q: What next?] The baby that don't is going to get his fur wet and his mother is going to have to spank him. [Q: What then?] He's going to say that he should have weared his napkin. [Q: Why not wear?] Because he didn't know how to tie it—no, his mother didn't want to choke his head.

Card 2. The father's pulling here, and the baby and the mother's pulling this way. The little baby's almost sliding off, and the father's ready to slide down the hill. [Q] Both are going to slide down both hills, they're hanging onto the rope so they won't slide down because their nails aren't big enough.

Card 3. The papa lion was thinking how to get a mouse and the mouse is looking out, and he don't see the mouse. Wow—he looks mean [points to lion]. [Q: What next?] The lion's going to hear because maybe there's wood. He's going to see the mouse and he's going to get him. [Q: What then?] The mouse will be dead and the lion will be bigger. The mouse will chop the lion's head in his chop teeth and the lion will fly up in the air. Then the baby mouse will be saved.

Card 4. The mother's hopping and the baby is riding a bike and the mother's purse is out and the purse could knock the baby on the bike and the bike bump the mother. There's a little baby in her pocket. They're going to have a picnic. The baby's holding a balloon and the mama can put up her feet and take the baby's balloon and pop it. The little baby in the pocket looks a little like me. I don't know where the father is. [Q: Where do you think?] He is in the woods jumping over a fence to kill something to eat tonight.

Card 5. Well, the big papa's . . . the two babies are in the little bed and the father and mother are in the papa's bed. Looks like they forgot to shut their window. The little babies are opening their eyes, just talking. [Q: What next?] They're going to get out of bed and the father will hear them and spank them. [Explained that it's just like when he visits his cousins.]

Card 6. The mother . . . is supposed to keep this little baby bear. The daddy and the mother are over there and they're supposed to be by the baby cuz he's scared. [Q: What baby do?] He'll run out and get lost and his father's going to have to get him. [Q: What thinking?] That he shouldn't have runned away.

Card 7. The lion was sleeping and the monkey made a noise and the lion jumped up and ran to get the monkey and the lion almost got the monkey's tail and the monkey's running. I didn't know lions liked to eat monkeys. [Q] The big lion is going to bite his tail and the monkey don't have a chance to get out of there. [Q] He's going to be dead. The lion will pick him up with his sharp teeth and eat him up—or the monkey could climb into a little hole. Then maybe the lion will climb up there and wait to eat the monkey.

Card 8. The boy and girl (left) are saying something, saying that the mother ain't dressed up. The baby's going to crawl over and hear and tell the mother and she'll get them out of the house.

Card 9. The little baby's looking outside because the mother and daddy forgot to shut the door. He thinks he should shut the door and run away. The mother will find the pillow under the covers. The baby will leave a note. [Q: Note?] It'll say the baby will run away to some other rabbits. [Q: Mother do?] She'll run out there and be lost and the father will have to get them both. [Q: Find them?] I guess he can, but I bet the little boy is so far away he comes around and jumps back in bed and the mother jumps back in bed and the father jumps back in bed. Then the baby goes out again [repeats the same sequence]. [Q: Why run away?] Because the mother and father ain't keeping care of him. [Q: What are they doing?] They're sleeping and I bet they didn't even say their prayers with him.

Card 10. The other dog's jumping on the other one [the little dog on the big one]. The bottom one is supposed to go on the potty and the other one won't let him go. [Q: Why?] Because he don't want him, he wants him to go on the floor so they can give him a lickin'. You know how big dogs are, they like to give little babies a lickin'. Boy, will the father be sorry! I bet the little baby's going to run away. [Q: What then?] He'll grow up and be the father. He can take care of himself. Boy!

The following adaptive mechanisms were identified from the analysis of Tommy's stories:

Reaction formation and Undoing   Fear and Anxiety
Isolation   Regression
Deception   Adequate Identification
Symbolization

Tommy's current school and behavioral difficulties appear to be closely linked to the present family structure in that he still longs for his real father and has not had time to adjust to the altered family situation or to accept the newcomer's usurpation of his father's role. Outstanding in this protocol are the frequent references to mother and father (stepfather?) as a couple who are seen as being so preoccupied with each other that they neglect the child. The child figures to get even by running away (cards 6, 9, and 10), which serves the added function of bringing the father (real?) back into the family. Most poignant are his comment, "I don't know where the father is" (on card 4 which follows immediately after his observation that the kangaroo baby looked like himself) and his statement on Card 6 that "The mother is supposed to keep the little baby bear" (which may have been the explanation given to him concerning custody arrangements, in addition to the wish to have mother to himself).

Although he feels abused and neglected and would like to do something rash to hurt the parents, even fantasies of oppositional, acting-out behaviors generate a considerable amount of guilt. There are many evidences of basic strengths, in that child characters recognize when rules have been broken and considerately leave notes to keep the family informed. Identification is in the positive direction, and he looks forward to growing up and becoming a father himself.

Illustrative Example: Childhood Psychosis

Jerry, a psychotic child, was 9 years and 8 months of age when admitted to an inpatient facility. He had an IQ on the WISC of 110 (Verbal = 100; Performance = 118). There were no indications of any organic problems. His responses to the 10 CAT cards were as follows:

Card 1. They're dreaming about this chicken in the soup. All them chickens are dreaming there's this big rooster in the soup.

Card 2. These guys are tugging the rope and that bear thinks that little bear should get out of the way. Little bear and two big bears; it ain't fair. [How feel?] Don't know; they're gonna win.

Card 3. It's a lion in a chair and the mouse thinks he should be in the chair and he ain't. [How feel?] Don't know. The lion's gonna get the chair; he doesn't know the mouse is there. [Happen?] The lion will still be in the chair; the mouse is in the crack.

Card 4. Two—three—kangaroos going to a picnic and uh . . . [What?] Don't know; gonna be a lot of cake. They're mad. [Why?] They don't know why they've won.

Card 5. A spooky house and there's an ocean in their bed. [Ocean?] It just came. Nothing except water, anybody else? [Happen?] Nothin'.

Card 9. * The rabbit's gonna get out of bed and go to the spooky house. [What happens then?] Going to get the treasure. [Get it?] Yes.

Card 7. A tiger's getting a monkey. [Why?] He's a robber and the lion is a member of the lion police. [Why get him?] He stole some grasshoppers. They'll put him in jail; he's scared. Grasshoppers are money in the jungle.

Card 8. Gonna rob again—these monkeys' grasshoppers—from the bank. They're all robbers. [Happen?] Nothin'; maybe get caught. It's fun. Mad at the bank.

Card 6. * Bear police of the Eighth National Bank are gonna get them monkeys and put 'em in jail. The bear police are mad. That's all.

Card 10. Dog's going to get thrown in the bathtub; he ain't clean. Another dog. Monkey and elephant robber; gonna throw them in the bathtub. [How feel?] Scared, gonna get thrown in the toilet. That's all.

The adaptive mechanisms identified in Jerry's stories were:

Denial	Controls weak or absent
Projection	No indications of identification
Regression	

Jerry's responses to the first four cards indicate some awareness of reality as depicted in the pictures. Beyond that point regressive and aggressive fantasies perseverate in a series of loose associations, with bizarre content and extremely tangential thinking. There is no real affective content; characters are viewed as mad or scared in an almost global, impersonal manner.

There is no mention of any parental figure or of children acting as children. He does not appear to identify with any character; rather, he remains an aloof and detached onlooker in a fluid world. What few defenses he has are very primitive: denial (omission of the usual story content and activities) and projection (addition of objects, characters, and details).

Children's Apperception Test-Human (CAT-H)

The human form of the CAT, shown in Figures 3.3 and 3.4, was developed particularly for use with children approaching the upper age limit for which the animal version was intended, and for younger children of superior intellectual ability (Bellak & Hurvich, 1966a,b). The same basic principles of administration, scoring, and interpretation are,

*The order of these cards was reversed in the examination.

FIGURE 3.3 Plates 1 through 5 of the Children's Apperception Test—Human (CAT-H).

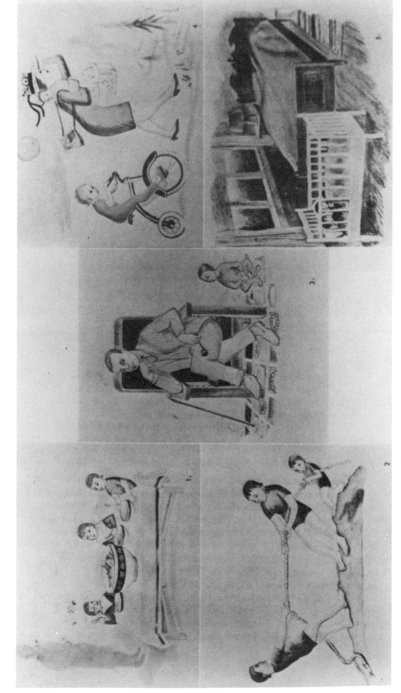

Source: Reproduced with the permission of Leopold Bellak and C.P.S., Inc., P.O. Box 83, Larchmont, NY 10538.

FIGURE 3.4 Plates 6 through 10 of the Children's Apperception Test—Human (CAT-H).

Source: Reproduced with the permission of Leopold Bellak and C.P.S., Inc., P.O. Box 83, Larchmont, NY 10538.

of course, applicable to both forms of the test, and either Bellak's or Haworth's scoring scheme can be used.

This author has administered both forms of the test to 22 children referred to a psychiatric clinic for a variety of emotional problems ranging from behavioral acting-out to borderline psychosis. Few differences were found between the two forms when scored on the Schedule of Adaptive Mechanisms. The categories most often used on both forms were Projection–Introjection, Weak Controls, and Confused Identification. The latter two dimensions are particularly characteristic responses for clinical groups, so it is gratifying to find that either form is capable of eliciting these responses. In those cases where Projection–Introjection was used on only one form, it was given considerably more often on the animal version.

The stories also were analyzed for the presence of four themes: oral deprivation, anal concerns, oedipal attachments, and oppositional tendencies. All of these are themes on which the original (animal) CAT cards were based. Oral deprivation and oedipal themes occurred more frequently in the animal stories (in a ratio of 3:2), while oppositional themes were more frequent on the human form (with a similar ratio).

Experience with both forms suggests that, when it is known that the child has experienced some traumatic interpersonal event (such as death of a parent, sexual molestation, or alcoholism in the family), the human form may elicit more clues as to the anxieties and fears associated with the trauma and the degree to which it is still interfering with adequate functioning. Obviously, the animal form has long been acknowledged as being useful in this respect, but for some children under some circumstances the human form may prove to be more effective in highlighting reactions to specific stresses.

The following stories were given by a 9-year-old girl who, at the age of 3, had been given up for adoption. The case history material suggested that she may have been the victim of sexual molestation in early childhood. She was referred for gorging her food, body scratching, persistent masturbation, and exposing herself when outdoors. The CAT was administered initially, followed by the CAT-H two and one-half weeks later. Except for cards 6 and 9, the animal stories were very brief, descriptive, and generally noncommittal, while by card 3 of the CAT-H she was well launched into a rich and revealing protocol.* The most significant parallel stories from the two sets are presented in the following list:

*The complete protocols are presented in M. R. Haworth, *The CAT: Facts about Fantasy.* New York: Grune & Stratton, 1966, pp. 291–293. Excerpts reproduced with permission of the publisher.

CAT

Card 3. I see a little mouse right down here. The lion is smoking a pipe. He's got a cane. That's all.

Card 4. Once upon a time a mother kangaroo went out for groceries, and she's coming home. Baby kangaroo got a balloon and a bike. They see some toadstools. I see some milk and cheese and meat.

Card 5. Once upon a time there lived four bears. Mother and father covered their whole self, even their heads. Baby bear was playing in bed.

Card 6. The same. Once upon a time there lived four bears. Now they're sleeping in a hole. Papa bear woke up and then baby bear woke up, and they said, "Let's go out for a walk." Then mother bear and other baby bear woke up. They found out Papa and other baby bear were gone. [Q] Mother bear and baby bear came and looked for them. Mother bear spanked other baby bear because she woke up first with Papa bear.

Card 7. Once upon a time there lived a monkey named Cheetah. A big tiger came along and was after him. [Q] Tiger going to chew him up.

Card 9. Once upon a time there lived Alice in Wonderland. There was a rabbit that got a broken leg. He had a beautiful house. When he was well he chased Alice again, and she got a

CAT-H

Card 3. Once upon a time in this family, having company for baby Sally's birthday. Next morning he came again and Sally got a spanking. He said, "Baby Sally, why did you break pipe?" She said, "I just was having some fun." [Q: He do?] He was a robber.

Card 4. Once upon a time, four lived in this family. A snowy day. The man had to carry home some bread and milk and cheese for his wife. When her husband came home, he was carrying a rabbit and their house was right around the corner, and a snowy night. That evening a robber came and stole all their clothes and their baby girl.

Card 5. Four lived in this family. Two baby boys, no, one boy and one girl. Mother and father slept together. It was Hallowe'en night and a goblin came in and took everything they got. Mother and father said, "Arrest those things, arrest that man." "Don't take off [all?] our clothes 'cause they're not for you."

Card 6. Once upon a time three lived in a cabin house; that means a tent. One night some animals came and tore down their tent and they were all scratched up. One was awake in the night and got up and shot every single animal.

Card 7. One day a little boy, Jack in the Beanstalk, he went up to the giant's palace, and the giant caught him, and says, "Oh, baby." [Q] Nothing.

Card 9. Once only one lived in this house. He was sick because his mother and father were dead. The telephone rang and he couldn't get out of bed cause . . . cause he was broken arm so she couldn't play. [Q: How break?] Bumped into a great big thing.

sick. [Q: How end?] He got married then and lived happy ever after.

Adaptive Mechanisms
Projection-Introjection

Adaptive Mechanisms
Isolation
Symbolization
Projection-Introjection
Fear-Anxiety

The animal stories were generally bland and unrevealing, except for the overtly oedipal situation described in card 6 and the highly suggestive reference to a sexual attack on card 9. By contrast, the human figures of the CAT-H served to uncover her memories of past traumatic experiences. Card 3 describes an intruder–robber who scolds a baby girl for *breaking his pipe*. On the next card, a happy family scene is disrupted by a robber who stole the baby girl and her clothes (or took off her clothes?). This theme persists into card 5, but with a much higher level of anxiety, first evidenced by a slip of the tongue, "Arrest those *things*," which she then changes to *"man."* The repressive barrier is finally breached with "Don't take *off* our clothes" rather than the probably-intended *"all* our clothes." Card 6 describes animals *scratching* the people and destroying their home. The usual attack theme on card 7 is embellished by the attacking giant's comment of "Oh, baby." But by card 9 she can recover and concludes a story of illness and parental death with a happy ending of marriage and living happily ever after.

CHILDREN'S APPERCEPTION TEST—SUPPLEMENT (CAT-S)

The CAT-S consists of 10 cutout pictures mounted on heavy cardboard, designed for use with very young children (Bellak & Bellak, 1952). It is also suitable for disturbed youngsters and children whose mental ages are at the preschool level. The cards can be presented one at a time or laid out on the table for the child to play with and talk about spontaneously. The pictures tend to elicit themes of peer play, school activities, trips to the doctor, and mother–child relationships. The 10 pictures are shown in Figures 3.5 and 3.6.

No new clinical material on the CAT-S has been published in recent years, and no formal research has been undertaken since its first appearance in 1952. For further information on this version the reader is referred to Bellak's (1971) description of the test, which includes protocols from normal children. In addition, Haworth (1966) has provided five clinical examples of young retarded subjects.

FIGURE 3.5 Cards 1 through 5 of the Children's Apperception Test—Supplement (CAT–S).

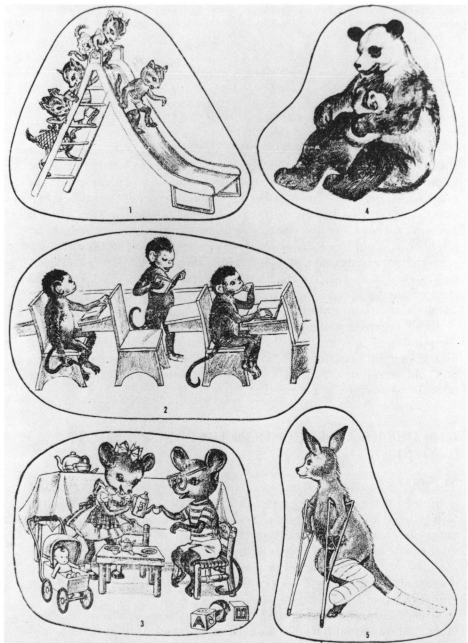

Source: Reproduced with the permission of Leopold Bellak and C.P.S., Inc., P.O. Box 83, Larchmont, NY 10538.

FIGURE 3.6 Cards 6 through 10 of the Children's Apperception Test—Supplement (CAT–S).

Source: Reproduced with the permission of Leopold Bellak and C.P.S., Inc., P.O. Box 83 Larchmont, NY 10538.

THE CAT AS PART OF THE TEST BATTERY

While it would be redundant to caution against using the results from only one projective instrument as a basis for the personality evaluation of a child, the question as to which group of tests to select is worth consideration. Clinical experience suggests that there are at least two tests that should be part of every battery and serve to complement each other since they tap different aspects of personality functioning. Generally, the CAT can be expected to throw light on interpersonal and familial relationships, ego functioning, sources of discomfort, and evidence of conflicts and past traumas. The Rorschach explores deeper levels of personality, emotional responsiveness and mechanisms for control, the extent of reality contact, and available defenses.

Research

The importance of the order in which tests are administered has received far too little attention. Magnussen (1967) used the CAT in his investigation of the effect of animal-related tests on the subsequent appearance of animal content on the Rorschach. Twenty children (aged 6 to 13) were given the Rorschach, Draw-an-Animal (DAA), and CAT, in that order, while 20 carefully matched subjects were tested in the sequence of DAA, CAT, and Rorschach. Significantly more animal content was found on the Rorschach when the DAA and CAT preceded its administration.

Williams (1968) used the CAT along with the Rorschach, WISC, and Bene-Anthony Family Relations Test in a study of children separated from their parents. (The complete discussion of the CAT aspects of the study will be reviewed later, with other sociocultural studies.) Her comparisons between CAT and Rorschach responses showed that the CAT elicited stories of loneliness, desertion, and severe punishment by parents, along with atypical views of family relationships, while the Rorschach served to reveal more of the dynamic personality factors. When compared to their nondeprived controls, these 5- and 6-year-olds gave significantly more color responses (especially CF and C), as well as perceptions of blackness and darkness (C'), "sinister" responses (ogres, monsters, atomic bombs), and "autistic" responses (magical events, escapist fantasies).

An extensive battery of tests also has been used by a group of French psychologists with normal and disturbed children. Perron, Rausch de Traubenberg, and Chabert (1973) studied 25 normal 6-year-olds with a test battery composed of the Rorschach, CAT, DPI (Perron's Dynamique Personnelle et Images), von Staabs's Sceno-Test, and other drawings (free choice, and a child witn parents). The focus of the study was on children's views of their parents. Two aspects were considered: (1) modes of referring to parental images (descriptive, role and status, implicit meanings, and psychoanalytic connotations) and (2) levels of elaboration (viewed as a continuum from the superficial, manifest aspects to expressions arising from the unconscious). The complete protocols are presented for one subject, along with discussions of the results from each test and comparisons of the types of material secured from the different tests.

A comparative study of prepsychotic* and psychotic children by a similar group of French psychologists (Rausch de Traubenberg, Lambert-Boizou, Bloch-Lainé, Chabert, des Ligneris, & Ponroy, 1973) will be discussed in greater detail, with special reference to the CAT, later in this chapter in the section on diagnostic studies. Their complete battery included (1) an intelligence test (WISC or Terman-Merrill, 1937); (2) perceptual (Bender, Rey) and graphomotor tests; (3) Rorschach; (4) CAT or TAT (depending on age and maturity); (5) the Sceno-Test; (6) free drawings; and (7) for some of the subjects, the Patte Noire.

As with Williams' (1968) study, these investigators noted that different levels of personality organization were tapped by the different tests according to the degree of structure, or lack thereof, in the individual instruments. In summarizing results from all the tests in the battery, the authors found that the prepsychotic child is able to reorganize in the face of disorganizing experiences and is more likely to respond to aspects of the external world in a relatively harmonious fashion. In contrast, the psychotic's responses are characterized by a remarkable heterogeneity. The prepsychotic has developed a sense of self that permits a superficial adaptation to everyday life, while the psychotic child remains at a primitive level with no precise definition of self. When fantasy does intrude, the prepsychotic never gives way to a total loss of control, while for the psychotic the sense of reality is radically altered and the capacity for restoration or recuperation is absent. It is as if the psychotic is blocked in unreal situations and cannot disengage from the grip of the primary process.

Illustrative Protocols: CAT versus Rorschach

Billy, 9 years old, was 5 when his parents divorced; his mother died later in the same year. He then lived with an aunt for two years. At 7½ he was transferred to a large home for boys.

While the following CAT results give several indications of Billy's longing for oral gratification, love, and parental attention, it is the

*The French "prepsychotic" group appears to resemble those children viewed as "borderline" or "borderline psychotic" in the United States.

Rorschach (which was administered first) that reveals the depth and intensity of his inner turmoil and his feelings with respect to the lack of warm, caring, familial relationships.

Rorschach

Free Association	Inquiry
I.1. Doesn't look like much of anything. [E encourages.] I still can't make anything out of it.	**I.1.** I can see a little design where the ink has marked over; can't tell where it ends. I made one like it in school.
II.1. Kind of bones with blood on, sort of.	**II.1.** Black part looks like bones, and down here it's bleeding and blood is splattering. The red part [lower red] splattered all over, like it's running down. [Q] Looks like the ribs.
II.2. Looks like a little face, sort of.	**II.2.** Kind of looks like a person, but here it's fluffed up [upper red].
III.1. Not much.	**III.1.** [Adds] Right here [entire lower center, card inverted]; if that wasn't there it would look like a peach when you cut the top part and don't take out the seed; keep making mistakes cutting the skin. [Q] The shape looks like it and the bottom kept poofing when trying to cut the skin off.
IV.1. This one here looks like kind of a worm.	**IV.1.** I saw a yellow one like it outside [entire lower center].
IV.2. Looks like a butterfly with part of his wings tore off.	**IV.2.** If I didn't want to see it as a worm it would look like a butterfly with its wings torn away.
V.1. This one looks like sort of a bat—legs.	**V.1.** Not the whole thing; take off this. The wing should come up more. [Q] Kind of grey in it.
VI.1. Can't make anything out of this.	
VII.1. This looks like part of the beginning of a dress that's been ripped up here.	**VII.1.** Down here it looks like a dress, and up here it comes together with straps but it looks like it's been cut in the center.
VIII.1. Some kind of an animal on a rock and trying to step here.	**VIII.1.** There's a cliff there, too; he's looking down to see how far down it is.

VIII.2. [Adds] Looks like a bone here [center]; like I seen on a rabbit once, backbone.

IX.1. These parts look like some kind of rock, with a face on the top end.

IX.1. Just looks like a rock. The missing spots are where people have been digging. Face of two men [lateral pink] that have fallen, like a statue people have been chipping at. It's some man.

X.1. These all look like bugs.

X.1. [Outer blue].

X.2. [Adds] Looks like part of a butterfly's wings with little eyes on it [lower green].

X.3. [Adds] Here is a stem with two seeds on it, with flowers on it [upper gray].

The Rorschach reveals a very anxious and insecure child who has not found adequate identification figures and does not feel close to anyone. The Fc and FC′ responses suggest a lonely, depressed, and sensitive boy whose affectional needs are not being met. As a result he may react in an immature and impulsive fashion (CF) at times.

The content of the record is striking, with its aura of emptiness (holes and vacant spaces), torn wings and clothing, bones, and splattered blood—all responses frequently found in protocols of children who have experienced the loss of their parents (Haworth, 1964). Humans are not seen on any of the early cards, except for a "little face" (card II.2); the "mother" card (VII.1) is described as a ripped and empty dress. When people do finally appear (card IX.1), they are seen as two cold, hard, stone "statues" that have fallen; emphasis is on the hardness of the rock, the holes where unseen people have been digging, and the chipping away at the stone. In effect, he has distanced himself from interpersonal relationships and retreated from emotional involvements.

CAT

Card 1. This looks like a rooster standing where they're at. The little birds are sitting. The mother is going to pull the bowl over and feed them. They're not little birds; they're chickens. They're holding their spoons. Shall I describe all of the table? [E: How feel?] Chickens are happy and real hungry.

Card 2. The papa bear and mama bear are fighting and baby is on mother's side. If mother falls, baby will fall first. There's a cliff on her side; on his [father's] side there ain't no cliff. [E: What happens?] They're both leaning back and in a little while they'll all fall backwards. It looks like the mother and baby are winning. They're on top of a mountain.

Card 3. There's a rug on the floor and he's sitting on the king's chair with a pipe. There's a mouse looking out of a hole. He has a pipe lit, looks like he's enjoying himself. Should I describe the chair? These people—they voted for him to be king so he could be king of the jungle. He got to be king. They bought a house for him, and a chair, and a pipe, and a cane. The mouse made a hole in the floor; he thought he could get something to eat. Looks like there are people working in front of him and he's watching them.

Card 4. A mother kangaroo and two babies. They're going on a picnic, maybe. Mother is hopping ahead of the biggest baby; he's trying to ride his trike. The smallest is in the pouch with a balloon in his hand. Their house is over here; they're probably going on a picnic—woods over here. They went someplace, to a kangaroo place, and they gave them some food and they're going on a picnic. After they get done, they'll go home and stay home.

Card 5. It looks like a story of the three bears—two baby bears in the baby bed. There's a three-way window, a lamp, and a desk. One baby is asleep and one is awake. Looks like people are in the bed, but probably ain't. [Q] They're in bed. One will get up and do something bad because Mother and Dad aren't in there and they'll get in trouble. (E: What did they do?) Probably got some toys out and played.

Card 6. Looks like the mama and papa bear. It's winter and they hibernate and they went to sleep. The baby bear hasn't gone to sleep yet; he's off in a corner by himself on some sticks. He's probably by the door so he can look out at the snow. [Q] Probably he didn't want to go to sleep yet. Probably wanted to stay awake for a couple of weeks and watch what happens in the snow—how strange it seems to him.

Card 7. This one looks like in the jungle, lots of leaves and trees and vines. The lion's jumping at the monkey to kill him. He's up in the tree; he jumped from the trees to the rocks and he pushed himself off the rock to get the monkey. Looks a little like the monkey might get away; he's reaching up for a vine to climb and the tiger's a little ways away—right by the tail. He takes him; after he kills him I don't know what he would do to him.

Card 8. Looks like there's a . . . two women there . . . and a picture of Grandma on the wall. The third one is either a boy drinking something. Over here one of the women are talking to the little girl, and one woman is drinking coffee and talking to one man. Probably she's telling the child to stay close to the house. That's all.

Card 9. Oh, this little rabbit here went to bed—little one or big one—looks like a big one. She left the door open and windows open. Maybe she's going to run away; maybe she's mad at her mother and will run away. The wind's blowing hard and it looks like there's some little animal on the . . . a little toy man. [Q] Probably she did something bad and she got a whipping.

Card 10. Oh, this dog and he's bad and they had company and father took him in the bathroom and is giving him a whipping. He's whining. There's a laundry bench there; a toilet. [E: What do bad?] He probably knocked over something on purpose to get their attention. [E: How feel?] He doesn't feel very good; it kinda looks like he's laughing, though.

The adaptive mechanisms noted in this series were as follows:

Reaction-formation and Undoing
Isolation
Symbolization
Adequate Identification

While Billy was much more verbal on the CAT than on the Rorschach, his responses reveal little of the depth of his underlying feelings; rather, he tends to distance himself from the threat of the familial activities portrayed by the animal figures by retreating behind a literal description of card details.

Nevertheless, the need for oral gratification is prominent (cards 1, 3, and 4), starting out with the mother as the solicitous provider to her hungry children. On card 3, the king (father?) has everything he needs to "enjoy himself," while the little mouse hopes to get at least some oral supplies. Themes of parental desertion or absence appear on both cards 5 and 6. On card 5, the parents should be in bed but they "probably" are not; this pessimism is continued on card 6, where the parents are present but asleep, with the little one being left out in the cold.

Child characters engage in several misbehaviors which, in turn, bring on parental punishment and feelings of guilt. (Does he feel his naughtiness may have caused his parents to separate and/or brought on mother's death?) The final statements on the last card reflect his longing for parental attention at all costs, his guilt, and the use of denial and bravado as defenses; no one must know how much he hurts inside.

RECENT RESEARCH

In 1966 the author reviewed all available published research on the CAT, as well as dissertations and unpublished papers (Haworth, 1966). Consequently, the discussion in this chapter will concentrate on research published since that time. In those first 17 years there were 54 published studies, while in the past 18 years there have been 29. The early studies were concerned with three major issues: the relative utility of animal versus human protagonists, normative studies, and comparisons between various diagnostic and sociocultural groups. The more recent research has focused on the new CAT-H and on aspects of the examining situation. There have been some further reports on longitudinal projects and a few additional studies of diagnostic and sociocultural samples. It is interesting that half of the recent research has come from countries outside the United States.

Research on the CAT-H

The introduction of a human form of the CAT in 1965 seems to have effectively called a halt to experimental studies on the relative theoretical merits of animal versus human characters for eliciting projective responses from young children. Whereas 15 such studies were published between 1950 and 1963, only one has appeared since that time. Simmons (1967) proceeded from the theory that very young children make little distinction between animals and humans in terms of appropriate activities and behaviors, leading in turn to a proclivity to identify with personalized animals. With increasing age and intellectual development, children would be expected to reject humanized animals as identification figures and turn instead to a preference for human models. Sixteen pairs of drawings were used in which any given animal was engaged in a natural action in one picture and in a humanized activity in the other. The subject was asked to select the one liked best in each pair. In the age range studied, 6 to 12 years, the younger children demonstrated no distinct preference, but by age 10 and beyond the personalized animals were rejected in favor of animal figures shown in their natural situations.

There have been three studies comparing the CAT with CAT-H since the human form appeared. The first, by Lawton (1966), served essentially as a normative study of the relative "pulling power" of the two sets. Both forms were administered, in balanced order, to 24 kindergarteners and 28 second graders with a two-week interval between tests. Protocols were scored with Haworth's Schedule of Adaptive Mechanisms, and comparisons were made of the most common themes for each card. Analysis of the relative use of defense mechanisms revealed no consistency between forms except for Projection-Introjection, which did show significant agreement between forms. The two forms elicited fairly similar themes for the corresponding cards, except for the presence of more aggressive responses on the animal version; for example, for card 2, the tug of war was seen more often as a fight on the animal card and as a game between peers on the human version; on card 3, the smaller figure was seen more often as the victim of an attack in the animal version.

Neuringer and Livesay (1970) made a comparison of the relative amounts of projective fantasy elicited by the two forms and assessed any differences in responses from children of differing levels of anxiety, on the assumption that the animal stimuli might be more effective with highly anxious children. Three groups of fourth-grade children were selected on the basis of scores on the Children's Manifest Anxiety Scale. Protocols were scored on five variables: number of words, number of emotional words, number of expressed negative emotions, Haworth's Schedule of Adaptive Mechanisms, and the Transcendence Index (Weisskopf, 1950). There were no significant differences on any of the measures that could be attributed to differences in anxiety level. Subjects gave longer stories to the CAT-H, while the CAT elicited more emotional words and more negative emotions. The two forms were comparable in demonstrating similar scores on Haworth's Schedule. The only significant difference between forms was found for the Transcendence Index, with the CAT protocols giving higher mean scores than the CAT-H. The authors concluded that there was no evidence that animal stimuli would prove more effective than human with highly anxious children, and that there were few differences in children's responses that could be attributed to any preference for one form over the other.

The TAT was used with 60 second-graders in comparisons with the CAT-H and the CAT by Myler, Rosenkrantz, and Holmes (1972). The protocols were evaluated by word count, the Transcendence Index, and ratings for creativity (introduction of characters, unusual activities) and organization (a tightly knit story in logical sequence). There were no significant differences between the CAT and CAT-H. The TAT was less effective than either of the other two tests on all measures, with significant differences from both "child" tests on the Transcendence Index, and for word count in the CAT-TAT comparison.

It is worth highlighting the fact that these studies all conclude that any differences in projective power between the two forms are very slight indeed, consequently the two forms can be considered as essentially equivalent. As Bellak and Hurvich (1966a) have suggested in the CAT-H manual, this newer version of the test can be used as the only instrument or introduced as an alternate form if the animal version has not proved satisfactory due to the age of the child, the paucity of the protocol, or any unsatisfactory testing conditions that may appear to have inhibited the child on the initial exposure.

Aspects of Test Administration

Several of the recent studies have addressed issues in connection with administering the tests, especially at the younger age levels. Passman and Lautmann (1982) administered the CAT to children 23 to 35 months of age and to a second group 41 to 45 months of age. Either the mother, father, or a security blanket was present for the first half of the session. For the younger age group, the presence of a parent for the initial portion of testing was more productive than provision of the blanket; for the older group there were no differences in verbal responsiveness between parent or blanket. For both groups, productivity increased from the parent-present to the parent-absent parts of the session. Thus the presence of a parent during the initial phase of testing appears to provide a sense of security which then facilitates the establishment of rapport with the examiner once the parent has left the room.

Dandridge and Faust (1973) used a standard set of CAT cards with 3- and 4-year-olds, plus a set in which each card was cut into a simple jigsaw puzzle. With the latter set, the child was instructed first to put the puzzle together before being asked to tell a story. Protocols were scored for enumeration, description, interpretation, and identification. The puzzle form elicited significantly more interpretive and descriptive responses than did the standard set.

Erikson and Rørorsgaard (1979) have addressed the question of the most effective role for the examiner to take in encouraging the child's participation. They have proposed a method whereby the examiner takes a more active role, communicating with the child by play-acting through the characters in the stories.

A study by Newmark, Wheeler, Newmark, and Stabler (1975) was concerned with the relative amount of anxiety a child experiences during administration of the CAT, Rorschach, Sentence Completion, and WISC. The subjects, 9-year-olds, were given the State–Trait Anxiety Inventory for Children before and after each test, with one-day intervals between tests. There were no significant differences in trait anxiety for any of the tests. For the CAT and the Sentence Completion there were no significant changes in state anxiety, in contrast to significant increases in state anxiety after administration of the Rorschach and the WISC.

The coping styles of young children when confronted with the requirements of responding to the CAT have been of concern to a group at the Menninger Foundation, as reported by Moriarty (1968). They were interested in the quality and intensity of the child's reactions to the testing situation and the resulting effect on overall functioning. Evidence of considerable stress was found, revealed particularly in speaking (especially in boys) and in reduction in clarity and intensity of voice quality (in girls). Boys were three times more apt to be restless and hyperactive than were girls. The most frequently observed defenses at this age were denial, repression, avoidance–withdrawal, and the projection of aggression. In conclusion, Moriarty emphasized that

> For all of our preschool subjects, the interpersonal relationship with the examiner in a new, unfamiliar and bewildering situation, along with the potential conflict stimulated by card content, was exceedingly stressful. . . .

Such expressions of tension were understandable in terms of the artificiality of the examining situation, insofar as the child participated not out of his own need, but from adult pressures already experienced by most young children as excessive. Furthermore, he was asked for verbal responses and insights which pressed his developing language capacity and his attention span. He had no choice but to comply, but did this according to his own perceptual style. It is the examination of this style which is the meat of his responsiveness and which cannot be fully standardized. (Moriarty, 1968, p. 418)

Normative and Longitudinal Studies

A review of the CAT literature since 1966 has revealed only two studies concerned with normative responses and/or developmental progressions, and two follow-up, continuation reports of ongoing longitudinal studies of normal children.

Bradfer-Blomart (1970) compared the CAT responses of 50 boys and 50 girls, all 8 years of age. There were few sex differences, although boys were less likely to oppose adult control than were girls. Boys also gave more common responses but showed fewer aggressive feelings, while girls were found to be more mature in their manner of responding.

Schroth (1977) examined the CATs of 80 normal schoolchildren, 6 to 10 years of age, using the Associative Elaboration and Integration Scales initially developed by Slemon, Holzworth, Lewis, and Sitko (1976) for the TAT. Progressions with age were found for both scales. The Associative Elaboration Scale (embellishments, affective reactions, details not shown on the card) yielded significantly higher scores at age levels beyond 7 years. Similarly, the Integration Scale (theme and plot combined in an integrated whole) showed significant differences, with ages 9 and 10 scoring higher than the younger age levels.

The most extensive longitudinal study of the CAT has been carried out by Witherspoon (1968) and his students. They have followed 80 children from ages 3 through 11 years. Of major concern was the development of methods for objectively scoring and analyzing the protocols. Initially the stories were coded for the presence of the following dynamics: orality, anality, sibling rivalry, oedipal conflicts, aggression, fear, sexuality, and identification with parents. Ten years later, when some 500 subsequent stories were evaluated for the same dynamics, results similar to the initial ones were found; namely, parental identifications, aggression, and orality were revealed most often on the CAT, with card 5 being the only one to elicit oedipal themes. Sex differences were minimal. In a later effort to move away from an approach based largely on psychoanalytic principles to a more objective picture of personality development, a set of basic factors was derived from factor-analytic studies of developmental behavioral data. Nine scoring categories emerged that could be used in the content analysis of CAT responses: Schizothymia (antisocial, aggressive, socially undesirable), Emotionality (affective involvement), Character-integrity (self-discipline, responsibility), Basic Needs (sleeping, eating), Sex Role (gender or sex role), Activity (ongoing movement, verbal behavior), Description (enumeration, naming), Self-reference ("I," "me," "we," etc.), Evasion (no response, card rejection, conversation with examiner). When these categories were applied to 30 protocols, the first four occurred only rarely at any age level; Sex Role and Activity responses increased with increasing age; the last three categories (Description, Self-reference, and Evasion) decreased markedly with age.

Moriarty (1968) and the Menninger group evaluated children's coping maneuvers during the testing situation through the preschool and latency years (with the CAT) and on into prepuberty and adolescence (with the TAT). As mentioned in the preceding section on aspects of test administration, some degree of denial, repression, avoidance, and projection was found in the preschool records. During latency, these same children exhibited a wider range of coping mechanisms along with more realistic and conforming behaviors, more control of affect, and fewer expressions of aggression and hostility. Coping styles during prepuberty and adolescence showed increasing subtlety and differentiation, with redefinition of identity and more concern with cognitive, academic aspects. Some of the preschool children had been found to make exceptionally free use of fantasy and imagination along with a clear recognition of reality. This creative, elaborative style was still evident in their CAT responses during latency, but in prepuberty (with the TAT) only half of this subgroup continued to use rich fantasy in their stories.

Diagnostic Groups

The CAT–H was administered by Porterfield (1969) to preschool stutterers matched with nonstuttering classmates and a group of nonstuttering children referred to a clinic for attention-getting and negativistic behaviors. Using the Schedule of Adaptive Mechanisms, he found that the stutterers received significantly higher scores on Repression-Denial and Symbolization, while the normal nonstutterers scored higher on Projection–Introjection. There were no differences between the stutterers and the clinic-referred nonstutterers.

In studies from overseas, Bose and Benerjee (1969) in India studied the CAT responses of institutionalized handicapped children of varying intellectual levels and, in a subsequent study, orthopedically handicapped, nonretarded children from 7 to 12 years of age (Bose & Biswas, 1972). Also in India, Sen Mazumdar and Solanki (1979) found significant differences between large groups of emotionally disturbed and normal subjects when the CAT (or TAT, depending on subject's age) protocols were compared on four criteria: unfavorable press, security versus insecurity, rationalization, and optimistic outcomes. Guinand, Delfosse, and Bradfer-Blomart (1969) found that children with educational or minor neurotic problems gave more evidence in their CAT stories of conflicts, hostility, and defensiveness than did normal children.

In France, Rausch de Traubenberg et al. (1973) used the CAT as one of a battery of tests administered to 25 prepsychotic children (5 to 11 years of age) and to 22 psychotic children (6 to 12 years of age). They reported that the prepsychotic responses were characterized by initially adequate recognition and perception of the figures on the cards, which soon gave way to fantasy interpretations. By the end of the story, however, the child often was able to return to the reality level. For the psychotics, primary process material intervened much more readily, the structuring of time and place was usually deviant, or the child resorted to reciting dates, names, or numbers.

The prepsychotics' stories were characterized by a rich fantasy of an archaic type; fantasies of being devoured at the oral-sadistic level; and expressions of fear of annihilation or abandonment. There were many regressive themes of eating, drinking, and sleeping and of escaping into an imaginary, magical world. Little distinction was made between the aggressor and the one aggressed against, and there was little differentiation of paternal and maternal roles, although the basic recognition of the differences between the sexes was apparent. In most cases there was a mother–child relationship, with mother alternating between good and bad, while the paternal image was nonexistent or viewed only at the phallic level. In contrast, psychotic children saw parental images with indifference; parents served only a social function, and oedipal themes appeared merely as artifacts of the described situation. In terms of defense mechanisms, the prepsychotics employed adaptive defenses and maintained contact with objective reality. The psychotics' defenses were largely projection, projective identification, and denial of reality, with recourse to magical thinking and arbitrary rationalizations.

Sociocultural Studies

Parental Loss. The effects of parental loss were studied by Williams (1961) with a sample of 54 children aged 5 to 11 years. Not only had these children suffered loss of their parents at an early age, but each had been transferred from a foster home to a Children's Reception Center (CRC) because of unsatisfactory relations with the foster parents. The control sample consisted of 74 children who had experienced continuous family life until an emergency crisis required temporary care at the CRC. The CAT was administered as part of the test battery to those children who were 5 and 6 years of age (20 from the breakdown group and 21 controls). There were no differences between groups in terms of purely descriptive stories. The loss group gave significantly more stories of unrealistic family relationships and of loneliness and rejection of child characters. The control group gave significantly more stories concerning normal family relationships.

In an overview of the content of the stories from the parentally deprived group, Williams (1961) particularly noted an emphasis on severe punishments by parent figures and themes of parental desertion, in addition to the loneliness and rejection of the child characters. She uses this story, given for card 9, as a typical example:

> A little rabbit sitting up on a cot. He's supposed to be asleep but he's not, he's wide awake because Father Christmas saw him and never gave him no toys. He is cold and lonely and he has a bad cough. His Mummy and Daddy were nasty. They didn't look after him. They left him alone. (Williams, 1968, pp. 138–139)

A group of 24 orphaned boys aged 6 to 10 was administered the Indian adaptation of the CAT by Singh and Akhtar (1970). The stories were generally realistic but they lacked imagination and originality. The environment was seen as hostile; there were concerns about punishment and physical harm; and there was a high interest in food and the need for affiliation. Identification was made with male figures, and superegos were severe.

Kibbutz versus Moshav Children. Rabin (1968) compared the CAT responses of 43 children (5 and 6 years of age) raised in an Israeli kibbutz with those of 36 children who were living with their parents in a moshav village (a rural cooperative-type settlement). In view of the different parenting experiences of the two groups, reactions to parental figures in the cards was of primary interest. Kibbutz boys consistently mentioned father and mother figures more often than did moshav boys, and they saw the parents as more positive and affectionate toward children. There were no differences between girls in the two groups in terms of mentioning parent figures, but the kibbutz girls saw the parents as being more positive toward child figures. Kibbutz boys used more oral themes, and kibbutz girls expressed more aggression than did their respective controls. There were no major differences between kibbutz and moshav subjects in terms of omission of figures, while both girls and boys from the kibbutz made more use of denial (not describing the most obvious perceptions of figures or situations).

Rabin (1968) places these findings in the context of his longitudinal study of the personality development of children raised in the kibbutz, wherein kibbutz infants appeared to show developmental delays in ego development when compared to nonkibbutz controls, while, by 10 years of age, the kibbutz children had caught up with and, in some areas, surpassed the controls in terms of personality and emotional adjustment. Rabin suggests that the emphasis on parental figures and oral themes in the CAT stories given by the kibbutz boys may indicate a reaction to their less close contact with the actual parents. This trend toward dependency is later reversed in adolescence, where TAT stories show little concern for family and an extreme independence.

Thai versus British Children. The CATs of 80 Thai and 40 British children between the ages of 4 and 6 were studied by Kline and Svaste-Xuto (1981). A Thai psychologist selected the cards most likely to be understood by Thai subjects, namely cards 2, 3, 7, 9, and 10. Protocols were examined for the presence or absence of specific features characteristic of each card. There were no sex differences, but several significant cultural differences were noted on cards 2, 7, and 10. On card 2, British children saw the contest as mother and child pulling against a family member or a friend, with the single figure winning; Thai children saw the pair as friends and as the winners. On card 7, British children thought the monkey would be caught and killed, while the Thai children felt the monkey could escape although it would get hurt. British children saw the figures on card 10 as a parent and child; the Thai children saw them as mother and father, or brother and sister, or as friends. The authors suggest that the differing responses may be reflective of differing perceptions of parental figures in the two cultures and of the greater importance of peers to Thai children.

Philippine Barrio. Ilan and Resurreccion-Ventura (1971) administered the Philippine CAT to kindergarten children from a college community and to children from a barrio. The children from the college community gave more responses of identification with the mother and concerns about toileting, while the barrio children showed more interest and concern centered on aspects of sexuality.

SUMMARY

After 35 years, the animal version of the CAT continues to play a major role in the area of picture–story tests for young children. The human form (CAT–H) has not generated as much research interest as did the former, but results from the few comparative studies suggest that the two forms are basically equivalent. Methods of scoring have been discussed as well as factors to be considered when interpreting the results. The role of the CAT as part of the test battery has been the focus of two large research projects in England and in France. Other recent research efforts have concentrated on aspects of test administration, normative and longitudinal studies, various diagnostic groupings, .and comparative studies of children with differing sociocultural experiences.

REFERENCES

Bellak, L. (1955). *Short-form: Bellak TAT and CAT blank.* Larchmont, NY: C.P.S.

Bellak, L. (1971). *The T.A.T. and C.A.T. in clinical use* (2nd ed.). New York: Grune & Stratton.

Bellak, L., & Bellak, S. S. (1952). *Manual for the supplement to the Children's Apperception Test (C.A.T.-S).* Larchmont, NY: C.P.S.

Bellak, L., & Bellak, S. S. (1961). *Children's Apperception Test (C.A.T.), manual* (4th ed.). Larchmont, NY: C.P.S.

Bellak, L., & Hurvich, M. S. (1966a). *C.A.T.-H. Children's Apperception Test (human figures), manual.* Larchmont, NY: C.P.S.

Bellak, L., & Hurvich, M. S. (1966b). A human modification of the Children's Apperception Test (CAT–H). *Journal of Projective Techniques and Personality Assessment, 30,* 228–242.

Bose, S., & Benerjee, S. N. (1969). A resolution on the personality make-up of some institutionalized physically handicapped children by the Children's Apperception Test. *Journal of Psychological Researches, 13,* 32–36. (From *Psychological Abstracts,* 1971, *45,* Abstract No. 4696.)

Bose, S., & Biswas, C. (1972). A study on the social world of some physically handicapped children. *Indian Journal of Applied Psychology, 9,* 20–23. (From *Psychological Abstracts,* 1974, *52,* Abstract No. 1310.)

Bradfer-Blomart, J. (1970). Analyse des thèmes fournis au CAT par des garçons de huit ans: Comparaison des récits d'un groupe de garçons et de filles du même age. *Enfance, 2,* 215–234. (From *Psychological Abstracts,* 1971, *46,* Abstract No. 4681.)

Dandridge, M. C., & Faust, W. L. (1973). The Children's Apperception Test: Puzzle and regular form. *Journal of Personality Assessment, 37,* 244–247.

Erikson, H., & Rørorsgaard, O. (1979). [An alternate way of administering CAT.] *Tidsskrift for Norsk Psykologforening, 16,* 484–492. (*Psychological Abstracts,* 1981, *65,* Abstract No. 174.)

Guinand, M., Delfosse, F. K., & Bradfer-Blomart, J. (1969). Utilization de la notion de banalité et d'originalité dans l' interprétation de récits fournis on test C.A.T. par des filles de 8 ans. *Enfance, 5,* 309–337. (From *Psychological Abstracts,* 1970, *44,* Abstract No. 16386.)

Haworth, M. R. (1963). A schedule for the analysis of CAT responses. *Journal of Projective Techniques and Personality Assessment, 27,* 181–184.

Haworth, M. R. (1964). Parental loss in children as reflected in projective responses. *Journal of Projective Techniques and Personality Assessment, 28,* 32–45.

Haworth, M. R. (1965). *A schedule of adaptive mechanisms in CAT responses.* Larchmont, NY: C.P.S.

Haworth, M. R. (1966). *The CAT: Facts about fantasy.* New York: Grune & Stratton.

Ilan, L. C., & Resurreccion-Ventura, E. (1971). Responses of preschool children to the Philippine Children's Apperception Test (PCAT): A preliminary study. *Philippine Journal of Psychology, 4,* 44–52. (From *Psychological Abstracts,* 1973, *49,* Abstract No. 611.)

Kline, P., & Svaste-Xuto, B. (1981). The responses of Thai and British children to the Children's Apperception Test. *Journal of Social Psychology, 113,* 137–138.

Langmay, A. V. (1975a). Responses of elementary school children to the Philippine Children's Apperception Test (PCAT). *Philippine Journal of Mental Health, 6,* 9–16. (From *Psychological Abstracts,* 1980, *63,* Abstract No. 800.)

Langmay, A. V. (1975b). Studies on a Philippine Children's Apperception Test (PCAT): 1. Construction and development administration. *Philippine Journal of Mental Health, 6,* 18–25. (From *Psychological Abstracts,* 1979, *62,* Abstract No. 12648.)

Lawton, M. J. (1966). Animal and Human CATs with a school sample. *Journal of Projective Techniques and Personality Assessment, 30,* 243–246.

Magnussen, M. G. (1967). Effect of test order upon children's Rorschach animal content. *Journal of Projective Techniques and Personality Assessment, 31,* 41–43.

Moriarty, A. E. (1968). Normal preschoolers' reactions to the CAT: Some implications for later development. *Journal of Projective Techniques and Personality Assessment, 32,* 413–419.

Myler, B., Rosenkrantz, A., & Holmes, G. (1972). A comparison of the TAT, CAT and CAT–H among second grade girls. *Journal of Projective Techniques and Personality Assessment, 36,* 440–444.

Neuringer, C., & Livesay, R. C. (1970). Projective fantasy on the CAT and CAT–H. *Journal of Projective Techniques and Personality Assessment, 34,* 487–491.

Newmark, C. S., Wheeler, D., Newmark, L., & Stabler, B. (1975). Test-induced anxiety with children. *Journal of Personality Assessment, 39,* 409–413.

Passman, R. H., & Lautmann, L. A. (1982). Fathers', mothers' and security blankets' effects on the responsiveness of young children during projective testing. *Journal of Consulting and Clinical Psychology, 50,* 310–312.

Perron, R., Rausch de Traubenberg, N., & Chabert, C. (1973). Les images parentales. Niveaux d'élaboration et niveaux d'expression dans diverses épreuves projectives. *Psychologie Française, 18,* 175–194.

Porterfield, C. L. (1969). Adaptive mechanisms of young disadvantaged stutterers and nonstutterers. *Journal of Projective Techniques and Personality Assessment, 33,* 372–375.

Rabin, A. I. (1968). Children's Apperception Test findings with Kibbutz and non-

Kibbutz preschoolers. *Journal of Projective Techniques and Personality Assessment, 32,* 420–424.

Rausch de Traubenberg, N., Lambert-Boizou, M. F., Block-Laine, F., Chabert, C., des Ligneris, J., & Ponroy, R. (1973). Organisation prépsychotique et psychotique de la personnalité chez l'enfant à travers les techniques projectives. *Psychologie Française, 18,* 213–231.

Schroth, M. L. (1977). The use of the Associative Elaboration and Integration Scales for evaluating CAT protocols. *Journal of Psychology, 97,* 29–35.

Sen Mazumdar, D. P., & Solanki, P. S. (1979). A comparative study of emotionally disturbed children and normal children on selected criteria of projective apperception tests (TAT/CAT). *Indian Journal of Clinical Psychology, 6,* 115–117. (From *Psychological Abstracts,* 1981, *65,* Abstract No. 6877.)

Simmons, D. D. (1967). Children's preferences for humanized versus natural animals. *Journal of Projective Techniques and Personality Assessment, 31,* 39–41.

Singh, U. P., & Akhtar, S. N. (1970). The Children's Apperception Test in the study of orphans. *Psychology Annual, 4,* 1–6. (From *Psychological Abstracts,* 1976, *46,* Abstract No. 2744.)

Slemon, A. G., Holzworth, E. J., Lewis, J., & Sitko, M. (1976). Associative Elaboration and Integration Scales for evaluating TAT protocols. *Journal of Personality Assessment, 40,* 365–369.

Strnadová, M., & Bŏs, P. (1977). [CATO: A semi-projective test for the assessment of interpersonal relations in the child's family and his social environment.] *Psychológia a Patopsychológie Dietařa, 12,* 449–457. (From *Psychological Abstracts,* 1979, *62,* Abstract No. 10153.)

Terman, L. M., & Merrill, M. A. (1937) *Measuring intelligence.* Boston: Houghton Mifflin.

Weisskopf, E. (1950). A transcendence index as a proposed measure in the TAT. *Journal of Psychology, 29,* 379–390.

Williams, J. M. (1961). Children who break down in foster homes: A psychological study of patterns of personality growth in grossly deprived children. *Journal of Child Psychology and Psychiatry, 2,* 5–20.

Williams, J. M. (1968). *Rorschach with children.* London: Pergamon Press.

Witherspoon, R. L. (1968). Development of objective scoring methods for longitudinal CAT data. *Journal of Projective Techniques and Personality Assessment, 32,* 406–412.

4

The Michigan Picture Test—Revised

Max L. Hutt

The original Michigan Picture Test was first published in 1953 (Science Research Associates, 1953), consisting of 16 cards, one of which is blank. The Michigan Picture Test—Revised (MPT-R) was published in 1980 (Hutt, 1980a), consisting of 15 cards, one of which is blank. The revision was based on the original research program and findings, carried out over an intensive three-year period and comprising a research population drawn from 17 public schools and 11 state child guidance centers, all in Michigan, selected to represent a distribution characteristic of the socio-economic variables of the state and cultural and geographic features of that population. The sample was restricted to children enrolled in the third, fifth, seventh, and ninth grades. The major features of the revision were the exclusion of one of the original test cards (since it was no longer appropriate in view of cultural changes) and an extensive reorganization of the user's manual so as to provide (1) greater clarification of the research findings, (2) more adequate instructions for scoring and inter-pretation, and (3) inclusion of more recent research findings on compara-bility of norms.

The major objective of the revised test remains the same: the rapid and objective differentiation of emotionally disturbed schoolchildren from well-adjusted schoolchildren by means of a small sample of thematic stories based on four core cards. Our research data indicate that this objective has been attained; moreover, the clinician may use either the four core cards or samplings of other cards to delineate areas of interest, such as types of conflict present, content of emotional problems, and other aspects of adjustment patterns.

TEST MATERIALS

As will be noted later (see section on standardization and research findings) the test pictures were selected to meet carefully defined a priori criteria and statistically significant findings. At this point the test cards will be described and designated with "C" for core card, as well as "B" for boys, "G" for girls, and "X" for both sexes. Their descriptions are as follows:

Card 1 (C, X). Family scene at breakfast. The father, mother, son, and daughter are eating breakfast. Tends to elicit themes concerning familial harmony and discord.

Card 2 (X). Boy and girl in field. The scene depicts a preadolescent boy and girl, possibly appearing shy towards each other. Many aspects of heterosexual relations are elicited by this card.

Card 3G (G). Woman and child on a sofa. The woman "appears" to be talking (sternly?) to her child; the child is turned away. Themes concerning mother–daughter relationships, often with a disapproving mother, are evoked.

Card 3B (B). Father and son. A seated, stern-looking man is looking up at a somewhat crestfallen boy standing in front of him. Themes similar to those on Card 3G, concerning father–son conflict, often are provoked by this card.

Card 4 (X). Bathroom scene. A man (father) is helping his young son and daughter (both about three to four years of age) after they have emerged from the bathtub. Frequent themes involve oedipal wishes and fears.

Card 5 (C, X). Preadolescent children playing checkers. Two children are playing while others, boys and girls, are observing intently. Themes of competition, failure, success, and power often are stimulated.

Card 6 (X). Young children walking up a country road. Various forms of fantasy, especially themes concerning adventure and differentiation from family, are elicited.

Card 7G (G). Young girl leaning on school desk. The usual themes are fantasy, especially endless fantasy.

Card 7B (B). Young boy gazing into the distance. Themes similar to 7G are called forth.

Card 8 (C, X). Lightning in the dark. Themes concerning basic anxiety, abandonment, and helplessness are frequent. In some children, blocking or avoidance occurs.

Card 9G (G). Father and daughter in serious discussion. Themes concern father–daughter relationships, with many variations in content.

Card 9B (B). Stern man with young boy. The man is frequently perceived as an authority figure, perhaps a school principal. The boy is perceived as contrite or subdued.

Card 10 G (G). Girl at desk in school classroom. Frequent themes involve conflict and fantasy about schoolwork and school problems.

Card 10 B (B). Young boy and uniformed man confronting woman in doorway. A very productive card, evoking varied themes concerning apprehension, relationships with mother, and antisocial wishes/tendencies.

Card 11 (C, X). Blank card. As with most thematic tests, this blank card provides the stimulus for unstructured fantasy. It provides an opportunity for the subject to project without specific, a priori, limitations.

It has been found that the most frequent areas of concern/conflict that are elicited by these test cards are (1) interpersonal relations with peers, (2) interpersonal relations with family members, (3) achievement and failure, (4) sexual wishes and anxieties, (5) school attitudes and phobias, (6) reactions to authority, (7) identity problems, and (8) feelings about the body.

The Michigan Picture Test (Hutt, 1980a) provides detailed instructions for administering, scoring, and both quantitative and qualitative analysis. Norms are provided for grades 3 through 9. A record form is also provided for recording objective findings as well as for qualitative analysis.

TEST ADMINISTRATION

The examiner may wish to administer either the core series (four cards) or the full series, depending on the purposes for which the test is given. The core series was designed to provide a rapid, nonthreatening examination that would yield objective scores related to degree of emotional adjustment. It was hoped that well-validated scores, based on critical personality factors, would assist in differentiating the well-adjusted from the poorly adjusted schoolchildren in the applicable age range. Test administration of the core series usually takes from 10 to 20 minutes. Scoring, once the scoring criteria are learned, usually takes about 5 minutes. As our findings indicate, data from the core series yield fairly valid differentiation of well-adjusted from poorly adjusted schoolchildren.

Core cards 1, 5, 8, and 11 are administered in that order. The examiner also may wish to administer card 6 if an additional objective index is desired (see later section on uses for the MPT–R). The test is designed to be administered individually, although, as all users of apperceptive tests are now aware, small-group administration is also possible.

The examiner simply presents each card in turn and says, "I'd like you to tell me a story about this picture. Just tell what is happening, how it came about, and how it ends." The examiner may wish to add, "You can also tell me how these people are feeling." This addition is usually not needed, since it has been found that most children will describe both feelings and actions. If the child is hesitant about beginning, some simple encouragement is usually all that is needed, such as, "Oh, just make up some sort of story about the picture, anything it makes you think of." When the blank card is presented, the examiner may say, "Here is a blank card. Let's see how good your imagination is. This time make up any kind of story you like about this blank card." None of these directions need to be followed literally; rather, the intent should be conveyed in whatever manner is appropriate for the particular child. If the child does not provide some outcome for the story, or if the antecedents of the action have not been described, the examiner may ask, "And how did it come out?" in the former instance and "How did this happen?" in the latter instance.

When administering the full series, the examiner should give the cards in their numerical order. Since the additional cards of the full series need not be scored, the examiner may wish to select only those cards which are of particular interest in a given instance. Thus the "full" series may consist of any number of cards not included in the core series, from a minimum of 5 cards to a maximum of 15 cards. (Of course, "X" cards may be administered to both sexes, while "B" cards will be used for boys and "G" cards will be used for girls. In this way, the examiner can explore the specific areas of personality interest.)

After all of the selected cards have been administered, the examiner may wish to clarify the meanings or implications of the stories that the subject has proffered, thereby conducting what is called an inquiry. Questions may be asked to elucidate the feelings of the characters, the further outcomes of their actions, and even the identities represented by the several characters. In this way, test data can be integrated with clinical applications, should this be desired (see the later section on the uses for the MPT-R).

As with any clinical procedure, the examiner should seek suitable rapport with the subject and carefully consider any special circumstances that might affect test results.

It is recommended that the subject's verbalizations be tape-recorded. Not only will the content of the proffered stories be more accurately recorded, but such factors as significant pauses and blockings, inflections, side remarks, and verbalizations between the examiner and the subject will be recorded for later evaluation with respect to their possible significance.

BRIEF HISTORY OF THE MPT-R

The MPT was developed under the impetus of Samuel W. Hartwell, who at the time was Assistant Director of the Department of Mental Health of the state of Michigan and who believed that an apperceptive test, with appropriately selected test cards, would be a highly useful clinical tool for both diagnosis and treatment. He designated a research committee to work on this project with Max L. Hutt as clinical and research consultant. After more than three years of intensive research efforts involving the psychologists in the central office and the collaboration of psychologists and others in the public schools and child guidance centers of Michigan, and after publication of preliminary research findings, the MPT was published in 1953.

The MPT was widely used for a number of years and was favorably received and reviewed by workers in the field (see, for example, Freeman, 1953, and Neuringer, 1968), but for unforeseen circumstances publication and distribution of the test ceased for a number of years. When the publisher decided to resume publication, Hutt undertook (1) to revise the manual in the light of criticisms that had been offered by users and (2) to cross-validate the norms and test materials in the light of changing cultural conditions.

The MPT-R was published in 1980 (Hutt, 1980a) and included all of the previous research data and normative data. One test card was deleted. Preliminary cross-validation data, based on a representative sample of schoolchildren and upon patients from a pediatric division of a major university hospital, indicated that normative data and previous research findings were validated. The MPT-R is therefore based on the original research data, with scoring procedures and normative data intact.

STANDARDIZATION AND RESEARCH FINDINGS

As noted previously, in developing the MPT-R more than 700 children in the state of Michigan were examined. Seventeen public schools, chosen to provide a representative socioeconomic and cultural sample of the state, and 11 child guidance clinics provided a sample of clinically validated cases of emotionally disturbed children.

There were two sets of criterion variables. For the schools, a Rating Scale for Pupil Adjustment was developed by the research staff (see Hutt, 1980a). This scale consisted of 11 items, each of which could be rated from one to five. An intercorrelational study of the items was conducted with a preliminary population. Teachers rated 86 pupils after they had

had at least 3 months of classroom observation. Analysis of the obtained intercorrelations yielded four clusters of items. A Total Emotional Adjustment Scale was developed and used as the criterion variable for the school population.

All of the statistical analyses were performed utilizing test data from schoolchildren and the criterion of adjustment based on scores on the Total Emotional Adjustment Scale. However, all of the obtained scores on the test were validated separately, using the clinical judgments obtained in clinical evaluations at the various child guidance centers. Thus, the objective indices (Tension Index, Verb Tense, and Direction of Forces) based on the core series of test cards were doubly validated, both against teacher ratings and against clinical evaluations. Final norms on the test were based on the total sample of schoolchildren. All other variables that were not found to achieve adequate statistically significant levels of validity but were found to be clinically useful for exploratory purposes were evaluated separately against clinical criteria. It should be noted that some of these exploratory variables were close to the level of achieving statistical significance; further research is needed either in modification of scoring criteria or more adequate definition of outcome criteria before these can be incorporated into the normative tables. The 1980 manual (Hutt, 1980a) includes all of the relevant data.

Test Cards

The areas to be "tapped" by the test cards were first selected after a critical review of research and clinical literature on child development. Over 1,000 pictures were first considered, and after preliminary evaluation by psychologists, 65 were selected for empirical study against our criteria (Adjustment Scale); two additional cross-validations led to the final selection. The method of analysis in the final two cross-validation studies employed statistical tests of significance for all of the test variables in differentiating well-adjusted from poorly adjusted children on subsamples of the population (Andrew, Walton, Hutt, & Hartwell, 1951). It also should be noted that all of the selected pictures met a priori criteria with respect to stimulus values (Hutt, 1980a).

Test Variables

In order to develop objectively scorable test variables, a search was made of relevant empirical and theoretical publications in the field. Based on this review and our own theoretical predilections we selected and carefully defined eight potentially useful variables that merited further study in a small population of both school and clinic cases, not utilized subsequently in the final validation. Refinements in definition of the variables and improved directions for scoring were made (Hartwell, Hutt, Andrew, & Walton, 1951). These redefined variables then were tested in the final validation process, using the remainder of our school and clinic populations. Three of the variables were found to discriminate significantly between well-adjusted and poorly adjusted children and met the tests of clinical judgment as well. The three are tension, verb tense, and direction of forces. The other variables either did not meet our criteria of statistical significance or failed to produce suitable distributions of scores at all age levels. However, several seemed so promising, as noted earlier, that we will present our research findings for them and suggest further use for exploratory purposes.

Tension Index. This index is based on the frequency of verbal expressions of seven defined needs: love, extrapunitiveness, intropunitiveness, succor, achievement, submissiveness, and personal adequacy. The score on the Tension Index is the arithmetical sum of these expressed needs on the four core cards. Normative data for both well-adjusted and poorly adjusted schoolchildren are presented in the user's manual (Hutt, 1980a), and critical scores, which are defined as scores that significantly distinguish between pupils who are well adjusted and those who are poorly adjusted, also are presented. For example, at the third-grade level, the mean number of defined needs that are expressed is 4.2 for the well-adjusted while the mean is 6.8 for the poorly adjusted. The difference is significant at the .05 level. For fifth-grade children, the comparative means are 4.7 and 7.1; the difference is statistically significant at the .01 level. For seventh and ninth graders combined, the respective means are 6.4 and 10.2 and the difference is significant at the .05 level.

Verb Tense. This is an interesting variable in several respects. From a developmental viewpoint, the relative use of past, present, and future tenses is interesting since the increasing use of both past and, especially, future tenses is correlated with healthy mental development. From the viewpoint of test construction and use, it is very simple to count the number of times each of the tenses is utilized. It is also fairly simple to compare and predict how the relative proportions of the three tenses vary with both developmental status and emotional well-being.

As expected, the most frequently used tense at all grade levels was the present tense; however, preferential use of both past and future tense varied irregularly with developmental status. The use of past tense increased from 7.5 percent in the third grade to 28.7 percent in the fifth grade, and then declined to 16.7 percent in the seventh and ninth grades. The use of future tense declined from 8.5 percent in the third grade to 3.2 percent in the fifth grade, and then increased to 6.0 percent in the seventh and ninth grades. It was decided to use the percent of use of each tense in relation to the total of all three tenses as the measure to be explored. Based on a study of our data, we determined the relative *critical percentages* for each tense that differentiated poorly adjusted from well-adjusted pupils. As illustrative of our findings, at grade five, a percentage of 43 and above in the use of past tense is indicative of poor adjustment, while a percentage of 52 and below in the use of present tense is also indicative of maladjustment. Our data indicated that at grade 5 these critical percentages differentiated well-adjusted from poorly adjusted children at the .01 level of significance. Unfortunately, perhaps due to the relatively infrequent use of future tense in the story protocols, critical percentages for future tense did not reach the level of statistical significance.

Direction of Forces. This variable was defined in terms of the direction of action of the central figure in each story. Three types of action were specified:

1. *Centrifugal.* The direction of force is outward; that is, the subject is exerting force toward the world.
2. *Centripetal.* The force is being exerted upon the central figure from the world.
3. *Neutral.* Neither of the other two types of forces is evident.

This test variable discriminated between well-adjusted and poorly adjusted children at all grade levels. Out of six tests of statistical significance for this variable, *p* reached the .001 in three instances, the .01 level in two others, and .05 in one instance. Not only does this objective index do a good job in screening for maladjustment, it is also significant to the clinician in helping to define the subject's typical stance in relation to the world: active versus passive.

Combined Maladjustment Index

A study of the interrelationships of the three primary test variables showed that these could be combined fruitfully to yield even more effective discrimination between well-adjusted and poorly adjusted groups. This index is simply the number of times an individual scores at or above the critical score (see next section) on each of the three primary variables.

Critical Scores

Tables were prepared to indicate the critical score for each variable. These scores were defined as scores that distinguish significantly between well-adjusted and poorly adjusted children. Although such scores yield some false positives, our data indicate that they add to the effectiveness in differentiating the two groups. Tables are provided in the user's manual (Hutt, 1980a) that indicate the probable effectiveness of these scores in differentiating well-adjusted from poorly adjusted pupils.

Interscorer Reliability

Since the calculation of scores for Verb Tense is simply a matter of accurate counting, no reliability studies of this variable were made; however, interscorer reliability was evaluated for the other variables. Two staff psychologists with different amounts of clinical experience separately scored 15 records at each grade level. Interscorer reliability was .98 at each grade level for the Tension Index. Interscorer reliability for Direction of Forces was .95 at grade 3; .87 at grade 5; and .91 at grades 7 and 9. These findings suggest that scoring is sufficiently reliable for the purpose of this test.

OTHER RESEARCH FINDINGS

Only the most pertinent studies will be reviewed briefly in this chapter; the reader may consult the revised user's manual (Hutt, 1980a) for greater detail. Andrew (1951) did an intensive, independent study on the effectiveness of the Tension Index in discriminating well-adjusted from poorly adjusted children and found that critical scores on this variable did discriminate significantly in the third and fifth grades. She also investigated the relevance of age, IQ, socioeconomic status, ordinal position in the family, number of children in the family, race, and the like. She found that the only extratest factors that were significantly related to poor adjustment were low IQ, socioeconomic status, and living apart from both natural parents. Her findings suggest that such extratest factors be taken into consideration in evaluating low scores on this variable.

Ringwall (1951), in a comprehensive study of 27 indexes that were being considered for inclusion in the scoring of our test, found that the scores on the Tension Index discriminated significantly between well-adjusted and poorly adjusted children at the fifth-grade level, as evaluated by a clinic staff.

FINDINGS ON OTHER VARIABLES

The research staff and others have explored several other test variables presumed to offer promise. One of these was a measure of Psychosexual Level. Although our own findings were promising, they did not reach the level of statistical significance required for inclusion in our final test protocol. It was noted, however, that, when significant or very large discrepancies on Psychosexual Level did occur, this was indicative of possible psychopathology and should be considered by the clinician. Our findings on this variable, therefore, are included in the revised manual (Hutt, 1980a).

Ringwall (1951) did find significant statistical discrimination on the Psychosexual Level variable, but felt it was not sufficient for individual diagnosis. On the other hand, Gurin (1952) conducted a more sophisticated study on this variable, using 13 categories of psychosexual manifestations. She was able to find evidence consistent with psychoanalytic theory concerning the latency period (when psychosexual tendencies are theorized to be repressed) and adolescence (when these drives are expressed much more openly). In short, this variable seems to have considerable value and needs further definition and research.

Another variable that showed some promise but failed to meet our criteria of significance was that of Interpersonal Relationships. It was hypothesized that the more frequent production of stories involving two people would be more characteristic of well-adjusted children. Our results were inconclusive but offered indications that this variable is worthy of further study.

It was felt that pronouns in reference to the self, as contrasted to other pronouns, might differentiate the two categories of adjustment that were studied. The revised user's manual (Hutt, 1980a) summarizes our findings on this variable; while our data are promising, they do not meet the tests of statistical significance.

Two other variables that were studied were the frequency of use of "Popular Objects" and the Level of Interpretation offered by respondents. Neither of these variables, as defined, turned out to differentiate the two levels of adjustment. Level of Interpretation, particularly, has received very favorable attention in the research literature on apperceptive tests; however, our findings could not confirm its significance.

USES FOR THE MPT-R

Our primary purpose in developing the MPT-R was to devise an apperceptive thematic test for the differential diagnosis of emotional maladjustment in schoolchildren. Most children are able to tell stories about the pictures without undue anxiety about revealing themselves; thus this procedure offers the psychologist or other mental health worker a means of evaluating, in a pleasant atmosphere, the presence of psychopathology. The scores obtained with the few cards in the core series are sufficiently reliable and valid for such screening purposes.

Nevertheless, no single test and no single score is sufficient for final diagnostic evaluation. As Hutt points out (1980b), scores obtained even from the most highly valid instruments, and normative data obtained even with the most representative samples, have serious limitations. At best they are only indications and involve assumptions such as that the individual being examined satisfies all of the precise criteria characteristic of the population on which the original scores and norms were obtained, and that the subject obtained that score from a comparable series of operations that were typical of that population. Therefore, in reaching a final diagnosis, whether the finding is positive or negative, other factors such as type of performance on the test, experiential background, motivation, and physical–medical history must be considered.

The MPT-R and similar tests involving thematic content have the clinical advantage of providing other, significant types of data. Analysis of the content, whether by formal qualitative analysis, such as the revised manual (Hutt, 1980a) suggests, or by scrutiny of the elicited stories in some other manner, may offer cues about the idiosyncratic nature of the child's performance, background, or motivation that the examiner then can consider in evaluating the test results. Thus, even when the test is used as a screening procedure, the test findings (the several scores, the content of the stories, and the variability in emotional tone demonstrated in the stories) can be quite revealing in the final evaluation. Moreover, other cards from the full test may be administered and scores on other test variables may be utilized in the continuing evaluation process.

The test also provides for psychotherapeutic opportunities. As is well known, the mere telling of a story has some cathartic value. The mental health worker can use the stories in various therapeutic ways when this is desirable. What we have called the "Inquiry" (see Hutt, 1980a) can be employed for therapeutic as well as diagnostic purposes. The themes of the stories, as well as their moods and outcomes, can offer leads for further discussion and counseling. In these and other ways, material from the test can be useful in exploring and in resolving particular problems that a child reveals.

The MPT-R also offers considerable opportunity for research purposes. Our objective indices provide only one way of conceptualizing significant test variables; many other ways need to be explored and other variables need to be considered. Of course, other types of pictures and other ways of analyzing particular variables need to be explored, as Ringwall (1951) and Gurin (1952) have demonstrated. And then there are the endless types of research areas in which a test such as the MPT-R can be employed. How do different cultures, races, and ethnic groups respond on this test? When do sex or developmental factors affect results and in what manner? How do children with differing psychopathologies respond, and how do such differing conditions affect the various scores?

How does the MPT–R compare with other diagnostic devices in effectiveness in the diagnostic process? How do situational factors affect test results? What about differing educational programs or therapeutic experiences? This is but a small sample of the research that waits to be done.

REFERENCES

Andrew, G. (1951, May). A survey of the mental health status of Battle Creek public school children. Unpublished report, Michigan State Department of Mental Health.

Andrew, G., Walton, R. E., Hartwell, S. W., & Hutt, M. L. (1951). The Michigan Picture Test: The stimulus value of the cards. *Journal of Consulting Psychology, 15*, 51–54.

Freeman, F. S. (1953). *Theory and practice of psychological testing* (Rev. ed.). New York: Holt.

Gurin, M. G. (1952). Differences between latents and adolescents: A psychoanalytic study utilizing the Michigan Picture Test. Annual proceedings of the Michigan Academy of Science, Arts, and Letters, Detroit, Michigan, *38*.

Hartwell, S. W., Hutt, M. L., Andrew, G., & Walton, W. E. (1951). The Michigan Picture Test: Diagnostic and therapeutic possibilities of a new projective test in child guidance. *American Journal of Orthopsychiatry, 21*, 124–137.

Hutt, M. L. (1980a). *The Michigan Picture Test—Revised.* New York: Grune & Stratton.

Hutt, M. L. (1980b). Microdiagnosis and the misuse of scores and standards. *Psychological Reports, 50*, 239–255.

Neuringer, C. (1968). A variety of thematic methods. In A. I. Rabin (Ed.), *Projective techniques in personality assessment.* New York: Springer.

Ringwall, E. (1951). Some picture story characteristics as a measure of personality traits. Unpublished doctoral dissertation, University of Michigan, Ann Arbor.

Science Research Associates. (1953). *Manual: The Michigan Picture Test.* Chicago: Author.

Walton, R. E., Hutt, M. L., Andrew, G., & Hartwell, W. W. (1951). A tension index of adjustment based on picture stories elicited by the Michigan Picture Test. *Journal of Abnormal and Social Psychology, 46*, 438–441.

5
The Separation Anxiety Test

Henry G. Hansburg

The Separation Anxiety Test (SAT) grew out of a project conceived by a team of psychiatric and psychological personnel in the mental hygiene clinic of the Jewish Child Care Association in New York City and developed and researched by the present author, beginning in 1965 and continuing to the present. The major purpose of the method was to develop an instrument that would differentiate the various patterns of response to separation experiences in children and adolescents ranging in age from 10 through midadolescence. It was hoped that such a method would be highly effective not only in determining the type of facility that would be most helpful in the placement of children but also as a tool in understanding aspects of personality not available in other methods. Since the Jewish Child Care Association was an agency caring for foster children in foster homes, group residences, group boarding homes, and an institutional setting, its population consisted entirely of children and adolescents separated from their biological parents. Therefore, since separation was an indigenous characteristic of this population, it would prove fruitful territory for studying separation experiences and making comparisons with nonseparated populations.

THEORETICAL UNDERPINNINGS

The theoretical background for the development of the SAT was derived largely from this author's many years of clinical experience with Freudian psychoanalytic concepts, chastened and revamped by the variety of revisions and additions by leaders in the field. Among these were Margaret Mahler, John Bowlby, Anna Freud, Peter Blos, Robert White, Erik

Erikson, Herman Witkin, Gerald Rochlin, and others whose concepts, taken together, made it possible to see many different aspects of separation problems. I arrived at the realization that separation anxiety was manifested in so many different ways that one could not hope to arrive at a reasonable study of it if one simply concentrated on the phenomenon of anxiety itself. My experience with separated children as well as earlier experiences with school-phobic children convinced me that a study of separation problems would require observation of the many-faceted reactions that accompanied separation experiences. Further, since separations were of such varied quality and intensity—some being daily, casual, and of relatively minor significance and others being startlingly severe, traumatic, and/or of prolonged duration, it was necessary to study the various reactions to separation under various circumstances of vastly different natures. It was also obvious that children who had suffered intense separations at very early ages, especially in infancy, would be most likely to react differently than those who experienced similar separations at later ages.

Consideration was given to the nature of the onset of adolescence as a stage in development that further complicated the effort to study separation problems. From the psychoanalytic viewpoint adolescence is considered a period of psychological separation more intense and more demanding than the latency period. Separated children not only have to deal with the circumstances of physical and geographical separation but also with the adolescent urges for psychological differentiation and individuation. The relative absence of the close physical ties and of the usual emotional nourishment to be derived from them raises significant questions with regard to the separated adolescent's capacity to achieve the necessary goals of adolescence without some impairment in development.

This author was further guided in deliberations by the likelihood that it would not be feasible to attempt to expose older children and adolescents to sample separation situations in the manner in which Mary Ainsworth (1979) was able to in her experiments with young children in strange situations. Patterns of behavioral and emotional response at later ages are already so complicated by social pressures that the revelation of separation reactions may be blocked easily. For this reason I sought a method that would provide vicarious separation experiences, bring out the expression of patterned reactions, and provide the opportunity of being reminded of past separation occurrences and feelings. It seemed likely, therefore, that much could be accomplished by depicting separation situations in the form of pictures. If such were the case, the questions were what kind of separation situations would be most pertinent, how they should be presented, how many samples should be created, how they should vary in quality and intensity, should they be in color or black and white, should emotional expression be shown in the pictures or avoided, and so forth.

DEVELOPMENT OF METHOD

In line with these deliberations, 12 pictures of separation situations were created. Originally, they were 6 inches square, but they later were reduced to 5 inches square. Black-and-white drawings were used rather than color photographs because color itself has emotional implications and photographs create more difficulties in dealing with emotional expression. Six of the 12 pictures were felt to be casual and typical enough to be considered mild stimuli, and six were strong enough and in some cases so devastating as to be considered powerful separation stimuli. The situations depicted are shown in Figure 5.1 and described as follows:

1. The child will live permanently with his grandmother.
2. The child is being transferred to a new class.
3. The family is moving to a new neighborhood.
4. The child is leaving his mother to go to school.
5. The child is leaving his parents to go to camp.
6. After an argument with the mother, the father is leaving.
7. The child's brother is a sailor leaving on a voyage.
8. The judge is placing the child in an institution.
9. The mother has just put this child to bed.
10. The child's mother is being taken to the hospital.
11. The child and the father are standing at the mother's coffin.
12. The child is running away from home.

It will be noted that the pictures place the child in the foreground, in order to stimulate the child's attention to this central figure. Wherever possible, the figures were presented in motion in order that their separation action would be brought into focus. Complete clarity of the separation situation was not always attained; for this reason the title of the separation situation was included at the bottom of each picture. This precluded the possibility of misinterpretation of the basic theme of each picture. While the intensity of the separation stimulus was seriously considered in arranging the order of administration of the pictures, it was decided not to put the pictures in the gradually ascending stimulus order. Thus, the first picture is a strong stimulus, the next four are mild followed by a strong, mild, strong, mild sequence and finally three

FIGURE 5.1   The 12 Drawings of the Separation Anxiety Test (SAT).*

*See text, page 87, for captions to drawings.

strong pictures. The reason for this order was a reflection of the idiosyncratic nature of the strength of a stimulus and its effect on various individuals. Nevertheless, four of the mild pictures occur among the first six and four of the strong ones appear among the last six.

TEST ADMINISTRATION AND SCORING

The method by which the children were to respond to the pictures was given very extensive study and preparation. Most projective tests depend largely on free association, but this technique is usually difficult to score and tends to encourage much subjective speculation by the test interpreter. After considering a number of techniques, it was decided to present a series of phrases for each picture, from which the subject could select as many as he wished. Each phrase represented an affective and/or cognitive reaction to the separation experience depicted in the picture. After reducing the number of phrases from a rather unwieldy 32 to 17, the final version was as follows (the words in parentheses do not appear on the test, just on the scoring chart):

The child feels . . .
1. that he will be much happier now (well-being)
2. that his parents don't love him any more (rejection)
3. like curling up in a corner by himself (withdrawal)
4. a terrible pain in his chest (somatic)
5. alone and miserable (grief or loneliness)
6. that he doesn't care what happens (evasive denial)
7. that he will do his best to get along (adaptation)
8. that his house will be a scary place to live in now (phobic)
9. that something bad is going to happen to him now (anxiety)
10. that it is all the fault of his neighbors (projection)
11. angry at somebody (anger)
12. that he won't be the same person any more (identity stress)
13. that if he had been a good child, this wouldn't have happened (intrapunitive)
14. that it's only a dream—it isn't really happening (fantasy)
15. like reading a book, watching TV, or playing games (sublimation)
16. sorry for his parents (empathy)
17. that he won't be able to concentrate on his schoolwork any more (intellectual dysfunction)

For each picture, the child is asked to read the phrases to himself and select as many of them as would describe how he believes the child in the picture feels.

The actual wording of these phrases was necessarily varied to suit the reality demands of each picture, and for each picture the order of presentation of the phrases was redistributed. Additionally, prior to the presentation of the phrases a series of mental-set questions was provided to stimulate recollection of separation events in the child's life. The following are some examples:

Did this ever happen to you?　　Now try to imagine how the
　　Yes　　　　No　　　　　　　child in the picture feels.
Can you imagine how you would
　　feel if it did happen?　Yes　No

The mental-set questions appear before the phrases of each of the 12 pictures. The answer to the first mental-set question, "Did this ever happen to you?" is recorded, resulting in 12 mental-set answers. (Responses to the other mental-set questions are also recorded for qualitative but not quantitative use.) If there are only four or less "yes" answers, the child's environment is deemed overprotective. If there are eight or more "yes" answers, the child is judged to have experienced traumatic separations.

The use of these techniques described has made it possible to obtain an objective scoring system. The total number of responses for each phrase may be added up, thereby producing a score for each phrase and enabling the examiner to see where the greatest emphases are and which responses are least selected. At the same time it is possible to determine how many responses are made to each picture and what the character of these responses is. Further, the number of responses for each group of mild and strong separation pictures can be calculated and compared. The total number of possible responses equals 204 (12×17); however, the median number of responses to the entire test actually is approximately one-fourth of this. In addition, of this total, 25 responses are considered as inappropriate; these serve as a measure of reality testing.

Although study of the 17-phrase response chart yielded some interesting information, it was found more diagnostic to combine these into patterns representing significant concepts derived from various psychoanalytic theoretical formulations, especially those of Mahler and Furer (1968) and Bowlby (1969). These consisted of those responses representing attachment need, individuation (self-reliance), hostility, painful tension (fear–anxiety–pain complex), reality avoidance (defensive withdrawal, evasion, and fantasy), self-esteem preoccupation (intellectual involvement), self-love loss (rejection and intrapunitiveness), and identity stress. These patterns proved to be very significant when analyzing the child's reactions to separation. An additional indicator of importance was the summation of the "yes" answers to the mental-set questions, from which it was possible to tell the frequency and intensity of the separations experienced by the child. These norm charts appear in the appendices of two Hansburg publications (Hansburg, 1972a, 1980b).

NORMS, RELIABILITY, AND VALIDITY

The normative reactions of this test were calculated in percentage terms. The number of responses for each pattern was conceived in terms of its ratio to the total number of responses to the entire test. This made it possible to compare the scores of persons with different total scores and with different number of responses to each pattern. Thus, if a child had a total of 50 responses to the entire test and 10 responses to the attachment pattern, his attachment score would be 20. The same score would be achieved by a child who had 15 responses to the attachment pattern and 75 responses to the entire test.

In the earlier studies using the SAT (Hansburg, 1980a), nearly 250 children had been examined, under the auspices of the Jewish Child Care Association. A number of these children were studied intensively in the psychiatric clinic, many were children who had lived for some time in the various residences of the agency and the Catholic Charities, and over 100 were obtained from intact families, to provide a more normative, contrasting population. The data obtained from these studies indicated an internal consistency coefficient of 0.885, which was accepted as a measure of reliability. In later years this coefficient was confirmed in test–retest (6-month waiting period) reliability of 0.84 by Black (1981). Individual-item consistency correlations ranged from 0.50 to 0.70, while most of the patterns showed similar reliability. Black found a number of higher test–retest reliabilities in the patterns.

Over the years there has been consistent proof that separation experiences stimulate attachment as well as the alarm emotions: fear, anxiety, and pain. Feelings of loneliness, rejection, or empathic reactions are so common as to represent at least 20 percent of the total responses to the test. For 157 children tested between July 1969 and April 1970, the median response of attachment was 22.1 percent, which was the highest of all patterns. The fear–anxiety–pain pattern median was 17.1 percent. These data generally support the theory that as separation experiences become more intense they trigger an alarm that causes a strong impetus in the direction of attachment. This reduces the drive toward exploration of the environment and what Mahler and Furer (1968) refer to as individuation and Bowlby (1973) calls self-reliance. This is shown by the median individuation response of 18 percent and the lowered individuation response on the strong pictures. Although these data are derived from adolescence, they accord well with Ainsworth's (1979) findings in infancy and early childhood. The reversal of the attachment and the individuation responses on the mild and strong pictures was quite noteworthy in the 1969-to-1970 data: On the mild pictures, 157 children gave 646 responses to attachment and 1,012 to individuation (self-reliance); on the strong pictures they gave 1,289 responses to attachment and 627 responses to individuation. This ratio was true of every one of the eight groups that comprised the 157 children.

ATTACHMENT AND SEPARATION ISSUES

This characteristic has been found to hold true in every research with the SAT that has been conducted since. Thus, when in a particular case this reversal does not hold true a pathognomic condition of the attachment system is posited. If the attachment responses to the mild pictures exceed the individuation responses on those pictures, a symbiotic factor in the adolescent is considered likely. This is further enhanced by very few individuation responses in relation to attachment responses on the strong separation pictures. If the attachment responses to all the pictures provide a high attachment percentage while the individuation responses fall below the level of the median area, an additional symbiotic indicator is present. As will be seen later, there are other factors in the test that must be considered before the problem of excessive attachment—or, as Bowlby (1973) appropriately categorizes it, "anxious attachment"—may be posited.

This alternating reaction to separation depending upon its intensity indicates that the attachment need is a compelling force in human behavior and will be aroused strongly when threats of separation are intensified. Further, when the casual and almost daily separations occur, individuals are more likely to pursue exploratory behavior, relatively confident of the availability of attachment figures. In psychoanalytic terminology one might say that object constancy and the incorporation of basically safe attachment figures provide the security necessary for individuation reactions. In Bowlby's (1969) theoretical framework, which he considers to be a revision of psychoanalytic theory, a secure base from an available attachment figure provides the model from which exploratory behavior may be pursued. Bowlby (1979) states, "An individual develops within himself one or more working models representing principal features of the world about him and of himself as an agent in it. Such working models determine his expectations and forecasts and provide him with tools for constructing plans of action" (p. 117).

I have coined the term "separation pain" to describe the fear–anxiety–pain reaction that often accompanies separations in varying degrees of strength. Normally, as noted previously, this group of responses shows a median of 17.1 percent of the total, although the variation among groups is considerable. Generally this response is lower than the attachment reactions but much stronger than the hostility pattern. Usually the pain responses to the mild pictures are not that much lower than on the strong pictures, with most youngsters increasing only slightly. In the original study it appeared that the increased separation stimulus on the strong pictures tended to transfer the strength of the affect to hostility. I have referred to the latter as "separation hostility." It was concluded that hostility is not a primary reaction to separation unless there has developed some degree of pathology due to deprivation of the attachment system.

When the hostility pattern becomes the dominant reaction to the test, especially when the attachment pattern is below the norms, a serious pathological indicator is present. This was found to be true in clinic cases and resulted in a diagnosis of homicidal tendencies when a separation was a serious threat to the individual. An interesting example of this was the case of a 16-year-old girl whom a psychologist recommended should be carefully supervised but who was permitted to babysit for a local family. The warning sparked by the test result went unheeded, and a fire set in the home by the girl nearly killed the child she was caring for (cf. Hansburg, 1972b).

Since the measurement of separation anxiety is complicated by many factors, some effort at developing a more simple score for it was sought. This has eventuated in the use of a comparison between two clusters involving four patterns: the patterns of attachment and separation pain in relation to the patterns of individuation and hostility. By subtracting the latter two patterns from the former two patterns a difference score is obtained that may be used as a measure of degree of separation anxiety. In addition, the resulting score tells us whether the individual reacts to separation experiences with heightened attachment need or with a trend toward detachment; either the person is anxious and needful for attachment or more detached and hostile. Varying degrees of these trends in the personality will be shown to exist. The more intense the attachment and pain responses in the presence of a lessening of individuation and hostile responses, the more we move in the direction of anxious attachment. The median score for this index is generally 9 percent; as the scores rise, the anxious attachment level rises. As the score lowers and drops into the minus column, hostile detachment becomes more evident. Many variations of this exist, especially those in which the hostility level is high but the individuation level is low, and those in which the pain level is high and the attachment level is low.

The pattern of reality avoidance, defensiveness, or separation denial has a number of significant aspects to it. It should be recognized that the resistance to the acceptance of the implications of a separation represents the most common defense that the ego can adopt. The pattern consists of withdrawal, fantasy, and evasion. When the percentage of these responses is high, it must be interpreted in terms of the patterning of attachment, pain, individuation, and hostility. In the average situation the withdrawal technique dominates the pattern and fantasy plays the secondary role. This is generally most true when attachment and pain dominate the protocol. When hostility and/or individuation are predominant, evasion is most likely to dominate the defensive patterning. Thus, high defensiveness, when present in the dominant attachment protocol, increases the extent of anxious attachment. When added to the individuation–hostility protocol, it contributes to the strength of the detachment. The dominance of evasion as a defense is most common in characterological disorders and is a poor indicator for treatment.

Three aspects of a self-evaluative system are part of the Separation Anxiety Test and show the effects of separation experiences on individuals' feelings about themselves. These aspects are self-esteem preoccupation, self-love, and identity. The degree of self-esteem preoccupation is shown negatively by the effect of separation on the powers of concentration and positively on the ability to sublimate. When these are reported in large quantities, whether positive or negative, it suggests concern with self-esteem heightened by separation.

Self-love is a more primary experience and depends more upon the very early experiences of feeling loved and cared for. Its effect begins in the first year of life and by three years of age becomes stronger with the increased awareness of object permanence in the Piagetian sense (Piaget, 1954) and object constancy in the Mahlerian sense (Mahler & Furer, 1968). This feeling of being cared about and loved is a profound feeling and is altered only by either seriously eroding experiences or by cataclysmic events. On the test, the feeling of loss of self-love is expressed by the rejecting and intrapunitive responses. When this percentage is high and tends to be higher than the percentage of the self-esteem preoccupation score, a depressive syndrome reaction to separation is posited. Such depressive reactions are common and tend to occur most frequently in anxious attachment syndromes rather than in the detached patternings. When they occur in the latter, the problem is generally more serious than in the former. The reason for this lies in the fundamentals of attachment theory (Bowlby, 1969), in which persons with strong capacities for attachment and sufficient pain levels are considered to be basically more reachable and more amenable to relationship and positive transference.

The depressive syndrome reaction adds to the anxious attachment category in the high-attachment, high-pain protocols.

It should be noted, in passing, that my own theoretical bias is to consider self-esteem as a less profound phenomenon than self-love. This bias is strongly related to the position taken by Robert White (1963) in his theoretical work on the ego and reality in psychoanalytic theory. Self-esteem is largely developed as a result of the feeling of being effective in dealing with the environment. It revolves around the experiences of rewards and punishments in relation to such efforts. Separation experiences are more likely to affect self-esteem than self-love in more normative situations, but a large percentage of the population is not so healthy as to avoid its effect on self-love. Thus it is likely that separation experiences will result in a depressive syndrome in at least 40 percent of the population.

The sense of identity, a factor in development most carefully studied by Erikson (1968), may be affected by separation. This feeling of who or what one is in relation to others (family, class, community) is apparently a part of the personality and of deep meaning in behavior. It is obvious that people with whom one has been close for a long time have considerable influence on the way the self is organized. The threat of the loss of such persons or the loss of one's place with such persons endangers the integrity of the self. Thus, if the subject chooses the response that "he won't be the same person any more," this represents a feeling of change in the identity of the self, referred to as "identity stress."

The median percentage of response to this statement—8.55 percent— was surprisingly high considering the fact that it represented only one response out of the 17. However, by ages 13 to 14, the percentage rose to approximately 12 percent. Further studies in later years on older adolescents and adults indicated that there was a considerable drop in this percentage. This suggested that the threat to identity from separations or fears of separation is a more serious problem in early adolescence and late latency and tends to recede with further personality development. This seems likely due to the fact that the sense of identity is in the process of formation in early adolescence and, once it is more firmly established, is less threatened by separation experiences.

INAPPROPRIATE-ABSURD REACTIONS

Twenty-five of the total responses to the 12 pictures have been marked as inappropriate or absurd reactions. For example, picture 4, entitled "the child is leaving his mother to go to school," elicits "somebody else is causing all this trouble." This response is so inappropriate to the picture and so farfetched as to be considered absurd. Generally, most adolescents of reasonable mental health will select no more than three such responses. More than three give reason to suspect poor reality testing and impaired judgment. This type of reality-testing problem differs from the defensive reactions in the reality-avoidance pattern discussed earlier. It is much more related to psychotic deteriorative processes, while the reality-avoidance pattern simply provides a picture of the relative strength of defensiveness. However, if we find a high level of defensiveness coupled with an excessive number of absurd responses, we can be fairly certain that we are dealing with a psychotic process.

FURTHER ISSUES OF INTERPRETATION

It has proven of value to examine the number of "yes" responses to the mental-set questions. It is expected that this response would occur most often on the mild separation pictures such as the school, sleep, and camp pictures and would occur least often on the strong separation pictures such as the judge or the death of the mother. If eight or more "yes" responses occur on the mental-set questions, we would have to assume that there have been separation traumas. By the same token, four or fewer "yes" answers would have to be interpreted as indicative of a relatively protected environmental experience. However, this is merely related to the child's report of separations; the record tells us much more about what has transpired in the child's inner psychic life.

The total number of the responses with the population we tested yielded a median of 57, with 21 percent more responses on the strong pictures than on the mild ones. A small number of responses suggests constriction and repression, while a large number of responses may represent in some cases a loosening of the personality. However, it is difficult to use the number of responses for diagnostic purposes because familial and cultural factors are frequently involved in the degree of responsiveness to the test. We can achieve some diagnostic insights, however, by examining the differences among the responses to the mild and strong pictures. Very small differences suggest poor judgment as well as difficulty in reacting normally to the strength of the stimulus. Over-reaction to mild stimuli represents extreme sensitivity, while underreaction to the strong stimuli indicates a blunting of affect. This can be determined only by studying the patterns to see where this has occurred. An interesting analogy might be made with the response to a physical stimulus. A light tap on a subject's hand might be reacted to by a violent scream, while a no greater reaction might proceed from a severe blow with a hammer. In such a case we definitely would state that the person was overreacting to a mild stimulus, since the violent scream is inappropriate to the light tap but perfectly reasonable to the hammer blow. An example of an underreaction to a strong stimulus on the Separation Anxiety Test may be observed readily if a youngster responds to the death-of-the-mother picture with relatively unfeeling and innocuous statements such as he feels "like reading a book or watching TV" and if he does not report any effect or stress. In this sense the difference between the responses to the mild and strong pictures may be of diagnostic significance.

It can be seen from the foregoing that the Separation Anxiety Test is a far more comprehensive instrument for the study of separation reactions than would be expected from the title. It is rich in its revelation of personality characteristics. I have enhanced further the diagnostic features of the test by utilizing a systems theory suggesting six varied systems having patterned effects stemming from separation experiences:

1. Attachment system
2. Individuation system
3. Fear–anxiety–pain system
4. Hostility system
5. Defensive system
6. Self-evaluative system

By developing an interactional plan for these systems, it is possible to refer to varied test protocols with not only a categorization in terms of the systems but also to infer certain significant dynamics.

I have suggested a continuum, ranging from severe anxious attachment to severe hostile detachment, which are the extreme categories. In between these are varied levels of anxious attachment and detachment. The number of relatively perfect protocols that might be characterized as quite healthy would be small and therefore create a U-shaped curve representing the distribution.

The implication of this method is to suggest that separation reactions are determined by complexes that surround the degree of attachment or detachment and provide a picture of the dynamic flow of affective and cognitive psychic experience. To categorize this flow I have suggested that we consider the following phrases as representative pathways to understanding the inner response and psychic reaction to separation:

1. Severe anxious attachment
2. Strong anxious attachment
3. Mild anxious attachment
4. Healthy pattern

5. Mild detachment
6. Dependent detachment
7. Hostile detachment

Within this grouping I have suggested certain syndromes, mainly the depressive syndrome and excessive self-sufficiency. The former is most common in the anxious attachment categories and the latter is found often in the detachment-dominated protocols.

The only effort thus far to study the stability and reliability of these categories was made by Black (1981). While he found considerable stability and high test–retest reliability to the patterns, he was unable to do so for these categories. The patterns are represented by attachment, individuation, hostility, and so forth, while the categories are meaningful combinations of the patterns, as noted on the last few pages. Black gave the test a second time six months later and was impressed with the reliability of the patterns, but the categories did not show this reliability. Unfortunately, Black determined the composition of the categories somewhat differently than described in Hansburg (1980b). This is the most likely reason for the reliability problem. On the other hand, Black ascribed the problem to a number of factors including differences in the populations (Black used older adolescents and adults) and the manner in which the norms were derived. The only category for which he found good stability was the depressive syndrome. In general, Black (1981) found the SAT to measure more profound and stable characteristics of the personality than self-report tests. The general evidence suggests that further clarification of the details that go into the definition of the categories will be required.

Another aspect of the problem of separation deals with the concept of deactivation of a system proposed by Bowlby (1980), here including the notion of deactivation of a *behavioral* system. I have referred to this concept (Hansburg, 1980b) largely in connection with the attachment system, although any psychological system can undergo either partial or considerable deactivation. It is shown on the SAT by a very low system score in any of the pattern areas. For example, in one case (Hansburg, 1980b), a 15-year-old boy gave only five responses out of 67 to the individuation pattern, resulting in a percentage of 7, at least 10 percent below the norm. This represents a considerable deactivation of the system of individuation. The interpretation of this one factor lay in a low level of capacity to function on his own. A strong dependency feature permeated his character. The term *deactivation* seems likely to be of considerable use because it implies the possibility of reactivation, while the terms *disability* or *personality damage* suggest or imply a more pessimistic view. The term is also more meaningful in a developmental sense.

CASE STUDIES

A couple of clinical vignettes may serve to highlight and integrate the material in this chapter and to illustrate the method.

Frank

At age 14, Frank was brought to me because he had occasional depressed feelings, which concerned his mother. After interviews with the boy I had the impression of a youngster who was within normal limits in personality development but who had some problems related to an active, ongoing family situation. On the SAT he gave a total of 63 responses, which is within normal limits. Of these, 22 were to the mild pictures and 41 to the strong ones, a difference of 19, which is 30 percent of the total and represents a strong reaction to the strong pictures. This is more common in closely knit family structures, according to my original research. A healthy balance between the attachment and individuation systems was demonstrated on the mild and strong pictures, with the bias in the direction of individuation and with minimal separation anxiety (an index of −5%). This index is much below the median of +9 percent. This is in the area of mild detachment. A strong personality core is suggested by a 23 percent attachment and a 28 percent individuation.

These scores indicate that Frank's inner capacity to respond adequately to object relations and the ability to utilize his inner resources in separation situations were very adequate. The fear–anxiety–pain index and the hostility index were both definitely below the norms, suggesting affect repression. The combination of all these factors placed Frank in the mild detachment group with evidence of excessive self-sufficiency. There were only three absurd responses, which is within normal limits, and the reality-avoidance level was only 7.9 percent. These indices, when compared to the strength shown in both the attachment and individuation levels, demonstrated a strong, reality-based individual.

What then were the problem areas that appeared on the test? There was evidence that the two areas of the self-evaluation system were affected adversely. Self-esteem preoccupation was high, at 14 percent, as was identity stress, at 14.7 percent. Since self-esteem and sense of identity are offset most readily by separation experiences, it was decided to concentrate in this area, recognizing that, although the report by the mother indicated that the boy was showing some depressive problems, there was no evidence of this on the Separation Anxiety Test. It became obvious during therapy sessions that Frank was really struggling with self-esteem and identity problems that were responsible for his occasional bouts of depressive moods and for some problems with his schoolwork. He improved rapidly within a short time after having had an opportunity to express his feelings about some problems in the home and about some social problems with his peers.

Abraham

A more serious situation was found in the case of Abraham, a Syrian Jewish boy who first came to me when he was 13 years of age. Attending a private parochial school, he had a spat with a boy in the school, wouldn't stop fighting when told to do so, had to be slapped by a teacher to get him to calm down, and then ran out of the building. He previously had been expelled from another school for similar uncontrolled incidents, despite repeated admonitions to desist from this behavior. The history showed a definite separation disorder: He would throw up when the mother left him with babysitters, so she was forced to take him with her wherever she went. The mother referred to him as being "spoiled." When he was older and placed in a summer camp he was so homesick and lonesome he had to be taken home. For the first three or four years at school he carried on wildly when left by the mother and tended to be nervous and tense.

At the time of referral, subsequent to the initial interview, Abraham was given the Separation Anxiety Test. The result was definitely pathological. Both the attachment and individuation percentages were below the norms (18% and 10%, respectively), which indicated a poor personality core and the likelihood of low-level functioning in both relationships and resourcefulness. The higher number of attachment responses than individuation responses on the mild pictures was a pathognomic, symbiotic indicator, while the almost equal individuation reactions on the mild and strong pictures were confirmatory of this. Forty-five percent of the responses were in the affective area (18% hostility and 27% fear–anxiety–pain), demonstrating a highly volatile emotional reaction to separation. The remainder of the protocol showed several more factors indicating the likelihood of serious dependency reactions. This included a depressive reaction involving high loss of self-love (12%) and low self-esteem preoccupation. This suggested a deep problem of self-love, indicating an early difficulty in adequate object constancy and raising the question of parental capacity for providing a sense of safety in their absence.

What also was suspect was the very large number of responses (93) to the test that indicated a looseness of control. Further, the larger than usual number of absurd responses (6) suggested reality-testing problems. The reality avoidance (separation denial) was within normal limits, although the patterning was abnormal. The attachment–individuation index was 17 (high separation-anxiety score), which is on the anxious attachment side; however, the total protocol comes very close to a diagnosis of dependent detachment, a condition that definitely will frustrate any therapist. This is even more true when we see the height of hostility in relation to attachment (both are at 18%).

The mixed picture presented by this case raises doubts about success with therapeutic intervention alone. I thus sought the aid of a psychopharmacologist who prescribed one of the phenothiazines in a mild dosage. I then introduced supportive therapy with a view to improving both the parents' and the school's handling of the boy's outbursts, and to helping the boy understand the nature of his anxiety and anger, especially the latter. The outbursts in the school stopped, the semester ended, and the boy was graduated. As happens in many such cases, the improvement of the situation had the effect of alleviating parental anxiety and thus leading to the cessation of therapy by the parents, against my recommendation. As expected, the symptoms returned while the boy was in the high-school setting, but nothing was done until two years later when the situation again became intolerable. This time the boy's resistance to coming for therapy, which had not existed previously, surfaced; he attended for one consultation and did not return. I never heard from the parents again.

Conclusion

A considerable variety of patterns is obtained from the SAT, and their interpretations are not always as simple as they appear in the case vignettes presented. With clinical experience the patterns become very meaningful and especially helpful in the interpretation of those adolescents whose problems appear to have originated during early or even later separations or threats of separation. Various adaptations have been developed for the test including (1) Klagsbrun and Bowlby's (1976) version for children aged four and five; (2) Varela's (1982) revision of the Klagsbrun-Bowlby Scale; (3) Duplak's (1983) revision for latency-age children who are nonreaders; (4) several foreign-language translations, including Mitchell (1980) in Spanish; (5) Brody's (1981) adaptation for third-grade children; and (6) Burger's (1981) revision for use with divorced males.

RECENT RESEARCH

Extensive research has been carried on with the SAT, not only with children and adolescents but also with young adults, older adults, and even with the elderly. Among the earlier studies are those done by the author, which will be found in another volume that is in preparation. They include a study in which the SAT was given to all the members of the family, including fathers and mothers and siblings; a study of the use of the test in the detection of self-destructive tendencies in early adolescence (Hansburg, 1976); a study of various groups of elderly men and women; and a study of a group of mothers.

A group of studies involving child abuse was done by graduate students at the California School of Professional Psychology in Los Angeles (DeLozier, 1982; Kaleita, 1980; Mitchell, 1980). Two of these studies dealt largely with the abusive mothers. DeLozier (1982) administered the test to a small group of 18 known abusive mothers and compared the results to a group of 18 mothers who were nonabusive. Analysis of demographic data showed the two groups to be similar. The degree of attachment disorders among the abusive mothers was found to be significantly different from the group of nonabusive mothers:

> In the clinical interpretation of the SAT protocols, the abusing mothers exhibited a significantly higher number of factors thought to indicate anxious attachment. Twelve of the 18 abusing mothers were found to be in the "severe" category, compared with only two controls. In contrast, only three abusing mothers were in the "mild" category, compared with 10 controls. Furthermore, when protocols indicating severe levels of anxious attachment and those indicating detachment were combined, the abusing group was found to demonstrate evidence of severe attachment pathology at significantly higher levels (χ^2, $df = 1$, corrected for continuity $= 7.31$, $p < .005$, one tailed) than the typical mother group. (p. 102)

Thus the depressive syndrome was twice as great among the abusive mothers.

Mitchell (1980), repeating DeLozier's study, but with 30 abusive Mexican-American mothers in comparison to 30 Mexican-American nonabusives, used different techniques of analysis of the SAT results. She emphasizes the extent of responsiveness to the separation stimuli demonstrated by the abusive mothers in comparison to controls and the inordinately large number of responses to the mild pictures in comparison to the strong ones. Among the abusive mothers, attachment responses were excessively high, while individuation responses were excessively low, with marked indicators of anxious attachment. The abusive mothers appeared much more alarmed by the pictures than the nonabusives, according to Mitchell. She agreed with DeLozier that depressive syndromes were more common among abusive mothers, who in addition were more prone to select inappropriate responses. Mitchell considered abusive mothers to show far less self-reliance and to be more needful than the nonabusives.

Kaleita (1980) concentrated on studying abused and neglected adolescents. Groups of over 30 abused and 30 neglected subjects were compared to a similar number of controls. Thorough statistical analysis indicated that the virtually opposite attachment needs existed with the youngsters as existed with their mothers. Here it was found that degrees of detachment, pseudo-self-sufficiency, and great variability in defensiveness were related to ethnic background. Kaleita stated:

> Each subject in the two maltreatment groups had documented histories of rejection, abandonment or separation. . . . It is suggested that this expression of "pseudo-independence" is centered around increasing uncertainty about the availability of attachment figures as well as cognitive representations developed from past experiences. Moreover, there is substantial evidence that a natural course of changing attachment–separation patterns is a general characteristic of this age. It would appear that intense anxiety from past and present separation experiences combined with the developmental tasks of this stage would combine to establish cyclical patterns of pathological conflict. An adolescent in these circumstances may, therefore, be compelled to adapt by becoming "pseudo-mature" and self-protective through avoidance of contact with others who would normally provide this function. (p. 116)

From these studies of abuse and neglect it would appear that the SAT has the ability to reveal attachment pathology of one type in abusive mothers and another type in abused adolescents.

Studies using the SAT with children of divorce have been reported by Miller (1980) and Brody (1981). Miller studied groups of 30 male and female children, aged 9 to 12, of divorced or separated parents. Expecting to find in comparison to controls a group of anxious, attached children on the SAT, she found instead a condition similar to what Kaleita (1980) found with the abused and neglected: pseudo-self-sufficiency. Further, Miller found greater hostility among these children. For the first time she used an index, suggested by this author, that was a measure of attachment–pain minus individuation–hostility. The mean difference for the intact group was 9.73 and for the separated/divorced group, 3.03. Thus, it was clear that there was an increased chance that the children of divorce would be under greater impetus to assert opposition to separation, to be more exploratory of the environment, and to be more hostile. It also would appear that in some cases hostility would dominate and in others individuation would be stronger. In intact families, it appears that separation occasions more dominance from either attachment need or the fear–anxiety–pain complex.

Brody (1981), using the SAT as part of her study, investigated the effects of divorce on eight-year-olds in four Catholic schools in Phoenix, Arizona. There were 53 in the divorce/separation group and 67 among the controls. One significant finding that corroborates Miller's results was the high level of individuation scores among the divorce group, especially the male children. Brody interpreted this in terms of Despert's (1953) remark that children with divorced or divorcing parents often have a strong show of independence which is really just a compensation for a greater need to be dependent. Among a section of girls she found increasing levels of hostility similar to what Miller found. The test appears to be highly sensitive to this increase in hostility and individuation where strong abusive or divorce situations intensify separation concerns.

Varela (1982), studying the relationship between maternal separation anxiety and the hospitalized child's separation anxiety, examined 30 children aged 4 to 7 who underwent surgery in a hospital, as well as their mothers. What was interesting was the use of a revision of both the SAT and the Klagsbrun-Bowlby Scale for young children. Using a complicated separation test index score (see Varela, 1982, for details) as a measure of both the child's and the mother's separation anxiety, she found a significant positive correlation between them: "The mother's Separation Test Index Score accounted for a significant proportion (21.88%) of the variance of the child's Separation Test Index Score (t (20) = 2.59, $p < .05$)" (p. 228). Studies of anxiety behavior were not revealing at all, but the test indexes were.

Of the many other interesting studies using the SAT, the following are illustrative of the use of the test with college-level students. Among the first to attempt this was Sherry (1980). Instead of being concerned with the mothers, he decided to study students whose fathers were absent from the home because of death or divorce, a problem he had noticed in his counseling work to be of some significance in poorly adjusted students. Testing 90 freshman students, 45 from father-absent families and 45 from intact ones, male and female, ages 18 and 19, after they had been at the university for five to six months, his data strongly indicated that father-absent subjects were less inclined to use separation as a springboard for independent action than freshmen from intact families. A trend also was present in which father absence was related to increased attachment seeking. He concluded that freshmen from father-absent homes are generally more anxiously attached.

Somewhat related to Sherry's work is the study of intimacy among college women by Levitz (1982). Studying 89 undergraduate women ranging in age from 18 to 25 at the University of Missouri, she found that the Separation Anxiety Test was able to differentiate the levels of intimacy of college women. Women in the high-intimacy group exhibited a mild degree of anxious attachment, whereas women in the two other groups, merger and low intimacy, displayed strong or severe degrees of anxious attachment. She states:

> Results of group comparisons on the individual subscales of the Separation Anxiety Test revealed that women in the high intimacy group had greater capacities for self-reliance, a lower need to defend against separation and a tendency toward lower levels of self-love loss than women in the merger and low intimacy groups. These results lend support to the theories that postulate that mature intimacy capacity is dependent upon the capacity to disengage from parental dependencies and achieve a sense of psychic independence. (p. 99)

Finally, I should like to mention a study of self-destructive tendencies in early adolescence (Hansburg, 1976), in which I examined five specially selected adolescents (boys and girls), aged 11½ to 15, who showed a pattern which I subsequently defined as severe anxious attachment with self-destructive implications. A comparison was made of the prevalence of the same pattern in 14 clinic cases and 30 cases from a random population of early adolescents. In this comparison, the 14 clinic cases were found to have the following characteristics, compared to the random population: (1) low individuation and high attachment on mild pictures, (2) a severe lowering of the total individuation percentage, (3) a very high combined level of hostility and pain reactions, (4) very strong separation denial, (5) a depressive syndrome including severe loss of self-love in relationship to a lower self-esteem preoccupation, and (6) a low identity stress response. The pattern appeared to be associated with self-destructive behavior of various types. Since the time of that study, the pattern has been found to be prevalent in abusive mothers, young adults who seek out cultist groups, and low-intimacy-level college women when compared to high-intimacy groups.

SUMMARY

In summary, it appears that the SAT is a highly sensitive instrument for uncovering disturbances of the attachment system in adolescents as well as in older persons. It has proven to be highly useful in settings devoted to clinical analysis, to treatment, and to placement of youngsters in residential facilities. Further, the method has been found very useful in research dealing with attachment, separation, and loss and is very amenable to adaptation at various age levels and to revisions for special research purposes.

REFERENCES

Ainsworth, M. D. S. (1979). *Patterns of attachment.* Hillsdale, NJ: L. Erlbaum Associates.

Black, H. M. (1981). *Trait anxiety and separation distress: An analysis of two measures in parents and their adolescent children.* Unpublished doctoral dissertation, California School of Professional Psychology, Los Angeles.

Blos, P. (1967). Second individuation in adolescence. *Psychoanalytic study of the child, 22,* 162–186.

Bowlby, J. (1969). *Attachment and loss (Vol I). Attachment.* New York: Basic Books.

Bowlby, J. (1973). *Attachment and loss (Vol II). Separation.* New York: Basic Books.

Bowlby, J. (1979). *The making and breaking of affectional bonds.* London: Tavistock Publications.

Brody, N. P. (1981). *The effects of parental divorce on third graders.* Unpublished doctoral dissertation, Loyola University, Chicago.

Burger, D. (1981). *Bowlby's theory of separation as it applies to separated and divorced males.* Unpublished doctoral dissertation, California School of Professional Psychology, San Diego.

DeLozier, P. P. (1982). Attachment theory and child abuse. In C. M. Parkes & J. S. Hinde (Eds.), *The place of attachment in human behavior* (pp. 95–117). New York: Basic Books.

Duplak, C. (1983). *Separation problems of learning disabled children.* Unpublished doctoral dissertation, New York University, New York, NY.

Erikson, E. H. (1968). Identity, youth and crisis. New York: Norton.

Freud, A. (1958). Adolescence. *Psychoanalytic Study of the Child, 13,* 255–278.

Hansburg, H. G. (1972a). Adolescent separation hostility: A prelude to violence. In *Abstract guide of XXth International Congress of Psychology* (p. 599). Tokyo.

Hansburg, H. G. (1972b). Separation problems of displaced children. In R. Parker (Ed.), *The emotional stress of war, violence and peace* (pp. 241–262). Pittsburgh: Stanwyx House.

Hansburg, H. G. (1976). *The use of the separation anxiety test in the detection of self-destructive tendencies in early adolescence.* In D. V. S. Sankar (Ed.), *Mental health in children* (Vol. III). Westbury, NY: PJD Publications.

Hansburg, H. G. (1980a). *Adolescent separation anxiety (Vol. I). A method for the study of adolescent separation problems.* Springfield, IL: Charles C Thomas, 1972. Reprinted: Melbourne, FL: R. E. Krieger.

Hansburg, H. G. (1980b). *Adolescent separation anxiety (Vol. II). Separation disorders.* Melbourne, FL: R. E. Krieger.

Kaleita, T. A. (1980). *The expression of attachment and separation anxiety in abused and neglected adolescents.* Unpublished doctoral dissertation, California School of Professional Psychology, Los Angeles.

Klagsbrun, M., & Bowlby, J. (1976). Responses to separation from parents. *British Journal of Projective Psychology, 21*(2), 7–27.

Levitz, E. M. (1982). *Separation–individuation resolution and intimacy capacity in college women.* Unpublished doctoral dissertation, University of Missouri, Columbia, MO.

Mahler, M. S., & Furer, M. (1968). *On human symbiosis and the vicissitudes of individuation (Vol. I). Infantile psychosis.* New York: International Universities Press.

Miller, J. B. (1980). *The effects of separation on latency age children as a consequence of separation–divorce.* Unpublished doctoral dissertation, California School of Professional Psychology, Los Angeles.

Mitchell, M. C. (1980). *An application of attachment theory to a socio-cultural perspective of physical child abuse in the Mexican-American community.* Unpublished doctoral dissertation, California School of Professional Psychology, Los Angeles.

Piaget, J. (1954). *The construction of reality in the child.* New York: Basic Books.

Rochlin, G. (1965). *Griefs and discontents.* Boston: Little, Brown.

Sherry, M. (1980). *Father absence and separation anxiety in college freshmen.* Unpublished doctoral dissertation, Michigan State University, East Lansing.

Varela, L. M. (1982). *The relationship between the hospitalized child's separation anxiety and maternal separation anxiety.* Unpublished doctoral dissertation, California School of Professional Psychology, Los Angeles.

White, R. (1963). *Ego and reality in psychoanalytic theory.* New York: International Universities Press.

Witkin, H. A., Fatterson, H. F., Dyk, R., Goodenough, E., & Karp, S. (1962). *Psychological differentiation.* New York: John Wiley.

III
Inkblot
Tests

6
Diagnostic Use
of the Rorschach
with Adolescents

Melvin Berg

Use of the Rorschach with adolescents, like the study of adolescent development itself, has been treated as a perplexing stepchild, at once a burden and yet lovingly coaxed into the family. In the vast Rorschach literature the emphasis on children and of course adults is considerably greater than that accorded to adolescents. The ambivalence and uncertainty surrounding the study of adolescence derives from its obscure and puzzling origins in the shadowland where physiological developments converge with sociological and psychological processes. Once the biological upheavals of pubescence have settled, leaving behind the foundations of physical and cognitive maturity, the journey into adulthood becomes less clear as it is no longer bounded by the concrete anchor points of physical change. Adolescence then becomes a matter of psychological growth as the young person proceeds with the hidden, internal work of forming a character and identity that will serve as his design for living in the world as an adult. The study of these psychological processes, both in healthy youth as well as those in whom the adolescent passage has gone astray, is a challenge to our diagnostic and clinical abilities.

The problems of using the Rorschach with children, with regard to administration, norms, and interpretation, are evident even to the neophyte and consequently have given rise to a vigorous study of these issues. However, the deceptive similarity of adolescents and adults often has lulled the psychologist into believing that specialized knowledge of this developmental epoch and its bearing upon Rorschach procedures and performance was not necessary. Most of the literature on the use of the

Rorschach with adolescents has been based on the effort to formulate nomothetic patterns representing the behavior of large populations of adolescents. The nomothetic approach has generated the thrust to produce normative data of ever increasing specificity, as well as construct validity studies that broaden our ability to interpret individual Rorschach determinants objectively. Less visible but of equal clinical significance are the advances that also have been made from another direction, the idiographic approach using naturalistic observation of clinical phenomena not readily transformed into quantitative elements. This chapter draws upon knowledge derived from nomothetic studies as well as clinically based methods that make use of clinical observation and inference as guided by developmental and personality theory. This synthesis aims at establishing a base of specialized knowledge necessary to using the Rorschach clinically in a manner that can contribute toward the understanding and treatment of adolescents.

IS RELIABLE RORSCHACH DIAGNOSIS OF ADOLESCENTS POSSIBLE?

In his landmark study, Hall (1904) sketched a picture of adolescence characterized by a chaotic and fluid mixture of contradictory traits, affects, levels of ego function, and character styles that to his mind defy understanding. Similarly, Rorschach practitioners who work with adolescents typically have exercised wary caution due to the difficulty in determining what is "normal," expectable, or pathological in this age group (Hirsch, 1970; Machover, 1961).

Adolescence has been viewed traditionally as a period of transition during which childhood patterns of adaptation are relinquished as new styles of coping are tailored for the tasks of adult life. Anna Freud (1958) describes the adolescent as typically vascillating between stable adjustment and symptom formation of a neurotic or psychotic variety as a result of the arousal of sexual and aggressive drives for which the embattled youth has not developed adequate defenses to master. Thus turmoil and volatile change are regarded as normative for the adolescent, who in the process of attempting to meet instinctual threats tries out a variety of adaptational solutions and develops temporary symptoms as efforts at conflict resolution are tried, discarded, or refined. Indeed, this classical view holds that the absence of internal reorganization involving temporary regression and upheaval is in itself suggestive of a maladaptive and defensive calcification of personality, which is "pathological" (Beres, 1961; Oldham, 1978). In support of the normative status of adolescent turmoil Livson and Peskin (1980) review a variety of longitudinal studies of normal adolescence showing that disequilibrium and fluidity are both statistically "normal" and in fact conducive to psychological development.

Rorschach studies have added to the evidence pointing toward the prevalence of turmoil during adolescence. The Rorschach records of adolescents display more regressive and primary-process thought than is found in adults (Schimek, 1974), as well as more indications of disordered thought (Weiner & Exner, 1978), both of which are indicative of psychological disorganization. From the standpoint of content, adolescent Rorschach performance is characterized by a preponderance of themes depicting aggression, decay, disease, fear, and alien creatures, all of which are regarded as ominous signs of grave internal unrest when found in the protocols of adults (Rychlak & O'Leary, 1965). Moreover, in support of the beneficial effects of adolescent disequilibrium Rychlak and O'Leary also found that the prevalence of these content categories correlated with the psychological adjustment of adolescents. Similarly, Hertz (1960), in her review of the literature on adolescent Rorschachs, describes several studies reporting that the protocols of adolescents reveal a high frequency of "neurotic signs" that have been found to be indicative of psychopathology in adult protocols. Finally, Ames, Metraux, and Walker (1971) demonstrate through a longitudinal Rorschach study a rhythmic cycling of constriction and expansiveness suggesting that adolescence is characterized by experimentation with various shifting and changing modes of psychological adaptation. These views of normative adolescent turmoil throw into question whether psychopathology can be reliably diagnosed by the Rorschach or any other means, since instability is the norm (Freud, 1958).

The normative status of adolescent turmoil is contested by many studies that show that psychological health in adolescence predicts adjustment in adulthood (Masterson, 1967, 1969; Mellsop, 1972; Robins, 1966; Vaillant, 1978). Adolescence is described as a typically quiescent period, strikingly lacking in turmoil, by Douvan and Adelson (1966), whose cross-sectional study included 3,000 adolescents from all strata of American society. A similar view of adolescence was presented in Offer's (1969) longitudinal study of adolescence based upon intensive interviews and psychological tests (Ostrov, 1975), in which it was found that the most psychologically healthy adolescents moved through this period smoothly and without anguish and instability, thus negating the inevitability of adolescent turmoil. Studies examining the reliability of Rorschach scoring categories in adolescence demonstrate a high level of temporal stability, approaching that found in adults, suggesting that volatile change is not typical for this period (Exner, 1980; Exner, Armbruster, & Viglionc, 1978; Kagan, 1960; Schimek, 1968).

The classical psychoanalytic position that adolescence necessitates tumultuous upheaval and the views of Offer (1969) and Douvan and Adelson (1966) depicting adolescence as a period of smooth transition both overgeneralize from select samples. The psychoanalytic position has been based largely upon a narrow sample of disturbed adolescents who were seen in intensive psychoanalytic treatment, while Offer's sample is also biased due to the exclusion of subjects who scored on the extreme ends of a variety of personality and adjustment variables. Furthermore, only 23 percent of Offer's sample did not experience serious psychological turmoil, suggesting that although upheavals are not *inevitable* they are *typical*. As suggested by Giovacchini (1973), the degree of turmoil experienced by adolescents varies and depends upon the extent of earlier trauma and psychological stability.

The lesson to be learned by those who use the Rorschach is that assessment of adolescents is inevitably difficult since the criteria for psychological well-being are not clear and some uncertain degree of turmoil is inevitable except for the fortunate few. However, several guidelines that have clinical and empirical validity for judging the severity of adolescent illness on the Rorschach can be posited. First, Machover (1961) evaluates the severity of disturbance as a function of disorganized cognition. This has been empirically validated by Weiner and Exner (1978), who found that clinic and control adolescents could be discriminated best on the basis of the traditional indicators of thought disorder. Second, slippage in reality testing and thinking that are not accompanied by either anxiety or awareness of the lapse must be viewed with concern as a sign of either long-standing regression or a developmental arrest of ego functions. Third, signs of an impaired capacity for attachment and empathic interpersonal relationships whereby human representations, in the thematic content, are inaccurately perceived or depicted as dehumanized and devalued should be regarded with concern. These indications of impaired capacity for empathic ties do not result from illnesses derived from conflict, but from serious developmental failures in the basic building blocks of adaptive personality organization. Fourth, when there is question about clinical status a repeat testing in six months to a year can help distinguish a temporary psychological maladjustment from a stabilizing pattern of illness.

Piotrowski (1962) recommends interpretive restraint in the analysis of an adolescent's Rorschachs such that leeway is granted for the youths' need to try out various modes of psychological adaptation. In order to assess the range within which adolescents can be expected to experiment and how this might be manifested through Rorschach behavior, familiarity with adolescent development is necessary. Similarly, age-indexed norms for Rorschach determinants help guide the clinician toward understanding the individual youth.

THE USE OF NORMS

The interpretation of adolescent protocols requires specialized normative data, as those for adults generally would portray the adolescent as more disturbed than is indeed the case. Ames et al. (1971) show that the typical Rorschach performance of adolescents from the standpoint of both content and structural determinants is highly deviant according to adult normative standards. Age-indexed norms inform the examiner whether the adolescent's Rorschach behavior is within the range of the statistically expectable. Normative data are presented by Hertz (1960), Ames et al. (1971), Levitt and Truumaa (1972), and Exner and Weiner (1982), all of whom carefully selected their samples to represent the distribution of the population on crucial demographic variables such as sex, socioeconomic status, geographic distribution, and minority group membership.

The availability of refined norms, although necessary, is not the touchstone for adequate interpretation. Defects within even the most sophisticated data and failure to recognize the limits of these data can plague interpretation. First, adolescent norms refer to a group of individuals who, although of the same age, are at vastly different points in the maturational process with regard to psychophysiological puberty. Thus, the currently available age groupings are actually heterogeneous and only grossly represent an appropriate developmental cohort for any single adolescent.

Second, normative data belie extensive variance in the use of all Rorschach determinants, which variance of course reflects the wide variation within the range of what is loosely regarded as "normal" psychological adaptation. Norms are an abstraction representing the qualities of an essentially mythical figure who is supposed to describe Everyman and subsequently adequately reflects the individual qualities of nobody. The routes to psychological equilibrium are legion, and wide deviations in psychological variables can be incorporated into balanced and used adaptively within stable and successful character styles that are vastly different. Piotrowski (1971) notes that single determinants on adolescent Rorschachs can be highly deviant statistically and yet serve as important components in an adaptive character structure.

Third, it is not clear that the use of Rorschach determinants results in normal distributions, the absence of which modifies the significance of the means and medians used in normative data.

Fourth, the use of norms as the only guide to inference making often leads toward a "sign" approach to Rorschach interpretation whereby personality functioning is fractionated into a conglomeration of discrete, static, and poorly integrated variables, with the result that the sum of the parts adds up to less than the whole person.

In conclusion, normative data must be used in a flexible manner and viewed merely as landmarks providing the examiner with a general sketch of the expectable range of usage of determinants by adolescents who are approximately of the same pubescent status. Norms are only a starting point for interpretation. The remainder of the interpretative effort relies on knowledge of adolescent development, personality theory, and psychopathology, in order to discern the meaning and relevance of the wealth of data made available through naturalistic, clinical observation of the testing process.

DEVELOPMENTAL TRENDS

A scrutiny of the changes in the performance of adolescents on the Rorschach illustrates the course of adolescent development. Although a comparison of a particular adolescent performance with that of his agemates in itself does not provide a definitive picture of his psychological functioning, it does offer one observation point for assessing how that individual is finding his way along the adolescent passage. The following trends, summarizing the findings of several studies, reveal the increasing approximation of adult norms in the manner with which the developing adolescent approaches the Rorschach task.

Productivity

The productivity of the adolescent increases over this period such that the average number of responses for the 10-year-old increases from 10 to 21 by 16 years of age (Levitt & Truumaa, 1972). Similarly, whereas over 25 percent of latency-age children refuse at least one card, refusals decrease to about 16 percent by age 16 (Ames et al., 1971). The rise in productivity reflects the growing cognitive capacity and flexibility of the adolescent, who becomes increasingly intellectually curious, assertive, and able to process information toward organizing ideas.

Location

The emphasis on globally perceived whole responses by the latency child blossoms into more articulated cognitive organization decreasing the mean number of W responses from 38 percent at 10 years of age to 22 percent at 16 (Levitt & Truumaa, 1972). The decline in the percentage of W responses indicates a greater capacity for abstraction, since the diffuse W's drop out and are replaced by those that are more differentiated and integrated (Goodman, 1973; Hertz, 1960).

The lower percentage also reflects the rise in D responses from a mean of 47 percent at 10 years of age to a mean of 51 percent at 16 (Exner & Weiner, 1982) causing the W:D ratio to approach the 1:3 level of the adult (Ames et al., 1971). Likewise, small details are used with more frequency, changing from an average of 7 percent at 10 years of age to 9 percent at 16 (Exner & Weiner, 1982). The growing capacity for abstract conceptualization parallels greater attunement to the practical, common, and concrete aspects of experience, that serve as the building blocks for the abstraction process. The greater interest in fine details is evidence for strengthened cognitive discipline, orderliness, exactitude, and control. These cognitive shifts contribute to the capacity for formal operations and symbolic logic.

Form

The constriction of the late-latency child gives way to heightened spontaneity, affective responsiveness, and increased complexity of conscious experience, as suggested by the reduction in F% from 50 at 12 years of age to 41 at 15 years of age (Hertz, 1960). This trend is part of the maturing capacity for refined cognition which can integrate affect, drive, and fantasy with the objective elements of reality. At the same time attunement to reality is sharpened so that the idiosyncratic and autistically personalized ways of organizing experience are tempered and channeled into consensually validated ideas, creative productions, and improved judgment. Subsequently, F+ responses surge from 70 percent at 10 years of age to 82 percent at 16 years of age (Levitt & Truumaa, 1972). Moreover, the expanding awareness of and ability to participate in and make productive use of the most conventional ways of organizing reality are reflected by the increase in P, which moves from a mean 4.2 at 10 years of age to 5.3 at 16 years of age (Levitt & Truumaa, 1972).

Movement

Human movement responses increase from 2 at 10 years of age to 3.2 at 16 years of age (Exner & Weiner, 1982), whereas FM slips from 2.7 to 2.4. The predominance of FM over M is reversed during early adolescence and continues into adulthood as the adolescent gains capacity for delay, use of fantasy to control drive and affective pressures, and empathic attunement to other people. The achievement of greater reflectiveness and ability to integrate drive pressure through the constructive use of fantasy and planful deliberation was noted by Hertz (1960), who referred to the "introversial swing" of middle adolescence. Surprisingly, the use of M remains uncorrelated to age, with the mean being just below one (Levitt & Truumaa , 1972) even in the face of the explosion of biological drives and the personality reorganization of adolescence.

Color

The growing capacity for modulation of affect is demonstrated by C falling from a mean of .22 per record at 10 years of age to .03 at 16 years of age (Levitt & Truumaa, 1972). CF inches downward slightly during the adolescent years (Ames et al., 1971), but in late adolescence and early adulthood FC begins to outstrip CF, usually by 15 years of age (Exner & Weiner, 1982). Infantile and narcissistic emotional expression decrease as affective discharge becomes more controlled and attuned to reality, social convention, and the experience of others.

Shading and Achromatic Color

Shading changes most strikingly of all the determinants, as it jumps from .7 responses per record at 10 years of age to 1.6 at 16 (Ames et al., 1971). This confirms the adolescent's heightened ability to gain conscious awareness of anxiety and conflict and use introspective reflection as a means of conflict resolution. The appearance of shading during adolescence is part of the "introversial swing" and demonstrates the expanded tolerance for anxiety.

C′ is used infrequently and appears in only 20 percent of adolescent records (Exner & Weiner, 1982), due to their typically manic posture and incipient capacity to tolerate depression without the threat of immobilization. The use of achromatic color in an adolescent Rorschach should be attended to carefully and often points toward depression derived from intense struggles over separation and the fear of abandonment.

Content

Human responses step up from a mean of 18 percent at 10 years of age to 21 percent at 16 (Levitt & Truumaa, 1972), as awareness of and empathic attunement to the human environment and the experience of others widen. Animal responses throughout adolescence remain quite stable at 45 percent until they decrease in late adolescence and early adulthood to approximately 39 percent (Exner & Weiner, 1982).

Responses depicting blood, aggression, and violence are given by 18 percent of adolescents, and fire responses occur on 20 percent of the records, attesting to the adolescent preoccupation with crude aggressive impulses and to their susceptibility to emotional pressures. Likewise, percepts of humanoid creatures (H), which are rare prior to puberty, starting at age 10 occur at a mean of nearly one per record (Ames et al., 1971) and often appear together with frequent reference to the blots appearing "weird" and "strange." These characteristics illustrate the adolescent's reaction to new instinctual stirrings and cognitive insights that have yet to be integrated and that give rise to fantasies charged with affect, drive, and a subsequent sense of estrangement from these new experiences. Interestingly, although anatomy percepts occur rather frequently, explicit sexual references are rare and when they do appear hint at a disruption of control and defense. Despite changes in sexual mores, sexual wishes remain laden with anxiety and are fended off more strenuously than aggression.

Disordered Thought

The classical indications of disordered thought on the Rorschach—including fabulized combinations, autistic logic, deviant verbalizations, perseveration, and personal references—have a high frequency, with the mean approaching one per record in 11-year-old subjects (Exner & Weiner, 1982). These lapses in thought organization fall off 50 percent by 16 years of age; however, the number at 16 years is still twice that found in an adult population (Exner, 1978). The prevalence of cognitive slippage reveals the unstable nature of adolescent thought organization and defense, which have yet to coalesce into reliable and reality-attuned structures. Nevertheless, these deviant thought processes are crucial in identifying pathologically disordered thought and ruptures in defense, since they appear with significantly higher frequency in disturbed adolescents as compared to a control group (Weiner & Exner, 1978).

DIFFERENTIAL DIAGNOSIS

Neurotic Disturbances

Neurotic conditions are characterized by intact personality structures that have developed and matured to a sufficient extent that they are able to maintain attunement to reality, adherence to logical modes of thought, modulation of impulses, empathic attachments, and an integrated and consistent identity. Although the basic structures of personality are intact in neurotic adolescents, they are characterized by conflict over unacceptable wishes and ideas that generate anxiety and symptoms as a misguided effort to resolve the conflict. Symptomatically, neurotic disturbances are manifested as anxiety disorders, phobias, psychophysiological disturbances, and obsessive–compulsive patterns. Although on occasion these adolescents pursue treatment on their own initiative, prompted by internal discomfort, they generally come to the attention of their parents or school authorities because of impaired academic functioning, social withdrawal, or phobias. Frequently the underlying anxiety is masked by drug abuse or psychosomatic illness.

Most empirical efforts to identify signs distinguishing neurotic adolescents have borne little fruit since neurosis encompasses a very broad range of illnesses that are comprised of many different symptom pictures, defense configurations, and character styles. Furthermore, to the extent that all adolescents—or people, for that matter—experience conflict, no individual is without neurotic features. The often-used "neurotic signs" developed by Miale and Harrower-Erickson (1940) to identify neurotic illness are of little value, for these are merely indicators of constriction and appear to be a function of psychological immaturity, as they normally decrease over the course of adolescence (Hertzman & Marguiles, 1943). These neurotic signs occur with such high frequency in normal adolescents that they lack usefulness as a basis for differential diagnosis (Ives, Grant, & Ranzoni, 1953). One study examining the Rorschach protocols of obsessive adolescents demonstrated that an obsessive *character style* can be discerned readily in adolescents (Goldfarb, 1943) and that the clinical picture is similar to that found in obsessional adults (Schafer, 1948). Nevertheless, Goldfarb did not identify adolescents suffering from a *symptomatic neurotic illness*, but those endowed with an obsessive character style.

Adolescents experiencing neurotic conflicts in which the equilibrium of defenses has been shaken so as to trigger actual neurotic symptoms present features on the Rorschach indicating dysphoria, anxiety, and defensive instability. First, extreme and exaggerated reliance upon either a repressive and hysterical or obsessive–compulsive approach to the Rorschach suggests a defensive posture that is rigidifying in response to tenuously contained conflict over impulses. Second, a plethora of content charged with affect and drive, particularly when these are depicted with forceful intensity, is suggestive of impulses overwhelming defenses. Third, when such content is accompanied by demonstrations of anxiety and discomfort, neurotic instability is highlighted. Fourth, actual content representations of vigorous conflict or a general tone of discomfort point toward a consciously experienced dysphoria often resulting from neurotic symptoms. Fifth, such dysphoria is often reflected in a usage of achromatic color and shading beyond what is normatively expected. Sixth, the appearance of more than one inanimate movement response alludes to the impingement of impulses that are outstripping coping maneuvers. Finally, the standard indicators of shock signal neurotic disequilibrium. In interpreting such features on the Rorschach as evidence of a symptomatic neurosis, the examiner must use caution and grant leeway for the occurrence of normative neurotic developments as a sequel to adolescent instinctual development.

The Rorschach often can make an important contribution to the evaluation of the obviously troubled adolescent by helping to rule out more severe psychopathology characterized by thought disorder, affective disturbance, or a nonpsychotic deformation of ego development, as is found in adolescents with severe personality disorders. Moreover, the Rorschach data can assist in constructing a working model of the adolescent that illustrates the psychological functioning of the adolescent in whom the neurotic disturbance has been identified, along with providing hints as to the purposes served by the neurotic symptoms. This model can be a guide to the cognitive and defensive style of the adolescent and the kinds of treatment interventions likely to be useful and acceptable to the youth.

Depression

Depression is normally experienced throughout adolescent development as the vast changes demanded of the youth stir temporary feelings of helplessness and major alterations of identity. The adolescent is called upon to give up his secure role as a child and the dependent manner in which he had been gratified, and he must relinquish his claim upon his parents and look to the expanding world of peers to meet his needs. Furthermore, the spurt of instinctual activity often stirs confusion and guilt, with depression in the aftermath. Thus, depression is a typical adolescent byproduct and in those who come for psychiatric assistance it usually plays a large role in the presenting symptomatic picture.

Determining the extent to which depression contributes to the psychological disturbance of the adolescent is complicated by several factors. First, depressive moods and the subsequent depletion of energy subdues the adolescent's more typically manic, labile, and unpredictable behavior, rendering her more acceptable and similar to adults. The dampening of energetic adolescent behavior may come as a relief to adults, who then fail to notice the inner struggle. Second, adolescents are generally reluctant to admit to depressive concerns, as these represent a failure to grow up and a threat to their narcissism and identity as one who will soon be an adult. Third, the admission of depression to adults and the implied request for assistance and nurturance challenge the adolescent's wish to assert autonomy and sever dependent ties with adults. Fourth, troubled adolescents experience a spectrum of depressive equivalents that cover over the inner crisis. The masquerade can take the form of denial, as in complaints about boredom and emptiness. A variety of physical symptoms, fatigue, and hypochondriacal worries can act as a discharge channel for depressive anxieties. Finally, hypomanic behavior, surges of activity, and flights into sexual promiscuity and drugs may be pursued as palliatives.

The Rorschach can help to identify depressive anxieties that are masked by these depressive equivalents. A pattern of constriction, inhibition, stereotypy, and hyperconventionality, when accompanied by the use of achromatic color, diffuse shading, and inanimate movement, is generated by depressive experience. Exner and Weiner (1982) offer empirical evidence that the use of vista responses, color shading, and a depleted "Egocentricity Index" (consisting of reflection responses and pairs) are structural indications of dysphoric introspection and impoverished narcissistic resources. Thematically the protocols of these adolescents display depressive content falling into three categories: morbid concerns with injury and damage; images referring to guilt, punishment, and superego pressure; and representations depicting abandonment and deprivation.

Suicide is the fifth most frequent cause of death within the middle and late adolescent age group (Copeland, 1974), and several Rorschach features discriminate those with suicide potential. Exner and Weiner (1982) have developed a constellation of suicide signs that can alert the clinician to potential danger. They have shown that a criterion of seven or more of their eight indicators discriminate with a hit rate of 71 percent. A similar configuration of signs yields a hit rate of 92 percent and a false-hit rate of 25 percent (Arffa, 1982). The high false-hit rate is due to these signs essentially identifying troubled adolescents, many of whom are not actively suicidal but who feel inadequate and overwhelmed such that they withdraw from the environment in the midst of depressive despair. Although these signs cannot be used to rule out suicide, they certainly highlight some components of suicidal behavior.

Once depression has been uncovered as disrupting the adolescent's functioning, the source of the depression still must be determined. Frequently depression appears as a result of cerebral impairment or encroaching schizophrenic decompensation, as well as guilt or abandonment concerns, and the Rorschach can assist in making these diagnostic distinctions. This differential discrimination, however, is only the beginning of the diagnostic task, for the psychological organization of the person who has succumbed to depressive pressures still must be described.

Schizophrenia

From mid adolescence onward, the rate of psychiatric admissions due to schizophrenia soars to 25 times the rate of incidence during childhood

(Holzman & Grinker, 1977). The correct diagnosis of a schizophrenic disorder during adolescence can have far-reaching consequences. Failure to discern a schizophrenic illness precludes treatment and can leave open the way to further and perhaps irreversible disorganization. Conversely, the false identification of schizophrenia can be gravely injurious to the adolescent's fledgling self-esteem and may give rise to an unnecessary hospitalization that in itself could provoke regression.

The differential diagnosis of schizophrenia is encumbered by a variety of factors, including the normative incomplete development of cognitive organization and defenses during adolescence. As a result, indicators of thought disorder and cognitive slippage suggestive of schizophrenia are found in normal adolescents (Ames et al., 1971; Weiner & Exner, 1978). Similarly, from the standpoint of content, adolescents normally offer responses depicting crude aggression, fear, alienation, and deterioration, which at a later age would arouse concern about psychotic deterioration (Rychlak & O'Leary, 1965). For example, whereas normal adolescents present features reminiscent of adult schizophrenics, schizophrenics in early adolescence may paradoxically appear less disorganized than normal youths. Instances of gross thought disorder have been found to decrease markedly as schizophrenics enter early adolescence (Cobrinik & Popper, 1961), as a result of the defensive constriction often accompanying earliest puberty.

During adolescence, schizophrenia can be confused readily with borderline disorder, drug psychosis, minimal brain dysfunction, and transitory confusional states (Noshpitz, 1980). Moreover, what overtly appears to be a conduct disorder often masks an incipient schizophrenia. Indeed, a retrospective examination of the high-school records of male schizophrenics diagnosed during adulthood reveals that the typical adjustment of these adolescents was characterized by unsocialized aggression (Watt, Lubensky, & McClelland, 1970). Despite these diagnostic curveballs, schizophrenic adolescents generally can be distinguished on the basis of a profusion of primary process thinking (Silverman, Lapkin, & Rosenbaum, 1962) and disordered thought (Bilett, Jones, & Whitaker, 1982).

Schizophrenic illness emerges on the adolescent Rorschach protocol through a pattern of impaired functioning in four areas: reality testing, thought organization, object relations, and affect modulation. First, impaired reality testing is suggested by an F+ percentage of below 60. Even one particularly poor F− that grossly violates the blot is ominous. A decrease in the use of Populars also points toward a rupture of reality moorings. The significance of weak form level when it occurs in the context of a specific content area, particularly in a lengthy record, is mollified, as it may suggest a nonschizophrenic regression due to a circumscribed conflict. These indicators of impaired reality testing also may occur in the protocols of some severely learning disabled adolescents or those who suffer cerebral deficits as a result of deficient perceptual organization; thus, the presence of impairments in other areas is necessary in order to make a differential diagnosis.

Second, the prevalence of the entire range of disordered thought and language is greater in schizophrenic adolescents. The manifestations of cognitive slippage, in order of increasing severity, are language misusage, fabulized combination, confabulation, autistic logic, and contamination (Blatt & Ritzler, 1974; Exner & Weiner, 1982). The pathonomic significance of these indicators of disruptions in logical thought, as is the case for failures in reality testing as well, is potentiated when they are accepted by the adolescent with bland lack of concern and a failure to look critically at the deviation. One exception is the negativistic youth who deliberately rejects convention and flouts reality as a means of rebelling against the demands of the testing situation and the adult world.

Third, a disturbance in interpersonal relations as a result of schizophrenic illness is manifested by indications of withdrawal and loss of attunement to the human environment. The absence of human percepts and movement responses is suggestive of retreat and the severance of interpersonal ties. Furthermore, the appearance of either perceptually distorted or peculiar human representations points toward impairment of empathic perception and rapport with others and the disruption of interpersonal relationships by idiosyncratic fantasies and primitive, unmodulated impulses.

Fourth, although also prominent in other clinical conditions, primitive affect organization is typically part of the adolescent schizophrenic illness. Poor modulation of affect is demonstrated through a prominence of CF and particularly C and Color Naming responses, or by a complete absence of reference to color. Extremely long reaction times and pauses, especially in the absence of depression, may point toward tenuously strained efforts to contain impulses. From the perspective of content, responses often depict unmodulated aggression and/or sexual preoccupations evincing the impaired capacity for drive containment and the smooth regulation of emotions.

Borderline Disorder

Borderline illness refers to an array of serious personality disorders that occupy a midway position between neurotic illness and the psychotic level of psychopathology (Berg, 1982a). The continua upon which neurotic, borderline, and psychotic functioning vary refer to the intactness of the executive and defensive functions of the ego as well as the level of maturity and capacity for interpersonal functioning and relationships.

Borderline personality organization can be manifested through a wide variety of character styles and symptom pictures, since the diagnostic category does not designate and cannot be based upon surface traits or behavioral symptoms; rather, it depends upon broad patterns in ego functioning and interpersonal relationships that must be abstracted and inferred from surface behavior. The borderline range of psychopathology encompasses infantile, narcissistic, antisocial, inadequate, and impulse-ridden personalities (Kernberg, 1976). Although in adults borderline disorder is distinct from psychosis and schizophrenia, the distinction is less clear in adolescence, where borderline illness may represent a transition toward later schizophrenic disorganization (Kernberg, 1978). The typically chaotic clinical picture presented by these adolescents due to ego weaknesses in affect modulation, anxiety tolerance, and impulse control can readily mislead the clinician toward a misdiagnosis of minimal brain dysfunction or attention deficit disorder as the primary illness (Rinsley, 1980a, 1980b). This diagnostic error has far-reaching detrimental ramifications, since long-term psychotherapy and often family therapy are necessary in order to help the borderline adolescent surmount his developmental failures.

Adolescent borderline disorder can be disclosed on the Rorschach through a gestalt of impairments in the realm of reality testing, thought organization, defense configuration, drive and affect modulation, interpersonal relations, and object representations (Berg, 1982b, 1983). First, although reality testing does not suffer to the extent found in schizophrenic adolescents, as manifested in grossly distorted F— percepts, nevertheless moderate though frequent lapses from sharp reality testing permeate the record. Generally these occur within the context of affective or drive arousal, as suggested by the content or determinants of the response or the adolescent's behavior, rather than their more widespread appearance in schizophrenic protocols. Subsequently, a pattern of uneven reality testing emerges, with sharply perceived responses juxtaposed with those reflecting moderately defective judgment. Although not necessarily contributing toward gross decrements in form level, responses often are embellished and fabulized with idiosyncratic fantasies.

Second, in borderline disorders lapses in thought organization typically occur, especially odd verbalizations, fabulized combinations, and autistic logic, whereas instances of the more severe varieties of disordered thought, including contaminations and confabulation, are restricted primarily to schizophrenia. Frequently the borderline adolescent flaunts such responses in a manner suggesting a narcissistic delight in violating consensual guidelines in favor of adhering to her infantile and idiosyncratic modes of thought. In contrast to schizophrenic adolescents, those within the borderline range are more able to empathize with the examiner's challenge and confrontation of their cognitive lapses and thus demonstrate a greater capacity for monitoring themselves, albeit usually at the behest of external promptings and structure.

Third, the defensive functioning of these youths is unstable and riddled by failures, giving rise to both fractures in thought organization, affect regulation, and drive containment. Thus, developmentally primitive defensive efforts, especially denial, avoidance, externalization, and projection, are called up such that card refusals are common, determinants other than form are avoided, and the cards become a projection screen for frightening fantasies of external malevolence. Externalization and projection often are dramatized in the testing interaction, as the adolescent blames the examiner for his difficulties or accuses him of ill intention. Finally, as demonstrated in the records of borderline adults (Lerner & Lerner, 1982), these adolescents display an impaired capacity for repression so that they fall back upon the more primitive defense of splitting, which involves the alternation between oppositely polarized affects, rather than a balanced state of ambivalence or simple repression of one or the other. Subsequently these adolescents vacillate chaotically between contrary emotions such as love and hate and elation and depression. This splitting of affect states is demonstrated largely through the content of responses whereby polarized and inconsistent representations, such as devils and angels, appear in concert.

Fourth, drives and affects are experienced by these adolescents with commanding force, which gives rise to labile, diffuse, and intense discharges readily channeled into action or emotional storms. Correspondingly, CF and C outweigh FC to an even greater extent than is typical for the adolescent's age group, and, where FC does appear, it is often spoiled by weakened form or the intrusion of idiosyncratic fantasy. Thematically these records seethe with indications of barely contained aggression, particularly in the form of images of oral destructiveness and explosions. Any manifestations of genital sexual concerns generally bely and mask the primary interest in oral gratification of infantile needs for nurturance.

Finally, from the standpoint of object representations and interpersonal functioning, human percepts are few and those that are offered depict a world peopled by unappealing and alien figures often referred to as appearing "weird." These strange and distorted human representations reflect the adolescent's limited capacity for relatedness, as her overwhelming need states prevent accurate perception as well as empathic attunement to others. In contrast to these devalued and frightening human representations, highly idealized images also appear as a result of the splitting of emotional experience whereby others are regarded with either untempered love, fear, or hate. Images depicting deprivation and anxiety over abandonment are frequent, as are representations of fused objects, such as Siamese twins, highlighting the infantile longing for merger with an omnipotent figure as a rescuer from annihilation due to separation from the parents.

Conduct Disorders and Delinquency

Adolescents with conduct disorders comprise 70 percent of the psychiatric referrals for this age group (Evans, 1982). Antisocial behavior has numerous etiologies and actually can occur in a variety of different diagnostic categories. Consequently, early Rorschach studies generally failed to identify delinquent adolescents (Boynton & Walsworth, 1943; Lindner, 1943; Schmidl, 1947). With improved sampling techniques and greater specificity of diagnostic criteria, however, some distinguishing characteristics of these adolescents have been discerned on the Rorschach.

The unstable affect and impulse control of these adolescents is revealed by their hair-trigger and gross responsiveness to color (Cox, 1951; Curtiss, Fezko, & Marohn, 1979; Ostrov, Offer, Marohn, & Rosenwein, 1972; Schactel, 1951). Despite Piotrowski's (1962) caution that the content of adolescent Rorschachs typically displays themes suggesting inadequate impulse control, and thus is not valid as a distinguishing feature of delinquent adolescents, a proliferation of aggressive content does characterize their Rorschach records (Gorlow, Zimet, & Fine, 1952; Ostrov, Offer, & Marohn, 1976). Similarly, a higher percentage of extensor—as opposed to flexor—movement responses is found in the records of conduct-disordered adolescents (Schlesinger, 1978), indicating their propensity for vigorous activity as a means of managing and discharging tension. High as well as low F percentages often are found in these youths, as some make faltering attempts to constrict in order to contain their action potential while others throw caution to the wind as they forsake deliberative judgment and evaluation of their experience.

In a massive study examining 500 juvenile delinquents, Schactel (1951) concluded that, while some determinants reflecting poor impulse control and impoverishment of ideation are prevalent, a global approach to interpretation focusing on the configuration of the entire Rorschach picture is the most robust method of clinical study. Such a configurational perspective brings to the forefront two broad categories of adolescents presenting delinquent behavior. First, the antisocial, narcissistic youth comprises the core of the conduct-disorder syndrome. These adolescents are glib and make only lackadaisical efforts lacking in perseverance, so that their thinking is superficial, arbitrary, banal, and stereotyped, as manifested by low R; high W, A, and P percentages; low F+ percentage; and a low EB. Their differentiation and synthesis of the blot into integrated percepts is minimal, as ideation is not valued by these adolescents who too readily resort to action as a means of discharging internal pressures (Bowlus & Shotwell, 1947). Second, these adolescents are typified by poor frustration tolerance and affect regulation, leading to impulsive behavior, as suggested by short reaction times, primitive color responsiveness, low M, and emphasis on animal movement. Third, the impoverishment of their interpersonal attachments is suggested by a low H percentage, few M, and a depiction of humans in a devalued manner. Finally, indications of anxiety (manifested by use of shading) and depression (as indicated by achromatic color) are absent, pointing toward the relative level of stability gained by these adolescents, who experience little internal conflict and distress except that which is blamed on the environment.

A large number of adolescents who present conduct disorders, however, are given to disruptive behavior by virtue of neurotic conflict rather than a narcissistic personality organization. These youngsters evince greater ideational capacity and impulse control than the antisocial group. The appearance of well-perceived M responses and a high H percentage point toward their investment in other people and a capacity for empathic relatedness. Their use of shading and achromatic color demonstrates (1) vulnerability to anxiety resulting from conflict and (2) depression and guilt for their inability to sufficiently repress, integrate, or sublimate their unruly impulses.

Minimal Brain Dysfunction and Learning Disability

Difficulties in academic performance are experienced by most adolescents referred for psychological evaluation. The impairment in learning may be due to mental deficiency, disinterest in academic achievement, psychiatric illness, or minimal brain dysfunction. Adolescents with minimal brain dysfunction often demonstrate poor concentration, impaired perceptual organization, impulsivity, hyperactivity, and inadequate affect controls, a constellation of deficits that can lead the examiner erroneously to infer psychiatric disturbances. Although the Rorschach is not a primary method for the diagnosis of learning disability or cerebral dysfunction, the test findings of these adolescents may help in a preliminary assessment, and certainly the Rorschach picture should be reliably identified and distinguished from psychiatric illness.

Most notably, poor adherence to the formal characteristics of the blot may be attributable to a defect in perceptual processing rather than an impairment in reality testing or a psychiatric illness. Poor form level, in the absence of other indicators of ego impairment such as thought disorder, peculiar or primitive thought content, language misusage, and impaired object relations, is suggestive of cerebral dysfunction. A group of signs, based upon those developed by Piotrowski (1937) to detect organic brain syndrome in adults, has been found useful in identifying adolescents with minimal brain dysfunction; these include R equal to or less than 20, F+ percentage less than 75, P percentage less than 17.5, Sum C equal to or less than 3, Color Naming, card rejection, and perseveration (Assael, Kohen-Raz, & Alpern, 1967).

Minimal brain dysfunction, particularly when it causes learning disability, can have a devastating effect upon the adolescent's developing identity and adaptive capacity. In assessing these adolescents, the clinician can use the Rorschach to determine the meaning and significance that the cognitive deficit has for the youth and its influence upon personality organization. The resulting description can be helpful to those who must design remedial educational strategies tailored to the individual adolescent and her psychological needs. Frequently the Rorschach protocols of these adolescents display manifestations of impoverished self-esteem, shame, and depression. Representations of damage and injury are often present as evidence of the adolescent's experience of herself as handicapped.

The protocol also may point toward a grandiose stance or one of chronic resentment being used to ward off a depressive response to the cognitive impairment. The capacity for impulse control and frustration tolerance can be assessed, providing information useful in planning educational strategies with regard to perseverance and how failure is managed. Although the specific intellectual deficit and neurological impairment cannot be identified by the Rorschach performance, the cognitive style used in organizing experience and approaching problems can be clarified and will give hints as to how the youth is most able to learn. Finally, the manner in which others are experienced and perceived, as revealed by Rorschach representations, can orient educators to problematic interpersonal dispositions potentially encumbering relationships in the educational setting.

Mental Deficiency

Mentally deficient adolescents who function in the borderline range of intelligence approach the Rorschach in a manner that can give the appearance of several psychiatric syndromes, due to their apparent constriction and stereotypy. These youngsters produce few responses and are limited in their use of determinants, as their functioning and experience are wanting in ideational and affective differentiation. Subsequently, F percentage is high while form accuracy is low, with arbitrary percepts erroneously often giving the impression of a psychotic disorder. Movement, achromatic color, and shading responses are generally absent, and color, when used, tends to be of the more primitive variety.

As with the learning-disabled adolescent, the Rorschach can yield useful clinical impressions regarding how the mentally deficient adolescent views himself and his limitations. Frequently these adolescents regard the environment with fear as they impotently struggle to master problems and social demands beyond their adaptive capacity. The extent to which the adolescent is gripped by a persecutory experience or is able to experience others as benign sources of assistance can be assessed with the Rorschach. It also can be useful to examine attitudes toward imminent adulthood and autonomy, as these demands often present a fearful stumbling block in the development of these youngsters, who often wish to cling to their role as a dependent child. A wide variety of symptoms and disordered conduct may cover over the fear these youngsters feel regarding their dependent longings and their rising sexual interests. The manner in which challenge is responded to and the defenses used to maintain self-esteem and regulate tension also can disclose information useful in helping to plan for the future of these adolescents. Whether challenge and stress engender a catastrophic reaction and disorganization, passive collapse, or constructive help-seeking can have bearing upon the adolescent's adaptive potential and capacity for independent functioning. Finally, the extent to which denial is relied upon can be assessed, to inform the clinician as to whether the youngster harbors unrealistic ambitions that must be challenged.

Although the Rorschach certainly cannot supply quantitative or finely tuned data pertaining to intellectual capacity, cognitive resources not tapped by standard tests of intelligence may be discovered and be a sign of greater intellectual capacity than was previously recognized. Developmental level, or the capacity to form differentiated and integrated percepts, is correlated with intelligence (Ridley & Bayton, 1983) and can divine hidden intellectual potential, particularly in subculture youths (Gerstein, Brodzinsky, & Reiskind, 1976). Furthermore, it has been found that form level (Apperson, Goldstein, & Williams, 1963), whole responses of good form level (Marsden, 1970), and responses depicting human or animal interaction (Rychlak & Guinouard, 1960) all correlate with standardized measures of intelligence. In the assessment of adolescents who have been designated intellectually deficient these measures should be attended to carefully, for convergent validation of the defect or for discrepancies. A meticulous examination of and inquiry into the apparently deficient youth's Rorschach performance may be encumbered, however, by the examiner's anxiety and guilt over the frustration experienced by the adolescent. The examiner must strike a fine balance between providing a thorough assessment and not overtaxing the youngster's capacities.

ADOLESCENT OBJECT RELATIONS

In studying object relations, one examines the images by which individuals represent themselves and others, along with the accompanying affects and defenses regulating interpersonal relationships. These object representations are the cognitive schemata structuring interpersonal experience and serving as the organizing principles and patterns according to which individuals relate to each other. The foundation of object representations is established in the early interactions of the child with his primary caretakers, and this becomes the basic template for the interpersonal relationships that follow throughout life.

The adolescent's object world undergoes important shifts as discrepant aspects of the personality are integrated into an identity upon which adult roles are based. The task of adolescent development calls for crystallizing a consistent identity and ways of maintaining and regulating self-esteem sanctioned by ego ideals and supported by cultural mores. Additionally, the adolescent must wrench himself away from his early childhood ties and establish adult relationships in the adult world founded upon his newly consolidated identity. The success with which the youth is able to master these developmental tasks is a useful perspective from which psychological functioning and health can be evaluated. The Rorschach can provide a clear view of the adolescent's object world by examining percepts, particularly those of animals and humans, as indicative of the manner in which he constructs his experience of himself and others. Thus, the examination of Rorschach object representations provides rich clinical information about how the adolescent, despite the diagnostic category, functions in the social environment.

The content of the adolescent's percepts reflects the qualities and inner experience attributed to self and others. The degree to which relationships between objects are portrayed on one end of the dimension as symbiotic and fused (e.g., Siamese twins) and on the other extreme as autonomous has been found to correlate with the capacity for autonomy and mutuality as revealed by the clinical history (Urist & Shill, 1982). Similarly, although in this instance demonstrated in an adult sample, the extent to which human percepts show the capacity to perceive others empathically and with accuracy and to experience them as benign and valuable in their own right correlates with therapists' ratings of overall psychological health (Krohn & Mayman, 1974).

An examination of the formal characteristics of human percepts establishes a trend throughout adolescence and early adulthood whereby people are perceived with increasing detail, accuracy, and wholeness (as opposed to Hd), in a manner compatibly combining the action described with the nature of the person depicted (Blatt, Brenneis, Schimek, & Glick,

1976). These findings suggest a line of development along which object representations become increasingly accurate, differentiated, and integrated, as is true for overall development as described by the theories of Werner and Piaget. The validity of these dimensions as indicative of psychological development and health has been supported in an adult sample, where these scales correlate with measures of reality testing and severity of psychopathology (Lerner & St. Peter, 1984). Blatt and Lerner (1983) have shown how adolescents from a variety of diagnostic categories can be differentiated by using the formal characteristics of object representations on the Rorschach as indicative of how the adolescent experiences both himself and others and even how thought and internal controls are organized. Moreover, a schematization of the adolescent's object world can be used as a means of predicting how the adolescent will experience treatment, the resistance likely to be marshalled, and the transference paradigms and countertransference traps likely to be generated once treatment begins (Lerner, 1983).

TOWARD DIAGNOSTIC UNDERSTANDING OF THE ADOLESCENT

Although categorization of the adolescent, in terms of the previously reviewed typological groupings, is useful for roughly designating the most prominent features of psychopathology and comparing these to known patterns of illness, this taxonomy is only a component of the diagnostic enterprise. For once the examiner has located the diagnostic region occupied by the adolescent's illness, the task of ideographic description—of determining in detail how the adolescent, as a person, functions psychologically—must begin. Thus, the Rorschach data can be used to illuminate "how the patient is ill, how ill the patient is, how he became ill and how his illness serves him" (Menninger, Mayman, & Pruyser, 1963, p. 7). From this perspective diagnosis is not the identification of a discrete disease entity in the medical sense but the elaboration of a working model of the adolescent person who is beset by illness. Whereas the developmental history, family interviews, and reports of functioning within the home and the community can contribute toward a longitudinal view of the adolescent across time and place, the Rorschach displays a cross-sectional view (Allen, 1981) revealing the structural, organizing principles by which the youth arranges his life.

The facets of the adolescent's functioning that diagnostic assessment must address include reality testing, thought organization, and the extent to which age-appropriate cognitive modalities have been achieved. The level of drive organization and whether genital aims have superseded infantile pleasures are indicative of maturational status; these are illustrated in the thematic content of responses. The types of defenses used to control anxiety and unacceptable wishes point toward the adolescent's success in being able to integrate realistically her needs with what the environment can offer and toward whether or not these needs can be sublimated into gratifying endeavors. A related issue is whether a consistent and stable character style and identity are forming upon which the adolescent can rely to meet her needs and the demands of the environment. The adolescent's ability to modulate affect and the manner in which this is done are a hallmark of the emerging adaptive capacity of the young adult. The nature of the adolescent's experience of herself and others and whether this leads toward empathic appreciation and accurate perception of others will determine the youngster's availability for intimate involvement. Finally, whether the adolescent has the means to experience herself as separate from others has bearing upon the readiness to relinquish infantile gratifications and move toward adult autonomy.

The clarification of these prominent lines of adolescent development does not rely upon any single Rorschach sign or determinant but is based on a gestalt construction involving constellations of various aspects of Rorschach performance, as described by Schafer (1954). Each source of information with potential bearing upon the important dimensions of psychological functioning does not always yield clear or convergent inferences that validate the others; in fact, often they are contradictory. The clinician then must stand back and view the Rorschach performance as a whole, against the backdrop of developmental history and all sources of information about the youth, and determine how the meaning of the individual elements is affected by the configuration of the whole.

For example, the adolescent's capacity to perceive clearly bounded and distinct percepts, the content of these percepts, as well as the style of relating to the examiner, all can contribute toward a description of the adolescent's identity and movement toward separation. Thus, percepts depicting fused objects like "a fetus in the womb" point toward symbiotic longings interfering with the process of forming an autonomous identity. Inferences also can be based upon the interpersonal aspects of the testing process.

THE INTERPERSONAL INTERACTION AS A SOURCE OF DATA

Along with the content and structural aspects of the adolescent's Rorschach performance, the interpersonal transaction with the examiner is a fertile source of clinical inferences. Psychological functioning takes place within the context of an interpersonal relationship, and the quality of the adolescent's performance on the Rorschach is both *contingent upon* and *revealed by* the form and quality of the relationship and interaction with the examiner. The Rorschach task is framed by the examiner's invitation to engage in an alliance aimed at exploring the psychological functioning of the adolescent, with the expectation that relief from psychological distress will accrue. The manner in which the adolescent perceives and responds to this offer and the relationship he constructs with the examiner is determined by the nature of his psychopathology, character style, and capacity to use therapeutic assistance (Berg, 1982b, 1984, 1985).

Despite efforts to adhere to the guidelines of standardized administration, all patients shape the relationship with the examiner to conform with their internal schema of the human object world and their typical adaptive efforts. Indeed, adolescents are most adept in doing this in forceful and dramatic ways. The examiner then finds that clinical exigency and the need to adjust and tactfully respond to the idiosyncrasies of the patient require that each testing process be in some ways unique and molded around the personality organization of the adolescent. This avails the examiner of two funds of data deriving from a scrutiny of the interpersonal transaction with the adolescent. First, the examiner can make note of the unique manner in which the adolescent meets the testing task and shapes the relationship with the examiner. The vicissitudes of this interpersonal process and how it *influences* or is *influenced by* the adolescent's Rorschach productions offer insight into the interdigitation of psychological functioning and the adaptation to the social context. For example, an examiner observed that his friendly approach during testing the limits caused an adolescent girl to constrict further such that her productions grew more stereotyped. It later became clear that this girl's feared sexual preoccupations rendered relationships dangerous and that her cognitive functioning was sterilized in order to ward off instinctual threats.

Second, the examiner can note the nature and the fate of the various interventions he selects, particularly during inquiry and testing the limits, which are aimed at supporting the adolescent's involvement in the diagnostic alliance, his investment in meeting up to the challenge of the task, and his capacity to reflect upon his performance. The range of interventions available to the examiner is wide; which ones are chosen depends upon the aspect of the adolescent's behavior requiring assistance in order to master the Rorschach task or the clinical hypotheses that might be clarified by the examiner's intervention. During the free-association phase, such interventions are generally not called for; however, highly constricted and oppositional adolescents on the one hand or those who are regressed and teetering on the edge of disorganization may necessitate the examiner intervening in some way to support the faltering ego functioning. During the inquiry the examiner must often devise ways of responding to the adolescent's frustration, dismay, or belligerence, as well as ways of helping him to clarify his thoughts in order to provide useful information about the nature of the percept and the psychological process producing it. Finally, during testing the limits, the examiner is free to intervene with an even greater degree of freedom aimed at investigating latent response tendencies, fantasies underlying selected percepts, and the adolescent's ability to monitor lapses in his reality attunement and thought organization.

Whatever manner the examiner uses to intervene will evoke a response in the adolescent that will serve as data upon which clinical inferences can be drawn. The examiner selects interventions that are designed to validate diagnostic hypotheses regarding the adolescent, and the tests of the hypotheses come about by observing the youngster's responses. Here the boundary between diagnosis and treatment becomes obscure:

> One can view the interaction between the patient and clinician as a *diagnostic process* or a *treatment process* depending upon one's purpose in making the discrimination. We treat through efforts at understanding and understand through observing the results of our efforts to treat, i.e., to change the situation. Diagnosis and treatment, therefore, are not different kinds of activities but are simply two points of view toward a clinical process. They are complementary points of view, neither complete without the other. (Schlesinger, 1973, p. 499)

A common transactional posture adopted by adolescents during the Rorschach is that of extreme negativism. Few adolescents spontaneously seek therapeutic assistance, much less psychological evaluation, but come under pressure from parents, school, or the legal system. The examiner, at least initally, is viewed as an agent of the overbearing adults who have shanghaied him to the consulting room. Adolescents are particularly averse to psychological evaluation and frequently object most strenuously to projective techniques like the Rorschach. Winnicott (1971) noted, "One thing that must be recognized at the start by those who explore in this area of psychology is the fact that the adolescent boy or girl does not want to be understood. Adults must hide among themselves what they come to understand of adolescents" (p. 40).

The administration of the Rorschach represents to the adolescent an assault on several fronts. First, the very fact that the assessment is being conducted on the adolescent challenges their frequent predilection to externalize responsibility for problems onto others, particularly parents. Second, the carefully guarded privacy of the adolescent is invaded, representing a potentially persecutory scrutiny of wishes and feelings with which the adolescent is barely familiar and not yet comfortable. Third, the evaluation arouses shame and narcissistic injury if it is regarded as an indication of a failure to grow up and achieve the long-cherished ideal of independence and freedom. Fourth, seeking assistance or being coerced to submit passively to the helpful administrations of an adult subverts the adolescent's wish to free himself from reliance upon adult caretaking. Subsequently, the examiner must navigate a careful course between being too invasive or controlling on the one hand and yet offering a genuine interest in establishing a diagnostic alliance on the other.

In the course of efforts made to involve the adolescent in a collaboration around the Rorschach, by virtue of how the youngster responds to the examiner's overtures, clues will emerge as to whether the adolescent's resistance and negativsim derive from intellectual deficiency, depressive inertia, schizophrenic disorganization, or a long-standing characterological style. Of course, not all adolescents come to the Rorschach in overt negativistic defiance, and the variety of maneuvers by which the diagnostic task and goal of self-exploration can be undermined or deflected are numerous. Similarly, the ways in which the examiner can meet and respond to these defenses and security operations, with the goal of facilitating self-disclosure and discovery, are equally varied. Whether and to what degree the examiner's attempts to engage the adolescent in a collaboration succeed or fail, the examiner will gain critical information. The success or failure of the examiner's overtures will leave in their wake information about the adolescent's ego functioning, interpersonal relationships, and ability to form a therapeutic alliance, as well as the manner in which he must be approached by helping adults if the alliance offered is to appear therapeutic and helpful indeed.

Thus, the Rorschach is not only a test of cognitive organization but also a meeting ground where the adolescent and the examiner engage each other in a task in order to observe and learn from what will happen. As the examiner presents the blots in order to observe the youngster's manner of psychological mastery, an interpersonal process is set in motion. This molar process is intimately enmeshed with how the adolescent manages the cognitive challenges of the inkblots themselves on the molecular dimensions of perception, thought organization, and affect regulation.

REFERENCES

Allen, J. G. (1981). The clinical psychologist as a diagnostic consultant. *Bulletin of the Menninger Clinic, 45*, 247–258.

Ames, L., Metraux, R., & Walker, R. (1971). *Adolescent Rorschach responses.* New York: Brunner Mazel.

Apperson, L., Goldstein, A., & Williams, W. (1963). Rorschach form level as an indicator of potentials in mentally retarded children. *Journal of Clinical Psychology, 19,* 320–321.

Arffa, S. (1982). Predicting adolescent suicidal behavior and the order of Rorschach measurement. *Journal of Personality Assessment, 46,* 563–568.

Assael, M., Kohen-Raz, R., & Alpern, S. (1967). Developmental analysis of EEG abnormalities in juvenile delinquents. *Diseases of the Nervous System, 28,* 49–55.

Beres, D. (1961). Character formation. In S. Lorand & H. Schneer (Eds.), *Adolescents: Psychoanalytic approach to problems and therapy* (pp. 1–15). New York: Paul Hoeber.

Berg, M. (1982a). Borderline psychopathology: On the frontiers of psychiatry. *Bulletin of the Menninger Clinic, 46,* 113–124.

Berg, M. (1982b). Psychological testing of the borderline patient: A guide for therapeutic action. *American Journal of Psychotherapy, 34,* 536–546.

Berg, M. (1983). Borderline psychopathology as displayed on psychological tests. *Journal of Personality Assessment, 47,* 120–133.

Berg, M. (1984). Expanding the parameters of psychological testing. *Bulletin of the Menninger Clinic, 48,* 10–24.

Berg, M. (1985). The feedback process in diagnostic psychological testing. *Bulletin of the Menninger Clinic, 49,* 52–69.

Bilett, J., Jones, N., & Whitaker, L. (1982). Exploring schizophrenic thinking in older adolescents with the WAIS, Rorschach and WIST. *Journal of Clinical Psychology, 38,* 232–243.

Blatt, S., Brenneis, B., Schimek, J., & Glick, M. (1976). Normal development and psychopathological impairment of the concept of the object on the Rorschach. *Journal of Abnormal Psychology, 85,* 364–373.

Blatt, S., & Lerner, H. (1983). The psychological assessment of object relations. *Journal of Personality Assessment, 47,* 7–28.

Blatt, S. J., & Ritzler, B. A. (1974). Thought disorders and boundary disturbances in psychosis. *Journal of Consulting & Clinical Psychology, 42,* 370–381.

Bowlus, D., & Shotwell, A. (1947). A Rorschach study of psychopathic delinquency. *American Journal of Mental Deficiency, 52,* 23–30.

Boynton, P., & Walsworth, B. (1943). Emotionality test scores of delinquent and nondelinquent girls. *Journal of Abnormal and Social Psychology, 38,* 87–92.

Cobrinik, L., & Popper, L. (1961). Developmental aspects of thought disturbance in schizophrenic children: A Rorschach study. *American Journal of Orthopsychiatry, 31,* 1970–1980.

Copeland, A. (1974). *Textbook of adolescent psychopathology and treatment.* Springfield, IL: Charles C. Thomas.

Cox, S. (1951). A factorial study of the Rorschach responses of normal and maladjusted boys. *Journal of Genetic Psychology, 79,* 95–113.

Curtiss, G., Fezko, M., & Marohn, R. (1979). Rorschach differences in normal and delinquent white male adolescents: A discriminant function analysis. *Journal of Youth and Adolescence, 8,* 379–392.

Douvan, E., & Adelson, J. (1966). *The adolescent experience.* New York: John Wiley.

Evans, J. (1982). *Adolescent and pre-adolescent psychiatry.* London: Academic Press.

Exner, J. E. (1978). *The Rorschach: Current research and advanced interpretation* (Vol. 2). New York: John Wiley.

Exner, J. E. (1980). But it's only an inkblot. *Journal of Personality Assessment, 44,* 562–577.

Exner, J. E., Armbruster, G. L., & Viglione, D. (1978). The temporal stability of tone Rorschach features. *Journal of Personality Assessment, 42,* 374–382.

Exner, J. E., & Weiner, I. (1982). *The Rorschach: Assessment of children and adolescents* (Vol. 3). New York: John Wiley.

Freud, A. (1958). Adolescence. *Psychoanalytic Study of the Child, 13,* 255–278.

Gerstein, A., Brodzinsky, D., & Reiskind, N. (1976). Perceptual integration on the Rorschach as an indicator of cognitive capacity: A developmental study of racial differences in a clinic population. *Journal of Consulting and Clinical Psychology, 44,* 760–765.

Giovacchini, P. L. (1973). The adolescent process and character formation. *Adolescent Psychiatry, 2,* 269–284.

Gluek, S., & Gluek, E. (1959). *Predicting delinquency and crime.* New York: Harvard University Press.

Goldfarb, W. (1943). A definition and validation of obsessional trends in the Rorschach examination of adolescents. *Rorschach Research Exchange, 7,* 81–108.

Goodman, L. (1973). Perceptual preferences in relation to aspects of personality. *Genetic Psychology Monographs, 88,* 111–132.

Gorlow, L., Zimet, C., & Fine, H. (1952). The validity of anxiety and hostilty Rorschach content scores among adolescents. *Journal of Consulting Psychology, 16,* 73–75.

Hall, G. S. (1904). *Adolescence: Its psychology and its relations to physiology, anthropology, sociology, sex, crime, religion and education.* New York: Appleton.

Hertz, M. (1960). The Rorschach in adolescence. In A. Rabin & M. Haworth (Eds.), *Projective techniques with children* (pp. 29–61). New York: Grune & Stratton.

Hertzman, M., & Marguiles, M. (1943). The value and the limitations of the so-called "neurotic signs." *Journal of Genetic Psychology, 62,* 189–215.

Hirsch, E. (1970). *The troubled adolescent.* New York: International Universities Press.

Holzman, P., & Grinker, R. (1977). Schizophrenia in adolescence. In S. Fernstein & P. Giovacchini (Eds.), *Adolescent Psychiatry (Vol. V)* (pp. 276–292). New York: Jason Aronson.

Ives, V., Grant, M. & Ranzoni, J. (1953). The "neurotic" Rorschachs of normal adolescents. *Journal of Genetic Psychology, 83,* 31–61.

Kagan, J. (1960). The long-term stability of selected Rorschach responses. *Journal of Consulting Psychology, 24,* 67–73.

Kernberg, O. (1976). *Object relations theory and clinical psychoanalysis.* New York: Jason Aronson.

Kernberg, O. (1978). The diagnosis of borderline conditions in adolescence. *Adolescent Psychiatry, 6,* 298–319.

Krohn, A., & Mayman, M. (1974). Object representations in dreams and projective tests. *Bulletin of the Menninger Clinic, 38,* 445–466.

Lerner, H. (1983). An object representation approach to psychostructural change: A clinical illustration. *Journal of Personality Assessment, 47,* 314–323.

Lerner, H., & Lerner, P. (1982). A comparative study of defensive structure in neurotic, borderline and schizophrenic patients. *Psychoanalysis and Contemporary Thought, 5,* 77–115.

Lerner, H., & St. Peter, S. (1984). Patterns of object relations in neurotic, borderline and schizophrenic patients. *Psychiatry, 47,* 77–92.

Levitt, E. E., & Truumaa, A. (1972). *The Rorschach technique with children and adolescents.* New York: Grune & Stratton.

Lindner, R. (1943). The Rorschach test and the diagnosis of psychopathic personality. *Journal of Criminal Psychopathology, 5,* 69–93.

Livson, N., & Peskin, H. (1980). Perspectives on adolescence from longitudinal research. In J. Adelson (Ed.), *Handbook of adolescent psychology* (pp. 47–98). New York: John Wiley.

Machover, S. (1961). Diagnostic and prognostic considerations in psychological tests. In S. Lorand & H. Schneer (Eds.), *Adolescents: Psychoanalytic approach to problems* (pp. 301–345). New York: Paul H. Hoeber.

Marsden, G. (1970). Intelligence and the Rorschach whole response. *Journal of Projective Techniques, 34,* 470–476.

Masterson, J. F. (1967). The symptomatic adolescent five years later: He didn't grow out of it. *American Journal of Psychiatry, 123,* 1338–1345.

Masterson, J. F. (1969). A point of view on diagnosis and treatment of adolescents. *Seminars in Psychiatry, 1,* 57–65.

Mellsop, G. (1972). Psychiatric patients seen as children and adults: Childhood predictors of adult illness. *Journal of Child Psychology and Psychiatry, 13,* 91–101.

Menninger, K., Mayman, M., & Pruyser, P. (1963). *The vital balance.* New York: Viking Press.

Miale, F. , & Harrower-Erickson, M. (1940). Personality structure in the psychoneuroses. *Rorschach Research Exchange, 4,* 71–74.

Noshpitz, J. (1980). Disturbances in early adolescent development. In S. Greenspan & G. Pollock (Eds.), *The course of life* (Vol. 2). Adelphi, MD: Mental Health Study Center.

Offer, D. (1969). *The psychological world of the teenager: A study of normal development.* New York: Basic Books.

Oldham, D. (1978). Adolescent turmoil. *Adolescent Psychiatry, 6,* 265–279.

Ostrov, E. (1975). Patterns of Rorschach test scores among three groups of adolescents. In D. Offer & J. Offer (Eds.), *From teenage to young manhood* (pp. 109–126). New York: Basic Books.

Ostrov, E., Offer, D., & Marohn, R. (1976). Hostility and impulsivity in normal and delinquent Rorschach responses. In S. Sankar (Ed.), *Mental health in children* (Vol. 2) (pp. 479–492). Westbury, NY: P. J. D. Publications.

Ostrov, E., Offer, D., Marohn, R., & Rosenwein, T. (1972). The "impulsivity index": Its application to juvenile delinquency. *Journal of Youth and Adolescence, 1,* 179–195.

Piotrowski, Z. (1937). The Rorschach inkblot method in organic disturbance of the central nervous system. *Journal of Nervous and Mental Disease, 86,* 525–537.

Piotrowski, Z. (1962). The relative pessimism of psychologists. *American Journal of Orthopsychiatry, 32,* 382–387.

Piotrowski, Z. (1971). Introduction. In L. Ames, R. Metraux, & R. Walker (Eds.), *Adolescent Rorschach responses.* New York: Brunner Mazel.

Ridley, S., & Bayton, J. (1983). Validity of two scoring systems for measuring cognitive development with the Rorschach. *Journal of Consulting and Clinical Psychology, 51,* 470–471.

Rinsley, D. (1980a). Treatment of the severely disturbed adolescent. New York: Jason Aronson.

Rinsley, D. (1980b). Diagnosis and treatment of borderline and narcissistic children and adolescents. *Bulletin of the Menninger Clinic, 44,* 147–170.

Robins, L. (1966). *Deviant children grown up.* Baltimore: Williams & Wilkins.

Rychlak, J., & Guinouard, D. (1960). Rorschach content, personality and popularity. *Journal of Projective Techniques, 24,* 322–332.

Rychlak, J., & O'Leary, L. (1965). Unhealthy content in the Rorschach responses of children and adolescents. *Journal of Projective Techniques, 29,* 354–368.

Schachtel, E. (1951). Notes on Rorschach tests of 500 juvenile delinquents and a control group of 500 non-delinquent adolescents. *Journal of Projective Techniques, 15,* 144–172.

Schafer, R. (1948). *Clinical application of psychological tests.* New York: International Universities Press.

Schafer, R. (1954). *Psychoanalytic interpretation in Rorschach testing.* New York: Grune & Stratton.

Schimek, J. (1968). A note on the long-range stability of selected Rorschach signs. *Journal of Projective Techniques and Personality Assessment, 32,* 63–65.

Schimek, J. (1974). Some developmental aspects of primary process manifestations in the Rorschach. *Journal of Personality Assessment, 33,* 226–229.

Schlesinger, H. (1973). Interaction of dynamic and reality factors in the diagnostic testing interview. *Bulletin of the Menninger Clinic, 37,* 495–517.

Schlesinger, L. (1978). Rorschach human movement responses of acting-out and withdrawn adolescents. *Perceptual and Motor Skills, 47,* 68–70.

Schmidl, F. (1947). The Rorschach test in juvenile delinquency research. *American Journal of Orthopsychiatry, 17,* 151–160.

Silverman, L., Lapkin, B., & Rosenbaum, I. (1962). Manifestations of primary process thinking in schizophrenia. *Journal of Projective Techniques, 26,* 117–127.

Urist, J., & Shill, M. (1982). Validity of the Rorschach Mutuality of Autonomy Scale: A replication using excerpted responses. *Journal of Personality Assessment, 46,* 450–454.

Vaillant, G. (1978). The natural history of male psychological health. *American Journal of Psychiatry, 135,* 653–659.

Watt, R., Lubensky, A., & McClelland, D. (1970). School adjustment and behavior of children hospitalized for schizophrenia as adults. *American Journal of Orthopsychiatry, 40,* 637–657.

Weiner, I. B., & Exner, J. (1978). Rorschach indices of disordered thinking in patient and nonpatient adolescents and adults. *Journal of Personality Assessment, 42,* 339–343.

Winnicott, D. (1971). Adolescence: Struggling through the doldrums. *Adolescent Psychiatry, 1,* 40–50.

7
Issues in the Use of the Rorschach with Children

Nina Rausch de Traubenberg

Testing conditions in the psychological examination of the child present a twofold situation combining two types of opposite yet complementary attitudes. Tests of efficiency and competence require adaptation to the requirements of reality: the best response with the shortest latency. On the other hand, projective techniques invite the free expression of imagination interwoven with the perceptual reality that shapes it.

In fact, all of the child's production, whether standardized or free, is situated between the two poles of the real and imaginary. The development of the child, intellectual or affective, is based on two fundamental needs: to adapt to external reality and its exigencies and to express internal reality—the needs, fears, and fantasies.

THE PLACE OF THE RORSCHACH
IN THE CHILD'S PRODUCTION

The child naturally perceives the appeal of fantasy and play and therefore creates and invents in accordance with his needs. In the case of the Rorschach card, he is confronted with external reality and with the obvious objective characteristics of shape, color, and structure in relation to a vertical axis of symmetry. But this external reality is not known reality, as the play is not really true. The child probably will relate the stimulus to a known object or give it a meaning from his own subjective and imaginary world. Therefore, the responses will have two phases, the first having its source in external reality and the second in internal reality. It is this situation that permits us to speak of the development of responses and their oscillation, showing us where the child is situated between the real and the imaginary.

TESTING CONDITIONS

The Rorschach is never the only test given to a child; it is given as part of a battery in which objective testing alternates with projectives. It is important that the child understand the differences in the attitudes required. It is equally important to know that the young child seeks more to establish a relationship than to express his abilities; also, that gestures, signs, and exclamations are part of the child's reactivity, expressing seduction, dependency, or aggression. All this makes it difficult to record the protocol and makes the inquiry rather uncertain. The child also soon gets tired and restless; unless he is overly obedient and submissive, it is difficult to hold his attention.

One should begin with the most simple inquiries; for example, "What could this be?" It often happens, however, especially with the shy and reticent child, that it is necessary to encourage and to repeat the question with each card. An original procedure of inquiry was proposed by Beizmann (1961), consisting of a graphic technique by which the child traces the blot and then is asked to construct his response. This technique greatly intensifies the reactions and provokes comments that clarify the responses, which also are accompanied by their corresponding emotional tone.

It is difficult to set the conditions of test administration once and for all. Any experienced clinician must modify the administration in accordance with the goals she sets for herself. We believe that under no circumstances should the productivity of the child be sacrificed to the procedure; however, one must be aware of the modifications introduced and of their effect upon the child's reactions and our interpretations.

THE RESPONSES: THE SCORING PROCESS

Whether the responses are made up exclusively of nouns or they are fabulized stories, the scoring system concerns only the core or the "body" of the response. Thus, the entire scoring system constitutes a framework that has been elaborated in different ways, and the qualitative aspects (contents given separately or qualified by epithet and subjective references) indicate the differences in the individual modes of functioning.

The scoring system used in France is, in fact, a combination of the propositions made by Rorschach and of a simplified form of Klopfer's (1946) scoring of shading and minor kinesthetic determinants (m, FM), the latter having been adopted in 1947. We shall mention these various factors only in order to comment on the particulars of their utilization by children. First, we note the importance of the verbalization, the frequency of exclamations, adjectives ("big, big, big"; "tiny, little"), and superlatives. This insistence shows the emotional resonance and gives a hint of the meaning of the story as well as the extent of the imagination.

MEANING OF THE RORSCHACH FACTORS

Modes of Apprehension, or Perceptual Modes

Perceptual modes define the location of the response. Of all the perceptual modes, the global mode (W) has been subject to the most research, so the determination of the extent of its structure is important in evaluating the child's association process. If American psychologists have explained the evolution of perception on the basis of the works of Werner (1948), European psychologists have leaned on Claparede (1938) and later on the work of Wallon (1947) in marking the phases of perceptual and conceptual differentiation. The ability to differentiate and the consciousness of the interpretation prove the evolution not only of perception but, more generally, of the individuation processes, in particular, the difficulties in delimiting the inside from the outside. W and Ws locations are used for the most primary themes of annihilation and destructive incorporation; for example, they are expressed directly by prepsychotic and psychotic children.

We also can discuss perceptual modes in terms of spaces used by the child in projecting the body image. This projection is facilitated by the structure of the stimulus, which is based on a vertical axis, a structure to which the child is particularly sensitive. She tries to slide into the perceptual space and in so doing places herself in a relational space.

Determinants or Modes of Expression

The child expresses herself essentially by means of forms. These forms are ways of knowing objective reality, but what is known is often determined too much by what is feared or desired. These F responses are called "dynamic" by Schachtel (1941) and are seen as equivalent to libidinal expression or expression of aggression ("sword," "dagger," "tiny animal"). Careful reading of these responses reveals the child's awareness of herself in relation to others, especially with regard to feeling powerful or weak. The evaluation of the quality of the form is made by using adult norms. This has the advantage of comparing development and progression of judgment but is not always adequate in the appreciation of unique cases.

The mode of expression of the child is also kinesthetic and includes human movement (M), animal movement (FM), and inanimate or object movement (m). The human movement responses have an absolutely primordial role in the child's Rorschach. They refer to two aspects: the construction of the body image and the way the libidinal energy is taken up by the image. Stated in another way, the awareness of the body image and the projection of a relationship are determined by the emotional development or libidinal stage, in relation to parental images as they appear in fantasy.

Reactions to color are particularly difficult to interpret (shading is almost never used). Colors provoke reactions of pleasure and displeasure, stimulate exploration, or in some cases give rise to representations. In our experience, it is impossible to attribute to children's color responses the same affective value that they have for the adult. The emotional experience is different with red and pastel stimuli and also in the presence of white or gray stimuli. One must note the sensitivity of the child to gray as a color.

The emotional responsiveness of children follows other paths than color alone; we have seen an articulation of the kinesthetic and chromatic poles where m and FM may mean C or CF.

The study of determinants used by children at different ages and in various pathological organizations raises the notion of the *interchangeability of modes of expression* in early childhood, as if the specificity of factors has not yet been elicited. Actually, it is just as easy to convey the meaning of destructiveness, for example, in form responses as it is in color or movement (e.g., "demolished bridge," "burnt house").

Content

The categories used by children mostly concern animals. A differentiated analysis of the animal figures must be made, either for research purposes or for the clinical study of individuals. Instead of making a simplistic classification of animals as "powerful," "dangerous," "devourers," or "aquatic," we must note the choices in relation to the blot and the characteristics that the child attributes to the animal. Plant life often is used by the child, especially the tree, which is associated with nature and its active phenomena such as "rain," "explosion," and "volcano," revealing a tumultuous period in his life.

The human world is either active or acted upon. The world of objects appears only after the age of seven.

Content takes the meaning of identification, through the power displayed or aggression feared, but one must be cautious in judging the significance, especially when the references concern forces of human or animal nonreality.

The task of analyzing the different response factors in various age groups and psychic organizations demonstrates the complexity of the meaning of the data. It may be inferred, therefore, that the ability to perceive objective reality is effective only if invested with meaning and fantasy material, and that any perceptual activity, even though it corresponds to the child's developmental stage, may be disorganized by the projection of the child's momentary underlying meaning. It also may be deduced that, through his verbalizations, his use of location, the expressed content, the way he responds to the explicit and implicit stimulus value of the inkblot, and his use of the material which he shapes, creates, and destroys, the child is looking for his identity in his body image and in his relations with others.

CLINICAL INTERPRETATION: HYPOTHESIS

The interpretive schema we are presenting depends on clinical experience and our working hypothesis. Our hypothesis is that the pressure of conflicts and the needs for expression and realization have repercussions at the mental, and perceptual, and emotional levels. As a matter of fact, the interactions between the mode of elaboration and the thematic aspects are decisive because they account for the contents and intensity of the libido, the strength of the ego, and the ways of resolving conflict. To try to elicit the modes of interaction is to grasp the manner in which perceptual activity is affected by the libido and also to mark the restorative role of the perceptive elements in the presence of high fantasy pressure. Experience shows an obvious relationship between the primitive nature of a libidinal stage and the deterioration of perceptual–cognitive activity. This occurs in cases of serious changes in psychic functioning. The question may be raised as to the mode or pattern of these interactions in less pathological organizations and particularly in the normal or normative personalities in which the expressions are much more modulated, the links are subtle, the oscillations are controlled, and in which fantasy is yet fully present.

METHOD OF INTERPRETATION

A systematic study of these interactions requires a precise review of interpretation. Two sets of data are analyzed. The first set of data concerns the mode of using the mental equipment in accordance with the stage of maturity; it involves productivity (R) and its variation and rhythm, the control of perceptual reality (W, D,), the mode of expression (F, M, C), and the prevalent contents and verbalization. The second set of data concerns the expression of what is lived, experienced, and felt. This set is quite extensive, so we will stress the main points in the following sections.

The Dominant Themes of Libidinal Development

The themes in the Rorschach are more difficult to interpret than in other projective techniques. Finding a thematic trend implies a psychoanalytic orientation consisting of ideas regarding the structure of personality and the phases of development.

The study of unstructured personalities has helped in the refinement of our analysis, as it was necessary to differentiate the psychotic child from the immature or severely retarded child. This orientation has facilitated the development of special attention to thematic issues and therefore to the importance of the expression of fantasy relating to what apparently is experienced in the first years of life.

The principal points of reference are the dyadic relationships (symbiotic or not); triangular relationships; and fantasy expressions relating to oral, anal, and phallic phases. All these elements are always referred to the entire protocol, regulated by the defense mechanisms that place them on a continuum ranging from normality to psychosis. It is actually normal when a young child confronts the experience of a psychological examination by expressing his conflicts relative to development not yet completed, with versatility appropriate to the specificity of the situation. In Rorschach protocols, it seems possible to spot some major expressions of libidinal development. The Rorschach also can reveal the expression of identity, orality, and anality, in their primitive and secondary forms, and, above all, the struggle against drives. The expression of genitality (either phallic with anal components or at the passive pole of aggressive drives) and castration anxiety are perceptible, and the presence of obvious sexual symbols also can be observed.

It is mainly this content that makes up the dominant themes, which can be assessed largely by taking into account the adjectives and epithets that come up at different response levels. It is evident that the question is that of dominance, and it is normal to find in the maturing child regressive movements that may be, for example, a function of the psychological examination, the transference, or of recent life experiences.

Libidinal development in itself is of no diagnostic value and should not be separated from its context.

Anxiety and Defense Mechanisms

A particular pathology, linked to phases of libidinal development, results in a precisely defined anxiety that is present in the images of the representations. Aside from this, one may observe a pure, raw anxiety, as intense as that of an adult. Besides facing certain inkblots—IV or IX, for example—responses deteriorate and become DW and F− and in turn may be indirect expressions of anxiety.

Of course, the defense mechanisms are less structured and less well defined in the child as compared with an adult. There are attitudes that have defensive significance and means of adaptation that find expression as much in behavior and verbal comments as in the content and manner of expression. These various expressions do not always converge, yet they are organized around the recourse to reality or the expression of affect or flight into fantasy. Recourse to reality is an adaptive mode used by all children (e.g., response to instructions, reference to the perceptual characteristics, search of the known, descriptive verbalization). It arises during the latency period, due to the development of preoperational and operational thinking. It becomes a significant defense mechanism only when it blocks any other approach and reduces the reactivity to a meager conformism. It may be similar to a repression attitude, especially if the content of the response is characterized by impulsiveness (e.g., card VI: "It's an animal's skin that is frightening; it's the stick that's frightening"). At this point, a characteristic defense mechanism may be organized that is akin to isolation, unless the movement of negation of reality causes too much anxiety (e.g., card IV: "It's a toad; it is big, it is frightening; no, toads are not like that; it is not a toad").

Recourse to affect and to the imaginary are attitudes found in young children. The expression of affect releases tension via subjective comments of pleasure and displeasure (e.g., card V: "A nice butterfly, it is nasty"; or card X: "It is a snake, it's so nice"). Contradiction is used as a defense mechanism and is effective because of the child's omnipotence.

In phobic reaction types, the affect of anxiety takes a defensive function and interferes with the expression of themes, but this greatly reduces the reactions.

Recourse to fantasy and imagination, when pushed to the extreme, constitutes an attempt to disengage and avoid conflict or anxiety by replacing reality with a magic world. In this case, there also is a denial of reality and an identification with the aggressor. All are ways of defending against the fear of annihilation.

Self-image and Self-representation

In her responses and orientation, the child presents different images of the self that indicate her autonomy and differentiation from the outer world, as well as the stage she has reached in the identification process. For example, the presentation of the self as a sexual being vis-à-vis the outside world is suggested in card VI ("A rocket taking off"), or it may reflect the power of a sadistic impulse ("Ho Chi Minh," "a dentist's chair"). On the other hand, there is the archaic and embryonic representation of the self in such responses as "a leaf and its stem," "clouds," or "a stick."

Actually, the 10 cards of the Rorschach test have different stimulus potential. They may represent the self whether the content is human or not; the manifestations can be direct or indirect, and the expression may be primitive or well developed. Let us take a few examples.

In card I (which calls forth in the young child the projection of the most urgent themes), the response, "a spider that swallowed a fly," shows the confusion of boundaries and the absence of autonomy by introducing the devouring theme. On the other hand, the response, "a big fly flying," is a more advanced level showing intact boundaries. The three-part combination in the blot encourages the projection of a triangular relationship, sometimes expressed directly, as in, "Dad and Mom going for a walk, holding their child's hand," in which the self-representation is obvious.

Card IV suggests an image of power that might be perceived at two levels: the power of authority and the magic level of being all-powerful over others. The expression of fear is quite normal in responses where the tiny or nonformal are suggested: "a germ," "a mollusk," or "clouds." One needs to be careful about cultural stereotypes given in a fanciful manner, for example, "Ogre," "Goliath," and "King Kong."

Card V is handled on a high level when the response is a whole animal. It is the choice of the animal (e.g., "dragonfly," "a large eagle") that differentiates the self-representation. This card evokes physical pain and projects into the affected organ (e.g., "heart under operation," "sick rabbit").

Self-representation in the color cards is rather understood through the resonance to the colors, therefore to the environment, and by the positive analysis of the large details (D) or the confusion and mixing of these details.

In card IX, for example, it is possible to visualize the interior of the body: "a stomach, there is a pipe, there is the food we have eaten, three stomachs, they are those of the three animals," where confusion between inside and outside is definite, whereas a direct representation of differentiated human images exists: "clowns fishing with a line," or reference to overpowerful images: "spitting devils." A nice image of well-being in dependency was given by a four-year-old girl: "an animal living with its mother."

These examples show that it is necessary to take into account the level of perceptual organization as well as the content in order to evaluate failures of identification or the possible access to it, as well as the different steps in searching for it.

Parental Images

Self-presentation and the level of its expression depend on the conditions of libidinal development, the level of the relation to the object, needs and fears, and the manner in which the parental images are experienced. For the child, her way of being in the world and her relationships with others are closely dependent upon her relationships with parental images. Whatever story she constructs about herself, it is always a reference to these images as they are fantasized.

These images are present throughout the test, but they can be elicited more directly via projections given to cards I, IV, VI, and VII. They may be given in human as well as animal content. Expression of these images can be simultaneously clear and open, camouflaged and archaic; there may be coexistence of a sexualized human action with half-animal, half-human, and humanized vegetative content and other things belonging to the world of fantasy, either benevolent or malevolent. These confusions are quite frequent as long as sexual identification is not achieved. The differentiation of parental images cannot be considered as complete as long as the boundaries between the self and the world are not established; parahuman images such as "witch" or "angel" are often given, expressing a world of omnipotence and the survival of a very tight link to an archaic mother image.

On the other hand, when the sexual identification has been achieved, the projective movements are better controlled and movements are reduced in number, the humans are identified with several roles, the need for self-presentation dominates via the affirmation of interests, the self-image is projected into the future, and references to parental images are less necessary. It is not surprising to find that, in this so-called latency period, the protocols are neutral and less dynamic and the responses are formal, where the repression and avoidance of drives seem to reinforce the autonomous functioning of the ego.

In order to attach an objective and more comprehensive understanding of the differentiation of human representation, we have devised a scale for the analysis of self-presentation (Rausch de Traubenberg & Saglade, 1984).

Mode of Adaptation

What we call the mode of adaptation is a functioning mode specific to each subject, evolved by the juxtaposition of the first set of data with the second set. This term embraces the modes of resolution of conflicts, integration of needs, and of the realization of potentials.

These modes cannot be cross-checked with the categories of functioning in terms of description, but may be related at a later stage.

INTERPRETIVE PATTERNS OF CHILDREN'S RORSCHACHS

It is the study of the psychological functioning of prepsychotic and psychotic children that led us to conduct a systematic analysis of the Rorschach along the lines described here. It should be noted that ours is similar to the experience that marked the beginning of the work by Meyer and Caruth (1970). It is known that prepsychotic and psychotic children are able to maintain a certain level of objective reality comprehension, in spite of the intensity of their fantasy experience and the fears of annihilation (Engel, 1963; Rausch de Traubenberg, Boizou, Bloch-Laine, Chabert, DesLigneris, & Ponroy, 1973).

We studied the Rorschach in terms of the development of projective activity and the evolution of thematic data involving fantasy. The interaction between these two sets of data informs us regarding the strength of the ego and the modes of conflict resolution. The perceptual mode is inflected, even deteriorated and disorganized, by the theme; whereas under other circumstances, it plays a constructive role by containing and controlling imagination. Any noticeable unevenness, positive or negative, is due to the pressure of fantasy life.

The disturbing role of fantasy is known; regressive movements, failure of control, and the intrusion of primary mechanisms are easily detected. But the need for the expression of fantasy also has an organizing function quite visible in the Rorschachs of young children and adolescents. A very vivid conflict may lead to the acting out of a scenario. On card I, for example, a response of the W.M.H. type seems to be overelaborated compared to an ordinary child's response. There is an overarticulation that results from the intensity of the conflict and is not always a sign of maturity.

The existence of these interactions must alert us to the oscillations of the levels of response in relation to the cards. Reduction in response quality is not always pathological but may be a sign of originality or nonconformity. An excess of organization of response elements is not always positive.

Perceptual activity and fantasy life are involved jointly in the game that forges the child's Rorschach response. In this game appear the needs of the child to be regarded as differentiated or undifferentiated, dependent or autonomous, aggressor or victim. In short, the aim is to determine his position in relation to others.

The interpretation of the child's Rorschach is a pattern in terms of interference between perceptual activity and fantasy activity. The elaboration of responses to the Rorschach is based on these different positions.

The Rorschach test is widely used in clinical settings, but it can be of value only when employed in the spirit of a dialogue between theoretical research and clinical application. Although a review of the research in Europe and the United States is beyond the scope of the present work, brief mention of a few of the issues and concerns of recent research may be made.

A book by Exner and Weiner (1982) concerns children and adolescents, reporting not only normative data for the various test factors but also studies of such psychopathological conditions as schizophrenia and depression. In France, the work of Rausch de Traubenberg and Boizu (1977) presents studies of various categories of neurotic psychotic or prepsychotic pathologies, as well as of problem children at different ages and levels of immaturity. Mention also should be made of the work in Italy (Tognazzo, Farini & Passi, 1984) on the diminution of aggressive content in the Rorschach as a function of age in children 4 to 10 years old. Also, Russ's (1980) work discusses the relationship between the level of primary process—judged from the Rorschach—and cognitive efficiency and scholastic competence.

CHILDREN'S VERSUS ADULTS' RESPONSES

In conclusion, the question often is raised as to how the stimuli are handled differently by the child as compared with the adult. The handling of the stimuli is different because the child's need for expression is primary and comes before the apprehension of objective reality. The cards are integrated into a subjective world and interpreted in terms of personal experience. The individual is closely impacted by the dynamics of development.

The manipulation of the stimuli is different also, because of the spatial appeal that meets the child's need to build himself, to organize space in relation to his own body, and to differentiate himself from it.

Perceptual activities and fantasy evoked by these stimuli originally have no distinct reality but are jointly involved in the formulation of the response; hence the richness and specificity of the child's Rorschach.

REFERENCES

Beizmann, C. (1961). *Le Rorschach chez l'enfant de 3 á 10 ans, étude clinique et génétique de la perception enfantine.* Neuchâtel, France: Delachaux et Niestlé.

Claparede, E. (1938). A propos d'un cas de perception syncrétique. *Archives de Psychologie, 37,* 373.

Engel, M. (1963). Psychological testing of borderline psychotic children. *Archives of General Psychiatry, 8,* 426–434.

Exner, J. E., & Weiner, J. B. (1982). *Assessment of children and adolescents* (Vol. 3). *The Rorschach: A comprehensive system.* New York: John Wiley.

Klopfer, B. (1946). *The Rorschach technique.* New York: World Book Company.

Meyer, M. M., & Caruth, E. (1970). Rorschach indices of ego processes. In B. Klopfer, M. M. Meyer, & F. B. Brawer (Eds.), *Developments in the Rorschach technique* (Vol. 3) (pp. 47–98). New York: Harcourt Brace Jovanovich.

Rausch de Traubenberg, N., & Boizou, M. F. (1977). *Le Rorschach en clinique infantile, l'imaginaire et le réel chez l'enfant.* Paris, France: Dunod.

Rausch de Traubenberg, N., Boizou, M. F., Bloch-Laine, F., Chabert, C., Des Ligneris, J., & Ponroy, R. (1973). Organization pré-psychotique et psychotique de la personnalité chez l'enfant á travers les techniques projectives. *Psychologie Francaise, 18,* 213–231.

Rausch de Traubenberg, N., & Sanglade, A. (1984). Représentation de soi et relation d'objet au Rorschach: Grille de representation de soi. *Revue de Psychologie Appliquée, 34*(1), 41–57.

Russ, S. (1980). Primary process integration on the Rorschach and achievement in children. *Journal of Personality Assessment, 44*(4), 338–344.

Schachtel, E. G. (1941). The dynamic perception and the symbolism of form. *Psychiatry, 4,* 76–96.

Tognazzo, D. P., Farini, M. A., & Passi, B. (1984). *Les contenus fantasmatiques anxieux et aggressifs au test de Rorschach chez 350 enfants italiens de 4 à 10 ans.* Onzième congrès international de Rorschach et des méthodes projectives. Barcelona (in press).

Wallon, H. (1947). *Les origines de la pensée chez l'énfant* (Vol. 1). Paris: Presses Universitaires de France.

Werner, H. (1948). *Comparative psychology of mental development.* Revised edition. Chicago: Follett Publishing Company.

8
Recent Research on the Rorschach Test with Children

Zoli Zlotogorski

Projective instruments enable the psychologist to explore the dynamics of a child's personality by gathering empirical data on both the subject's perceptual–cognitive world and her inner fantasy world. Exner and Weiner (1982) have ably pointed out that the former are representative samples of behavior, while the latter are representative samples, symbolic of behavior. In this manner, the well-trained clinician can formulate hypotheses concerning a child's personality functioning based on solid empirical evidence (Weiner, 1977). Ideally, testing should occur in a playroom setting, with the projective instruments being a part of a comprehensive battery and interview. Thus, associative (Rorschach) and expressive (play) techniques may be complemented by construction (TAT) and ordering (psychometric) techniques so as to allow the child maximum freedom and spontaneity.

The Rorschach test with children has a long research and clinical history. Early work in this area was characterized by a twofold focus on developmental norms and symbolic interpretations (Halpern, 1953). Ames and her colleagues (Ames, Metraux, Rodell, & Walker, 1952) were pioneers in a series of studies that collected normative data on young children's Rorschach responses. This was followed by a further study of adolescent Rorschach responses (Ames, Metraux, & Walker, 1959). In these studies, 650 Connecticut children aged 2 to 10 years and 700 adolescents aged 10 to 16 served as the subjects. A more comprehensive study was completed recently by Exner and Weiner (1982), in which they collected 1,870 protocols from children aged 5 to 16. Although his was not a truly stratified random sample, it represents the most comprehensive undertaking to date and provides the clinician with a wealth of normative data. Before proceeding with a review of the relevant research in this area, let us turn our attention to methods of administration and other methodological issues.

ADMINISTRATION OF THE RORSCHACH TO CHILDREN

There are two methods of administering the Rorschach to children. In the first, free association to each of the 10 inkblots is followed by an inquiry referring back to the responses. The second method advocates a standard inquiry immediately following the free association to each card. Although some (Ames et al., 1952; Halpern, 1953) suggest that the latter method is particularly useful with younger children, Exner and Weiner (1982) found it unnecessary for all but a small percentage of their sample. Further, they report that this small percentage was largely made up of seriously disturbed children. In addition, the latter method may be considered a confounding variable that seriously limits the comparison of results to normative tables.

The preferred method for administration includes initial establishment of rapport, a brief discussion of interests and school, a brief explanation about the process of testing, and introduction of the test. The Rorschach cards may be called inkblots, a term with which most children are familiar. The examiner should be seated beside the child, and the first card should be presented with the standard questions, "What might this be? What does it look like?" The initial anxiety of the test situation itself is allayed to some extent when this brief procedure is followed by the actual test administration. Newmark, Wheeler, Newmark, & Stabler (1975) found that state anxiety rose more following the Rorschach and intelligence tests than with the Children's Apperception Test or the Sentence Completion Test. Thus, the recommended order of administration of tests in a battery begins with the more structured and proceeds to the less structured tests.

An interesting investigation was conducted by Stone and Dellis (1960), who posited an inverse relationship between the depth of personality tapped and the degree of stimulus structure for a given test. They report that a greater degree of psychopathology was elicited by the unstructured tests (Draw-A-Person, Rorschach); thus, it is essential that the examiner devote sufficient time to easing the mistrust and anxiety the child often feels during testing. Rapport-building, which need not be prolonged, can ease the situational anxiety appreciably. Irons (1981) found that familiarity with the examiner had no appreciable effect on test performance. Although Bohm (1958) warns that the external features of the examiner may affect the protocol, Tuma and McCraw (1975) found no significant differences in productivity when they varied the sex of the examiner.

Finally, the most crucial issue of Rorschach administration with children is the developmental frame of reference for interpretation. The ability to "think on a sliding scale" (Bohm, 1958, p. 312) is a necessary prerequisite. In other words, the clinician must consider the expected developmental progression in the subject's perceptual–cognitive world. Normative tables for children aged 5 to 16 (Exner & Weiner, 1982) are essential in the interpretive process. Deviations from the mean values provide important clues; that is, "Rorschach behavior means what it means regardless of the age of the subject" (p. 14). Thus, the protocol of a young child that indicates an F+ percentage of 25 is significant, despite our impressions that children generally fantasize. A significantly depressed F+ percentage indicates that the child's perception of reality is faulty and hampers her ability to interact effectively with the environment.

Developmental progression is clearly noted in the child's perceptual–cognitive style. The global perception of the younger child is gradually replaced by recognition of obvious detail. As the child attains the ability for formal operational thought, ability to analyze data systematically is enhanced. Further, changes in affective control are expected as intellectual and visual–motor development progress. Thus we would expect the older child to have greater ability to mediate affect with a fair degree of control and delay (FC). The young child, on the other hand, is not expected to react in such a manner.

COGNITIVE FUNCTIONING AND SCHOOL PERFORMANCE

A number of researchers recently have begun to investigate the utility of the Rorschach as an assessment tool in academic and school settings. The conceptual framework that underlies much of this work hypothesizes that there is a direct relationship between the degree of secondary process development and school achievement. Accordingly, the child who is able to deal successfully with drive-laden impulses through play and fantasy is seen as more capable, open, and flexible.

Russ (1980) administered the Rorschach and a standardized reading test to 51 second graders using Holt's and Havel's (1977) Primary Process scoring system. The subjects in this study were seven- and eight-year-olds who had a mean IQ of 106. Two raters scored the protocols, and the interrater reliability was judged to be sufficient. Russ reported that two measures, Defense Effectiveness and Adaptive Regression, were correlated significantly and positively with achievement. In addition, the study found that a measure of reality perception (extended F+ percentage) was not correlated significantly with reading scores. This latter finding was not supported by Adheidt (1980) who reported a significantly lower F+ percentage for poor readers. Her study examined the Rorschachs of 25 second-grade children with average intelligence or better. Poor readers had greater difficulty forming clear perceptual gestalts and had poorer organizational abilities. This finding was in substantial agreement with an earlier study by Ames et al. (1952), who reported a higher F+ percentage and less reliance on pure form (F%) percepts for the better readers.

Exner and Weiner (1982) note that a child of limited intelligence will produce an impoverished Rorschach. The characteristics of such a protocol will be a brief record dominated by form responses of relatively poor quality accompanied by a narrow range of content. In addition color naming and a paucity of popular responses are common. Given these "typical" characteristics, an atypical protocol would warrant further exploration. Thus, Ames et al. (1952) suggested that the presence of even one complex whole response may indicate good intellectual potential.

Gerstein, Brodzinsky, & Reiskind (1976) questioned the efficacy of IQ scores as true representatives of available talent. Eighty-seven white children and 86 black children served as the subjects in their study. The subjects were divided into three age groups (7 years to 8 years, 11 months; 10 years to 11 years, 11 months; 13 years to 14 years, 11 months) and further divided at each age level according to Full Scale WISC IQ (70–89; 90–109). Rorschach protocols were scored by three blind raters, using Friedman's (1953) developmental scoring categories. Gerstein et al. (1976) report that black children had higher perceptual-integration scores in comparison to their white counterparts; however, this finding was accounted for by higher performance of low-IQ black subjects, while no differences were reported for the average-IQ group of black or white children. The authors concluded that some children may have intellectual capacities that are not reflected adequately in standard intelligence tests.

A similar investigation was conducted by Smith (1981), who hypothesized that there would be a significant increase in the number and complexity of whole responses upon the attainment of formal operational thought. Subjects included 30 second-grade students and 30 sixth-grade students, all of average intelligence. A number of Piagetian tasks were employed to assess the level of cognitive functioning, and Rorschachs then were administered to each child. Whole responses were scored using the Friedman (1953) scoring system, and interscorer reliability was found to be satisfactory ($r = .94$). The results indicated that a significant and positive relationship exists between children's stage of cognitive development and the number and complexity of whole responses.

Other studies (Allison & Blatt, 1964; Kissel, 1965) using the Friedman (1953) scoring system found that traditional IQ measures related significantly to the production of high-level whole responses. Blatt and Allison (1963) have cautioned that a limitation of most studies is that they seek to relate whole responses to intelligence, yet fail to differentiate the quality of whole responses while considering the quantity of such responses. Underlying this argument is a hypothesized developmental sequence that posits a movement from poorly defined whole blot responses, to articulation of details, to integration of well-defined details. A rigorous examination of this hypothesis was conducted by Weisz, Quinlan, O'Neill, and O'Neill (1978). In their study, a female experimenter administered the Peabody Picture Vocabulary Test (PPVT) and the Rorschach to 60 children. In a second session, a month later, a male experimenter administered the Children's Embedded Figures Test (CEFT), the Gestalt Completion Test, the Closure Speed Test, and the Visual Recognition of Incomplete Objects Test. The PPVT was used to assess mental age levels, and the principal experimental design was a 2×2 in which mental age (MA) and chronological age (CA) were orthogonal. Rorschachs were scored for Form Accuracy, Complexity, and Developmental Level, with interscorer reliability found to be quite high ($r = .93$; $r = .96$; $r = .90$). The researchers reported that all Rorschachs and perceptual measures were significantly correlated with MA. A stepwise multiple regression of MA on the four structured-test and three Rorschach variables was calculated, and the CEFT accounted for 52 percent of the variance ($p < .001$). Factor analysis on the matrix of intercorrelations yielded two principal factors. All four of the structured tests loaded on the first factor, accounting for 51 percent of the total variance, while the three Rorschach variables loaded highest on the second factor, accounting for 17 percent of the total variance. The researchers concluded that, while the Rorschach variables are correlated with intellectual level (MA), this relationship is eclipsed by the strong relationship between intellectual level and perceptual ability, as assessed through structured tests. In fact, controlling for CEFT performance reduced the correlation between Rorschach measures and MA to nonsignificance.

In summary, it would appear that the efforts to predict level of intellectual development from Rorschach protocols is fraught with pitfalls. Nevertheless, its utility is still quite substantial in educational planning. Here, the educator/clinician can provide relevant personality data and help identify special assets and liabilities. In fact, Exner and Weiner (1982) observed that this may be especially the case for children whose intellectual protocols show little if any variation in Wechsler subtest performance.

A final area of research focuses on behavioral problems within the school setting. Schlesinger (1978) studied 40 adolescent Rorschach protocols of 20 withdrawn and 20 acting-out hospitalized adolescents. No significant differences were reported between the number of human movement responses generated by either group. The acting-out group showed a significant preference for active fantasy, as compared with their counterparts. In a more recent study, Crain and Smoke (1981) studied the aggressive content of Rorschach protocols. They report more aggressive content (fighting) among their normal ($N = 42$) children. Their comparison group of 42 children, drawn from a clinic population, evidenced more orally aggressive and victim content. Exner and Weiner (1982) question whether research supports any hypothesis directly related to behavior. Clearly, with younger children, the differentiation between behavioral problems stemming from characterological versus neurotic personality structure is problematic. Exner and Weiner (1982) report that normal young children (12 and under) often give protocols that resemble character disorders; that is, they are self-centered, have poor impulse control, have higher secondary determinants, have a larger number of white-space responses, have fewer human responses, and have poor form quality. Therefore, they believe that accurate assessment is at best difficult.

Gordon and Oshman (1981) predicted a lower rate of movement responses in hyperactive children, based on their impaired ability for delay. The hyperactive children produced significantly fewer movement responses than either their agemates or their matched controls in Exner's sample. They also showed significantly more animal content and significantly less human content. However, the clinician must be wary of the assessment of minimal brain dysfunction or hyperactivity based on Rorschach indices. The limitation of the Rorschach in this area is that it is a measure of personality functioning. Berry and Cook (1980) assert that nothing definitive can be said in regard to personality characteristics that are unique to organically dysfunctional children.

Lest the reader conclude too hastily that the Rorschach has only limited utility in school settings, a note of clarification should be added. Erikson (1950) has pointed out eloquently that the developmental task facing the school-age child is the mastery of the inorganic laws of the tool worlds. With the emergence of the psychosocial crisis of industry versus inferiority, the central theme for personality development becomes "I am what I learn" (Erikson, 1959, p. 82). For the school-age child, competence lies in mastering the "three R's." Failure to achieve competence in these areas, whether due to organic dysfunction or maladaptive behaviors, leads to indelible scars on the child's self-perception. This inability to perform and gain mastery is often characterized by the school-age epitaph of "dumb." It is in this area that the robust nature of the data provided by the Rorschach has been too often overlooked.

By the second or third grade, many learning disabled children have already internalized a faulty conception of themselves that hampers their efforts and motivation. Regrettably, this misperception often is shared by parents and educators. Thus, the value of the Rorschach and other projective techniques lies in providing a greater understanding of the child's needs, attitudes, and potentials. The dyslexic child may have a rich inner fantasy world; the hyperactive child, a detailed and idiosyncratic approach. For each the range may extend from feelings of low self-esteem and depression to the vagaries of their unique perceptual cognitive approach to the environment. Clearly, these data are essential, for the emotional well-being of the child is a critical variable in the learning process. It is in this manner that projective material can aid educators and parents in helping the child "exercise dexterity and intelligence in the completion of tasks, unimpaired by infantile inferiority" (Erikson, 1964, p. 124).

PERSONALITY FUNCTIONING

Francis-Williams (1968) studied institutionalized young English children and found that early emotional deprivation was reflected by a paucity of affective responses on the Rorschach. In addition, these protocols evidenced a large number of poor-quality movement responses. Fantasy was dominated by poor form level involving mythical or fabulous creatures that were often sinister in attitude. In a more systematic study, Cohen and Weiner (1977) investigated the personality characteristics of 82 boys who had lived in a home for deprived but nondelinquent, nonretarded youths. They found that boys institutionalized prior to age 10 gave color responses that showed little degree of control or delay. However, this study failed to account for differences in developmental progression, as the boys, aged 10 to 17, were classified only as to age of first separation.

Lifshitz (1975) investigated the relationship of family structure to the functioning of 136 Israeli children (aged 9 years 6 months to 14). Thirty-four of his subjects had lost their fathers to war. The Rorschach was scored for form level (defined or diffuse) and location (integrated or balanced). No significant differences on these variables were found, suggesting that the quality of parenting may mitigate the traumatic loss endured by these children. Another inquiry on the effect of family structures on the personality functioning of children was conducted by Fisher and Fisher (1976), who sought to determine whether introversive parents produce introversive modes of perception in their children. Their data indicate that the children of introversive fathers were more likely to be introversive, whereas no such correlation could be found for introversive mothers.

Moelis, Wright, and Fisher (1977) developed a symbiosis scale for studying the effects of enmeshed family structures. Children from such homes have been found to be dependent and to have difficulty with issues of separation and individuation, autonomy, and personal identity. The symbiosis scale has a four-part classification system that includes part responses, touching, death themes, and oral content. It was hypothesized that children reared in a symbiosis-inducing family would obtain higher scores on the symbiosis scale, compared to a nonsymbiosis-inducing family setting. In a validation study, the scale successfully differentiated between the two groups; however, in a study of more severely maladaptive (borderline and psychotic) children, no differences were found.

The study of object relations and object representations in the Rorschach literature has contributed significantly to a growing body of literature on borderline syndromes. Blatt, Brenneis, Schimek, and Glick (1976) developed a scale for evaluating the content of Rorschach responses in terms of object representations. The scale considers all human and humanlike responses in terms of their attributes, form quality, motivation, integration, content, and the nature of any action involved. In a series of studies (Blatt et al., 1976; Blatt & Lerner, 1983; Ritzler, Zambianco, Harder, & Kaskey, 1980), the progression along the continuum of pathology for object representations has been explored. Blatt and Lerner (1983) report that the nonparanoid schizophrenic's objects are inaccurately perceived, inert, and unmotivated, with inappropriate attributes. In anaclitic depression, objects are perceived accurately but the themes of malevolence and deprivation in mother–child interactions are frequent. The borderline patient may present an initial, well-articulated, and accurate response pattern that deteriorates as stress takes its toll on the fragile personality structure. The depressed patient alternates between highly elaborate and well-articulated responses to those that are seriously impaired. Finally, in the hysterical perceptual style, objects are well articulated and elaborated but this articulation is primarily in terms of external, physical details rather than more personal attributes. The study of object representations provides "important information about the developmental level of personality organization and the quality of interpersonal relationships to which an individual is predisposed" (Blatt & Lerner, 1983, p. 25).

A special area of interest in the study of object representations is that of children who suffer from a variety of somatic illnesses. Fallstrom and Vegelius (1978) studied 16 diabetics and 16 matched controls. They report disturbed body image to be related to the diabetic syndrome. Thirty-two girls aged 7 to 15, with the diagnosis of diabetes mellitus and with duration of the disease exceeding one year, were the subjects of their study. The dichotomized data were subjected to a discriminant analysis, developed by the authors, on the differences between obtained and reference scores. Penetration responses were found to be higher in the diabetic group and hypothesized to be significantly correlated with disturbed body image. These findings are in marked contrast to an earlier study conducted by McGraw and Tuma (1977). In their study of 25 diabetic children compared to 25 controls, no significant differences in the number of penetration responses were found. They also report no differences in barrier, anxiety, or hostility responses. Nonsignificant results were attributed by the authors to their control for total responsivity on the protocols. However, it appears that response productivity is accounted for by the Fallstrom and Vegelius (1978) statistical analysis.

SUICIDE POTENTIAL AND DEPRESSION

The incidence of suicide has increased 300 percent in children and adolescents in the last 25 years (Klagsbrun, 1981). Suicidal children are apt to be depressed, experience free-floating anxiety, and may be involved in substance abuse. It appears that, while these children are often depressed and frustrated and show impaired impulse control, the absence of this constellation in overt behavior does not preclude the presence of a suicide potential. Since children may be unable to articulate their feelings, the Rorschach has proved a useful tool in assessing the underlying suicide potential.

In an earlier study, Exner (1974) developed a constellation of eight variables in which the presence of seven variables correctly identified 71 percent of children who committed suicide. Thirty-nine protocols of children who made suicide attempts within 60 days after the assessment were analyzed. The children's suicide constellation, given in the following list, indicates some overlap and some differences with the suicide constellation for adults, generally due to developmental factors.

$FV + VF + V + FD > 2$ $X^{+}\% < .70$
Color shading blend > 0 Pure $H = 0$
$3r + (2)/R < .35$ Affective ratio $< .40$
$Z_d > \pm 4$ Lambda $< .35$ or > 1.2

Suicidal children are expected to have higher organizational difference (Z_d) scores, higher secondary determinants, less modulated affective control, lower responsivity, and lower human content responses than nonsuicidal children. In addition, there is a heightened desire to avoid emotionally laden stimuli (Afr.) and an inability to evade them successfully (Lambda). Again, it should be noted that the absence of these indicators from a protocol does not preclude the presence of suicidal tendencies. "Elements such as distress, frustration and anger when combined with problems in ideational or emotional impulse control, can easily set the stage for the more spontaneous decision to self-destruction that often characterizes this event among younger people" (Exner, 1982, pp. 190–191).

Arffa (1982) successfully used a multiple-sign approach in her study of 48 psychiatrically hospitalized adolescents, who were divided into four groups according to the sequence of suicidal behavior. The composite score, based on Exner and Wylie's (1977) work plus two additional signs, emerged as a highly stable method of identifying suicidal behavior of a moderate lethality level.

In addition to the structural analysis we have just reviewed, a number of researchers have investigated the relationship between specific content areas and suicide potential. Neuringer (1974) found no studies in which suicidal ideation was expressed directly, leading him to hypothesize that this expression may be inhibited. However, suicidal individuals may provide content that includes motivation, abstraction, and aggressive ideation. Blatt and Ritzler (1974) have related the presence of transparencies, translucencies, or cross-sectional responses to suicide potential; and Rierdan, Land, and Eddy (1978) have reported a significantly higher number of these responses for suicidal individuals.

Although the reported incidence of self-inflicted death among children is low, there is a growing body of evidence that suggests that childhood depression is widespread. Exner and McCoy (1981)* developed the Morbid (MOR) content score based on the following criteria: identification of the object as dead or destroyed; identification of the object as being injured, broken, or damaged; and attribution of a clearly depressive feeling or characteristic to an object. After interscorer reliability was satisfactorily established, Exner conducted a series of studies designed to test the utility of the MOR scoring category. Generally, he reported (Exner & Weiner, 1982) that children who were diagnosed as depressed appeared to give a greater frequency of such responses than controls. The MOR score probably reflects the extent to which the dysphoric experience pervades ideational activity.

---

*Rorschach Workshops, 11 Bearer Dr., Bayville, N.Y. 11709.

Following the work on this special scoring category, Exner and his associates (Exner & Weiner, 1982) turned their attention to the formulation of a depression index. Rorschach data of some 91 adolescents with behavior problems were reviewed with the objective of creating two distinct groups. A depressed group (N = 24) was defined by the presence of no fewer than four of the five structural variables shown in the following list, and a nondepressed group (N = 55) was defined by the absence of at least four of these five variables:

FV + VF + V + FD > 2   Greater right-side eb
Color Shading Blend > 0   Special Score MOR > 2
Egocentricity Index < .35

The following results were obtained after a year of management-oriented intervention. A significant reduction of unwanted behavior problems was reported for the nondepressed subjects, with no such reduction for the depressed group.

The issue of chronic versus reactive depression in children is still elusive, despite the data supplied by the depression index. Children often mask the traditional symptoms of dysphoria, since they often are unable to contain feelings of distress. Thus, the externalization of the conflictual material may take the forms of somatic complaints, hyperactivity, temper tantrums, and antisocial and aggressive acting out. However, Exner and Weiner (1982) suggest that the presence of vista responses and a low egocentricity index are two variables that appear to be influenced by situational distress. Conversely, the presence of inanimate object movement (m) and shading (Y) in the absence of vista and texture, and with a low egocentricity index, probably signals a reactive depression.

CONCLUDING REMARKS

Halpern (1960) has noted that the Rorschach serves at least two important functions in the evaluation of the personality of children. First, it provides a comprehensive personality picture upon which clinical diagnosis can be based. Second, it sheds much light on the course of personality development. The considerable research reported since the establishment of the comprehensive scoring system has strengthened the Rorschach as a reliable instrument and gives it a "new lease on life" (Rabin, 1980). Exner's (1982) recent contribution of normative data on more than 1,800 children extends this lease well into the next decade. Rabin (Buros, 1972), in a review of the Rorschach, noted that, "although research activity in the area has abated and concern with diagnosis among clinicians is lessened, Rorschach's ten inkblots persist in providing important stimulation to psychologists in producing increasingly challenging and useful research and applications" (pp. 443-446).

REFERENCES

Aheidt, P. (1980). The effect of reading ability on Rorschach performance. *Journal of Personality Assessment, 44*(1), 3-9.

Allison, J. S., & Blatt, S. J. (1964). The relationship of Rorschach whole responses to intelligence. *Journal of Projective Techniques, 28,* 255-260.

Ames, L. B., Metraux, R. W., Rodell, J. R., & Walker, R. N. (1952). *Child Rorschach responses: Developmental trends from two to ten years.* New York: Hoeber.

Ames, L. B., Metraux, R. W., & Walker, R. N. (1959). *Adolescent Rorschach responses.* New York: Hoeber.

Arffa, S. (1982). Predicting adolescent suicidal behavior and the order of Rorschach measurement. *Journal of Personality Assessment, 46*(6), 563-568.

Berry, K., & Cook, V. J. (1980). Personality and behavior. In H. E. Rie & E. D. Rie (Eds.), *Handbook of minimal brain dysfunctions.* New York: John Wiley.

Blatt, S. J., & Allison, J. (1963). Methodological considerations in Rorschach research: The W responses as an expression of abstractive and integrative strivings. *Journal of Projective Techniques, 27,* 269-278.

Blatt, S. J., Brenneis, C. B., Schimek, J. G., & Glick, M. (1976). Normal development and psychopathological impairment of the concept of the object on the Rorschach. *Journal of Abnormal Psychology, 85*(4), 364-373.

Blatt, S. J., & Lerner, H. (1983). The psychological assessment of object representation. *Journal of Personality Assessment, 47*(1), 7-28.

Blatt, S. J., & Ritzler, B. A. (1974). Thought disorder and boundary disturbances in psychosis. *Journal of Consulting and Clinical Psychology, 42,* 370-381.

Bohm, E. (1958). *Rorschach test diagnosis.* New York: Grune & Stratton.

Buros, O. K. (Ed.). (1972). *The seventh mental measurements yearbook.* Highland Park, NJ: Gryphon.

Cohen, L., & Weiner, F. J. (1977). Adolescent Rorschach responses as a function of age at first institutionalization. *Journal of Personality Assessment, 41*(3), 227-229.

Crain, W. C., & Smoke, L. (1981). Rorschach aggressive content in normal and problematic children. *Journal of Personality Assessment, 45*(1), 2-4.

Erikson, E. H. (1950). *Childhood and society.* New York: W. W. Norton.

Erikson, E. H. (1959). *Identity and the life cycle: Selected papers. Psychological issues* (Monograph No. 1, Vol. 1). New York: International Universities Press.

Erikson, E. H. (1963). *Childhood and society* (2nd ed.). New York: Norton.

Erikson, E. H. (1964). *Insight and responsibility.* New York: Norton.

Exner, J. E. (1974). *The Rorschach: A comprehensive system* (Vol. 1). New York: John Wiley.

Exner, J. E., & McCoy, R. (1981). *An experimental score for morbid content (MOR)*. Workshops Study 269 (unpublished). Rorschach Workshops.

Exner, J. E., & Weiner, I. B. (1982). *The Rorschach: A comprehensive system* (Vol. 3). New York: John Wiley.

Exner, J. E., & Wylie, J. (1977). Some Rorschach data concerning suicide. *Journal of Personality Assessment, 41,* 339-348.

Fallstrom, K., & Vegelius, J. (1978). A discriminatory analysis based on dichotomized Rorschach scores of diabetic children. *International Journal of Rehabilitation Research, 1*(3), 321-327.

Fisher, S., & Fisher, R. (1976). Parental correlates of Rorschach human movement responses in children. *Perceptual and Motor Skills, 42,* 31-34.

Francis-Williams, J. (1968). *Rorschach with children*. Oxford: Pergamon.

Friedman, H. (1953). Perceptual regression in schizophrenia: An hypothesis suggested by the use of the Rorschach test. *Journal of Projective Techniques, 17,* 171-186.

Gerstein, A. I., Brodzinsky, D. M., & Reiskind, N. (1976). Perceptual integration on the Rorchach as an indicator of cognitive capacity: A developmental study of racial differences in a clinic population. *Journal of Consulting and Clinical Psychology, 44*(5), 760-765.

Gordon, M., & Oshman, E. (1981). Rorschach indices of children classified as hyperactive. *Perceptual and Motor Skills, 52,* 703-707.

Halpern, F. (1953). *A clinical approach to children's Rorschachs*. New York: Grune & Stratton.

Halpern, F. (1960). The Rorschach test with children. In A. I. Rabin & M. Haworth (Eds.), *Projective techniques with children* (pp. 14-28). New York: Grune & Stratton.

Holt, R. R., & Havel, J. (1977). A method for assessing primary and secondary process in the Rorschach. In M. A. Rickens-Ousiankina (Ed.), *Rorschach Psychology* (pp. 375-420). New York: Krieger.

Irons, D. (1981). The effect of familiarity with the examiner on WISC-R verbal, performance and full scale scores. *Psychology in the Schools, 18,* 496-499.

Kissel, S. (1965). A brief note on the relationship between Rorschach developmental level and intelligence. *Journal of Projective Techniques and Personality Assessment, 29,* 454-455.

Klagsbrun, F. (1981). *Too young to die: Youth and suicide*. New York: Pocket Books.

Lifshitz, M. (1975). Social differentiation and organization of the Rorschach in fatherless and two-parented children. *Journal of Clinical Psychology, 31*(1), 126-130.

McGraw, R. K., & Tuma, J. M. (1977). Rorschach content categories of juvenile diabetics. *Psychological Reports, 40,* 818.

Moelis, I., Wright, D. M., & Fisher, S. (1977). The symbiosis scale: Inkblot responses of children from symbiotically and non-symbiotically oriented families. *Journal of Personality Assessment, 41*(3), 238-247.

Neuringer, C. (1974). Suicide and the Rorschach: A useful postscript. *Journal of Personality Assessment, 38,* 535–539.

Newmark, C. S., Wheeler, D., Newmark, L., & Stabler, B. (1975). Test induced anxiety with children. *Journal of Personality Assessment, 39*(4), 409–413.

Rabin, A. I. (1980). The Rorschach: A new lease on life. *Contemporary Psychology, 25,* 52–53.

Rierdan, J., Land, E., & Eddy, S. (1978). Suicide and transparency responses: A replication. *Journal of Consulting and Clinical Psychology, 46,* 1162–1163.

Ritzler, B., Zambianco, D., Harder, D., & Kaskey, M. (1980). Psychotic patterns of the concept of the object on the Rorschach test. *Journal of Abnormal Psychology, 89*(1), 46–55.

Russ, S. W. (1980). Primary process integration on the Rorschach and achievement in children. *Journal of Personality Assessment, 44*(4), 338–343.

Schlesinger, L. B. (1978). Rorschach human movement responses of acting-out and withdrawn adolescents. *Perceptual and Motor Skills, 47,* 68–70.

Smith, N. M. (1981). The relationship between Rorschach whole response and level of cognitive functioning. *Journal of Personality Assessment, 45*(1), 13–19.

Stone, H. K., & Dellis, N. P. (1960). An exploratory investigation into the levels hypothesis. *Journal of Projective Techniques, 24,* 333–340.

Tuma, J. M., & McCraw, R. K. (1975). Influences of examiner differences on Rorschach productivity in children. *Journal of Personality Assessment, 39*(4), 362–367.

Weiner, I. B. (1977). Approaches to Rorschach validation. In M. A. Rickers-Ousiankina (Ed.), *Rorschach Psychology* (pp. 575–608). New York: Krieger.

Weisz, J. R., Quinlan, D. M., O'Neill, P., & O'Neill, P. C. (1978). The Rorschach and structured tests of perception as indices of intellectual development in mentally retarded and nonretarded children. *Journal of Experimental Child Psychology, 25,* 326–336.

9
The Holtzman Inkblot Technique with Children and Adolescents

Wayne H. Holtzman

The Holtzman Inkblot Technique (HIT) was developed to overcome psychometric limitations in the Rorschach by constructing completely new sets of inkblots. During the 10-year period following World War II, major interest in the Rorschach was expressed by graduate students, many of whom had learned a little about the Rorschach while serving in the armed services. Hundreds of studies during this period piled up a wave of criticism from which the Rorschach movement never fully recovered. While much of this early research was either irrelevant or poorly conceived, an impressive number of well-designed validity studies generally yielded negative results. The growing realization that the Rorschach had inherent psychometric weaknesses came to a head in a symposium on failures of the Rorschach that was sponsored by the Society for Projective Techniques (Zubin, 1954).

DEVELOPMENT OF THE HOLTZMAN INKBLOT TECHNIQUE

Unlike the Rorschach, which has only 10 inkblots in a single form, the Holtzman Inkblot Technique (HIT) consists of two parallel forms, A and B, each of which contains 45 inkblots constituting the test series and two practice blots, X and Y, that are identical in both forms. The inkblots were drawn from a large pool of several thousand, many of which were created by an artist working with special papers and inks that produced brilliant colors and rich shading. Only about one blot in 50 survived initial screening by a group of judges who were familiar with the Rorschach.

Construction and testing of these initial inkblots was divided into three cycles for purposes of gathering data, each cycle containing a set of 45 untried inkblots. Shading, color, form, the symmetry or asymmetry of the inkblot, and white space for figure–ground reversals were used as the primary characteristics of the blots in the selection process. These stimulus qualities were chosen to ensure sufficient variation of response to yield reliable scores. Earlier work had indicated that somewhere between 40 and 50 inkblots with one response per blot elicited from the subject could be completed in less than an hour by most individuals.

The three experimental sets of blots were given to samples of patients in a mental hospital as well as samples of college students, since these two groups represent opposite extremes on several important variables from earlier Rorschach studies. The main goal was to select from among these 135 inkblots the 90 best ones for the final two forms. Criteria for choosing each blot were based upon analyses of six major scoring variables: Location, Color, Shading, Movement, Form Definiteness, and Form Appropriateness. Of equal importance in this item analysis was a new score called Pathognomic Verbalization, a score designed to capture bizarre and disordered thought processes as they are manifest in responding to inkblots.

Selection of inkblots for the final version of the HIT was aimed at maximizing the reliability of these scores as well as maximizing the discriminatory power of the final forms in differentiating superior normals from mental-hospital patients. The two parallel forms were constructed by pairing blots on stimulus qualities as well as item characteristics from the scores and then randomly assigning members of each pair to either Form A or Form B. Two inkblots, X and Y, were chosen as trial or warm-up blots, since each of them evokes very common responses. The final order of presentation for the 45 inkblots in each form was arranged so that most of the "best" inkblots appear rather early in the series.

Preliminary studies were conducted on college students in order to develop the scoring system, to determine the examiner effects, if any, upon subject response, and to perfect the procedures for administration before going to the great expense of reproducing the original blots and obtaining standardization data on thousands of cases across the country.

By 1959, the technique was sufficiently well developed to embark on a major standardization program, using printed versions of the original inkblots. Nearly 2,000 individual protocols were collected during the two-year standardization study on samples ranging from five-year-olds to mature adults and from chronic schizophrenic patients to mentally retarded individuals. Through the cooperation of psychologists in other settings across the country, 15 different, well-defined populations were sampled to provide the standardization data. Five of these samples were normal children: 122 five-year-olds drawn from nursery schools; 60 children in grades two through six from a middle-class, private school; 72 fourth-graders from Hamden, Connecticut; 197 seventh-graders from four Texas communities other than Austin; and 72 eleventh-graders from Chicago high schools. This last sample was given both the Rorschach and Holtzman inkblots by Mrs. Samuel J. Beck in a comparative study of the two methods.

Other samples in the initial standardization data consisted of 80 firemen representative of lower-middle-class, semiskilled workmen; 140 average adult women obtained by random house-to-house canvassing in two Texas communities; 143 college students from the University of Texas who were given both Form A and Form B with an interval of one week between testing periods; 92 superior students at the University of Texas; 66 freshmen from Austin College, most of whom were given the alternate form of the HIT by the same examiner a year later; 99 chronic schizophrenic men from the Waco VA Hospital; 51 schizophrenics from the Montrose VA Hospital; 50 mentally retarded students from Woodward State School in Iowa; 50 mentally retarded adults from Austin State School; and finally, 90 depressed patients from 11 VA Hospitals participating in a national chemotherapy project. A total of 1,384 individuals responded to one or both forms of the HIT, providing a firm basis for determining the means, standard deviations, and intercorrelations as well as percentile norms for 22 scores that had been developed.

The standardization data also were used for a number of methodological studies, including investigations of scorer agreement, internal-consistency reliability, test–retest stability, and intergroup differences, as a preliminary basis for differential diagnosis. The results of these studies, together with percentile norms and recommendations for use of the HIT in clinical assessment or for research studies, were published by Holtzman, Thorpe, Swartz, & Herron (1961a,b). While retaining the clinical sensitivity of the Rorschach blots, the HIT yields 22 variables that can be objectively defined, reliably scored, and efficiently handled by statistical methods. For the first time, it permits the clinician, the psychometrician, and the experimentalist to work with the same technique.

Greater reliability and objectivity of scoring are obtained because of the large number of inkblots and the fact that the subject is limited to one response per blot. The scoring guide further increases objectivity by making interscorer differences negligible on most of the major variables.

The existence of two parallel forms permits accurate retesting to evaluate change in a subject over time.

Since the publication of the HIT by the Psychological Corporation in 1961, hundreds of studies have been reported in the literature. An annotated bibliography containing over 660 entries provides a valuable reference for the serious student of the technique (Swartz, Reinehr, & Holtzman, 1983a). Our own work has focused largely upon the use of the HIT, in combination with many other cognitive, perceptual, and personality tests, for the study of child development in two cultures—Mexico and the United States. Data on over 800 children and their families have been obtained through annual, repeated testing over a period of six years, providing an unusually rich set of information on child development among schoolchildren in Mexico City and Austin, Texas (Holtzman, Diaz-Guerrero, & Swartz, 1975). Some of the findings from this study that are particularly relevant to the use of the HIT in the assessment of children and adolescents will be presented later.

DESCRIPTION OF THE TEST MATERIALS

Standard materials for the HIT consist of two parallel series, Form A and Form B, the accompanying printed record forms and summary sheets, and the *Guide for Administration and Scoring* (Holtzman, Thorpe, Swartz, & Herron, 1961).* Sets of 35-mm slides are available for use with the group method of administration, as developed by Swartz and Holtzman (1963). A computer-based scoring program for the group method, as developed by Gorham (1967), is also available. A handbook (Hill, 1972) for clinical application of the HIT and a workbook (Hill & Piexotto, 1973) have been published as guides for clinicians. The original monograph and the scoring guide have been translated into a number of different foreign languages. Since 1977, a programmed test and other HIT materials have been available in a multivolume series in German (Hartmann & Rosenstiel, 1977).

The inkblots are printed on thin but tough white cardboard, 5½ × 8½ inches in size. Cards X and Y contain practice blots that are usually not scored. These two cards appear at the beginning of both Forms A and B. Card X is a massive achromatic blot that looks like a bat or butterfly to most people. Very few individuals reject this card, although some prefer to use a smaller area rather than the whole blot. Card Y is suggestive of a person's torso to most people. Red spots of ink introduce the subject to

---

*Materials for the Holtzman Inkblot Technique can be obtained from the Psychological Corporation, 7500 Old Oak Boulevard, Cleveland, OH 44130.

color and often evoke responses such as "spots of blood," either given alone or integrated with the torso.

Cards 1 and 2 in both Forms A and B are achromatic and sufficiently broken up to make a whole response difficult unless there is integration of detail or unless the subject gives a very vague concept or one in which the form of the concept fails to fit the form of the inkblot. Both cards have popular responses in smaller areas of the blot, helping to discourage any tendency to give only whole responses. Card 3 is irregular in form and has a large red "sunburst" splotch overlaid on an amorphous black inkblot. It is very difficult to give a form-definite, form-appropriate whole response to card 3 because of the chaotic, unstructured nature of this inkblot. Card 4 is just the opposite, containing several finely detailed popular concepts that can be interrelated, together with color and shading that produces a vistalike effect. Responses such as "battle scene" or "cowboy watching a sunset" are typical of card 4A, and "knight carrying a spear and shield" is typical of card 4B.

Cards 5A and 5B are asymmetrical, grayish-colored blots unlike any in the Rorschach. By penetrating the charcoallike quality of these blots, one can distinguish a number of detailed objects. Together with several similar, rather wispy, amorphous, asymmetrical blots later in the series, these cards are difficult, particularly for the individual who is searching for definite concepts having good form or who wishes to use the entire blot.

The remaining inkblots cover a wide range of stimulus variation, giving the individual ample opportunity to reveal certain aspects of his mental processes and personality by projecting his thoughts onto otherwise meaningless inkblots. Twelve of the inkblots in Form A are black or gray, 2 are monochromatic, 11 are black with a bright color also present, and the remaining 20 are multicolored. Most of the blots have rich shading variations that help to elicit texture responses. A similar distribution of color, shading, and form qualities is present in Form B.

ADMINISTRATION AND SCORING

Standard procedures for administering the HIT have been developed so that published normative data may be used as aids to interpretation. Instructions for use have been designed to make the task as simple as possible while ensuring that sufficient information will be elicited to produce reliable scores for major variables. The instructions differ from those for the Rorschach in the following ways: (1) the examiner instructs the examinee to give only one response per card; (2) a brief inquiry is given immediately after each response; (3) permissible questions by the examiner during inquiry are limited both in number and in scope and are asked rather routinely to avoid inadvertent verbal conditioning of certain determinants or content. Three kinds of questions are permissible as part of the brief inquiry in the standard administration. The actual wording used can vary a great deal, so that the inquiry becomes a natural part of the conversation between examiner and subject. Typical phrasing would be as follows:

"Where in the blot do you see a———?"

"What is there about the blot that makes it look like a———?"

"Is there anything else you care to tell me about it?"

After establishing rapport, the examiner picks up the cards one at a time, handing each one in upright position to the subject. The instructions given to the subject should be informal and should stress the following points: (1) these inkblots were not made to look like anything in particular; (2) different people see different things in each inkblot; and (3) only one response for each card is desired. The examiner uses a standard record form for recording the responses and scoring. To facilitate the recording of the location of the response, schematic diagrams for the inkblots are included on the record form. As each response is given, the examiner outlines a specific area used. Adjacent to the diagram is a blank space for recording the verbatim response or a shortened version of it.

Usually the subject comprehends the nature of the task very quickly and the actual inquiry can be kept to a minimum. A skilled examiner, sensitive to subtle nuances in the examiner–subject interaction, can control the flow of conversation by stimulating a reticent individual and slowing down a verbose person.

In spite of the many interesting variations in test administration that can be attempted, there is much to be said for adhering closely to the standard method of administration. This method has proved highly practical and yields objective, reliable scores on a number of important variables. Currently published normative data and statistical studies of value in the interpretation of the protocols assume close adherence to the standard method of administration.

One exception to the standard method of administration has been successfully developed for young children, whose attention span is short and who therefore may get restless halfway through the testing session. As in the case of the 122 five-year-olds from Austin nursery schools, the examiner may interrupt the testing session temporarily after 20 to 30 cards, returning to finish the task after interpolated activity of a relaxing kind. In testing young children, the task can be structured as a playful, gamelike activity, heightening the child's interest in attending to it. This technique has been used successfully for some children as young as three years of age, although no norms are available below the age of five.

In the course of standardization, 22 quantitative variables were developed to cover nearly all of the important scoring categories and dimensions commonly employed with the Rorschach. The name, abbreviation, brief definition, and scoring weights for these variables are given in Table 9.1. Summary scores for the individual variables are obtained by adding the weights for a given variable across the 45 inkblots in either Form A or

TABLE 9.1 Names, Abbreviations, Brief Definitions, and Scoring Weights for 22 HIT Variables

Reaction Time (RT). The time in seconds from the presentation of the inkblot to the beginning of the primary response.

Rejection (R). Score 1 when subject returns inkblot to examiner without giving a scorable response; otherwise, score 0.

Location (L). Tendency to break down blot into smaller fragments. Score 0 for use of the whole blot, 1 for large area, and 2 for smaller area.

Space (S). Score 1 for true figure–ground reversals; otherwise, score 0.

Form Definiteness (FD). The definiteness of the form of the concept reported, regardless of the goodness of fit to the inkblot. A 5-point scale with 0 for very vague and 4 for highly specific.

Form Appropriateness (FA). The goodness of fit of the form of the percept to the form of the inkblot. Score 0 for poor, 1 for fair, and 2 for good.

Color (C). The apparent primacy of color (including black, gray, or white) as a response determinant. Score 0 for no use of color, 1 for use secondary to form (like Rorschach FC), 2 when used as primary determinant but some form present (like CF), and 3 when used as primary determinant with no form present (like C).

Shading (Sh). The apparent primacy of shading as a response determinant (texture, depth, or vista). Score 0 for no use of shading, 1 when used in secondary manner, and 2 when used as primary determinant with little or no form present.

Movement (M). The energy level of movement or potential movement ascribed to the percept, regardless of content. Score 0 for none, 1 for static potential, 2 for casual, 3 for dynamic, and 4 for violent movement.

Pathognomic Verbalization (V). Degree of autistic, bizarre thinking evident in the response, as rated on a 5-point scale. Score 0 where no pathology is present. The nine categories of V and the range of scoring weights for each are as follows: Fabulation, 1; Fabulized Combination, 2, 3, 4; Queer Response, 1, 2, 3; Incoherence, 4; Autistic Logic, 1, 2, 3, 4; Contamination, 2, 3, 4; Self-reference, 2, 3, 4; Deterioration Color, 2, 3, 4; Absurd Response, 3.

Anatomy (At). Degree of "gutlike" quality in the content. Score 0 for none; 1 for bones, x-rays, or medical drawings; and 2 for visceral and crude anatomy.

Sex (Sx). Degree of sexual quality in the content. Score 0 for no sexual reference, 1 for socially accepted sexual activity or expressions (buttocks, bust, kissing), and 2 for blatant sexual content (penis, vagina).

Form B. Three of the variables routinely are "corrected" for the number of rejections, in order to provide an estimate of what the total score would have been if the subject had given a response to each of the 45 inkblots.

Scoring agreement is uniformly high when trained scorers are compared. Intercorrelations between two independent scorers ranged from .89 to .995, with a median value of .98 in a sample of 40 schizophrenic protocols. When only beginning scorers are compared after training on a dozen protocols, average scoring reliability for all variables yields a median value of .86 in a large sample of normal adolescents. The more

TABLE 9.1 *(Continued)*

Abstract (Ab). Degree of abstract quality in the content. Score 0 for none, 1 for abstract elements along with other elements having form, and 2 for purely abstract content ("Bright colors remind me of gaiety").

Anxiety (Ax). Signs of anxiety in the fantasy content, as indicated by emotions and attitudes, expressive behavior, symbolism, or cultural stereotypes of fear. Score 0 for none, 1 for questionable or indirect signs, and 2 for overt or clear-cut evidence.

Hostility (Hs). Signs of hostility in the fantasy content. Scored on a 4-point scale ranging from 0 for none to 3 for direct, violent, interpersonal destruction.

Barrier (Br). Score 1 for reference to any protective covering, membrane, shell, or skin that might be symbolically related to the perception of body-image boundaries; otherwise, score 0.

Penetration (Pn). Score 1 for concept that might be symbolic of an individual's feeling that his body exterior is of little protective value and can be easily penetrated; otherwise, score 0.

Balance (B). Score 1 where there is overt concern for the symmetry–asymmetry feature of the inkblot; otherwise, score 0.

Popular (P). Each form contains 25 inkblots in which one or more popular percepts occur. "Popular" in the standardization studies means that a percept had to occur at least 14 percent of the time among normal subjects. Score 1 for popular core concepts (or their precision alternatives) as listed in the scoring manual; otherwise, score 0.

Integration (I). Score 1 for the organization of two or more adequately perceived blot elements into a larger whole; otherwise, score 0.

Human (H). Degree of human quality in the content of response. Score 0 for none; 1 for parts of humans, distortions, or cartoons; and 2 for whole human beings or elaborated human faces.

Animal (A). Degree of animal quality in the content. Score 0 for none (including animal objects and microscopic life); 1 for animal parts, bugs, or insects; and 2 for whole animals.

Source: W. H. Holtzman, R. Diaz-Guerrero, and J. D. Swartz (1975). *Personality Development in Two Cultures: A Cross-Cultural Longitudinal Study of Children in Mexico and the United States.* Austin: University of Texas Press. Copyright 1975 by the Hogg Foundation for Mental Health.

difficult variables to score, such as Pathognomic Verbalization, Form Appropriateness, Barrier, and Penetration, require a greater degree of training. Qualified clinicians and research investigators, however, should have no difficulty achieving completely satisfactory reliability in scoring HIT protocols, provided they follow carefully the *Guide for Administration and Scoring* (Holtzman et al., 1961).

RELIABILITY OF HIT SCORES FOR CHILDREN AND ADOLESCENTS

Both internal consistency and parallel forms reliability based on repeated testing have been reported in great detail elsewhere (Holtzman et al., 1961a,b, 1975). Split-half reliabilites, determined by computing the correlations between scores based on odd-numbered and even-numbered blots, are generally high. The four scores with highest internal consistency (generally about .90), regardless of population sampled, ranging from five-year-old children to schizophrenic adults, are Reaction Time, Rejection, Location, and Form Definiteness. Eight additional scores that have internal consistency reliability generally higher than .80 are Form Appropriateness, Color, Shading, Movement, Pathognomic Verbalization, Human, Animal, and Anatomy. Odd-even reliability coefficients for the symbolic content scores—Anxiety, Hostility, Barrier, and Penetration—are only slightly lower on the average and are more variable. Four scores—Space, Sex, Abstract, and Balance—occur too infrequently for accurate estimates of reliability, leaving only Popular as a score with relatively unsatisfactory internal consistency.

The most pertinent reliability measure for most clinical applications is the stability of an individual's score across time. Unlike the Rorschach, where spuriously high results are obtained due to retesting with the same inkblots, the HIT has truly parallel forms that provide conservative but realistic estimates of reliability of measurement over time. The best measure of such stability is the intraclass correlation obtained in a Latin-square design where a random half of the subjects are given Form A before B, while the other half receive B before A. The most extensive studies of this kind on college students yielded stability coefficients ranging from a low of .36 for Popular to a high of .82 for Location, with an interval of one week between testing.

Similar studies on other normal subjects with time intervals between testing sessions ranging from three months to five years provide additional evidence of the stability of HIT scores across time. The most extensive data come out of a major cross-cultural study of over 800 children in Mexico and the United States, involving repeated measures with alternate forms six years in a row (Holtzman et al., 1975). Begun during the 1962–1963 school year in Austin, Texas, 133 first-graders, 142 fourth-graders, and 142 seventh-graders were tested with the HIT as part of a large battery of perceptual, cognitive, and personality tests. Annual testing took place on the anniversary date of the initial testing until six years of repeated measurement had been completed. The basic design of this study is given in Table 9.2.

A complete replication of the Austin longitudinal project was begun in Mexico City in 1964, under the direction of Rogelio Diaz-Guerrero and his associates. Split-half reliability coefficients for 17 HIT scores in the first year of testing for these large samples of children in Mexico and the United States are given in Table 9.3. From these statistics, it is clear that scores on the HIT generally have high reliability for schoolchildren of all ages, as well as adults.

The results for internal consistency of HIT scores among preschool children are equally high, as evidenced by the results obtained for the 122 five-year-olds tested in Austin nursery schools as part of the standardization sample. Split-half reliability coefficients ranged from .53 for Penetration to .97 for Reaction Time. The median or average reliability for all variables among the five-year-olds was .86.

Scores on the HIT, the Human Figure Drawing Test, and the Vocabulary and Block Design subtests of the Wechsler Intelligence Scale for Children in the cross-cultural longitudinal project provide an unparalleled opportunity to examine the degree of test–retest stability of these measures over time intervals varying from one to five years and for schoolchildren of all ages. On a theoretical basis, one would anticipate that the magnitude of such correlations would fall somewhere in the middle ranges, say from .40 to .80. Correlations much higher than this would indicate rather rigid, unchanging personal characteristics, while

TABLE 9.2 Overlapping Longitudinal Design for Six Years of Repeated Testing

Group	Initial Age[a]	School Grades Covered
I	6.7 years	1 2 3 4 5 6
II	9.7 years	4 5 6 7 8 9
III	12.7 years	7 8 9 10 11 12

[a]The starting ages of 6 years, 8 months, 9 years, 8 months, and 12 years, 8 months were chosen when a pilot study revealed most children in the public schools of Texas reach these exact ages at some time during the school year. Actual testing took place within 30 days of the age specified.

Source: W. H. Holtzman, R. Diaz-Guerrero, & J. D. Swartz (1975). *Personality Development in Two Cultures: A Cross-Cultural Longitudinal Study of School Children in Mexico and the United States.* Austin: University of Texas Press. Copyright 1975 by the Hogg Foundation for Mental Health.

TABLE 9.3 Split-half Reliability Coefficients for 17 HIT Variables

	Mexico			United States		
Age of Child: (No. of Cases):	6 (147)	9 (141)	12 (149)	6 (133)	9 (142)	12 (142)
Reaction Time	.94	.94	.96	.92	.97	.97
Rejection	.95	.87	.91	.90	.93	.88
Location	.94	.95	.95	.95	.97	.95
Form Definiteness	.91	.88	.89	.90	.80	.86
Form Appropriateness	.90	.82	.77	.86	.81	.67
Color	.94	.84	.78	.93	.83	.85
Shading	.61	.55	.58	.74	.58	.78
Movement	.84	.83	.85	.86	.87	.88
Pathognomic Verbalization	.86	.52	.87	.90	.76	.79
Integration	.57	.69	.77	.58	.85	.82
Human	.84	.81	.79	.82	.81	.83
Animal	.92	.83	.71	.80	.73	.72
Anatomy	.83	.86	.75	.91	.80	.69
Anxiety	.92	.73	.70	.78	.68	.80
Hostility	.95	.63	.66	.88	.72	.78
Barrier	.70	.57	.46	.75	.51	.52
Penetration	.52	.69	.63	.81	.75	.63

Source: W. H. Holtzman, R. Diaz-Guerrero, and J. D. Swartz (1975). *Personality Development in Two Cultures: A Cross-Cultural Longitudinal Study of School Children in Mexico and the United States.* Austin: University of Texas Press. Copyright 1975 by the Hogg Foundation for Mental Health.

correlations much lower would reveal instability sufficiently serious to question the enduring nature of the measured personality traits over time. Among young children, one would expect lower stability coefficients than among adolescents or adults, since personality and cognitive development are proceeding more rapidly at the younger ages. Finally, on a theoretical basis, one also would expect that stability would drop gradually as the interval of time between testing increased from one to five years.

The most stable of all inkblot scores is Location. The complete set of test–retest correlations for Location is presented in Table 9.4, to illustrate the power of this methodology for estimating stability across time. With the exception of the youngest children in the first year, the test–retest correlations for Location are high in both Mexico and the United States, ranging into the .80s for the older children, even after several years of testing. It is interesting to note in Table 9.4 that, even after an interval of five years, the stability of Location is still moderately high, averaging .46 for all six groups combined.

It should be pointed out that the availability of parallel forms for the HIT means that an interval of two years takes place before the child

TABLE 9.4 HIT Location Test–Retest Correlations[a]

	Mexico			United States		
Years Correlated	I	II	III	I	II	III
1 & 2	.27	.57	.66	.28	.72	.76
1 & 3	.20	.49	.60	.27	.62	.70
1 & 4	.25	.49	.58	.26	.59	.69
1 & 5	.24	.46	.56	.26	.51	.67
1 & 6	.50	.26	.51	.33	.56	.59
2 & 3	.58	.70	.71	.50	.77	.84
2 & 4	.49	.73	.72	.54	.68	.81
2 & 5	.42	.64	.67	.46	.58	.76
2 & 6	.23	.57	.52	.49	.62	.75
3 & 4	.64	.75	.76	.68	.78	.82
3 & 5	.56	.70	.74	.70	.80	.80
3 & 6	.44	.63	.55	.64	.77	.75
4 & 5	.60	.77	.85	.71	.76	.86
4 & 6	.62	.73	.68	.68	.80	.86
5 & 6	.63	.76	.74	.79	.86	.85

[a]Table covers six years of repeated testing; groups I, II, and III started in year 1 at ages 6.7, 9.7, and 12.7, respectively.
Source: W. H. Holtzman, R. Diaz-Guerrero, and J. D. Swartz (1975). *Personality Development in Two Cultures: A Cross-Cultural Longitudinal Study of School Children in Mexico and the United States.* Austin: University of Texas Press. Copyright 1975 by the Hogg Foundation for Mental Health.

responds again to the identical form. Two years is a sufficiently long time for memory of the initial responses to fade almost completely. The use of a staggered longitudinal design with overlapping groups, as noted in Table 9.2, also makes possible the isolation of any practice or adaptation effects, regardless of the form used. A detailed analysis of the differences that can be attributed to culture, age, and sex and to trial of repeated testing has been reported elsewhere (Holtzman et al., 1975). Only selected highlights of the findings are presented here.

In a major analysis of variance of Location scores, noticeable adaptation to repeated testing was indeed found over the six-year period, as illustrated in Figure 9.1. Mexican children tended to use smaller areas of the inkblot than did American children. Similarly, children of all ages in both cultures tended to use smaller detail areas more often than whole inkblots, as the test was repeated. The amount of adaptation is much greater for the Mexican children in the first two years of testing, as evidenced by the significantly different curves presented in Figure 9.1. Of all the variables analyzed, only Location shows this adaptation effect over years of testing, and even then the stability of individual differences through time is unusually high.

FIGURE 9.1   Location as a function of culture and year of testing.

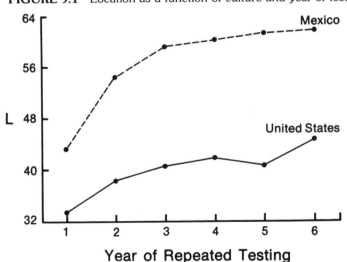

Year of Repeated Testing

Source: W. H. Holtzman, R. Diaz-Guerrero, and J. D. Swartz (1975). *Personality Development in Two Cultures: A Cross-Cultural Longitudinal Study of School Children in Mexico and the United States.* Austin: University of Texas Press. Copyright 1975 by the Hogg Foundation for Mental Health.

Close behind Location in stability are Reaction Time, Form Definiteness, Movement, and Human. These variables compare favorably with scores on Vocabulary and Block Design and with the Harris-Goodenough developmental score on Human Figure Drawing, with respect to stability over a long period of time. Of the 17 HIT scores sufficiently well distributed to permit the use of product–moment correlation coefficients, 6 have generally low stability coefficients ranging from insignificant values into the .40s and .50s, with an occasional value into the .60s and .70s; these are Rejection, Form Appropriateness, Shading, Pathognomic Verbalization, Barrier, and Penetration. Four variables—Space, Sex, Abstract, and Balance—generally occur too infrequently in samples of children to yield data amenable to treatment by correlation methods. No analysis was made of Popular, since it was scored only for the American children.

The following generalizations concerning the stability of inkblot variables among children and adolescents can be drawn from these findings:

1. Test–retest stability generally increases with an increase in the age of the child. Older adolescents tend to have the highest degree of stability, while children of any age show higher test–retest stability in the later years of testing than in the initial years.
2. Test–retest stability drops off in a regular fashion with increasing size of the interval between tests.
3. Test–retest stability is generally slightly higher for American children than for Mexicans, regardless of age group. This cross-cultural difference is particularly marked for Integration, Hostility, and Barrier.
4. Most of the HIT scores show a sufficiently high degree of stability across time to justify their use as predictors of later behavior. (A successful example of such a study over a nine-year period is reported later in this chapter.) At the same time, the test–retest correlations are not so high as to suggest any kind of fixed traits that remain relatively invariant as the child grows older.

VALIDITY OF THE HIT FOR CHILDREN AND ADOLESCENTS

Several hundred studies have been published bearing upon the relationships between scores on HIT variables and independent measures of personality. While most have been with adults, many have dealt specifically with children or adolescents. Extensive reviews have appeared recently (Holtzman, 1981; Holtzman & Swartz, 1983), and a comprehensive annotated bibliography containing all known references to the HIT through 1982 (Swartz et al., 1983a) contains abstracts of these articles. Only representative highlights of these many findings as they pertain to use of the HIT with children and adolescents are provided here. Since factor analyses of intercorrelations among the 22 HIT variables have indicated that, with few exceptions, these scores tend to cluster into meaningful factors, the findings with respect to validity will be arranged according to these more general dimensions.

Factor 1. Perceptual Maturity and Integrated Ideational Activity: Movement, Integration, Human, and Barrier

High scores on these four variables taken together are indicative of well-organized ideational activity, good imaginative capacity, and well-differentiated ego boundaries. All four variables increase with age among children and are significantly higher among college graduates than average adults, indicating a strong component of cognitive ability and creativity (Swartz, Reinehr, & Holtzman, 1983b). Studies have shown repeatedly that these variables are indicative of creative potential. They show significant relationships with reading comprehension among children, even after general intelligence has been held constant (Laird, Laosa, & Swartz, 1973).

The energy level of movement ascribed to the percept, regardless of content, has some other interesting correlates. A high score on Movement is associated with perceived empathy in counselors, while low Movement is associated with the reverse (Mueller & Abeles, 1964). The degree of eye contact and smiling among psychiatric patients when interviewed is also related to high Movement scores (Lefcourt, Telegdi, Willows, & Buckspan, 1972). Movement is correlated with the discharge or inhibition of cognitive energy, according to Covan (1976). Increased perception of movement in inkblots follows experimental inhibition of cognitive responses, while discharge of cognitive processes in a series of free-association tasks leads to a sharp decrease in reported perception of movement in inkblots. Dream deprivation, whether induced by drugs (Lerner, 1966) or prevented by interrupting rapid-eye movements (Feldstein, 1973), results in higher Movement scores. These findings support Rorschach's views on the fundamental similarity between movement and dreams due to the centrality of kinesthetic experience in both, an outcome that is also consistent with Heinz Werner's (1957) sensory tonic theory of perception.

Movement has a particularly strong cognitive component among young children. In the first year of testing for six-year-olds in the longitudinal study, the complete battery of tests for the Wechsler Intelligence

Scale for Children (WISC) was given. Factor analyses of intercorrelations among the various cognitive tests were done, with Movement included as an extra variable. Among the American children, Movement was clearly a major part of the first factor defined by the Verbal subtests from the WISC. Movement did not show up heavily loaded on a similar factor for the Mexicans until the nine-year-olds were analyzed. Similar results were found for the twelve-year-old Mexican children. No complete analyses could be made for the American nine- and twelve-year-olds, since they had not been given the complete WISC test battery. Movement deals with that component of verbal ability characterized by a lively, active imagination and the ability to project outward from one's fantasies. In this sense, it deals particularly with the expressive, imaginative aspects of verbal ability rather than with factual information, word meanings, and analytic problem solving.

Human content also has some special meaning worthy of note. As one would expect from projective theory, a high score on Human suggests high social interest, while lack of any Human content indicates the opposite (Fernald & Linden, 1966).

One of the most interesting of the symbolic content scores is Barrier, developed by Fisher and Cleveland (1958). The score is given for references to any protective covering, membrane, shell, or skin that might be symbolically related to the perception of body-image boundaries. High Barrier is indicative of strong ego identity, while low Barrier suggests diffusion. High Barrier is related to being influential and independent in group processes (Cleveland & Morton, 1962), adjusting well to physical disablement (Fisher, 1963), being able to tolerate pain (Nichols & Tursky, 1967), and having a positive evaluation of one's own body (Conquest, 1963). These findings are consistent with others showing that low Barrier is related to juvenile delinquency (Megargee, 1965).

Factor 3. Psychopathology of Thought: Pathognomic Verbalization, Anxiety, and Hostility

Dealing with unbridled fantasies, affective expressivity, and loose imagination, these three variables, frequently also associated with Movement, constitute an important cluster of scores indicative of psychopathology. Among children, moderately high scores on these three variables may be a good sign rather than bad. In most factor analyses of inkblot variables among children, this factor often proves to be highly correlated with factor 1, indicating creativity and imaginative capacity rather than psychopathology.

Even among children, however, very high scores on these variables are indicative of future emotional disturbance, as demonstrated by a long-term follow-up study of the six-year-olds tested in Austin. Nine years after the initial testing of the 133 first-graders in Austin, 46 children were located within the Austin schools and rated on personal adjustment by school personnel (Currie, Holtzman, & Swartz, 1974). Seven of the children were uniformly judged to have very serious emotional problems, seven were judged to be mildly maladjusted, 18 were seen as generally well adjusted, and 14 showed no signs of any problems. The mean scores on Pathognomic Verbalization, Anxiety, and Hostility from the HIT protocols of six years earlier for the seven most disturbed children were two standard deviations higher than the means for children judged to be well adjusted or only mildly maladjusted. Low Form Appropriateness was also associated with emotional disturbance. Interestingly enough, from the many tests in the original battery, the only other one that correlated significantly with later emotional disturbance in these children was the Koppitz Scale, based on 30 emotional indicators in human figure drawings.

Pathognomic Verbalization is the best single indicator of psychopathology. Among adolescents and adults, the bizarre perception and autistic logic underlying high scores on this variable are characteristic either of schizophrenia or extreme artistic license in responding to inkblots. Highly creative, successful artists do tend to get much higher scores than average individuals on Pathognomic Verbalization (Holtzman, Swartz, & Thorpe, 1971), but the quality of the response is noticeably different. Normal individuals tend to give fabulations with notable affectivity, mildly fabulized combinations of otherwise acceptable percepts, or even occasional queer responses that often are described in a playful manner. Schizophrenics, on the other hand, manifest a loss of distance between themselves and the inkblots, often giving severely fabulized combinations, contaminations, queer responses, or special kinds of autistic logic that show faulty, fantastic reasoning as a justification for the response. Embellishing a response with highly personal meaning by self-reference is particularly characteristic of psychotic thinking when manifest repeatedly (Swartz, 1970). A predominance of absurd responses is characteristic of mentally retarded individuals, while a predominance of deteriorated color associations is indicative of severe disintegration.

Among young children, moderately high scores on Pathognomic Verbalization simply may indicate immature thought processes coupled with uncontrolled fantasies and loose imagination, rather than serious psychopathology. While few of the cases in either the Mexican or the American sample received scores on Pathognomic Verbalization so high as to indicate serious psychopathology, the presence of some Pathognomic Verbalization among young children might indeed be taken as a good sign, provided the qualitative nature of the disordered thinking reveals primarily fabulized combinations and invalid integrations rather than bizarre perceptions.

The importance of Pathognomic Verbalization in psychodiagnosis can be illustrated best by an individual case drawn from our files of school-children in the Austin longitudinal study. While being tested with the HIT in the third year of repeated study, this young, apparently normal teenage boy shifted abruptly from normal responses one-third of the way through the test, thereafter giving responses heavily loaded with Pathognomic Verbalization. It is important to note that his responses to the first 12 inkblots and in the previous testing sessions over the past two years were generally normal, although under a high degree of self-control. Even in the remainder of this testing session, he continued to maintain an outward appearance of control, being polite, cooperative, and attentive. While we were quite concerned about the sudden deterioration in the quality of his responses, nothing was said to his parents or authorities because of the research nature of the data collection. Some months later, we learned to our dismay that the boy killed his father and was hospitalized for treatment as a schizophrenic patient. The incipient psychosis was not apparent in his general behavior or other tests, although it was clearly revealed by his Pathognomic Verbalization score on the HIT.

Signs of anxiety or hostility in the fantasy content form the basis for the Anxiety or Hostility score. Moderate-level scores on both of these symbolic content scales are normal, particularly in young children, but very high scores should be interpreted as having likely clinical significance. Zero or low positive correlations can be expected between each of these two variables and anxiety or hostility scales based upon self-report inventories. The most important evidence of their validity comes from experimental studies. Subjects who rapidly acquire the conditioned eyelid response have higher Anxiety scores than those who do not condition easily (Herron, 1965). Individuals with high Anxiety are less tolerant of pain (Nichols & Tursky, 1967). Individuals who show a marked increase in Hostility scores after experiencing frustrating situations are those who also show a predisposition to hostility as measured by factor 1 of the Buss-Durkee Inventory (Rosenstiel, 1973). Both Anxiety and Hostility scores are directly related to the observed interpersonal distance characteristic of an individual in an experimental setting; the higher the inkblot scores, the greater the distance (Greenberg, Aronow, & Rauchway, 1977). These findings are all consistent with the theoretical conception of these symbolic content scores. While the meaning of Anxiety and Hostility scores may be complex, it is clear that very high scores, even among children, have sufficient validity to justify clinical interpretation.

Factor 2. Perceptual Sensitivity: Color, Shading, and Form Definiteness (reversed)

The clustering together of Color and Shading with Form Definiteness (reversed) is inevitable. As with scoring systems for the Rorschach, the greater the predominance of color or shading over form in a response, the higher the score. Among younger children, significant negative loadings on this factor also appear for Animal, suggesting that many children tend to use color and shading as a determinant only when they cannot find a familiar animal form. The positive pole on this factor indicates overreactivity to the stimulus determinants, while the negative pole shows primary concern for form alone as a response determinant.

Among normal subjects, a high Color score has been found related to impulsivity (Holtzman, 1950) and to increased expression of affect (Mayfield, 1968). In her clinical use of the HIT, Hill (1972) recommends paying attention to the quality of the Color responses—particularly those given to inkblots having a high stimulus strength for Color—in making interpretations about the lability of affect.

There is little experimental evidence bearing upon the validity of Shading or Form Definiteness, the other two variables that measure degree of perceptual sensitivity. Nor is there much information from correlational studies with other personality measures that would indicate the independent meaning of these variables for assessment purposes. To be sure, there is a consensus among Rorschach clinicians concerning the use of these scores for personality assessment, but the scientific evidence is too tenuous at this time to justify any confident interpretations, particularly among children.

Other Factors

The remaining three factors are less important and vary somewhat in their patterning from one population to another. Location and Form Appropriateness generally appear as defining variables for factor 4. A high score on Location results when an individual uses smaller areas of the inkblot while ignoring the rest. This perceptual style makes it easier to find percepts that have good form. The combination of low score on Location with high score on Form Appropriateness is less common and indicates a high level of perceptual maturity and organization, particularly when accompanied by high scores on Integration.

Reaction Time and Rejection tend to be associated in a single factor (factor 5), since both measure the extent of inhibition or outright perceptual inability. Both variables must be taken into account with other inkblot scores, rather than interpreted alone.

Three scores—Sex, Anatomy, and Penetration—deal with bodily preoc-cupation and occasionally are clustered together in one factor (factor 6) for this reason. Blatant sex responses are relatively rare but significant when they do appear, especially among children. Very high Anatomy scores are also quite unusual and significant. High Anatomy scores have been found to be closely associated with a high degree of somatic preoccu-pation among hospitalized patients, confirming the theoretical interpre-tation of Anatomy (Endicott & Jortner, 1967). Penetration frequently also loads on factor 3, concerned with psychopathology, suggesting that high scores on Penetration generally should be interpreted as pathological. In one longitudinal study of schizophrenics undergoing treatment, a signif-icant drop in Penetration accompanied a drop in the morbidity of the patients (Cleveland, 1960). Other special content scores have been devel-oped that deserve mention, such as those for measuring suspiciousness and depression that have been validated by Endicott (1972).

NOSOLOGICAL AND NORMATIVE STUDIES WITH THE HIT

Closely related to the clinical validity of individual variables within the HIT is the use of patterns of scores for differential diagnosis. The origi-nal standardization data on 15 different populations are presented in percentile norms for eight major reference groups ranging from five-year-olds to superior adults and including psychiatric patients as well as mental retardates. Chronic schizophrenics differ from normal reference groups on almost all of the standard HIT variables. Even without Pa-thognomic Verbalization, Moseley (1963) was able to develop an objective approach based upon linear combinations of 16 HIT scores that classi-fied accurately 82 percent of the normals from schizophrenics, 71 percent of the normals from depressed patients, and 78 percent of the depressives from schizophrenics. Adding Pathognomic Verbalization in a two-stage model for use with doubtful cases, the efficiency of this objective ap-proach to differential diagnosis was improved even more. More impor-tantly, when cross-validated, the procedure held up completely. Others have had similar success in differentiating schizophrenics, neurotics, normals, or organics by various combinations of HIT scores (Barnes, 1964; Hill, 1972; Shukla, 1976).

Conners (1965) reported a number of highly significant differences between emotionally disturbed children seen in an outpatient clinic and normal controls of the same age and background. In Connors' study, disturbed children got higher scores on Rejection and Anatomy and lower scores on all other variables except Pathognomic Verbalization,

Sex, Abstract, Hostility, Penetration, and Balance. Using HIT factor scores, Connors found that neurotic children appeared to be more differentiated in response and more inhibited than were hyperkinetic children.

Percentile norms for the HIT have been published for emotionally disturbed children and adolescents and for male juvenile delinquents (Hill, 1972). Additional normative data for four representative groups of children and adolescents seen in clinical practice have been published by Morgan (1968). The norms for emotionally disturbed children published by Hill are based upon HIT protocols collected by Conners (1965) in clinical studies of 99 emotionally disturbed children and 114 neurotic adolescents. The norms for male juvenile delinquents are based on 75 cases collected by Megargee (1965). When taken together with the earlier sets of norms for mental retardates and for normal children and adolescents, the percentile norms that are available for the HIT provide a rich source of useful information to be used in psychodiagnosis and personality assessment.

In her handbook, Hill (1972) also provides detailed suggestions on how best to interpret HIT scores, as well as qualitative aspects of content with respect to cognitive functioning, affective functioning, and self-identity. A detailed case analysis of an adolescent making a schizoid adjustment to his problems is provided to illustrate the method. A second case analysis of an adolescent with brain damage and a third concerning a 17-year-old diagnosed as a process schizophrenic are also useful to the clinician interested in employing the HIT for individual assessment of adolescents.

USE OF THE HIT FOR CROSS-CULTURAL RESEARCH

Use of the HIT in research studies of differences in personality development among children of different cultures is particularly appropriate because of the relatively universal nature of the technique. The method has been translated into a number of languages and is relatively culture free. The technique has been used successfully for both adults and children in cultures as widely varied as primitive groups in New Guinea, Aleutian Eskimos, peasant children in Latin America, and children from modern, industrialized societies. Our own work has concentrated upon factors related to personality and cognitive development among children in Mexico and the United States. Of all the measures used in the cross-cultural longitudinal study, the HIT yielded the most striking differences between Mexican and American children.

One finding is of particular interest, since it sheds considerable light upon the possible use of the HIT for measuring an important coping style. The most significant differences between Mexican and American children—regardless of the age, sex, or socioeconomic status of the child—were found for seven HIT scores: Reaction Time, Pathognomic Verbalization, Location, Movement, Integration, Anxiety, and Hostility. Mexicans had a slower response time; had less pathology, anxiety, hostility, or movement in their fantasy expressions; tended to use more small details within the blots for their responses; and showed lower ability to integrate the parts into a meaningful whole than did the American children. These differences tend to narrow with increasing age.

Most of the differences between the Mexican and American children on the HIT can be understood better in terms of coping style than of any other concept. When the Americans, particularly the young children, attempted to deal with all aspects of the inkblots in an active fashion, they failed more often than the Mexican children, resulting in more responses showing deviant thinking. An active style of coping, with all of its cognitive and behavioral implications, involves perceiving problems as existing in the physical and social environment. The best way to resolve such problems is to modify the environment. A passive style of coping assumes that, while problems may be posed by the environment, the best way to cope with them is to change one's self to adapt to circumstances. American children tend to be more actively independent and to struggle for a mastery of problems and challenges in their environment, whereas Mexican children are more passively obedient, adapting to stresses in the environment rather than trying to change them.

CONCLUSION

The Holtzman Inkblot Technique was developed originally to bridge the gap between the intuitively oriented clinician and the scientific determinism of the academician. In order to achieve a higher degree of psychometric reliability and validity, the HIT is more demanding of the clinician than the Rorschach. The accrual of scientific evidence for clinical application is a slow process with which many practitioners are impatient. Since there are nine times as many inkblots in the combined forms of the HIT as there are in the Rorschach, the basic testing materials are significantly more costly. But the time and effort on the part of the clinician in administering, scoring, and interpreting the HIT need not be any greater than for the Rorschach, once a clinician has mastered the technique. Those who have learned the method well have been enthusiastic about its value for both clinical and research purposes. Many clinicians find the HIT difficult or cumbersome because of 45 inkblots instead of 10, or because of only one response per card rather than as many as the subject wishes to give. Yet these are the very features that produce superior psychometric qualities, rendering the technique more suitable for rigorous scientific validity as well as for processing with modern computer technology.

REFERENCES

Barnes, C. M. (1964). Prediction of brain damage using the Holtzman Inkblot Technique and other selected variables. *Dissertation Abstracts, 24,* 4789. (University Microfilms No. 64-3350.)

Cleveland, S. E. (1960). Body image changes associated with personality reorganization. *Journal of Consulting Psychology, 13*(2), 256–261.

Cleveland, S. E., & Morton, R. B. (1962). Group behavior and body image: A follow-up study. *Human Relations, 15,* 77–85.

Conners, C. K. (1965). Effects of brief psychotherapy, drugs, and type of disturbance on Holtzman Inkblot scores in children. *Proceedings of the 73rd Annual Convention of the American Psychological Association,* 201–202.

Conquest, R. A. (1963). *An investigation of body image variables in patients with the diagnosis of schizophrenic reaction.* Unpublished doctoral dissertation, Western Reserve University, Cleveland, OH.

Covan, F. L. (1976). *The perception of movement in inkblots following cognitive inhibition.* Unpublished doctoral dissertation, Yeshiva University, New York.

Currie, S. F., Holtzman, W. H., & Swartz, J. D. (1974). Early indicators of personality traits viewed retrospectively. *Journal of School Psychology, 12*(1), 51–59.

Endicott, N. A. (1972). The Holtzman Inkblot Technique content measures of depression and suspiciousness. *Journal of Personality Assessment, 36*(5), 424–426.

Endicott, N. A., & Jortner, S. (1967). Correlates of somatic concern derived from psychological tests. *Journal of Nervous and Mental Disease, 144*(2), 133–138.

Feldstein, S. (1973). REM deprivation: The effects of inkblot perception and fantasy processes. Doctoral dissertation, The City University of New York, 1972. *Dissertation Abstracts International, 33,* 3934B–3935B (Order No. 73-2835).

Fernald, P. S., & Linden, J. D. (1966). The human content response in the Holtzman Inkblot Technique. *Journal of Projective Techniques and Personality Assessment, 30,* 441–446.

Fisher, S. (1963). A further appraisal of the body boundary concept. *Journal of Consulting Psychology, 27,* 62–74.

Fisher, S., & Cleveland, S. E. (1958). *Body image and personality.* Princeton, NJ: Van Nostrand.

Gorham, D. R. (1967). Computer use in psychological testing. *Memorias del XIth Congreso Interamericano de Psicologia, 9,* 1–7. Mexico, D.F.: Universidad Nacional Autonoma de Mexico.

Greenberg, E., Aronow, E., & Rauchway, A. (1977). Inkblot content and interpersonal distance. *Journal of Clinical Psychology, 33*(3), 882–887.

Hartmann, H. A., & Rosenstiel, L. von. (Eds.) (1977). *Lehrbuch der Holtzman Inkblot-Technik (HIT)*. Bern/Stuttgart/Wien: Hans Huber.

Herron, E. W. (1965). Personality factors associated with the acquisition of the conditioned eyelid response. *Journal of Personality and Social Psychology, 2*(5), 775–777.

Hill, E. F. (1972). *The Holtzman Inkblot Technique: A handbook for clinical application.* San Francisco: Jossey-Bass.

Hill, E. F., & Piexotto, H. E. (1973). *Workbook for the Holtzman Inkblot Technique.* New York: The Psychological Corporation.

Holtzman, W. H. (1950). The Rorschach test in the assessment of the normal superior adult. Unpublished doctoral dissertation, Stanford University, Palo Alto, CA.

Holtzman, W. H. (1981). Holtzman Inkblot Technique (HIT). In A. I. Rabin (Ed.), *Assessment with projective techniques: A concise introduction* (47–83). New York: Springer.

Holtzman, W. H., Diaz-Guerrero, R., & Swartz, J. D. (1975). *Personality development in two cultures: A cross-cultural longitudinal study of school children in Mexico and the United States.* Austin, TX: University of Texas Press.

Holtzman, W. H., & Swartz, J. D. (1983). The Holtzman Inkblot Technique: A review of 25 years of research. *Zeitschrift fur Differentielle und Diagnostische Psychologie, 4*(3), 241–259.

Holtzman, W. H., Swartz, J. D., & Thorpe, J. S. (1971). Artists, architects, and engineers: Three contrasting modes of visual experience and their psychological correlates. *Journal of Personality, 39*(3), 432–449.

Holtzman, W. H., Thorpe, J. S., Swartz, J. D., & Herron, E. W. (1961a). *Administration and scoring guide.* Cleveland, OH: The Psychological Corporation.

Holtzman, W. H., Thorpe, J. S., Swartz, J. D., & Herron, E. W. (1961b). *Inkblot perception and personality.* Austin, TX: University of Texas Press.

Laird, D. R., Laosa, L. M., & Swartz, J. D. (1973). Inkblot perception and reading achievement in children: A developmental analysis. *British Journal of Projective Psychology and Personality Study, 18*(2), 25–31.

Lefcourt, H. M., Telegdi, M. S., Willows, D., and Buckspan, B. (1972). Eye contact and the human movement response. *Journal of Social Psychology, 88*(2), 303–304.

Lerner, B. (1966). Rorschach movement and dreams: A validation study using drug-induced dream deprivation. *Journal of Abnormal Psychology, 71*(2), 75–86.

Mayfield, D. G. (1968). Holtzman Inkblot Technique in acute experimental alcohol intoxication. *Journal of Projective Techniques and Personality Assessment, 32*(5), 491–494.

Megargee, E. I. (1965). The relation between barrier scores and aggressive behavior. *Journal of Abnormal Psychology, 70*(4), 307–311.

Morgan, A. B. (1968). Some age norms obtained for the Holtzman Inkblot Technique administered in a clinical setting. *Journal of Projective Techniques and Personality Assessment, 32*, 165–172.

Moseley, E. C. (1963). Psychodiagnosis on the basis of the Holtzman Inkblot Technique. *Journal of Projective Techniques and Personality Assessment, 17,* 86–91.

Mueller, W. J., & Abeles, N. (1964). The components of empathy and their relationship to the projection of human movement responses. *Journal of Projective Techniques and Personality Assessment, 28*(3), 322–330.

Nichols, D. C., & Tursky, B. (1967). Body image, anxiety, and tolerance for experimental pain. *Psychosomatic Medicine, 29,* 103–110.

Rosenstiel, L. von. (1973). Increase in hostility responses in the HIT after frustration. *Journal of Personality Assessment, 37*(1), 22–24.

Shukla, T. R. (1976). Psychodiagnostic efficacy of the HIT under Indian conditions: A normative study. *Indian Journal of Clinical Psychology, 3*(2), 189–198.

Swartz, J. D. (1970). Pathognomic verbalizations in normals, psychotics, and mental retardates. Doctoral dissertation, University of Texas at Austin, 1969. *Dissertation Abstracts International, 20,* 5703B–5704B (Order No. 70-10, 872).

Swartz, J. D., & Holtzman, W. H. (1963). Group method of administration for the Holtzman Inkblot Technique. *Journal of Clinical Psychology, 19,* 433–441.

Swartz, J. D., Reinehr, R. C., & Holtzman, W. H. (1983a). *Holtzman Inkblot Technique, 1956-1982: An annotated bibliography.* Austin, TX: Hogg Foundation for Mental Health.

Swartz, J. D., Reinehr, R. C., & Holtzman, W. H. (1983b). Personality development through the lifespan: Assessment by means of the Holtzman Inkblot Technique. In C. D. Spielberger & J. N. Butcher (Eds.), *Advances in personality assessment* (Vol. 3). Hillsdale, NJ: Lawrence Erlbaum Assoc.

Werner, H. (1957). *Comparative psychology of mental development.* New York: International Universities Press.

Zubin, J. (1954). Failures of the Rorschach technique. *Journal of Projective Techniques, 18,* 303–315.

IV
Verbal
Methods

10
Story- and Sentence-Completion Techniques

*Zoli Zlotogorski and
Edythe Wiggs*

STORY-COMPLETION TECHNIQUES

A story-completion technique may be defined as a verbal stimulus consisting of at least one complete sentence that represents the beginning of a story plot to be completed by the examinee. Hartshorne and May (1928) used this technique in an early investigation of character and deceit, while Piaget (1932) employed story completions in a study of moral judgment. The story-completion technique developed further when Madeline Thomas (1937) employed it as a subtle method of investigation that could be applied in clinical settings. Fifteen stories were selected to further this clinical method of investigation. At approximately the same time, Louisa Duss (1940) created the Duss (Despert) Fables, which were designed to elicit data on specific emotional conflicts in children of various ages. More recent work involving the story-completion technique has included its development as a clinical tool (Engel, 1958; Sargent, 1953), an investigation of aggression and failure in schoolchildren (Beardslee, 1960), and a large cross-cultural study of children's views of interpersonal conflict (Anderson & Anderson, 1954, 1961).

In this section, we will discuss the Madeline Thomas stories and the Louisa Duss Fables and review briefly their clinical and research applications.

Madeline Thomas Stories (MTS)

In administering the MTS, the examiner suggests to the child that the two of them make up some stories together. Wursten (1960) recommends that the approach should be flexible and adapted to the particular child. Since it is a clinical method rather than a test, the clinician must be prepared to facilitate the child's expression of emotional conflicts, preoccupations, and projections in the form of fantasies and stories. The beginnings of the stories, given in the following list, are read to the child, whose responses are recorded verbatim. Although all of the examples in the list are for boys, the character is changed to a girl when the child being examined is a girl.

1. A boy goes to school. During recess he does not play with the other children, he stays by himself in a corner. Why?
2. A boy fights with his brother. Mother comes. What is going to happen?
3. A boy is at the table with his parents. Father suddenly gets angry. Why?
4. One day, Mother and Father are a bit angry with each ot! ?r. They have been arguing. Why?
5. Sometimes he likes to tell funny stories, (a) to his friends, (b) to his parents. What kind?
6. A boy has gotten bad grades in school. He returns home. To whom is he going to show his report card? Who is going to scold him most?
7. It is Sunday. This boy has been taken for a ride with Mother and Father. Upon their return home, Mother is sad. Why?
8. This boy has a friend whom he likes very much. One day his friend tells him, (a) "Come with me, I am going to show you something, but it is a secret. Don't tell anybody." What is he going to show him? (b) "Listen, I am going to tell you something, but it is a secret, don't tell anybody." What is he going to tell him?
9. It is evening. The boy is in bed, the day is ended, the light turned off. (a) What does he do before going to sleep? (b) What is he thinking about? (c) One evening he cries; he is sad. What about?
10. Then he goes to sleep. What does he dream about?
11. He wakes up in the middle of the night. He is very much afraid. What of?
12. He goes back to sleep, and this time has a very nice dream. A good fairy comes to him and says, "I can do anything for you! Tell me what you want; I am going to touch you with my magic rod, and all you may wish for is going to come true!" What does he ask for?

13. The boy is growing up. Is he anxious to be a big boy soon, or would he rather remain a little boy for awhile? Why? What is he going to be when he grows up?
14. Among all the fairy tales that have been told to him, which one does he like best of all?
15. Do you remember when you were a little boy? Which is the first thing that you can remember now?

The MTS involves identification with an imagined situation and character. Thus, story 1 gives the child an opportunity to discuss issues of rejection, possible fears, and shame or guilt. Story 2 may elicit themes of sibling rivalry and possible feelings of differential treatment by mother, while story 7 asks the child to interpret the mood of the mother and project some concerns in his relationship with her.

Thomas (1937) initially studied a group of 31 children who were boarders in a children's home. Construct validity was investigated by comparing her findings to reports and descriptions provided by teachers and staff. Regrettably, the data reported are insufficient to establish construct validity clearly, although they did indicate a reasonable degree of general agreement between measures. Mills (1953) studied 50 children from kindergarten through the sixth grade, employing the MTS. He reported that the stories elicited valuable clinical material about the emotional lives of the children. Although the research data are scarce, the MTS seems to maintain its utility as a relatively unthreatening technique that permits us to explore the child's fantasy life.

Duss (Despert) Fables

Louisa Duss (1940) administered the 10 stories in the following list to 43 children varying in age from 3 to 15. Duss used the following six criteria as indicators of some specific emotional conflict in the child: (1) immediate and unexpected response; (2) preservation of the complex in other fables; (3) whispered responses, given rapidly; (4) refusal to answer to one of the fables; (5) silence and resistance; and (6) the subject wishes to start the examination all over. The intent of the fables is to provide the opportunity to project dynamically meaningful material. In this manner, the bird fable (#1) elicits information on attachment behavior, while the fable concerning a walk in the woods (#8) focuses on oedipal issues. For a more detailed analysis of each fable, the reader is advised to consult Mosse (1954), who provides sample responses and numerous diagnostic interpretations. Again, note that the sex of the child in the story would be tailored to fit the sex of the child being examined.

1. A daddy and mommy bird and their little baby bird are sleeping in a nest on a branch of a tree. All of a sudden a big wind comes along and shakes the tree, and the nest falls to the ground. The three birds wake up brusquely. The daddy flies to a pine tree, the mother to another pine tree. What is the little bird going to do? She already knows how to fly a little bit.

2. It is the daddy's and mommy's wedding anniversary. They love each other very much and are having a beautiful party. During the party the child gets up and all alone goes to the very end of the back yard. Why?

3. There is a mother sheep and her baby lamb in the meadow. All day long the little lamb plays next to the mother. Every evening the mother gives the lamb good warm milk, which she likes very much. But she also eats grass. One day, someone brings to the mother sheep a very tiny lamb who is hungry and needs to be fed some milk. But the mother sheep does not have enough milk for both the lambs, and she says to her big lamb, "I don't have enough milk for both of you, so you go and eat the fresh grass." What does this lamb do? (To judge only the weaning complex, leave out the arrival of the little lamb and say that the mother sheep no longer has any milk and that the lamb must now start to eat grass.)

4. A funeral procession is passing by in the village street and people are asking, "Who has died?" Someone answers, "It is someone in the family who lives over there in that house." Who is it? (One can mention the members of the family.)

5. Here is a child who says very softly, "Oh, but I am afraid!" What is she afraid of?

6. A child has a little elephant, which she loves very much. The elephant is very pretty with its long trunk. One day when she returns from a walk, the child comes into her room and finds that her elephant has changed. In what way has the elephant changed? And why is he changed?

7. A child has succeeded in making something out of clay (a tower), which she finds very, very pretty. What does she do with it? Her mother asks her to give it to her. She is free to decide. Will she give it to her mother?

8. A girl took a very nice walk in the woods alone with her father (or his mother, for a boy). They had lots of fun together. When she returned home, the girl found that her mother did not look as she usually did. Why? (Similarly, upon returning a boy finds that his father doesn't look the same as usual.)

9. A child comes home from school (or from a walk). Mother says to her, "Don't start your homework right away—I have something to tell you!" What is the mother going to say to the child?

10. A child wakes up in the morning all tired and says, "Oh, what a bad dream I've had!" What did she dream about?

Despert (1946) translated (from French to English) the fables as part of a study of 50 stutterers and a later study (Despert, 1949) on dreams in preschool-age children. Piexotto (1956) investigated the test–retest reliability of the fables, which she followed with a study (1957) in which she collected normative data on 442 children (aged 6 to 14) based on response frequency. Each fable was discussed in terms of its usefulness in eliciting atypical responses, its appropriateness for various age levels, and its reliability. Piexotto concluded, from these studies, that the fables seem most suitable for children under eight years of age.

The Insight Test

A story-completion technique suitable for adolescents was developed by Sargent (1953) and later modified by Engel (1958) for use with younger children. The Insight Test features a series of story beginnings that are structured around relationships with family, the other sex, and peers, as well as around vocational, religious, and health concerns. Story completions are scored on three principal dimensions: affect, defense, and malignancy. The affect category is used for expressions of aggression, mood, and anxiety, while the defense category covers qualifying words (perhaps, maybe, but) and evaluative indicators such as judging and generalizing. Finally, the malignancy category includes personalizations, bizarre content, irrelevant feelings, and unreal solutions.

Utility of Story-completion Techniques

Story-completion techniques have developed, in part, to facilitate clinical diagnosis. In order to fulfill this promise a considerable amount of research would have to be undertaken; however, to date, little work has been done. Even so, these tests still have considerable utility and offer idiographic data on a child's coping abilities.

Beyond their clinical utility, story-completion techniques have been used in a variety of research designs. Beardslee (1960a, 1960b) used story completions to study denial of both failure and aggression in two groups of 96 schoolchildren. This study was part of a broader research effort that compared adults' and children's coping mechanisms (Miller & Swanson, 1960). Beardslee (1960) manipulated feelings of failure and compared stories completed before and after the failure experience. Denial of failure was measured by the occurrence of an unrealistic resolution to the problem presented in the story. The tendency to increase denial, on posttest, was associated with harsh and inconsistent discipline in the home. Miller and Swanson (1960) also demonstrate the utility of the story-completion method in a research design. They cite advantages such as the veiled intention of the test, the latitude given the child in completing the stories, and efficiency of administration.

In their extensive research, Anderson and Anderson (1954, 1961) used 11 stories dealing with interpersonal conflict. The story-completion technique was administered to 9,546 children in seven countries. The stories focused on issues such as parental and teacher–child relationships. One such story, for example, concerns a child's playing on the way home from the store, which results in loss of the groceries. Another deals with money missing from a teacher's desk. Anderson and Anderson examined outcomes in terms of problem solving, decision-making, and reactions to authority.

Although currently little used as a research technique, the story-completion method seems to be a useful addition to the clinician's repertoire. It is nonthreatening to most children and gives the clinician an opportunity to explore some focal problems as well as potential problem-solving techniques used by the child.

SENTENCE-COMPLETION METHODS

There are two precursors to the present-day sentence-completion technique. The first, word association, was introduced and furthered by Jung's studies, which were designed to explore Freud's theory of repression. The second had its origins in the work of Ebbinghaus (1897), Kelley (1917), and Traube (1916), who used it to measure intellectual variables. In the early study of memory, incomplete sentences were employed as recall measures or recognition measures. In other words, either the subject was instructed to fill in the blanks from memory (recall) or he was instructed to select from alternative completions (recognition). As early as 1910, Wells (1954) reported the use of a "series of phrase-completions." Most reviewers, however, agree that the first systematic use of the sentence-completion technique in the area of personality assessment was in the late 1920s and early 1930s (Payne, 1928; Tendler, 1930). These early investigations found them of value as indices of response style and emotional reactions, with rather diverse populations (Bell, 1948; Forer, 1960; Rhode, 1957; Rotter, 1951; Sacks & Levy, 1959).

Wide use of the sentence-completion method, as well as most projective techniques, actually began as a result of the demands engendered by

World War II for diagnosis and diagnostic tools. Flexibility and economy were two features of the sentence-completion method, which greatly enhanced its popularity. In the past three decades, there has been a spate of sentence-completion devices, which have proved to be useful tools for both research and clinical purposes.

Underlying Assumptions

Common to all sentence-completion methods, as well as other projective methods, is the projective hypothesis, which Frank (1939, 1948) defines as follows: When an individual is forced to impose meaning or order on an ambiguous stimulus complex, his response is a "projection" of his "feelings, anger, beliefs, attitudes and desires" (Frank, 1948, p. 66). The child is said to reveal general personality styles as well as clues about specific conflicts and problem areas.

Incomplete sentences are less amorphous than inkblots, yet they allow greater variability of subject response than do such procedures as word associations. Sacks and Levy (1959) cite 10 responses they obtained to the stub, "The way my father treated my mother made me feel . . . " Five of the responses were positive in tone, five were negative. Content ranged from "very happy" through "rather indifferent" to "like killing him" and "he was a sucker." Response latencies varied from four to thirty-five seconds. This is an impressive demonstration of individual differences, with strong implications for personality assessment.

Psychodynamic considerations may well enter into the construction of a sentence-completion test, but other areas may be examined as well. The test can be focused on specific criteria, and items with content validity can be developed. Clinically oriented techniques, like the Sacks Sentence Completion Test (Sacks & Levy, 1959) or the Stein Sentence Completion Test (Stein, 1949), contain items specific to personality-relevant areas. Others, like that developed by Kovac (1979), are designed to test creativity.

A second assumption is that the child's responses to the sentence stubs are not shaped consciously by attitudes and beliefs devoid of deeper psychic meaning. Goldberg (1965) notes the theoretical controversy underlying this assumption. What level of personality does the sentence completion tap? In other words, if we conceptualize different levels of psychic functioning and organization, then where do the child's responses to the sentence stubs fit in? Meltzoff (1951) attacked the problem experimentally by manipulating situational factors. He found that response set and social desirability were factors in the obtained results. Siipola (1968) imposed time pressure and found a significant increase in ego-alien content. Jourard (1969) noted the effect of pronoun stems, standard nonpersonal stems, and impersonal stems upon projection.

Materials

By now it should be apparent that, while there may be one sentence-completion method, there are many sentence-completion tests. Materials depend on the focus of the inquiry. In other words, the sentence stems may vary according to the questions of interest and concerns of the researcher or clinician.

Most tests contain between 40 and 100 stems. Format is fairly consistent across sentence-completion tests. Instructions and demographic information normally are followed by a numbered list of sentence stems. Stubs are printed on the left of the page with a sufficient but limited amount of space for the subject's response. Finally, it should be noted that, as in other testing situations, an adequately lighted and quiet workspace as well as writing materials should be provided.

Administration

Any sentence-completion test can be administered individually or to groups of varying size, in a quiet, comfortable, and well-lit room. Instructions are printed on the sentence-completion blank and may be repeated aloud by the examiner.

Sentence completions are usually power tests, rather than speed tests. Although it is valuable to note the time taken, the clinician should be aware that time saving is directly related to response brevity (Cromwell & Lundy, 1954; Goldberg, 1965). The Rotter Incomplete Sentence Blank (Rotter & Rafferty, 1950) instructs the subject to express his "real feelings," while the Rhode Sentence Completion Method (Rhode, 1957) combines the speed criteria with the instruction of writing the "first thing that comes to mind," as does the Forer Structured Sentence Completion Test (Forer, 1950, 1960).

Evaluation and Interpretation

There are a number of ways of evaluating responses reported in the literature. The assessment of nonmeaningful properties of the sentence-completion response is called *formal analysis*. Benton, Windle, and Erdice (1957) have reported seven such methods, including length of completion, use of personal pronouns, time of reaction for completion, verb/adjective ratio, range of words used, grammatical errors, and first word use. Though some early research was conducted using formal analysis, most evaluation and interpretation is carried out by *content analysis*.

Rather than being a monolithic approach, content analyses of sentence-completion responses are many and varied. In the present review we will limit our discussion to the Forer Sentence Completion Test (Forer,

1960), although the reader is well advised to read earlier reviews of the major sentence-completion techniques (Goldberg, 1965; Rabin & Zlotogorski, 1981).

The Forer Sentence Completion Test (FSCT) has no formal scoring system; thus the emphasis is on description rather than quantification. Nonetheless, the evaluatory structure provided is detailed enough to make quantification a relatively easy next step. The FSCT contains 100 purposely structured stems forcing the child to deal with specific material. A few representative items are:

He felt proud that he _____.   When my mother came home,
If I think the class is too hard for   I _____.
  me, I _____.   I wish that my father _____.
School is _____.

Forer groups responses into four categories:

1. Interpersonal attitudes
2. Wishes
3. Causes of one's own feeling or action
4. Reaction to external states

A specially designed checklist is used to help organize the materials gathered from the test. The structure of the test allows the assignment of specific items to specific attitudes, reactions, and motivational areas. Given this structure, any deviation from the formal aspects of completion normally indicates "the presence of highly personalized elements in the associative process" (Forer, 1950, p. 25).

Personality Research

Goldberg (1965), in a review of the status of sentence-completion methods, notes that they are used relatively more as clinical than as research instruments. Given their flexibility and ease of construction, this is somewhat of a puzzle. In recent years, there is evidence of greater interest in sentence-completion methods, especially in the area of personality research. Here, we will review three distinct areas of personality research that employ the versatility of sentence-completion methods. These are emotional development, long-term stability of feelings, and ego development.

Emotional Development. Sentence-completion techniques remain one of the most popular clinical tools in assessing the functioning of children. Derichs (1977) conducted a study designed to assess the utility of this technique as compared to clinical interview information gleaned from meeting with parent and child. A 56-item test was constructed, with 17 items on a short form written in the first person and the remainder on a longer form written in the third person. He reports a significant difference between the amount of information obtained from the test and that obtained in previous consultations with the family. The areas of information included school behavior, fear of failure, pride in achievement, deprivation of attention, attitude toward the family, need for and the lack of contact, and tendencies toward aggression and/or withdrawal.

Lanyon (1972) constructed a sentence-completion test designed to rate hostility, anxiety, and dependency. Stems were based on strict behavioral definitions and administered to 1,017 12- to 14-year-olds. A number ($N =$ 228) of students were rated further by their teachers for the three variables. Lanyon reports that discriminant validity was demonstrated for the hostility scale but not for the anxiety and dependency scales. However, it should be noted that stems employed were highly structured with a clear stimulus pull; for example,

When people are not paying attention to me————.
When I feel like mouthing off in class————.

A more recent study by Rabinowitz and Shouval (1977) also examined the expression of hostility. They administered the Rotter Incomplete Sentence Blank (RISB) to 203 freshmen and sophomores in high school. The subjects then were subgrouped according to fantasy level (high and low) and level of aggression, as determined by peer and teacher ratings. The RISB successfully reflected the heightened hostility level of the aggressive subgroups. Aggression also was the focus of a study of juvenile delinquents conducted by Spiva (1969). The boys were divided into two groups: "winners" and "losers." The latter group was seen by peers and staff raters as marked by a sense of helplessness and confusion. Spiva reports that the RISB results for the "losers" indicated deficits in ego functioning and poor ability to cope with and control aggression.

Coping strategies were the focus of an investigation by Mar'i and Levi (1979) employing the Shanan Sentence Completion Test (SSCT). The SSCT (Shanan & Nissan, 1961) consists of 65 incomplete sentences and is built around four basic categories: (1) the ability to identify and express external goals, (2) the ability to detect and express external problems, (3) the readiness to cope actively with problems, and (4) self-esteem. In their study, 234 eighth graders in three Arab villages were given the SSCT in order to assess the relative effects of modernization versus the effects of minority status as a result of the reunification in 1967. They concluded that modernization tended to overcome the deleterious effects of minority status.

The flexibility of sentence-completion techniques is highlighted by the series of studies employing the SSCT. It has predicted successful coping with a wide variety of specific stresses, including level of social integration (Shanan, 1967), differentiating between the mentally ill and healthy (Shanan & Nissan, 1961), scholastic success (Shanan, Adler, & Adler, 1975; Shanan, Kedar, Eliakim, Oster, & Prywes, 1970, 1973), and adaptation to immigration (Shanan & Sharon, 1974).

Long-term Stability of Feelings. Rabin (1977), in a twenty-year longitudinal study, explored the endurance of sentiments from late adolescence to adult maturity. The focal question of his study was how this enduringness compares with the reported data that deal with stability and consistency of broader personality characteristics over time. A 51-item adaptation of the Sacks and Levy Sentence Completion Test was administered to both kibbutz and nonkibbutz subjects in 1955 and 1975. The subsample on which the data were obtained consisted of a group of 18 persons that was equally divided as to sex and type of family origin. The subjects were 17 to 18 years old during the original testing and in their late thirties upon retest.

The items in the test were grouped into eight different areas (e.g., father, mother, family, past, etc.), and the completions were rated with respect to affect involved: positive, negative, or neutral. Of the eight total areas, data analysis revealed two coefficients of correlation that were statistically significant. Attitudes toward father changed in a direction opposite to the original ones held during late adolescence, while attitudes toward sex were significantly consistent over the twenty-year time span.

In addition to this study, Rabin (1965) has conducted a series of cross-sectional comparative studies of kibbutz and nonkibbutz children, using sentence-completion techniques as one of his instruments. They proved to be useful tools in evaluating differences along personality dimensions between these groups from different environments. In effect, the kibbutz studies showed the versatility of the sentence-completion test in both a cross-sectional and longitudinal study.

Ego Development. In a series of studies, Loevinger and her colleagues (Loevinger & Wessler, 1970; Loevinger, Wessler, & Redmore, 1970) have used the sentence-completion test to evaluate levels of ego development. This work is based on the assumption that each person has a core level of ego functioning. Her hierarchy of stages of ego development includes seven basic levels spanning the lifetime. The strategy of the Washington University Sentence Completion Test (WU-SCT) is to determine this core level, based on the distribution of ratings of a subject's responses to the 36 sentence stems. The authors provide a detailed scoring manual, complete with numerous examples of each level being presented. Interrater reliability for both expert and less experienced raters was studied and found to be quite good. Median interrater correlations for items were .75; for the core ego level score it was .85.

Validity studies (Loevinger & Wessler, 1970) of the scoring system involved structured interviews of adults and comparison of children at different age levels. Ego development ratings then were compared to the levels obtained from the sentence-completion test and found to correlate quite highly. Redmore and Waldman (1975) reported on two studies evaluating the reliability of the test as a function of subject response. Their findings indicate some susceptibility of the sentence-completion test to systematic error stemming from the subject's motivational set.

Further construct validity for the WU-SCT was provided in a longitudinal study of ego development (Martin & Redmore, 1978). Thirty-two lower- and lower-middle-class black subjects were tested for ego development at the sixth and twelfth grades. Martin and Redmore report a significant correlation between grade and ego level, which they believe provides evidence for the developmental nature of the ego through an invariant order of stages.

In another study, Hauser (1976) attempted to investigate the relationship between observable behaviors and ego levels. He administered the WU-SCT, accompanied by structured interviews, to 98 adolescent females. Subjects were divided into preconformist and postconformist groups, based on the WU-SCT. Preconformist subjects may be characterized as those who are self-protective, tend to be manipulative, conform to rules to avoid being caught, and have a simplistic cognitive style. Those at the postconformist level are more aware of themselves as members of a group and have long-term goals and ideals, more differentiated feelings and motives, and more complex cognitive processes (Loevinger & Blasi, 1976). Preconformist subjects were reported to show significantly more sexually flirtatious behavior and lower levels of warmth and availability. Postconformist subjects, on the other hand, evidenced lower levels of erotically toned behaviors and significantly higher levels of available interactions.

In a similar study, Lorr and Manning (1978) administered the WU-SCT and the Interpersonal Style Inventory to 423 females and 225 male adolescents. They found that levels of ego development were inversely related to closed mindedness and belief in chance as the agent in what happens to a person.

Alternate forms and methods of administration of the WU-SCT have been studied as well. McCammon (1981) administered both an oral and written form of the test to 40 sixth graders and 40 tenth graders in a counterbalanced design. Although the oral form is easiest, the written form was found to be satisfactory, even for the younger subjects in this study. Holt (1980) administered a shortened, 12-item WU-SCT to a large sample of 16- to 26-year-olds. He reports that the short form could substitute effectively for the long form in research projects. Given the growing body of data on the reliability, validity, and versatility of this test over the past decade, the WU-SCT continues to have great potential as both a clinical and a research instrument.

The WU-SCT also has evidenced its utility in studies related to intellectual development. Hirsch (1979) administered the WU-SCT to 93 fifth- and sixth-graders and found their level of ego development to be significantly related to peer ratings of honesty and intellectual functioning. The relationship between intellectual development and level of ego development was also the focus of a study by Sheridan (1978). In his study of 50 educable mentally retarded (Mean IQ = 66) adolescents, the Kohlberg Test of Moral Reasoning and the WU-SCT successfully discriminated between those individuals who were most and least likely to succeed in employment.

Loevinger has repeatedly suggested that her hierarchy is conceptually distinct from the concept of psychological adjustment; however, she has speculated that "there may be differences in the kind of pathology or present symptom characteristic for different ego levels" (Loevinger & Wessler, 1970, p. 427). Gold (1980) designed a study to assess the relationship between Loevinger's hierarchy of ego development stages and symptom patterns as measured by the Minnesota Multiphasic Personality Inventory. A total of 250 high-school students between the ages of 14 and 15, 125 boys and girls, served as subjects. Gold hypothesized that certain symptom patterns were more prevalent at certain points of the ego development hierarchy than at others. The existence of all but one of these parallels was supported by the data. These results clearly indicate a greater degree of maladjustment among preconformists than those at other levels of ego development. A similar study by Adams and Shea (1979) investigated the relationship between stages of identity status and ego development. The Marcia (1966) Ego-Identity Status Interview was administered to 294 college students. Identity-achievement students (more advanced than those with low achievement) were found to be more advanced in their ego stage development and their level of internal locus of control.

SUMMARY

Both story- and sentence-completion techniques remain useful and valuable tools in the clinician's armamentum. Although research using the former is rare, the economy and flexibility of the latter have continued to attract researchers in a wide variety of settings. In summary, completion methods are valuable instruments in the assessment of personality.

REFERENCES

Adams, G. R., & Shea, J. A. (1979). The relationship between identity status, locus of control, and ego development. *Journal of Youth and Adolescence, 8*(1), 81-89.

Anderson, H. H., & Anderson, G. L. (1954). Children's perception of social conflict situations: A study of adolescent children in Germany. *American Journal of Orthopsychiatry, 24,* 246-257.

Anderson, H. H., & Anderson, G. L. (1961). Image of the teacher by adolescent children in seven countries. *American Journal of Orthopsychiatry, 31,* 481-492.

Beardslee, B. J. (1960a). Mechanisms of defense II: Denial of failure. In D. R. Miller & G. E. Swanson (Eds.), *Inner conflict and defense* (pp. 213-230). New York: Holt.

Beardslee, B. J. (1960b). Mechanisms of defense IV: Aggression and the second family of defenses. In D. R. Miller & G. E. Swanson (Eds.), *Inner conflict and defense* (pp. 256-271). New York: Holt.

Bell, J. E. (1948). *Projective techniques.* New York: Longmans, Green.

Benton, A. L., Windle, C. D., & Erdice, E. A. (1957). *A review of sentence completion techniques.* (Project NR 151-175.) Washington, DC: Office of Naval Research.

Cromwell, R. L., & Lundy, R. M. (1954). Productivity of clinical hypotheses on a sentence completion test. *Journal of Consulting Psychology, 18,* 421-424.

Derichs, Von G. (1977). Satzerganzungsvergahren als instrument des intake. *Prax Kinder, 26,* 142-148.

Despert, J. L. (1946). Psychosomatic study of fifty stuttering children. *American Journal of Orthopsychiatry, 16,* 100-113.

Despert, J. L. (1949). Dreams in children of preschool age. *Psychoanalytic Study of the Child, 3*(4), 141-180.

Duss, L. (1940). La methode des fables en psychanalyse. *Archives Psychologie, 28,* 1-51.

Ebbinghaus, H. (1897). Uber eine neue methode in prufung geisiger fahigkeiten und ihre anwendung bei schulkindern. *Zeitschrift fur Psychologie und Physiologie des Sinnsorganen, 13,* 401-457.

Engel, M. (1958). The development and application of the Children's Insight Test. *Journal of Projective Techniques, 22,* 13-25.

Engel, M., & Rechenberg, W. (1961). Studies in the reliability of the Children's Insight Test. *Journal of Projective Techniques, 25,* 158-163.

Forer, B. R. (1950). A structured sentence completion test. *Journal of Projective Techniques, 14,* 15-30.

Forer, B. R. (1960). Word association and sentence completion methods. In A. I. Rabin & M. R. Haworth (Eds.), *Projective techniques with children* (pp. 210-224). New York: Grune & Stratton.

Frank, L. K. (1939). Toward a projective psychology. *Journal of Projective Techniques, 24,* 246-253.

Frank, L. K. (1948). *Projective methods.* Springfield, IL: Charles C Thomas.

Gold, S. N. (1980). Relations between level of ego development and adjustment patterns in adolescents. *Journal of Personality Development, 44*(6), 630–638.

Goldberg, P. A. (1965). A review of sentence completion methods in personality assessment. *Journal of Projective Techniques and Personality Assessment, 29,* 12–45.

Hartshorne, H., & May, M. A. (1928). *Studies in the nature of character* (Vol. 1). *Studies in deceit.* New York: Macmillan.

Hauser, S. T. (1976). Loevinger's model and measure of ego development: A critical review. *Psychological Bulletin, 83*(5), 928–955.

Hirsch, R. (1979). Some correlates of ego development in children: An application of Loevinger's ego development measure. (Doctoral Dissertation, University of Maryland, 1979.) *Dissertation Abstracts International, 40*(5-A), 2534A.

Holt, R. R. (1980). Loevinger's measure of ego development: Reliability and national norms for male and female short forms. *Journal of Personality and Social Psychology, 39*(5), 909–920.

Jourard, S. M. (1969). The effects of experimenter's self-disclosure on subject's behavior. In C. D. Spielberger (Ed.), *Current topics in clinical and community psychology* (Vol. 1) (pp. 109–150). New York: Academic Press.

Kelley, T. J. (1917). Individual testing with completion test exercises. *Teacher's College Records, 18,* 371–382.

Kovac, T. (1979). Newer methodological approaches to children's creativity. *Studia Psychologica, 21*(4), 300–307.

Lanyon, B. J. (1972). Empirical construction and validation of a sentence completion test for hostility, anxiety and dependency. *Journal of Consulting and Clinical Psychology, 39*(3), 420–428.

Loevinger, J., & Blasi, A. (1976). *Ego development.* San Francisco: Jossey-Bass.

Loevinger, J., & Wessler, R. (1970). *Measuring ego development* (Vol. 1.). *Construction of a sentence completion test.* San Francisco: Jossey-Bass.

Loevinger, J., Wessler, R., & Redmore, C. (1970). *Measuring ego development* (Vol. 2). *Scoring manual for women and girls.* San Francisco: Jossey-Bass.

Lorr, M., & Manning, T. (1978). Measurement of ego development by sentence completion and personality test. *Journal of Clinical Psychology, 34*(2), 354–360.

Marcia, J. E. (1966). Development and validation of ego identity status. *Journal of Personality and Social Psychology, 3,* 551–558.

Mar'i, S. H., & Levi, A. M. (1979). Modernization or minority status: The coping style of Israel's Arabs. *Journal of Cross Cultural Psychology, 10*(3), 375–389.

Martin, J., & Redmore, C. (1978). A longitudinal study of ego development. *Developmental Psychology, 14*(2), 189–190.

McCammon, E. P. (1981). Comparison of oral and written forms of the sentence completion test for ego development. *Developmental Psychology, 17*(2), 233–235.

Meltzoff, J. (1951). The effect of mental set and item structure upon response to a projective test. *Journal of Abnormal and Social Psychology, 46,* 177–189.

Miller, D. R. , & Swanson, G. E. (1960). *Inner conflict and defense.* New York: Holt.

Mills, E. S. (1953). The Madeline Thomas completion stories test. *Journal of Consulting Psychology, 17,* 139–141.

Mosse, H. L. (1954). The Duess Test. *American Journal of Psychotherapy, 8,* 251–264.

Payne, A. F. (1928). *Sentence completion.* New York: New York Guidance Clinics.

Piaget, J. (1932). *The moral judgment of the child.* New York: Harcourt, Brace.

Piexotto, H. E. (1956). Reliability on the Despert fables, a story completion projective test for children. *Journal of Clinical Psychology, 12,* 75–78.

Piexotto, H. E. (1957). Popular responses for the Despert fables. *Journal of Clinical Psychology, 13,* 73–79.

Rabin, A. I. (1965). *Growing up in the kibbutz.* New York: Springer.

Rabin, A. I. (1977). Enduring sentiments: The continuity of personality over time. *Journal of Personality Assessment, 41*(6), 564–572.

Rabin, A. I., & Zlotogorski, Z. (1981). Completion methods, word association, sentence and story completion. In A. I. Rabin (Ed.), *Assessment with projective techniques: A concise introduction* (pp. 121–150). New York: Springer.

Rabinowitz, A., & Shouval, R. (1977). Fantasy as a medium for the reduction of trait versus state aggression. *Journal of Research in Personality, 11,* 180–190.

Redmore, C. D., & Waldman, K. (1975). Reliability of a sentence completion measure of ego development. *Journal of Personality Assessment, 39,* 236–243.

Rhode, A. R. (1957). *The sentence completion method: Its diagnostic and clinical application to mental disorders.* New York: Ronald Press.

Rotter, J. B. (1951). Word association and sentence completion methods. In H. H. Anderson & G. L. Anderson (Eds.), *An introduction to projective techniques* (pp. 279–311). New York: Prentice-Hall.

Rotter, J. B., & Rafferty, J. E. (1950). *Manual: The Rotter Incomplete Sentence Blank.* New York: Psychological Corporation.

Sacks, J. M., & Levy, S. (1959). The sentence completion test. In L. E. Abt & L. Bellak (Eds.), *Projective psychology* (pp. 357–402). New York: Knopf.

Sargent, H. D. (1953). *The insight test.* New York: Grune & Stratton.

Shanan, J. (1967). Active coping behavior. *Megamot, 16*(2–3), 188–196.

Shanan, J., Adler, C., & Adler, E. (1975). Coping style and rehabilitation. *Bitachen Sociale, 9*(10), 53–66.

Shanan, J., Kedar, H., Eliakim, M., Oster, C., & Prywes, M. (1970). Psychological tests in the selection of medical students. *Israeli Journal of Medical Science, 6*(1), 132–144.

Shanan, J., Kedar, H., Eliakim, M., Oster, C., & Prywes, M. (1973). *A follow-up study on selection for medical school.* Unpublished manuscript. Hebrew University of Jerusalem.

Shanan, J., & Nissan, S. (1961). Sentence completion as a tool of assessing and studying personality. *Megamot, 11,* 232–252.

Shanan J., & Sharon, M. (1974). *Immigrant student's adjustment to new life conditions during their first year of residence in Israel.* Unpublished manuscript, Hebrew University of Jerusalem.

Sheridan, S. J. (1978, June). Level of moral reasoning and ego development as factors in predicted vocational success with the mentally retarded. *Resources in Education.*

Siipola, E. M. (1968). Incongruence of sentence completions under time pressure and freedom. *Journal of Projective Techniques and Personality Assessment, 24,* 333–340.

Spiva, P. G. (1969). The loser syndrome in juvenile delinquents. *Dissertation Abstracts International, 29*(7-B), 2641.

Stein, M. I. (1949). The record and a sentence completion test. *Journal of Consulting Psychology, 13,* 448–449.

Tendler, A. D. (1930). A preliminary report on a test for emotional insight. *Journal of Applied Psychology, 14,* 123–126.

Thomas, M. (1937). Methode des histoires a completer pour le depiste des complexes et des conflits affectifs enfantins. *Archives Psychologie, 26,* 209–284.

Traube, M. R. (1916). *Completion test language scales.* New York: Columbia University Press.

Wells, F. L. (1954). Foreword. In J. Q. Holsopple & F. R. Miale (Eds.), *Sentence completion.* Springfield, IL: Charles C Thomas.

Wood, F. A. (1969). An investigation of presenting incomplete sentences stimuli. *Journal of Abnormal Psychology, 74,* 71–74.

Wursten, H. (1960). Story completions: Madeline Thomas and similar methods. In A. I. Rabin & M. R. Haworth (Eds.), *Projective techniques with children.* New York: Grune & Stratton.

11
Projective and Clinical Aspects of Intelligence Tests

Martha A. Karson

In this chapter we will discuss the projective and clinical aspects of various sections of intellectual measures used with children. We will look at the projective data from intellectual measures for both diagnostic and therapeutic frameworks. It is important to remember that the behavior exhibited during psychological evaluation is a sampling of behavior observed in day-to-day settings. It is representative of the conflicts, affects, desires, and fears of any person, but is particularly evident in its expression of how children view the world or see their own situation.

All behavior may be interpreted projectively. When involved in clinical assessment both the assessed and the assessor emit many responses that may be interpreted as projections of feeling states, needs, drives, problems, or fantasized solutions. The behaviors that occur in assessment are interesting bases for hypotheses about diagnostic labels or outcomes. Particular responses to a given instrument are added to observed behaviors in developing an emergent, interactive picture of the child's personality. When the child presented for psychological evaluation enters the psychologist's view, the projective evaluation begins. Before the introductions are even completed, one can look at projective hypotheses about the child: How does her gaze meet one's eyes? Does the child seem subdued or active? Is the position of the parent physically coercive or accepting of the child? Does the child speak, and is he audible? Is the separation from the parent at the start of testing easy/too easy/difficult? All of these initial observations form a part of the basis for projective hypotheses that will be derived during the total assessment. The examiner needs to process these data continually as evaluation proceeds.

Previous authors of work concerning the interpretation of psychological test responses have concurred with Sattler (1974), who states that

> the child's apprehension of the test questions, coupled with his answer, involves a complex chain of psychological processes. In fact, it may not be possible ever to state precisely which factor or factors have contributed to successful performances. In addition, a process used by one child to answer a question may not be the same process used by another child to answer the question. (p. 127)

Conceptually, then, the psychological examiner must be attuned to the idiosyncratic nature of a child's responses and attempt to build a coherent picture of the situational and the more permanent behavior and personality structures. The content of responses, the stylistic similarities in responses across subtests or across different measures, and the delivery style of responses all give clues to be interpreted.

Projective evaluation also focuses on behavioral cues as well as the overt verbal responses to testing items. Is the child ambivalent about choosing a place to sit? Does he have difficulty starting a requested task? What is the examiner's experience of the level of anxiety in the child? All of these observations aid the development of a coherent understanding of the child. The behavioral cues seen in the process of assessment are very important clues about the child's defenses, typical strategies for coping, and underlying needs. For example, does the child wait for the adult to initiate all conversation? Does he appear reluctant to initiate responses to test items? Does he give sketchy, quick, and impulsive drawings when such a task is entertained? These are cues frequently associated with passive, anxious, and withdrawn children who may feel uncertain about their position in the world, both in relation to adults and to other children. The same stance also may be observed in a child who always waits for the examiner to turn the Bender stimulus cards, the pages of the WISC–R Picture Completion Book, or to accommodate the change of page on the Stanford-Binet small picture book.

It is hoped that these examples will help the reader to recognize that the notion that all behavior may be projectively evaluated is not an empty one. All of our day-to-day behavior becomes a part of the expression of our underlying personality traits, as well as expressive of conflicts, needs, desires, and defenses. The careful analysis of individual responses, subtest or year-level groupings of responses, and a total protocol must be a part of the projective picture derived in a complete psychological evaluation of any child.

Now let us examine the individual intellectual measures of WISC–R; WPPSI; Stanford-Binet, Form L-M; and Kaufman-ABC. In each of these we will attempt to show some of the evident cues for formulating hypotheses of a projective nature about a diagnostic category.

THE INTELLECTUAL MEASURES: INTRODUCTION

The tests chosen in this chapter as examples of projective analysis of intellectual measures are the WISC-R; WPPSI; Stanford-Binet, Form L-M; and the Kaufman-ABC. Some general statements about all of the measures and the hypotheses derived from the varying forms of analysis seem in order.

As is adequately documented in many sources, including Palmer (1970), Sattler (1974), and Kaufman (1979), the total protocols for intellectual evaluations may be analyzed in a variety of fashions that yield hypotheses not only about learning or intellectual processes but also about emotional states or affects. Faced with a completed protocol, obviously the first task is to score correctly, total the scores, and derive the scaled scores from the protocol. Once this metric kind of exercise is finished, the clinician may proceed to an analysis of profiles of subtest scores or varying ways of looking at strengths and weaknesses within the total protocol (Kaufman, 1979).

Kaufman (1979) addresses the need to individualize interpretations. Using the WISC-R as his bespoken example, he states:

> Individualization demands a flexible examiner, one who is not wedded to a particular approach. . . . With experience, a well-trained examiner will be able to shift from one approach to another to find the best explanations for the observed fluctuations in a child's profile. Experience is also a prime requisite for interpreting children's behaviors during a testing session and for inferring cause–effect relationships between behaviors and test performance. (p. 15)

In this chapter we will concern ourselves with the individual response cues that are given on the various subtests of the chosen instruments and how these individual responses may be analyzed contextually to derive a sense of a child's needs, affects, and "personality pattern."

WECHSLER INTELLIGENCE SCALE FOR CHILDREN—REVISED (WISC-R)

The first instrument to be presented is the WISC-R. This instrument has been subjected to a wide variety of different analyses (e.g., Bannatyne, 1971; Blatt & Allison, 1968; Glasser & Zimmerman, 1967; Holt, 1967;

Kaufman, 1979; Meeker, 1969; Palmer, 1970; and Sattler, 1974). The approaches have been factor analytic, scatter analytic, comparisons of strengths and weaknesses in relation to mean subtest scores, and comparisons among and between subtests. In this section we will attempt to demonstrate the content and nature of specific responses and subtest "wholes" that lend themselves to projective interpretation.

Information Subtest

On the Information subtest of the WISC-R, a common hypothesis regarding learning problems may be derived by checking to see if a child with average overall intellectual functioning shows particular difficulty with knowing the number of days in a week, the number of items in a dozen, the seasons of the year, the direction in which the sun sets, and, at a higher level, the distance from New York to Los Angeles or the number of pounds in a ton. All of these are clues about the child's stability in locating herself in time and space, as well as her capabilities in regard to numerical concepts. It is important, therefore, to look at each subtest to see which items are passed or failed and to discover if any pattern exists among the passes and failures on a particular subtest.

The child who is uncertain about the environment and shows low awareness of relational, number, and physical properties may well be a child who is having ego difficulties. The ego, as the reader knows, serves as the "executive" of the personality, and an important ego function is to organize the world perceptually. Difficulties with such understandings as are contained in the Information subtest, therefore, not only express possible learning disability patterns but also show the child's possible difficulties with ego functions and with appropriate defensive structures.

Another common cue from the Information subtest is that of personalizing a referent. For example, the child who is struggling with some issues regarding superego formation and religious ideation may respond to the question, "In which direction does the sun set?" with a response such as, "Only the Lord knows"; or, when asked who invented the electric lightbulb, might respond, "Jesus Christ." To the question, "Who discovered America?" a response might be "God." The response in and of itself is not indicative of singular psychopathology but is suggestive of some of the areas of conflict with which the child may be dealing. The sensitive clinician is quick to note these areas and make use of them in further evaluation, either in interview or in more directly projective work at some other point in testing.

Other personalized referents on Information may relate to family interaction issues. For example, the child who answers an item such as, "What does the stomach do?" with a response such as, "My mother hasn't told me that yet," may be giving clear cues about the ways in which ideas may be experienced or transmitted between persons or generations. Several responses indicating the child's unwillingness or inability to function without direct parental involvement could demonstrate symbiotic ties or difficulties in separation and individuation.

Picture Completion Subtest

On the Picture Completion subtest, hypotheses regarding isolation and depressive feelings may be derived from the child's fairly common statement, when shown an item containing a suit coat or an umbrella or telephone, that the person is missing from that item. Feelings of low instrumentality or capability in the world may be indicated by a response to the picture of a screw that "the screwdriver is missing" or a response to the telephone item that "this phone won't work; the numbers are wrong." Again, one does not assume disturbances in functioning based on one or two responses. These examples of projective responses are merely ways that one might start developing further hypotheses regarding the feelings, conflicts, or issues facing a particular child at the time of a particular evaluation. All individual responses must be corroborated with additional evidence from other parts of the protocol, from interviews, or from more structured projective testing. Many different patterns may emerge, and the task of the examiner is to utilize all testing data and case history material to achieve the most powerful hunches and hypotheses about the child's functioning.

Similarities Subtest

On the Similarities subtest the presence of highly personalized responses to the items relating to beer and wine, anger and joy, or elbow and knee are not uncommon. The child may be experiencing enough press of the need in certain areas that responses of a highly personalized nature or stories regarding family issues may emerge. These stories are usually fairly obvious and blatant in their content and give rise to clear expression of difficulties at home or problems with significant issues in the environment, such as alcoholism worries, worries about physical abuse, or worries about difficulties in "capping feelings" that may lead to a dangerous position for a child. The danger is in the denial of feeling and the subsequent repression.

The similarities subtest also yields other interpretations. The item "first and last" elicited the following response from a 10-year-old boy: "It's like my family—the same as my brother and me. He's always first and me last." This response indicated an area of inquiry that provided much information usable in the subsequent therapy decisions.

The items "mountain-lake" and "liberty and justice" are frequently good indicators of a child's need for distance from present interpersonal stresses. Responses that show yearning for pleasant times or faraway places frequently emerge to these concepts, particularly because they approach the upper levels of difficulty for many children and therefore elicit more affective rather than "learned response" material.

Picture Arrangement Subtest

The projective applications of Picture Arrangement are evident in various rearrangements of how stories are commonly told. It is always desirable to ask a child to "tell me your story" as she completes a particular item. In this way, the psychologist is able to discover a number of the relevant variables that have determined the child's choice of picture arrangement. From a projective stance these often are interpreted in a highly individualized manner, and asking for the story in a verbal fashion allows the examiner to understand the child's affective tone more completely. For example, on the item "sleeper," a common incorrect arrangement puts the pictures in the order of H, U, R, S. This story arrangement frequently elicits from children stories of family discord. The way in which it is elicited is that the father is seen as comfortable and happy in his work environment, but then angry upon returning home and dealing with his wife. He is also seen as angry when the alarm goes off and as constantly rushed and harrassed as he attempts to return to the more benign environment. This interpretation of events on the part of a child is immediately suggestive of what some of the interpersonal stresses may be in the child's family situation.

Family conflict is also frequently interpreted from item 10, "gardener"; asking the child to tell a story about the arrangement S, M, R, W, O again elicits feelings of stress in the adult marital relationship. In this instance of correct sequence, the most common story told is of happiness and pleasure while alone fishing, returning happily to his house to tiptoe by the work laid out for him by the woman, and finally digging the hole to plant the flower as requested. But the notion most heavily emphasized is the happiness when being separate or isolated and the difficulties when adults are attempting to interact.

Both of these examples also give clear information about the feelings toward mothers by the fathers. While the structure of the stimulus cards is overtly sexist, the information from the child will show how issues of "female nagging, direction giving, or control" are dealt with in a child's experience.

The critical variable in utilizing the Picture Arrangement subtest projectively is to understand the child's unique construction of events. In projective work it is not the cognitions but the underlying affects and needs that determine the response, and we are looking for ways to understand more clearly the idiosyncratic construction of the child's personality.

Therefore, if a child is involved in the Picture Arrangement subtest, it is always desirable to ask the child to tell the story back to the psychologist as the child understands and sees it. This kind of completion technique allows the psychologist access to a good deal of intrapsychic as well as interpersonal data.

Arithmetic Subtest

The Arithmetic subtest on the WISC–R is a common area in which one might see anxiety expressed about school performance or school achievement. It is not unusual in this culture for children at a fairly early age to develop some feelings of inadequacy regarding their mathematical academic skills. Female children in particular show some difficulties with anxiety on this subtest at a fairly early age, and talking with them about particular items that make them anxious is often helpful in determining what areas need to be addressed interpersonally.

The issue of personal referents or appealing to outside influences can be seen in a child's response to an item not known, with such comments as, "We don't do that until third grade," "My teacher hasn't shown us how to do those yet," or "I could ask my brother." Children who have to use outside sources or potential targets of blame for their difficulties may be showing us the problems they experience with not being all-knowing or omnipotent. A child needs to come to grips with a view of himself as less than perfection but still a good person and, when that view has formed, also to be able to see others as less than perfect but still able to be helpful and to function well in the world.

Glasser and Zimmerman (1967) summarize the interpretations of the WISC (1949) for the Arithmetic subtest, and there seems little reason to not pursue the same hypotheses for the WISC–R (1967). They state that "the authority dominated child who is eager to please may do quite well while the resistant child who refuses to even try may do very poorly" (Wechsler, 1974, p. 59). They further suggest that high scores may indicate a teacher-oriented student, or the subtest may be subject to vacillation because of transient emotional reactions. The transient emotional variation is also supported by Kaufman's (1979) work on the third factor, showing Arithmetic to be a subtest quickly affected by difficulties in attentional variables or by anxiety in the testing situation.

Block Design Subtest

On the Block Design subtests of the WISC–R and WPPSI, less projective information is immediately evident from examining the items. There are, however, interesting kinds of data to be obtained from discovering which items lead to error. Fairly consistent difficulties with oblique angles, not directly accountable for by other perceptual deviations, are often representative of phallic concerns or difficulties with positive feelings of being effective within the environment. While this hypothesis may seem farfetched at times, the reader is encouraged to think of psychodynamic interpretations surrounding both Bender figures and the Block Design as similar. It is evident from clinical work that children feeling particularly vulnerable and noneffective in their interpersonal world will have distinct difficulty being effectual at the completion of the Block Design subtest.

The ability to analyze the requirements of the Block Design card and then synthesize the blocks both perceptually and motorically to reproduce the stimulus show us much about the smoothness of the child's cognitive and affective functioning. Severe childhood psychopathology may be seen on this subtest when verbal associations are offered. For example, the child who uses the Block Design card in the same fashion as the Rorschach stimulus may offer associations such as, "This looks like an arrow about to pierce somebody" or "This looks like an island all alone in the middle of a big ocean."

Vulnerability or loss of effective defenses may be posited from difficulties on the Block Design subtest, and it is important to entertain the projective use of the data obtained on the Block Design task in order to see how such projective inferences compare with other sources of information.

It is also important to note on all of the timed subtests, most notably Block Design and Picture Arrangement or Picture Completion from the WISC–R, that the child's expression of anxiety about timing of the subtests needs to be taken into account as part of the defensive structure or part of the underlying issues. Children who are very anxious about timing frequently spoil designs or become so involved in the timing by the examiner that they are unable to be successful at completion of the task. Children who greatly distort their sense of the timing on these subtests also may be showing difficulty with reality testing. Cues to such difficulties are a child's statement, "That took forever" or "I bet no one is as fast as I am."

Behavior exhibited during the completion of the Block Design task is also important. The child who aimlessly pushes the blocks around and then looks appealingly at the examiner may be expressing the feeling that adults always will finish an assigned task for a child. The continual spinning of the blocks may be indicative of anxiety in the child, while quick acceptance of a noncorrect design as a completion may reveal a nonreflective child who has difficulty self-correcting an assigned task, either as an expression of anxiety and low self-esteem or as a typical response to the demand of authority.

Children's verbal behavior during this subtest is also revealing. Self-derogation in such forms as, "I never can do these things" or "My brother is much better at this than me" are fairly commonly observed manifestations pointing to lower self-esteem, dependency on others for completion of tasks, or secondary gain from placing others in more powerful, knowledgeable positions.

Vocabulary Subtest

The Vocabulary items from the major intellectual measures are obviously a good source of projective data. They come to represent completion items or associative responses that move more closely to underlying processes in a child's personality. The ways in which we construct our verbal reality are related closely to our needs and drives, and the verbatim recording of a child's Vocabulary response often will give us many clues about areas of conflict or difficulty in a child's life. The length of the response as well as the content of the response generally are regarded as important. A child displaying obsessive and ruminating kinds of tendencies often will give long circumlocutions before arriving at the central defining words.

In addition, direct information often is given about difficulties while the subtest is being administered. For example, a seven-year-old child confided to the psychologist as a definition of "alphabet" that his parents were very upset with him because he did not know all his letters. Frequently the important part of Vocabulary items is to use them as stimulus words that allow the psychologist not only to determine the cognitive content of the child's verbal capabilities but also to use that stimulus word as an associative technique that then will elicit much underlying material. In another example, an eight-year-old girl responded to "gamble" by saying, "It's trying to win money off others—it's like betting that you're better than others"; to "thief" with, "It's like how my father came and took all the furniture when my mother and I were away and she said he was a thief"; and to "prevent" with, "It's like being able to stop something. I wish I could stop my father from leaving us." She obviously had associated to the Vocabulary items her major current concerns about the dissolution of her parents' marriage and her worries about her fate in the separation and divorce. This kind of example clearly gives the psychologist much more information than the breadth and depth of the child's vocabulary.

Vocabulary items also will reveal neologisms or unusual constructions or definitions that sometimes are seen in seriously disturbed youngsters.

From the interpretive stance, vocabulary items should be examined to discover the structure or character of the language. Children who have significant difficulty with reality testing often will have idiosyncratic uses of words or unusual combinations that have personalized referents or meanings. Examples from the WISC–R are seen in responses to items such as "nonsense" ("What my mother says I am filled with"), "gamble" ("What my father shouldn't do"), "nuisance" ("What I am in school"), "seclude" ("When I have to spend the whole day in my room") or "join" ("The other kids never ask me").

The vocabulary items show cultural advantage and disadvantage, give a fairly revealing picture of the child's self-view, and often show us much about the child's experience of the home environment. Vocabulary items also reveal much about the seriously disturbed child when the child responds to the stimulus word by giving slang associations, running together of syllables incoherently, or perseverating in the same definition for a number of words.

Object Assembly Subtest

The Object Assembly subtest is one with high intrinsic interest for most children. Emotional issues may be pulled out by the presence of the mutilated figures or car. These may relate to idiosyncratic responses for children. However, it also screens for the ability to use concrete reality in the production of a correct response. Therefore, the child who is somewhat action oriented and who enjoys hands-on tasks will give evidence of pleasure in this task, and the kind of concrete reality that is used by a child successful in Object Assembly will be differentiated readily from the concrete behavior of the neurologically impaired child who may place the pieces in a trial-and-error arrangement with no recognition of the gestalt they are attempting to achieve.

Physically impaired children's approach to Object Assembly items as either a gestalt or as a series of fragmented pieces is also an important determinant of how the child organizes her own view of the world and her own perception of her body in relation to the world. The difficulties in Object Assembly may show up as inability to complete a particular puzzle or inability to orient parts of the puzzle correctly, which may relate to the area of physical impairment for the child. This kind of sign often may be used as corroborating evidence for the same difficulty in a construction task such as Draw-a-Man or the Kinetic Family Drawing.

An approach to Object Assembly that is not successful and is chaotic in completion may represent both the child's neurological and affective state. For example, a seizure-disordered boy of nine could not connect his immediate perception that he needed to "build a car" with the actions to complete the puzzle. He tried for nearly the whole allotted time, then said to the examiner, "I know it's supposed to be a car, but I can't make it come out right." He became visibly depressed and was unable to be successful in any items for the rest of the testing session. He subsequently returned for completion of the evaluation and still remembered the car item and wished to "try it again." The examiner obliged, and he again experienced frustration and inability to complete the item. The comments he offered about his difficulties with the neurological issues and how these difficulties made him feel led us to a diagnostic and treatment plan that emphasized ways to help him circumvent such situations in the classroom and at home by rewarding the good learning behavior seen perceptually but not demanding the perceptual–motor completion of things like puzzles, designs, or mazes. Counseling that focused on the positive things he could do also diminished the lowered self-esteem and the obsessive return to situations in which he was unable to be successful.

As with all projective material, it is important to utilize several sources in order to forward a formal hypothesis about the child's affective functioning, and it is particularly important that the multiple corroboration of projective findings be pursued when children have frank physical impairments as well as internal ego problems or defensive lacks.

Comprehension Subtest

The Comprehension subtest on the WISC–R is a very fruitful place to search for signs of developing moral and social awareness and also to look for difficulties in personality processes that might lead us to suggest characterological problems with children. For example, the child who responds to the question, "What is the thing to do if a boy (girl) much smaller than yourself tries to start a fight with you?" with an answer such as "Beat up on her," "Clean his clock," or "Fight but don't get caught" is probably a child who does not understand the social contract regarding fair fighting and size. It also is indicative of problems in the development of a moral code.

Other items that need to be analyzed in relation to characterological problems are the questions, "What are some reasons why we need policemen?" "What are you supposed to do if you find someone's wallet or pocketbook in a store?" and "Why are criminals locked up?"

Responses to the Comprehension subtest not only tap the characterological or social and moral development of the child but also indicate the practical capability available to the child. Knowledge gained from daily social experience must be put together with formal educational variables to yield plans for action. Therefore, the approach adopted in solving these daily social problems frequently reflects the themes of personality that are of concern to the child. Glasser and Zimmerman (1967), in relation to the WISC, point out the themes of guilt and punishment, exploitation, disobedience, acting out, and preoccupation with dependency or victimization. All of these appear to be equally applicable to the WISC–R subtest.

In the interpretation of the Comprehension subtest it is well to keep in mind that the referent group for the moral code on these subtests is heavily loaded in the direction of middle-class expectations, and the scoring system does not allow the inclusion of other social variables in judging the appropriateness of the child's response. All of these intellectual measures are clearly culturally laden. One needs to determine the unique configuration of the child's personality and world and on the basis of such a determination offer projective hypotheses about moral development, conscience, or superego. When we are comparing the child's response to an "unexplicitly stated norm," it is important to remember that such comparisons reflect our own values and cannot be deemed "culture-free."

Coding Subtest

Coding from the WISC–R is used projectively as a possible measure of anxiety interference. Since functioning in this area commonly is disrupted by the presence of high anxiety, the presence of difficulties or low scores on any one of the items offers further credence to a possibility of internally held anxious response. It should be remembered that the Coding subtest makes relatively little contribution to the measurement of general intelligence; however, as Kaufman (1979) points out, Coding is a measure of learning ability related to copying tasks. It is therefore easy to see how compliance to demand may affect the capability the child demonstrates on Coding. A high score also is viewed as a capability to accept and internalize social standards (Glasser & Zimmerman, 1967). More pathological responses are interpreted from skipping squares, rubbing the model figures with a finger, associating verbal cues to the visual symbols, or going through the protocol to complete all of one symbol before starting another.

Digit Span Subtest

The Digit Span subtest measures attention and, to some degree, anxiety, but it has low overall yield for interpretive data. This is true primarily because the subtest is vulnerable to temporary disturbances of concentration and attention. One can interpret low scores, however, as indicating the presence of anxiety, and noncompliance to the task may reveal a negativistic or depressive stance.

It is hoped that the myriad of examples cited in this section offer some possibilities for ways that material from intellectual measures such as the WISC-R may be interpreted projectively. All of these interpretations become helpful in the formulation of diagnostic hypotheses regarding a child. They also are useful in relation to planning intervention or treatment programs. It should be noted that the child's projective material frequently gives direct information about the ensuing dilemmas that will arise in treatment. Let us examine two case assessments utilizing the WISC-R as the intellectual measure, to see how projective responses give clues as to the needed direction in treatment or intervention.

Two Case Assessments Using the WISC-R

An eight-year-old girl who was referred for evaluation and possible treatment because of her exceptionally obsessive and phobic behavior surrounding bedtime ritual was seen by the psychologist. The intellectual measure utilized with this girl was the WISC-R, and the responses of note that were seen on many percepts related to fear about her female status. For instance, on the Information subtest, to the item "stomach," she offered the response that it was where babies were made. She missed items with female percepts on Picture Completion, such as the doll in the mirror, the sock on the girl, and the ear on the girl. Her explanation of the way in which the elbow and the knee were alike was that they were both sharp points of the body that could hurt someone else. She saw item 2 on Picture Arrangement as surprise on the part of the woman that the man had forgotten to protect the picnic basket from theft of the "chicken" by the dog. Vocabulary items "thief" and "brave" elicited the information that a thief was someone who "stole into the house to take something away that was very valuable to you" and that "brave" was "some girl who was not afraid to stay alone at night." There were difficulties with the timed completion of the girl item on Object Assembly, and the Comprehension item offering the most projective material was item 7, "In what ways is a house built of brick or stone better than one built of wood?" To this item the girl responded that a house of brick or stone would keep one safer and you would not have to be afraid to stay alone inside it.

Using all of these projective responses as corroborating evidence for the themes as seen on the Roberts Apperception Test and on the Kinetic Family Drawing, the psychologist offered the therapist the interpretation that treatment issues needed to surround the child's fantasized or real experience of inappropriate sexual behavior within her family. It appeared that her extremely ritualized nighttime behavior was designed to ward off the anxiety she felt about sexual material that was either direct behavior or was being stimulated in fantasy. After approximately eight months of therapy focusing on the child's overly close relationship with an older male sibling and her extremely tight relationship with her mother, much of the obsessive and anxious behavior dropped out.

This example is used as a way of pointing up the importance of "fine-tooth combing" a protocol for existing projective patterns and using them as ways of formulating hypotheses about diagnosis as well as about needed treatment. In this instance the dilemmas of treatment were focused clearly in the child's lowered self-esteem about her female status, her concern about sexual behavior, and her obsessive rumination about punishment or guilt for sexual fantasy or sexual behavior. The items were not immediately available upon intake or upon projective evaluation but, with the additional support of these responses from an intellectual measure, an adequate diagnostic formulation and a treatment plan were reached.

Another example that points out the kinds of dilemmas that are evident from examining projective material on an intellectual measure is seen in the following case in which the evaluation utilized both the WISC–R and the Stanford-Binet, Form L-M (Terman & Merrill, 1973).

A boy of 10 was referred for psychological evaluation and possible treatment. At the time of evaluation there were vast discrepancies noted in previous intellectual testing, which had utilized both the Stanford-Binet and the WISC–R. The WISC–R consistently gave lower overall intellectual functioning measures than did the Stanford-Binet. This appeared unusual to the psychologist, for a child of 10; therefore, a new evaluation was indicated. The measure chosen for this evaluation was also the WISC–R, so that the current results could be compared with the past measures.

As the evaluation proceeded, certain items seemed significant: The child showed concern about "secrets," which came out on the Comprehension subtest in relation to the questions, "Why is it important for the government to hire people to inspect meat and meat packing plants?" "Why is it usually better to give money to a well-known charity than to a street beggar?" and "Why is it good to hold elections by secret ballot?" In all of these items he demonstrated a good deal of confusion about who might be entitled to know what information. On the Vocabulary subtest his responses to words such as "prevent," "contagious," "hazardous," and "espionage" all suggested a child with bright intellectual capabilities but one who was extremely concerned about who should know what material. Picture Arrangement also elicited stories about persons needing to keep information from others.

At this point the parents were interviewed because of the continuingly puzzling nature of the boy's responses. During the course of the interview they revealed reluctantly that this boy had been adopted as an infant and had not been informed of his adoption. However, other relatives in the family had offered some hints through the years that his condition of coming to the family might not be the same as the other siblings. As the boy grew older he became more and more concerned about the issue of his origins and more and more convinced, on an affective, feeling level, that there was something unique or different about him. The parents had been unwilling to reveal the story of how he had come into the family, and it was only after much consistent work with them, as well as with the boy, that some willingness to discuss this in a family session was achieved.

This example clearly shows how a long-standing issue in the family came to be expressed in a boy's individual responses on intellectual items that were interpretable projectively. It also set the tenor for the nature and course of therapy in that every new item that came up needed to be discussed in view of the history of "secrets" within both the boy and the family. Eventually this very rigidly held defensive structure loosened, and we began to see far better functioning, both with peers in the school environment and in the family environment.

WECHSLER PRESCHOOL AND PRIMARY SCALE OF INTELLIGENCE (WPPSI)

The WPPSI is published for use with children between the ages of four and six and one half years. It is similar to the WISC in form and content, with separate Verbal and Performance scales. There are three subtests on the WPPSI (Wechsler, 1967) that do *not* appear on the WISC–R, namely, Sentences, Animal House, and Geometric Design, and we will limit our interpretive sections to these subtests. Much less is known, obviously, about the interpretation applications of the three newer subtests. On the subtests that are common to both WISC–R and WPPSI, it is recommended by Sattler (1974) that, with certain reservations, the interpretations applied to the WISC–R subtest with the same name be used with the WPPSI. Interpretations from the three unique subtests will be offered here from clinical practice and observation.

Sentences Subtest

The Sentences subtest (supplementary) from the WPPSI appears to be primarily a memory test. The interpretation as well as the scoring require considerable skill, including careful transcription of responses. Interpretations of a clinical nature may be gleaned from both the length of the sentence that the child repeats as well as a close analysis of the missed words, transpositions, additions, or substitutions.

At the ages for which the test is standardized it is common for children to offer spontaneous comments about their own lives, stimulated by the context of the sentence they are asked to repeat. For example, "The bad dog ran after the cat" may elicit stories of animals at home and tales of how these animals are treated. Such information emerges in the less personalized context of animal discussion but may well be a comment about how people treat each other in the family. "Peter would like to have new boots and a cowboy suit" may give clues not only about current economic status but also about the way resources are allocated in a family. The dynamic theme possibilities are evident, including guilt and retribution, delay of gratification, obsessive trends, and possible stories about family relationships.

Animal House Subtest

The Animal House subtest and Animal House retest are considered to measure memory, attention span, goal awareness, concentration, and finger and manual dexterity (Sattler, 1974, p. 225). Children frequently personalize the referents on the Animal House subtest, giving names to the stimuli from their own experience. It also happens that children seem to hesitate or take more time with the figures representing particular areas of concern. This subtest also gives an indication of anxiety about performance when children recognize that they are being timed. This is particularly true for the child of school age (five to six and one half), who has become more aware of the demands of the world outside his home. Motivational factors and willingness to meet the expectations of adults are also interpretable from this subtest.

As with all projective interpretation, the examiner must take care to find multiple examples of support for hypotheses and must remember that all individual interpretations must be viewed within the total context of the administration, scoring, and interpretation of the entire intellectual measure.

The readministration of Animal House at the end of testing allows one to assess the amount of short-term learning that has occurred. Of clinical interest in the Animal House retest is the determination of where errors occur in the sequence and whether or not the elements of timing and adult pressure for compliance elicit the same responses from the child. A highly anxious child, for example, frequently will show the same level of disorganization on the retest when pressured to "see how much faster you can do it now."

Geometric Design Subtest

The Geometric Design subtest is considered to measure perceptual and visual–motor abilities. The interpretations possible on this subtest relate to the behavior of the child while completing the task and to the design drawn. The behavior appears to give the most projective information: Does she look to the adult for support about drawings? Does there appear to be resistance to the task, expressed either actively as "I don't want to do that" or passively as "I can't do it very well" followed by a waiting, noninvolved stance on the part of the child? In all drawing tasks, the behavior becomes the most evident projective information, and the interpretation of the behavior between the child and examiner gives the most clues about the underlying needs and affects.

Geometric Design is reported by Sattler (1974) to be the most difficult of all WPPSI subtests to score. An experienced examiner will utilize all the systems available from such sources as Koppitz (1963, 1975) to aid in the scoring and interpretation of the intellectual and projective material.

THE STANFORD-BINET, FORM L-M

The Stanford-Binet, Form L-M is widely used in clinical settings, though not as much as the WISC–R. In examining the strengths and weaknesses of the measure for clinical assessment purposes, it is useful to consult Sattler (1974) regarding the characteristics of the scale. He notes that, by ordering the data into a classification scheme that he devised, one may determine the following areas as diagnostic: language, memory, conceptual thinking, reasoning, numerical reasoning, visual–motor ability, and social intelligence. Each item from the Stanford-Binet at a given year level then may be classified. The projective implications of such a scheme are evident: A check may be made of when the data for a particular child shows strength or weakness that allows the examiner to pursue projective hypotheses.

To utilize an evident example, look at these responses that fall within Sattler's (1974) designation of social intelligence on the Stanford-Binet. They include "obeying simple commands," "response to pictures," "comprehension I," "comprehension II," "aesthetic comparison," "materials," "comprehension III," "picture absurdities," "comprehension IV," "naming days of week," "finding reasons," and "problem situations." Looking at an individual child's responses within this framework allows the examiner to pursue projective material from the intellectual measure in a systematic fashion. The use of such a systematic approach offers the possibility of a greater utility for the Stanford-Binet in the personality area than was previously easily available.

The Stanford-Binet, then, is useful in personality assessment in all three of the ways that Blatt and Allison (1981) point out in their work with the projective hypothesis and intelligence tests: (1) for examining the content of responses to the intellectual measure, (2) for exploring the style of responses or the quality and nature of the clinical transaction, and (3) for analyzing the structure or organization of psychological functions as indicated in the patterning of diverse abilities.

There are some drawbacks to the use of the Stanford-Binet that must be considered in making projective hypotheses. It has been noted extensively that Form L-M is too heavily weighted with verbal materials. The child who has difficulty in the verbal functions, or most particularly the verbal abstract functions, will offer scanty material for interpretation under the rubric of content; and the examiner will need to rely more heavily on the nature of the clinical transaction in order to draw interpretive material.

The Stanford-Binet also is criticized as not measuring originality and creative abilities. This objection is less serious to the projective clinician in that measuring originality is not a goal; instead, the clinician wishes to assess its presence and examine the content of responses without concern for whether these responses pass or fail as part of the I.Q. measure.

Let's look at some other areas and examples of interpretation from the Stanford-Binet. Under the category of numerical reasoning, a number of hypotheses about anxiety can be derived. As the mathematical portions of the test are administered, the examiner may see dramatic shifts in the level of anxiety for the child. Defensive styles also are elicited easily by the mathematical questions. The child may offer excuses for herself such as, "I'm not old enough," "My mother/father/teacher hasn't shown me how to do that yet," or "I bet no one else can do that either, huh?"

The pattern of successes is also important in mathematical operations on the Binet. It is important to observe the content, the "how" of an operation, and the outcome patterns, most particularly in evaluations concerned with a child showing learning problems or learning disability. In Counting on the Stanford-Binet, the examiner checks to see if the child has developed one-to-one correspondence, or the capability to associate one number counted aloud with one representative of the stimulus. This finding is interesting projectively in determining the establishment of object constancy. Does the child show capability of moving from the concrete representation of problems through fingers or blocks to a more abstract verbally mediated level of problem solving? And, are there particular operations with which the child has consistent difficulty? All of these clues are projective in nature and give some kind of direction to one's thinking about the issue of diagnostic outcome.

Anxiety as well as the capability for preplanning are seen in the Mazes,

Completion of Man, and the Plan of Search items from the Stanford-Binet. These are more clearly visually mediated indicators of capability to preplan and capability to bind anxiety by using one's visual and motor skills. It is important to observe how these tasks are completed, not only in relation to hypotheses about anxiety, but also in relation to hypotheses about possible learning disability problems.

Characterological signs from items on the Stanford-Binet are also important projective material. These diagnostic cues emerge from Finding Reasons, Abstract Words, and Comprehension III and IV. Answers to questions such as "Give two reasons why children should obey their parents" or "What do we mean by (revenge, conquer, obedience, curiosity, grief, etc.)" all yield important information regarding a child's concept of herself in relation to the social norms.

Such information is both developmental in a stage sense and informative in a projective sense. For instance, the query, "What is the thing to do if another boy/girl hits you without meaning to do it?" tells us not only about the child's ability to control aggressive impulses but also about the presence or development of a moral code that takes into account intent of the other as well as the severity of the infraction against the prevailing ethic.

A final caution about characterological signs: Before deciding on the basis of Comprehension items *only* that characterological issues exist, it is important to remember that these responses are affected by degree of urbanization of the child's environment, the subcultural heritage of the child, and the socioeconomic level of the child's family. There are many situations in which the "commonly accepted ethic" is neither functional nor ego syntonic. In these cases careful evaluation of all aspects of the child's protocol as well as environment needs to be pursued.

Ongoing family conflicts also are elicited frequently by the opportunity to define vocabulary words or abstract words. For example, a common response to "straw" often centers around the story of "The Three Little Pigs." When any questioning is done about straw in relation to "The Three Little Pigs," children who are feeling that their home environment is particularly tenuous or shaky often will give associations that clearly indicate that. For example, one child told the psychologist that "Our house is made of straw or sand and I don't know which will go first." Elaboration indicated the child's concept of the tenuous nature of the parents' marriage and her direct concern that one or the other parent was going to leave the environment fairly quickly. In this response the definition of the word straw served as a shorthand route to a major emotional conflict active in the child's life.

In particular cases, the items Mutilated Pictures or Completion of Man are interpretable in relation to a child's current life situation or major stressing event. For example, a six-year-old girl with severe motor limitations as a result of cerebral palsy responded to the wagon item in Mutilated Pictures by saying, "This wagon can't go, it's just like me." The self-concept of this child was of her handicapping condition as more important than her "personhood." This became the major focus of treatment, the goal of which was to help her see herself first as a person, then secondarily as a person with a handicapping condition that was an impediment to some of her functioning but not a determinant of her self-worth.

The Mutilated Pictures also are frequent representations of body difficulty as transferred to a physical object in the environment. Children with anomalous appearance often may offer associations to the Mutilated Pictures suggesting how they see their handicapping condition in relation to the world. Not only will the anomalous-appearing child or the one with a frank handicap offer responses available to interpretation, but many times normal-looking children will give verbal responses to Mutilated Pictures or associations to the Completion of Man task suggesting that these also represent their self-concept or view of ego capabilities in relation to the world at large.

Case Assessment Using the Stanford-Binet

A girl of seven and one half years was referred by her parents for psychological evaluation. The presenting concerns were excessive daydreaming, general unhappiness, and problems with accepting the arrival of a new baby sister, even though "she had been looking forward to having a little brother or sister."

She was evaluated for school problems and possible need for psychotherapy, using drawings, the Stanford-Binet, an achievement measure, and a structured play session. Projective material from the Stanford-Binet emerged in Naming the Days of the Week, Memory for Stories, and Comprehension IV. The specific responses were: (1) she was unable to recall all the days of the week, systematically omitting the weekend days when she was home with the family; (2) in Memory for Stories, she had a complete blanking of responses to questions, even though she demonstrated excellent reading skill when asked to read the passage aloud; (3) on Comprehension IV, to "What should you do if you found on the streets a three-year-old baby that was lost from its parents?" she responded that the baby should "be left there, because the parents probably know right where he is." She seemed to take sadistic pleasure in describing the child's discomfiture at its situation. Further, she could generate many fearsome things that "probably" would befall the baby. These responses gave numerous clues about the nature of the child's difficulties in the present. However, as with all projective material, it needed separate corroboration. This was amply forthcoming in her drawings and the doll play.

Approximately 15 sessions of treatment helped the girl to cope more adequately with her daydreaming and unhappiness. She played out her anger, rejection, and displacement fantasies most vociferously and subsequently was able to adopt a more sublimated and less disturbed and disturbing mode of functioning within the family and school setting.

Conclusions

It should be mentioned at this point that the interpretive stance of the examiner must always separate observable behavior, about which one offers interpretations, from the specific content or response to a test item. The behavioral cues represent specific clues that are part of the matrix of diagnostic understanding. However, the truly "projective" part of the evaluation is derived from the responses that fit into what is the typical stance of the personality. Responses are projective not only in the psychopathological sense but also in the attributive or autistic sense. As Rabin (1981) points out, in projective testing the broader term "externalization" is more appropriate, helping us to avoid thinking of the projective responses in only the psychopathological sense and allowing the examiner to "ferret out trends of the whole range of defense mechanisms from projective test data, including the defense mechanisms of projection itself" (Rabin, 1981, p. 10).

THE KAUFMAN ASSESSMENT BATTERY FOR CHILDREN (K-ABC)

Kaufman and Kaufman (1983) have presented, in their K-ABC, a new measure for child assessment that bears clinical promise. Both test behavior and content of performance on the 16 subtests give promise of yielding valuable projective information from the intellectual measure. The interpretive manual for the K-ABC offers a psychological analysis for each of the 16 subtests. At the present time, most of the observations are in the realm of "clinically valuable behavior," rather than interpretations of the content of responses. As the test is used in more settings, individual content of responses will gain more face validity and become at least consensually validated.

The major areas of intellectual–affective performance from which interpretations may be drawn are impulsivity and distractibility, noted in the subtests Magic Window, Face Recognition, Number Recall, Word

Order, Matrix Analogies, Spatial Memory, Photo Series, and Arithmetic. The effects of acculturation or richness of the early environment are seen in subtests of Expressive Vocabulary, Faces and Places, Riddles, Reading/Decoding, and Reading/Understanding. In all of these culturally loaded subtests, performance may be hindered by shy, inhibited behavior or reticence to try out a response. Kaufman and Kaufman (1983) attempt to sort out anxiety from the impulsive distractible dimension of behavior. Anxiety is more clearly seen in the subtests Word Order, Spatial Memory, Arithmetic, Number Recall, and Triangles. The presence of flexibility in thinking style is imputed by good performance on Triangles, Word Order, Matrix Analogies, and Riddles. Finally, the child who is capable of systematic planning or development of strategies will do well on Photo Series, Spatial Memory, Matrix Analogies, Word Order, Triangles, Hand Movements, and Face Recognition.

A desirable additional feature of the K-ABC is the possibility of comparing responses and scores on a given subtest with the related ones on the WISC–R or WPPSI. This measure is usable with children between 2½ and 12½ years and is designed to include novel tasks, to be relatively easy to administer and score, to produce findings that can be translated to educational intervention, and to be sensitive to the needs of exceptional and minority-group children. The authors' overall goal has been to provide a psychometric measure with clinical richness. Particularly rich in projective material are the subtests Gestalt Closure, Face Recognition, Photo Series, and Riddles. Gestalt Closure functions much like an ink-blot stimulus, and the responses lend themselves readily to clinical interpretation. The authors suggest the use of clinically productive subtests in a second Testing the Limits administration and the combing of such responses for projective material.

As more experience with the K-ABC is gained, it is evident that more hypotheses about underlying dynamics of an individual child may be offered from specific content of responses as well as from the style the protocol evinces. A present, more global analysis of the total subtest will give way to a more complex idiographic and nomothetic analysis.

SUMMARY

This chapter has attempted to show some of the ways in which projective material may be derived successfully from standard measures of intellectual functioning. The measures we have discussed most extensively—the WISC–R , WPPSI, Stanford-Binet, and K-ABC—are the most commonly used intellectual measures in the United States. Persons performing psychological assessments are generally familiar with these test measures, and it should appear evident that there are many possibilities for interpretation, not only of total test protocols, but also of individual responses, in order to arrive at coherent hypotheses regarding affective or intrapsychic functioning. Clinical observations of behavior also provide important clues to the diagnostic picture. We also have tried to show by example what some of the more common "different" responses might be and how these responses can be utilized by drawing corroborating evidence from a variety of sources in order to formulate diagnostic statements. The clinician is encouraged to use all sources of data in a projective as well as a psychometric analysis. It is important that psychologists be sensitive to the clues offered by children in a few responses and that they then find ways to generalize hypotheses about the nature of these responses that allow them to gain further insight into the child's functioning. As we said at the beginning of this chapter, all behavior may be interpreted projectively. It is important that the sensitive examiner view the content of individual responses, the totality of the subtest or year-level patterns, and the context of all behavior during evaluation. By such careful use of data, we should be better able to serve the best interests of the children we evaluate.

REFERENCES

Bannatyne, A. (1971). *Language, reading, and learning disabilities.* Springfield, IL: Charles C. Thomas.

Blatt, S. J., & Allison, J. (1968). The intelligence test in personality testing. In A. I. Rabin (Ed.), *Projective Techniques in Personality Assessment* (pp. 421–460). New York: Springer.

Blatt, S. J., & Allison, J. (1981). The intelligence test in personality assessment. In A. I. Rabin (Ed.), *Assessment with projective techniques* (pp. 187–232). New York: Springer.

Fromm, E. (1960). Projective aspects of intelligence testing. In A. I. Rabin & M. Haworth (Eds.), *Projective techniques with children* (pp. 225–237). New York: Grune & Stratton.

Glasser, A., & Zimmerman, I. (1967). *Clinical interpretation of the Wechsler Intelligence Scale for Children.* New York: Grune & Stratton.

Holt, R. R. (1967). Diagnostic testing: Present status and future prospects. *Journal of Nervous and Mental Disease, 144,* 444–465.

Kaufman, A. (1979). *Intelligent testing with the WISC-R.* New York: John Wiley.

Kaufman, A., & Kaufman, N. (1983). *Kaufman Assessment Battery for Children.* Circle Pines, MN: American Guidance Service.

Koppitz, E. M. (1963). *The Bender gestalt test for young children* (Vol. 2). New York: Grune & Stratton.

Koppitz, E. M. (1975). *The Bender gestalt test for young children* (Vol. 2) (2nd ed.). New York: Grune & Stratton.

Meeker, M. N. (1969). *The structure of intellect.* Columbus, OH: Charles E. Merrill.

Palmer, J. O. (1970). *The psychological assessment of children.* New York: John Wiley.

Rabin, A. I. (1981). Projective methods: A historical introduction. In A. I. Rabin (Ed.), *Assessment with projective techniques* (pp. 1–22). New York: Springer.

Sattler, J. (1974). *Assessment of children's intelligence.* Philadelphia: W. B. Saunders.

Terman, L., & Merrill, M. (1973). *Manual for the third revision of the Stanford-Binet Intelligence Scale.* Geneva, IL: Houghton-Mifflin.

Wechsler, D. (1967). *Manual for the Wechsler Preschool and Primary Scale of Intelligence.* New York: The Psychological Corporation.

Wechsler, D. (1974). *Manual for the Wechsler Intelligence Scale for Children—Revised.* New York: The Psychological Corporation.

V
Other
Methods

12
Graphic Techniques with Children and Adolescents*

Emanuel F. Hammer

Numerous clinicians have stated the projective-expressive principle: Rorschach through inkblots; Murray, regarding stories made up to pictures (TAT); Machover, involving drawing a person of each sex; and Buck, through drawing a house, a tree, and a person. It was neither a psychologist nor a psychiatrist, however, but a novelist who stated this psychological truth more broadly, who captured the universal: "Every man's work, whether it be literature or music or pictures or architecture, or anything else, is always a portrait of himself, and the more he tries to conceal himself, the more clearly will his character appear in spite of him" (Butler).

It was also a novelist who sensed the relatively purer authenticity of projection via drawings—a subsemantic channel—over the verbal techniques. Among the notable women of French letters still among us, Nathalie Sarraute has devoted her career to underscoring the understanding that feelings are altered by being passed through the filter of language. In her recent book *Childhood*, Mme. Sarraute (1984) looks back to her early years, from the vantage point of having entered her eighties, and has this to say about the effects of language on the tentativeness of feeling: "Scarcely does this formless thing, all timid and trembling, try to show its face than all powerful language, always ready to intervene so as

*Portions of this chapter appeared originally in E. F. Hammer, Acting out and its prediction by projective drawing assessment, in L. Abt and S. Weissman (Eds.), *Acting Out: Theoretical and Clinical Aspects* (pp. 288–319). New York: Grune & Stratton, 1965. Used with permission.

239

to re-establish order—its own order—jumps on it and crushes it." Elsewhere, during a panel discussion, she extended her comments: "There is always a kind of drying out produced by language."

Life was before language. The pictorial, drawing on a process that preceded language, retains more of the juice of feelings. And so children and adolescents relate more to, put more of themselves into, graphic than verbal projective techniques. Words are more distant abstractions than are pictures. The child tends naturally to order his experiences visually. When one observes the drawings of children, one sees things that they would never have been able to express in words, even if they had been fully conscious of some of the feelings that toss or distress them. Similarly, some patients have real difficulties communicating their dreams. "I could draw it," the dreamer frequently says, "but I don't know how to say it."

There is another aspect to projective drawings about which the creative artist can inform us. As Vincent van Gogh observed, "Real artists paint things not as they are, but as they feel them." So, too, do two other groups: children and, second only to them, adolescents. From the research vantage point, it is, interestingly, just those two groups, children and youths, who, when serving as subjects for studies, yield more positive validating results for projective drawing hypotheses than do the studies employing adult subjects (see Koppitz, 1966; Springer, 1941; Vande & Eisen, 1962).

THE GRAPHIC TECHNIQUES' ADVANTAGES

This writer has found that children with emotional difficulties can be led more easily from drawing to verbal expression. Drawings also serve as a means of more easily establishing rapport and as good "ice breakers" with the shy or negative child. The drawing task allows uncomfortable subjects to exclude the examiner, in a relative sense, during the initial phase of getting used to the new surroundings and to the stranger on the other side of the desk.

Both children and primitive people consistently draw elements that they consider essential and drop out others that do not concern them. They then include aspects that are known to be there but are not visible. The goal, thus, of both children and primitive people is not "objective realism" but what Luquet (1913) calls "mental realism."

Projective drawings, basically a nonverbal technique, have the obvious advantage of greater relative applicability not only to young children but to the more poorly educated child, the mentally defective child, the non-

English-speaking child, the mute, the painfully shy or withdrawn child, the child with a predominantly concrete orientation, and the child from a relatively barren and underprivileged sociocultural background who frequently is wracked by feelings of inadequacy concerning his capacity for verbal expression. Furthermore, we may add to this list the case of the child referred for a psychological evaluation because of remedial reading problems. Children with reading difficulties often show compensatory adeptness in artistic ability to make articulate their emotional and social problems and needs.

PROJECTIVE ASPECTS OF DRAWINGS

At first, drawings were employed by clinicians as a form of intelligence scale based mainly on the number of details put into the drawings. Soon, however, it became apparent that the drawings were tapping personality factors in addition to intellectual capabilities. In fact, emotional factors *even more* than intellectual ones constantly were pressing into view. In quantitative analysis, in crediting a drawing for the inclusion of a hand, the same score was given for a balled-up, clenched fist as for a delicate and open hand in a feminine gesture patting the cheek, and so important qualitative clues to the functioning of the total personality were being ignored. The subject was granted identical quantitative credit whether he drew his person with the arms crossed defiantly over the chest, hanging flexibly at the sides, or placed timidly behind the back, but the fact that these several arm positions had vastly different affective implications was not taken into account, and much valuable diagnostic material was overlooked. Similarly, the large range of facial expressions and the size and placement of the object on the page seemed to offer more information about nonintellectual components than about intellectual capabilities.

ADMINISTRATION OF A DRAWING TEST

In Buck's H-T-P technique (Buck, 1948), a no. 2 pencil and a sheet of paper are handed the subject. His drawing of a house is requested, with the longer axis of the sheet placed horizontally before the subject. His drawings of a tree and person, in turn, are then obtained on separate sheets of paper, with the longer axis placed vertically. The subject is asked to draw as well as he can, but he is not told what kind of house, tree, and person to draw. Recently I have begun to ask the subject to imagine he is that house, or that tree, or that person, and to speak for it.

If the subject protests that he is not an artist, he is assured that the H-T-P is not a test of artistic ability at all but that we are interested, rather, in how he does things. Any questions he asks are reflected back to him in such a way as to indicate that there is no right or wrong method of proceeding but that he may do the drawing in any manner he wishes.

After he draws the person, the subject is handed another sheet of paper and this time told to draw a person of the sex opposite to that of the first person drawn. In addition, the subject may be asked to draw the most unpleasant thing he can think of, or to draw a person in the rain, the latter tapping the sense of self when in stress situations. Then the drawings of a house, a tree, and a person of each sex are repeated, this time in crayon. With children, we occasionally may also ask for a drawing of an animal and the drawing of a family (Hammer, 1980).

Burns (1982) has modified the Draw-a-Family by adding an action—or, as he terms it, a kinetic—dimension. The instructions to the subject are simple: "Draw everyone in your family doing something." The results, however, are often rich and dramatic, bringing forth, for instance, a child's panic in response to an alcoholic father, feelings of isolation in a rejecting family, or massive withdrawal from threatening others in the household. Aspects elicited regarding self and family interactions are those of intimacy or distance, emotional tone in setting, and feelings of who is closest to whom. Are family members interacting or touching, or are they isolated from each other? Which member is facing which other member? Are certain family members, or the self-figure, using one or another activity to show off, or hide, or lure, or gain protection from a parent or sibling? Which family member is dominant and which secondary? Which are happy, sad, suffering, bored, cruel, rigid, detached, enraged, subservient, or trusting? Are members of the family comfortable or strained with each other, and what are their messages toward each other?

To elicit further cues to "reading" a subject's family drawing, Burns (1982) suggests the clinician ask himself (and I would add that we ask the subject), What if the drawing came to life? What would be happening? Who would go, who would stay? Who would nurture? Who would hate? Who would love? What feelings are flowing from the father, or mother, or siblings, or self?

THE GRAPHIC PROJECTION:
HOW IT ALL WORKS

In terms of expressive aspects, children's movements have diagnostic potential whether they are gross (as in the play therapy room) or confined (as on the drawing page). A child may withdraw into a corner of the room or sit on the edge of the chair, as though he were ready to run away; if he is given a big sheet of paper, he may follow suit by drawing cautiously in one corner of the page only. At the other extreme, a child may sit at a table as though he wished to occupy the whole space, showing no consideration for the other children there. No paper is big enough for him either, and his drawings expand beyond the drawing sheet. Projective drawings thus "capture" and record expressive movements on paper.

Whereas the aggressive child draws big, dangerous arms with long fingers, the inadequate or withdrawn child forgets to draw hands at all, as though the subject had not experienced helping hands when he needed them, or as if hands were guilty things that may be used to do something that is labeled as taboo in our culture.

As a reflection of their virility strivings, adolescent males frequently draw soldiers or cowboys as symbols of status attained through the use of force and aggression. Adolescent females project themselves as shapely in gowns or in bathing suits, or carrying flowers (the latter particularly in prepuberty), with femininity and/or attractiveness emphasized.

With adolescents, drawings assume the character of an overemphasized, exaggerated portrait of strength or importance. Within the normal range, adolescents tend to draw themselves as more forceful, more glamorous, bigger, or older than they actually are—a depiction indicative of their own wishes about themselves. They put into the picture a promise of that reality which they desire.

ACTING OUT: A MAJOR PROBLEM FOR PROJECTIVE EVALUATION

Perhaps the most pressing among the perplexities with which adolescents present us are questions of whether or not they act out and, if they do, in what manner they will do it.

The prediction of imminent aggressive acts—of assaultiveness, homicidal potential, suicidal risk, rape—is the most practical of all the challenges with which the diagnostician is ever confronted. It is here that we face issues of life and death, the problems of urgency and immediacy. It is here we wrestle with the most awesome of decisions, involving either depriving a person of his or her liberty (and recommending hospitalization) or risking the clinical judgment that he or she will not seriously harm others or self.

In the discussion that follows we will see that *clues* to acting out are at times available in projective drawing, to be picked up, if only tentatively and speculatively, if one is sensitized to such subtleties.

Direct Acting Out on Paper

To start with the grosser and less subtle indications brought out in drawings, let us consider instances of acting out *directly* on the drawing page itself.

An adolescent boy, referred because of excessive truancy, the flouting of rules in school, and generally rebellious behavior, reflected his characteristic role in life in his drawing of a person as presented in Figure 12-1. The drawn male is dressed in a soldier's outfit as a reflection of the subject's need for greater status and recognition as a male than he feels he possesses. The drawn person turns his back on the world, much as the subject himself has done, and introduces a regulation into the picture merely to break it. His adding the sign, "No Spitting," just so that the drawn person may disobey it, clearly parallels the subject's seeking out rules and regulations merely to break them, to prove to himself and others that they do not apply to him, that he is outside the sphere that authority encompasses, that he is bigger and better than the rules and the people who make them.

For his drawing of a female, he offers us Figure 12.2, a female whose face is smeared and debased. He describes her as "A young girl, flat as a board, trying out her new nonsmear lipstick and it smears." Here again we note that he directly acts out his anger on the drawn page, besmirching the figure's face in an aggressive laying on of the crayon. (We note, also, that he amputates one of her hands where it should attach to the wrist.)

When we get to the Unpleasant Concept test (the subject is asked to draw the most unpleasant thing he can think of) we note that he once again acts out—and this time all the more directly—his need to debase and vent his acute rage (see Figure 12.3). Where subjects popularly offer the concept of war, disease, or death, this subject instead draws a man with a ludicrously elongated nose, a huge penis hanging out of his open pants, and then stabs him with a long sword running through his body. He then adds the tag, "Dad."

In clinical practice, we generally may assume that a subject who acts out this violently on paper—and particularly when this acting out reaches such inappropriate extremes—also would be prone to act out the same needs to depreciate others, to search out rules and regulations to break, and to release his accumulated anger at the immediate world around him.

Figure 12.4 represents another case of intense and multiple statements of a theme, mounting up to suggest the likelihood of his theme bubbling over into acting out. This figure was drawn by an adolescent boy who happened to be one of a group of subjects studied in an effort to get a normative population from a local high school.

FIGURE 12.1   A "person" by an adolescent boy.

The expansion of the shoulders into exaggerated, sharply pointed, aggressive corners, the knife in the hand, the gun carried in the belt, the rough clothing and cap, the piercing eye, the sharp nose, and the mustache pulled down into a depiction of walrus tusks more than soft hair all add up to a reflection of an individual who is drastically motivated to prove himself aggressive, dangerous, and prone to violence. The fact that the feet are particularly out-sized and the shoes taken off suggests the primitiveness of his impulses, the subject apparently having shed considerations of social restraint and more sublimated behavior. When we add

FIGURE 12.2   Boy's drawing of a female.

the fact that the entire figure seems to be pulled off balance by the aggressively pointed shoulder, we get a picture of an individual who suffers from a feeling of emotional instability that may be triggered quite easily into aggressive behavior. At the same time, the absence of the crotch area and the two breastlike pockets convey his deeper doubts about masculinity that lie beneath the compensatory aggressivity.

After seeing so graphic a rendition of a compensatory and hostile theme, the writer consulted the school records and found that this youngster was indeed known to act out, having gotten into trouble for numerous fights in school, once having thrown a blackboard eraser through a closed school window, and recently having mugged a fellow student for money in the school bathroom.

Let us turn next to an example provided in the drawing of a tree, shown in Figure 12.5, that was offered by a 12-year-old boy who had been referred because he had been observed picking up baby pigs with the prongs of a pitchfork, throwing down baby chicks and crushing them under the heel of his shoe, and at one time setting fire to a bale of hay underneath a cow. On top of this, he recently had released a tractor to roll down a hill onto some children. (Fortunately, the children dodged the vehicle in time.)

His drawn tree speaks as eloquently as does his behavior. It is a graphic communication saying in distinct and unequivocal language, "Keep away from me!" Spearlike branches with thornlike "leaves" decorate a

FIGURE 12.3 Boy draws "Dad" in response to instructions to draw the "most unpleasant thing."

FIGURE 12.4   Drawing of a man by another adolescent boy.

sharply pointed tree trunk. The branches reach out aggressively in a promise of inflicting significant harm to all those who come within reach. The drawing is steeped in sadism, aggression, and angry resentment.

   Similarly, the drawing of a house in the House-Tree-Person (H-T-P) technique also may catch clues to potential acting out. One 12-year-old boy (see Figure 12.6) heralded his eventual running away from home by drawing a house in which a child was escaping through the top window, while a lower window was depicted as slammed down on the mother's neck, pinning her there. In spite of the family's beginning to involve itself in therapy at that point, four months thereafter the youngster actually did run away from home, and it was not until a couple of days later that he was found asleep in a park.

At times the implications for acting out may be gotten more from the strained efforts at control than from the direct depiction of the impulses themselves. Figure 12.7 was offered by a 15-year-old youth who was brought to the clinic because, according to his mother, he had threatened to kill her. The initial question that raised itself in our minds was of a differential diagnosis between vocalization on the part of an adolescent who merely wanted to get his mother off his back versus an actual homicidal potential.

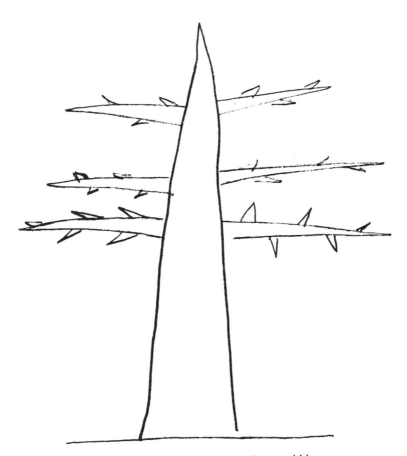

FIGURE 12.5 A "tree" by a 12-year-old boy.

FIGURE 12.6 A "house" by another 12-year-old boy.

The projective drawings administered at the time to the youngster provided rather vivid evidence on the side of the actual possibility of serious capacity for violence pressing forward in him. The strained facial expression, the exaggerated attempts to maintain control over bodily impulses, and the head pulling tensely to the side with the eyes reflecting acute inner strain and efforts at control are all brought to focus by the hands, which are presented almost as if to carry the suggestion of being manacled together to provide external controls against his lashing out in angry fury. To experience the actual kinesthetic feeling, the reader has only to reproduce the entire body position and twisted pull of the head on the neck, along with the facial expression, to feel in one's own musculature the struggle between control versus intense aggression within. Such a kinesthetic verification of the visual data also may convey a feeling of the immediacy of this potential eruption.

FIGURE 12.7 Drawing of a 15-year-old male.

The fact that his drawn tree (not shown) was presented as conspicuously off balance adds all the more to the personality picture of a youngster who felt his equilibrium was very much in jeopardy and who was shaky in maintaining defenses against his volcanic internal violence.

Following the emergence of this tension-flooded picture, the boy was referred to a mental hospital for more detailed observation. The impression of his therapist there later supported the implication that this was indeed a youngster who carried the active seeds of matricide.

The next case is also an example of overemphasized control showing up in the drawings and providing the clues to potential acting out in overt behavior. Figure 12.8 was drawn by an exhibitionist. The hand is drawn tucked in under a belt that anchors it and keeps it from moving to engage in forbidden acts, perhaps of exposing himself. This reveals a strong conflict between impulse and control. In addition, when external controls have to be resorted to (such as strapping the hand down), we

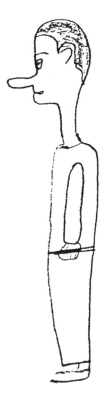

FIGURE 12.8   An exhibitionist's drawing.

may presume that internal controls are insufficient and the likelihood of acting out is all the more probable. This is supported by the fact that, while he draws the person with hands pinned, at the same time the person does engage in the exhibitionism of the extremely long, phallic-shaped nose; thus the impulses circumvent the efforts at control.

In all of the cases presented in this section, we may see that the stronger, the more frank, the more raw and unsublimated the expression of impulses that break through in the projective drawings, the more the defensive and adaptive operations of the ego may be presumed to be insufficient in their assimilative function and the greater the likelihood of acting-out behavior in everyday life.

SEQUENCE

By analyzing drawing test data in terms of the sequential emergence of drive derivatives, defense, and adaptation, we may witness dynamic and economic shifts. By examining a sample of ongoing drawing processes, we have an opportunity to study, in slow motion as it were, the structural features of conflict and defense.

In the microcosm of the interaction between a subject and the drawing page we have observed, for example, one subject give tiny shoulders to his drawn person, then erase them, and finally endow the drawn person with compensatory, overly-broad shoulders. This subject then looked at his drawing in a perplexed fashion, as if some automatic phenomena had taken over and he couldn't understand how this process got away from him. He commented, "I guess the shoulders expanded a little too much," as if "it" rather than he had done it. From this we may postulate that the subject's first reaction to a new situation is one of inferiority feelings which he then quickly attempts to cover up with a façade of capability and adequacy, which, however, he overdoes to the point of compensatory acting out that breaks away from him.

To illustrate the attempts at rigid control, punctuated by short erupting interludes, the following excerpt from the psychological report on a rather representative case is cited: In reproducing the Bender-Gestalt figures, the subject started out by making them noticeably small, but ended with the last two figures growing excessively large; this would tend to reflect strong needs at constrictive control over emotional impulses which, however, cannot remain successful for a prolonged time without cracking and allowing an impulsive release of uncontrolled affect and/or behavior.

Sequential analysis of the set of drawings may provide clues to the amount of drive or energy of the subject, and it also may provide data that allow an appraisal of the subject's control over this drive. Does the subject, for instance, break down under the emotionally tinged associations that are presumably aroused by the different drawing concepts, or is he able to handle himself well in these spheres? Does energy maintain itself, peter out, or erupt? Progressive psychomotor decrease, as he proceeds from one drawing to the next, suggests high fatigability. Progressive psychomotor increase suggests excessive stimulability and potential for acting out. A modulated, sustained energy level reflects more healthy personality integration.

Frequently subjects are somewhat disturbed initially but soon become calm and work efficiently as they proceed from the first to the last drawing. This is presumably simply "situational anxiety" and is not indicative of anything more serious.

PRESSURE

Pressure of pencil on paper, like size, has been found to be an indication of the subject's energy level (Hammer, 1980; Hetherington, 1952; Napoli, 1946). In regard to reliability, it was found by Hetherington (1952) that subjects are rather remarkably constant in their pressure.

Alschuler and Hattwick (1947) reported that children who drew with heavy strokes were usually more assertive and/or overtly aggressive than other children. Consistent with this, Pfister, as reported in Anastasi and Foley (1940), found that psychopaths, among the most troublesome of those who act out, characteristically employ heavy pressure.

One youth, examined by the present writer at a reformatory, drew his house, tree, and person with so fierce a digging at the paper that his pencil actually tore through the paper at various points along the line drawn. Several months later he stabbed a fellow inmate in a dispute over a card game, with a "knife" he had fashioned from a spoon.

STROKE

Alschuler and Hattwick (1947) found that children who drew with long strokes stood out for their controlled behavior, whereas children who worked with short strokes showed more impulsive behavior. Mira (1943) also writes that in general, the length of movement of a stroke tends to increase in inhibited subjects and decrease in excitable ones.

Krout (1950) found that straight lines were associated with aggressive moods and jagged lines (which incidentally appeared as the symbol of the most aggressive unit in Hitler's army) were associated with hostility, usually overt and acted out.

DETAILING

Children (or adults) who have the feeling that the world around them is uncertain, unpredictable, and/or dangerous tend to seek to defend themselves against inner or outer chaos by creating an excessively detailed, rigidly ordered, highly structured world. The drawings of these subjects will be very exact. These people tend to create rigid, repetitious elements in their drawings. There is nothing flowing or relaxed in the lines, the drawings, or in their presentation. Everything is put together by force, as though they feel that without this pressure everything would fall apart.

Too perfect a drawing performance, executed with unusual, exacting control and care, is offered by patients who range from obsessive-compulsive to incipient schizophrenics or early organics. But whatever the diagnosis, the "too-perfect" performance reflects the effort of these patients to hold themselves together against the threat of imminent disorganization. It is a direct manifestation of their hypervigilance and implies the presence of a relatively weak ego, so afraid of acting out a breakthrough of forbidden impulses that it dares not relax its constant vigilance.

The most frequent emotional accompaniment of the excessive detailing of one's drawing is a feeling of rigidity. Stiffly drawn trees or animals parallel the same quality in the drawn person. In this regard, the latter may be presented as standing rigidly at attention, with body and head very erect, legs pressed closely together, and arms straight and held close to the body. The kinesthetic emphasis in these projections is on the erect posture and on the rigid tension with which the posture is held, keeping impulses in. These drawing performances often express a most unfree— and hence uncertain but rigidly controlled—defensive attitude. This is the characteristic drawing performance of people to whom spontaneous release of emotions is an acute threat. Impulses, when they are released, are not smoothly integrated but tend toward the eruptive and uncontrolled.

SYMMETRY

Symmetry has long been regarded as one of the most elemental Gestalt principles. It is not surprising, therefore, that drawings that display an obvious lack of symmetry have been found to indicate equivalent feelings of personality imbalance, diminished integration, and hence increased chances of acting out.

PLACEMENT

In regard to placement on the horizontal axis of the page, Buck (1948) hypothesizes that the farther the midpoint of the drawing is to the right of the midpoint of the page, the more likely is the subject to exhibit stable, controlled behavior, to be willing to delay satisfaction of needs and drives, to prefer intellectual satisfactions to more emotional ones. Conversely, the further the midpoint of the drawing is to the left of the midpoint of the page, the greater is the likelihood that the subject tends to behave impulsively; to seek immediate, frank, and emotional satisfaction of his needs and drives; and to act out. Koch (1952), on the basis of his projective drawing work on the Tree Test in Switzerland, identifies the right side of the page with inhibition, which is consistent with Buck's concept suggesting control. Wolff (1946) found that subjects who were attracted to the right side of the page in their drawings showed introversion, while those attracted to the left side of the page showed extroversion. These findings also are consistent with Buck (1948), in that introversion is associated with the capacity to delay satisfaction, while extroversion is linked to the seeking of more immediate gratifications.

DISSOCIATION

Suggestions of dissociation, which are offered by incongruities between the graphic drawing and the verbal description of it, are perhaps the most pathognomonic of the clues to acting-out tendencies. This can be conveyed best by the following example.

A 17-year-old white male was referred to the clinic because he had been arrested for involvement in fights on the beach on several occasions and charged with felonious assault during racial riots. He had been transferred from high school to high school because of inability to relate to the black population in school. He was referred to the clinic with the idea of appraising his potential assaultiveness.

The essential problem for which we were asked to appraise this youth, namely his dangerousness, gained focus as we examined his performance as he moved through the projective drawing figures. He drew his first person, a female, as an extremely puny figure and then commented that it was "pretty skinny." He had left the top of the head out, and it came through that this was so that he could delay choosing whether to make it a male or female. He decided to refer the question to the examiner and asked, "It doesn't matter, does it, whether I make it a male or female, does it?. . . Which shall it be?" When this question was referred back to the patient, he elected to make it a female and added a curlicue of hair and earrings below. He then commented, "Holy Sweat, it looks like it went through the mill!" Here, in addition to the feeling of debasement, we note that he chose the neuter gender by which to refer to the figure.

The feelings of insufficiency, puniness, unimpressiveness, and confusion about psychosexual identification that came through in the first person drawing then were handled in an aggressive, compensatory maneuver in the following person drawing, shown in Figure 12.9. He emphasized the shoulder muscles and then opened the person's mouth wide in a sort of savage roar, where facial muscles strain, the arms go out to intensify the energy he is expelling, and the teeth are bared. To add to the aggressive quality, he then made the nose quite sharp. The demonstrative efforts to convey himself as angry, noteworthy, and certainly someone to be reckoned with were somewhat denied by the subtleties of the figure being empty, and thus without substance or the power he attempted to convey, and the fact that one arm appeared as if grafted at the elbow. Thus we get an image that is essentially empty and attempts to play a role of aggressive savagery and anger.

In regard to the question concerning his potential aggressiveness, the important quality that came through was not so much the aggressiveness

FIGURE 12.9 A "person" drawn by a 17-year-old male.

of his character armor but rather the *dissociated* aspects of this aggression. This dissociated ingredient was discerned when he described the drawn figure. When asked what the figure was doing, the subject commented, "Just standing there." This could not be dismissed as mere evasiveness, for the young man was frank, even vividly expressive, in his graphic communication. It was as if his consciousness did not recognize the clearly angry quality that came through around the edges of his awareness.

When we moved on to a consideration of his drawn tree, we found a sharp and somewhat unintegrated branch structure existed in among the foliage. In fact, this sharp, pointed branch was not blended with the tree but rather appeared to be a thing apart. Once more we got the feeling that aggressive qualities could be dissociated in him and surge outward, away from his control.

In summary, then, the uncertain quality conveyed in the first person drawing gave way to the compensatory masculine posturing of the second. This posturing was reinforced by anger to make it all the more impressive. But this rage, in turn, was handled by dissociation, unfortunately making it all the more dangerous and prone to being acted out.

Sometimes the clues to a state of dissociation of hostile impulses will come through within the drawing itself, without involving a disharmony between the drawing and its verbal description. Figure 12.10, with its massive, highly aggressive, mechanical-looking hands, attached as mere appendages at the end of the arms, illustrates this type of projection. The quality of automation, particularly in the area of the aggressive urges, suggests that these impulses are acted out automatically and without adequate integration with the personality.

CHROMATIC DRAWINGS

Color is perhaps the most dramatic of the variables to be analyzed in a drawing. Color is introduced into the projective-drawing task by asking the subject for a new set of drawings, this time in crayon. It has long been established that color symbolizes emotion, so its inclusion adds an additional affective element. The many experiments establishing this are too numerous to mention here, so an abbreviated sample will have to suffice. This would include Alschuler and Hattwick, 1947; Anastasi and Foley, 1943; Bieber and Herkines, 1948; Brick, 1944; Fox, 1952; Hammer, 1953, 1980; and Kadis, 1950.

Common parlance supports the experimental data. We speak of someone as being "red with rage"; we associate "yellow" with cowardice and fear; "blue" means depression; someone is "green with envy"; and a

FIGURE 12.10   A case of dissociation of hostile impulses.

person is "colorful" if he is in various ways freer than most in expressing unique personality ingredients and thus is generally at the opposite pole from the emotionally subdued or constricted personality, called "colorless."

Color stimulates people, as every fine-arts painter and advertising expert well knows. Asking a patient to draw in colored crayon moves us closer to being able to sample reactions to, and tolerance for, emotional situations—the very same situations in which acting out, if it is to be released, is apt to be triggered.

Moreover, the chromatic series of drawings is designed to supplement the achromatic series, to take advantage of the fact that two samples of behavior are always better than one. But the chromatic series is more than just a second sample, because the subject who produces it, I believe, must be in a somewhat more vulnerable state than he was when he produced his achromatic drawings. Even for the most well-adjusted subject, the achromatic series of drawings and the subsequent inquiry are an emotional experience, for many memories—pleasant and unpleasant—are aroused.

Thus the chromatic series becomes a behavioral sample that is obtained with the subject at a level of frustration that is different from that which obtained when the achromatic series was sought. If the achromatic series was a welcome catharsis (as it frequently is for the well-adjusted subject), the subject may be far less tense than she was at the beginning. In the average clinical case seen for differential diagnosis, however, this scarcely will be the case. Such a subject almost inevitably will be emotionally aroused enough so that his chromatic series will reveal still more about his basic needs, mechanisms of defense, and the like than the achromatic.

In the achromatic series, the subject is afforded every opportunity to employ corrective measures: He may erase as much as he likes, and the pencil is a relatively refined drawing instrument. In the chromatic drawings, the only corrective measure available is concealment with heavy shading, and the drawing instrument, the crayon, is relatively crude.

Thus, at the beginning, with the subject in relatively fuller possession of his defensive mechanisms, he is given tools that permit expressive defensiveness; in the second phase, by which time the subject will be more likely to have lost at least part of his defensive control (if he is going to lose it at all), he is provided with a grosser instrument and with an opportunity to express symbolically (through his choice and use of color) the emotions, the controls, and the lack of controls that have been aroused by the achromatic series and postdrawing interrogation.

Thus, when aggression is *relatively* more mildly conveyed in the achromatic rendition, as in Figure 12.11, but later is presented in frank and unvarnished fashion in the chromatic expression, as shown in Figure 12.12, our experience has been that such subjects can more or less get by

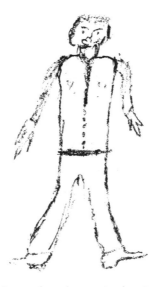

FIGURE 12.11 Adolescent's achromatic drawing of a person, done in pencil (compare with Figure 12.12).

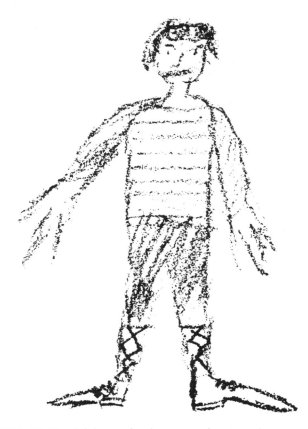

FIGURE 12.12 Adolescent's chromatic drawing of a person, done in crayon (compare with Figure 12.11).

in ordinary relations but tend to erupt into violence in emotionally charged situations.* Let us now examine the particulars of these two drawings.

*The patient had been charged with sexual assault, following a necking and petting session with a girl he had met at a dance and was now taking home. As he tried to advance to slipping his hand under her blouse, the girl objected; he, in an excited state, drew a knife and threatened her. The Probation Officer's report described the incident as follows: "He asked her to open her blouse, and she refused again. At this point the defendant ripped open her blouse with his hand. With the knife he cut her brassiere in the middle and fondled her breast. He made her bend down and he put his finger in her vagina. During the whole episode he made threats, and at one point banged the complainant's head against the side of the building. This knocked her down. He pulled her up, and wanted to open his zipper." At this point the victim was able to break away and run to safety.

As we follow this particular subject from his achromatic to his chromatic person drawing, we observe the heightening of many effects. The facial expression becomes more menacing; the hands become so large that they are elongated, pointed, spearlike entities that fairly shriek "hostility." The shoes turn into sort of Army-boot affairs that go up to almost the knees in conveying a feeling of brutality. All in all, the body image gives way to the pressing forward of a chromatic depiction of a monster. His raw feelings of aggression and rage are similarly apt to come charging forward in emotional situations.

CORROBORATING INFORMATION

A word of caution should be given here. The examples given in this chapter were presented as illustrations, as samples only. In actual clinical practice, the dangers of basing interpretive deductions on isolated bits of data are obvious. In practice, confirmation of interpretive speculation on the basis of one drawing must be checked against not only the other drawings but the entire projective battery, the case history, the clinical impression gleaned during the interview with the subject, and all other available information.

SUMMARY

Clues, then, to the possibility of acting out may be reflected in projective drawings by strong, open, and unsublimated expression of impulses breaking through to flood the drawing page; by too large a size of the drawing so that it presses out against the page's edges as the subject himself will similarly tend to act out against the confines of the environment; by sequential movement from expression of controls to exaggerated expression of impulses (in contrast to the opposite sequence); by pressure and savage digging of the pencil at the paper; by stroke detailing, dyssymmetry, placement, and evidence of dissociation; and by the triggering of the impulses in the chromatic expression.

As to the type of impulses apt to be released in the acted out behavior— whether aggressive, exhibitionistic, suicidal, or otherwise—this can be discerned in the content more than in the structure of the drawings.

The pencil or crayon stroke, at the moment of contact with the paper, thus carries, according to the American artist Robert Henri, the exact state of being of the subject at that time into the work, and there it is, to be seen and read.

REFERENCES

Alschuler, A., & Hattwick, W. (1947). *Painting and personality*. Chicago: University of Chicago Press.

Anastasi, A., & Foley, J. P. (1940). A survey of the literature on artistic behavior in the abnormal. *Psychological Monographs, 52,* 71.

Anastasi, A., & Foley, J. P. (1943). An analysis of spontaneous artistic productions by the abnormal. *Journal of Psychology, 28,* 297–313.

Bieber, I., & Herkimer, J. (1948). Art in psychotherapy. *American Journal of Psychiatry, 104,* 627–631.

Brick, M. (1944). The mental hygiene value of children's art work. *American Journal of Orthopsychiatry, 14,* 136–146.

Buck, J. N. (1948). The H-T-P technique: A quantitative and qualitative scoring manual. *Clinical Psychology Monographs, 5,* 1–120.

Burns, R. (1982). *Self-growth in families: Kinetic family drawings (K-F-D)*. New York: Brunner/Mazel.

Fox, R. (1952). Psychotherapeutics of alcoholism. In G. Bychowski and J. L. Despert (Eds.), *Specialized techniques in psychotherapy*. New York: Basic Books.

Hammer, E. F. (1953). The role of the H-T-P in the prognostic battery. *Journal of Clinical Psychology, 9,* 371–374.

Hammer, E. F. (1980). *The clinical application of projective drawings (5th ed.)*. Springfield, IL: Charles C Thomas.

Hetherington, R. (1952). The effects of E.C.T. on the drawings of depressed patients. *Journal of Mental Science, 98,* 450–453.

Kadis, A. (1950). Finger painting as a projective technique. In L. E. Abt & L. Bellak (Eds.), *Projective Psychology*. New York: Knopf.

Koch, C. (1952). *The tree test*. Berne: Hans Huber.

Koppitz, E. M. (1966). Emotional indicators in human figure drawings of children: A validation study. *Journal of Clinical Psychology, 22,* 313–315.

Krout, J. (1950). Symbol elaboration test. *Psychological Monographs, 4,* 404–405.

Luquet, G. H. (1913). *Les dessins d'un enfant*. Paris: F. Alcan.

Machover, K. (1953). Human figure drawings of children. *Journal of Projective Techniques, 17,* 85–91.

Mira, E. (1943). *Psychiatry in war*. New York: Norton.

Napoli, P. (1946). Fingerpainting and personality diagnosis. *Genetic Psychology Monographs, 34,* 129–231.

Sarraute, N. (1984). *Childhood*. London: John Calder.

Springer, N. N. (1941). A study of the drawings of maladjusted and adjusted children. *Journal of Genetic Psychology, 58,* 131–138.

Vane, J. R., & Eisen, V. W. (1962). The Good-enough Draw-A-Man test and signs of maladjustment in kindergarten children. *Journal of Clinical Psychology, 18,* 276–279.

Wolff, W. (1946). *The personality of the pre-school child*. New York: Grune & Stratton.

13
Projective
Play Techniques

Vita Krall

Play has existed as long as there have been children, and the theories of play have abounded from "pre-exercise" to "mastery" to "recapitulation" to "catharsis" (Piaget, 1962). Most comfortable to me for an understanding of play as we use it today in the diagnostic play situation is an integration of developmental with psychoanalytic theory.

Melanie Klein is the major and greatest proponent of the use of symbolic play of the child "to gain access to and liberate his phantasy" (Klein, 1948, p. 195). Because anxiety interferes with verbal expression, play is used to gain direct access to the child's unconscious (Klein, 1948). Klein's opinion is that the unconscious of the child is peopled by symbols in a way that it is not in adults. On this point she split early from Anna Freud (1947), who thought that the child was so closely related to parental figures that play was more expressive of the experiences of daily life. Anna Freud also criticized play as a form of free association, since the child lacks the purpose of the adult in controlling conscious interferences with associations.

Play may be used to interpret conflict and to bring it within the conscious control of the child. This point of view is a modification of the Anna Freud position, with the added recognition of the often limited verbal expression of children at younger ages, as well as their dependency on parental figures and their strong resistances (defenses).

The diagnostician who uses play as a projective tool to diagnose children's development and pathology may well want to take into account these various theoretical positions. Play is a universal in children, and Erikson (1964) has often been quoted for his description of "play disruption" in childhood as an occurrence that is symptomatic of disturbance. Play has structure and form, content and symbolism, and mirrors graphically—even within a single session—the developmental shifts and variabilities of each child's emotional, perceptual, and intellectual life. The interpretation of the play presented must take into account the age and intellectual level of the child and the vicissitudes of the mother–child relationship and the family environment, in order to interpret the conscious and unconscious symbols.

CHOICE OF MATERIALS

The choice of toys by which to gain access to the child's inner and outer world may vary some with the theoretical orientation, and it also varies, in amount at least, with the play environment that the diagnostician has available. Melanie Klein lists the following: "little wooden men and women, usually in two sizes; cars; wheelbarrows; swings; trains; airplanes; animals; trees; bricks; houses; fences; paper; scissors; a not too sharp knife; pencils; chalks or paints; glue; balls and marbles; plasticine; and string" (Klein, 1964, p. 119). Another pioneer, Virginia Axline (1947) lists "nursing bottles; a doll family; a doll house with house materials, including table, chairs, cot, doll bed, stove, tin dishes, pans, spoons, doll clothes, clothesline, clothespins, and clothes basket; a didee doll; a large rag doll; puppets; a puppet screen; crayons; clay; finger paints; sand; water; toy guns; peg-pounding sets; wooden mallet; paper dolls; little cars; airplanes; a table; an easel; an enamel-top table for finger painting and clay work; toy telephone; shelves; basin; small broom; mop; rags; drawing paper; finger-painting paper; old newspapers; inexpensive cutting paper; pictures of people, houses, animals, and other objects; and empty berry baskets to smash" (p. 56). Checker games and mechanical toys are discouraged.

Esman (1983) recommends "a good stock of paper for drawing and cutting; crayons and marking pens; plasticine or Play-Doh for modeling; blocks of various sizes (small and large) for building; small, flexible family dolls and a few pieces of doll furniture; a few hand puppets for dramatic play; a toy nursing bottle and a doll that can be dressed and undressed; a few cars and trucks; two toy guns; and a soft rubber or plastic ball. For latency age children, boys especially, a checker and chess set . . . and a set of plastic cowboys and Indians" (p. 16–17).

I have felt the need for orienting myself with this plethora of suggestions. Recent research has studied the actual toy preferences of children between the ages of two and twelve and found that the highest ranking toys combining popularity, communication value, fantasy stimulation, and dynamic spread were a doll family, soldiers, a gun, clay, paper and crayons, animals, planes, Nok-Out Bench, and trucks (Beiser, 1976).

My own approach to this problem has been to think of toys from a psychoanalytic framework. I am interested in toys that will elicit the widest array of structural, perceptual, intellectual, and symbolic play in the shortest amount of time. With a psychodynamic framework in mind, the many toys just named that are at times quite repetitive can be classified as follows:

1. Family toys: dolls, dollhouse, people puppets, soldiers.
2. Representational toys: cars, boats, planes, trucks.
3. Expressive toys: paper, paints, crayons, marking pencils.
4. Sensory toys: clay, play dough, plasticine.
5. Structured materials: building blocks, puzzles.
6. Motor toys: balls, ring toss, Nok-Out Bench.
7. Dependency toys (fuzzy toys): animals and puppet animals.
8. Aggressive toys: aggressive animals, Bobo the Clown, gun.

The advantage to the preceding classification is that it can be adapted to whatever space one has available. For the school psychologist who has to travel to a number of schools carrying all of these materials, one can make a selection from each of the categories. For example, take only a small set of dolls (eschew the dollhouse for a toy bed and a couple of chairs); a car or two, matchbox size; some paper and crayons; a stick of plasticine; and an animal, possibly an aggressive animal. An innovative school psychologist told me that if there is more than one session, she asks the child to name something she should bring next week, and this she does. All of these named materials can be carried in a shopping bag, or in a folding dollhouse suitcase such as the one designed by this author some years ago (Krall, 1953).

The next level of space is often the corner of the diagnostician's office. Here a corner is set aside as the play corner, with toys on a shelf, a small table and chairs for painting and crayoning. The diagnostician's desk can be declared off-limits and/or locked, or a screen can be set up to provide a more effective barrier for the play space.

If one has the luxury of a full playroom, then I have found the problem not to be space, but clutter. I know that over the years, working in play with so many children with different interests, I have added rather than subtracted from my menagerie. This has its advantages in terms of many choices being available for diagnostic purposes; but I have found also that it can be highly distracting, especially to either the younger child or the highly anxious one or the hyperalert, organically damaged child. In fact, one three-year-old told me quite directly that I had "too many toys" (and indeed I do). For choice of toy to be a meaningful clinical clue, one needs occasionally to straighten out the room, classify its contents, and eliminate some of the clutter; that is, make some choices.

SOME SPECIALIZED PROJECTIVE PLAY TECHNIQUES

One of the earlier projective play methods that has been developed is the World Test, invented by Charlotte Buhler (1949), adapted by Margaret Lowenfeld (1970), and now modified as the Sand Test (Aoki, 1981) or in Sweden, the Erica Test (Sjolund, 1981). The method uses a sandbox in which the child is instructed to build a world from miniature construction toys (houses, etc.), people, and animals. The results are interpreted on the basis of the elements used and the presence of symptoms of aggression, emptiness, distortion, and rigidity. Studies using the Sand Test in Japan have revealed good reliability. Aoki (1981) has demonstrated that better-adjusted children tend to change their productions in sand play, whereas delinquents and emotionally disturbed children persist in very similar creations, either because of the pressure of certain central issues for them or because of lack of flexibility.

The Erica Test from Sweden (Sjolund, 1981) interprets the sand play on the basis of choice of material; a formal analysis that categorizes the level of structure from recognizing and naming, indifferent placement, sorting, configuration, juxtaposition, conventional groupings, meaningful wholes, chaotic groupings, and bizarre groupings; and a thematic analysis.

The Miniature Life Toy Situation presents similar materials without the sand box (Lerner & Murphy, 1941; Murphy, 1956). The child is asked to play with construction and miniature play people to develop, in the microcosm, the macrocosm of her world. Interpretation is based on the toys chosen, space utilized, physical movements, affect, organization of the play, configuration and patterns of play, and content and themes of the play.

A recent test of symbolic play (imaginative play) by Lowe and Costello (1976) also has been validated by Udwin and Yule (1982). It reliably and validly discriminated between a language-delayed group and a normal control group of preschool boys in the dimension of imaginativeness in free play.

INTRODUCTION TO THE DIAGNOSTIC PLAY SESSION

Clinicians today strongly recognize the need to alert immediately the child being brought for diagnostic examination as to the purpose for being there. This is done routinely in the setting in which I work, whether the family has been able to explain the purpose to the child adequately or not. The child is helped to understand immediately that there is a problem that is making others, including himself, unhappy, and, further, that the diagnostician's purpose is to understand the child's pain, with his help, through his own play and words. If a child is in pain, the offer of help is understood and the child will respond.

Actually, I find that the diagnostic process begins with the first contact with the parent or parents and with their explanation of the process to the child. The child is motivated to reveal himself (or not to reveal himself) through these preparations. Given the tools of the playroom and the diagnostician, the child will be stimulated to demonstrate through his total organism that which he wishes to communicate. He may communicate as much by what he does not do as by what he does do. If there is no play disruption, he may reveal both his inner and outer world, and, through his relationship with the diagnostician, his emotional–social level of development.

INTERPRETATION OF PLAY

There has been much agreement across the various methods used, including free play, as to the components that form the basis of interpretations for projective play methods.

Age-level Development in Play

To begin to understand the play of children diagnostically, one must be acutely aware of the normative expectations for play and then to distinguish play presentations that are out of synchrony.

A recent research by Field, DeStefano, and Koweler (1982) describes the age-progression expectancy for play. The play sequence for 20 months through four years of age was reality play, to object fantasy, to person fantasy. They explain this progression from object to person fantasy on the basis of cognitive maturity and increasing ability to plan and to verbalize plans. They found the following sex differences: The girls engaged in verbal interactions, positive interactions, person fantasy, and announced fantasy play a greater proportion of the time than boys. Boys spent more time in object fantasy.

Gondor (1964) describes the sequence of fantasy in child psychotherapy as moving from a preoccupation with inanimate objects to interest in animals and finally human beings. Sarnoff (1976) traces the development of fantasy in early latency-age children as moving from amorphous monsters to figures that resemble people; monsters and ghosts change into witches and robbers. In later latency, preadolescents' fantasies are more preoccupied with the real objects in their lives. These progressions mirror the development of self and identifications, and the complexity of intellectual development from sensory-motor and concrete relations to objects, to person permanence and the internalized libidinal object (Mahler, 1967).

The Sears (Sears, P. S., 1951; Sears, R. R., 1947; Sears, Pintler, & Sears, 1946) studies of doll play sparked a number of studies with interesting results that are relevant here. Using a modified and standardized dollhouse presentation and varying some features of the dollhouse (standard doll family, realistic versus nonrealistic features, etc.), a number of findings emerge that facilitate decisions about a varied play setting. Phillips (1945) found that there was more exploration of the toy materials when they were of high realism, and more organizational play when the materials were of low realism. There were more changes in play themes and less continuity with low realism.

In lower-class 3½-year-old preschool children, McLoyd (1983) has found that highly structured toys elicit more noninteractive pretend play than minimally structured objects. There was also a sex difference, in that boys engaged in more fantastic themes and girls in more domestic themes.

Pulaski (1976) reports that, by the age of five, realistic structure of toys made very little difference. High-fantasy children were already more imaginative, regardless of structure of materials, than low-fantasy children, whose play was much more closely related to their daily lives.

In Robinson's (1946) study children using a doll family that duplicated their own (versus a standard doll family) were more inhibited in identifying with the duplicate characters, tending to refrain from socially unacceptable behavior. Pintler (1945) found that thematic aggression was reliably greater when there was high experimenter–child interaction. It began earlier in the session, with more unusual play. Length of session also influences play (Phillips, 1945). While there was more exploration and organization in the three shorter, 20-minute sessions, the longer, 60-minute session produced more tangential behavior and was of less interest and more frustrating to the children.

Structural Aspects

The analysis of the structural aspects of the child's play deals first with the child's use and organization of the space provided. Is there order or disorganization? Are structures such as fences or objects used to make boundaries? Are there gaps in the boundaries? Is there clarity or confusion in the use of space? Is the space disconnected and poorly arranged, or tightly enclosed and rigid, or open and fluid? From these observations we may make some inferences about the controls and the defenses and at the same time take into account the types of chaos that these children may be coming from in reality in their own homes.

Perception, Motility, and Cognition

The chronological age of the child may be a start at estimating developmental level and age expectancy for any particular child; however, it may not be sufficient. Usually the diagnostic play session is supplementary to a general evaluation, so that one knows at the start the approximate intellectual level of the child being evaluated. However, if this is absent, the play may be evaluated from a perceptual and cognitive point of view, and it also may supplement the other evaluations. The child's ability to perceive and organize the play materials (objects), as well as her fine- and large-motor coordination, can be observed. The ability to develop integrated and sequentially coherent fantasy can be evaluated for intellectual level, much as story themes from picture-story tests are evaluated. Language and language structure can be observed for intactness of syntax, articulation, and approximation to standard English. Here again, it is important to know the reality situation at home and whether standard English has been heard.

Content, Conflict, and Dynamics: Psychosexual Level of Conflict

We are interested in the themes or content of the play as it reveals the level of conflict from a psychosexual point of view. Here again the age of the child is an issue, and the expectation for a particular level of development is important to remember in interpreting any specific thematic content. Early preschool play is often involved with issues of feeding, bathing, and toileting in the representation of everyday life. However, it may be the particular preoccupation with such an event and its repetition that will reveal its importance for any particular child. In addition, it may be the particular doll figures that are depicted in that situation and in preceding and following sequences. For older children, remnants of previous psychosexual stages (oral, anal, phallic, oedipal, latency) may represent fixations or regressions that will be of particular importance in understanding the individual child's dynamics. The combination of preoccupations with specific conflict areas and with indicators of anxiety or defensiveness may help us pinpoint the child's central issues.

Object Relations

The choice of play material and the sequence of choice of material becomes an important interpretive element. From our hierarchy of materials suggested at the beginning, which does the child choose, to start?

How global or distant an object does he choose to play with? At what psychosexual level is the choice of material? Does it represent material evoking phallic aggression or sensory dependency neediness? Then, is there a shift in sequence as the play progresses, from distance objects to objects that express conflict or from objects to animals to people? Is the child freed by the end of the session to express direct affects with the toys, at the toys, or even at the diagnostician? One also may look for flow and discontinuity as well. The discontinuity may express the interplay of conflict expression, alternating with anxiety and defensiveness. One must ask, then, what preceded the inhibition and what followed it.

Relationships with the Diagnostician

One of the important aspects of projective play techniques is the relationship formed between the child and diagnostician and/or how the diagnostician is used in the play session. The diagnostician needs to make a decision as to the extent that she wishes to interact with the child during the play productions. My preference is to allow the child to make that choice, utilizing the extent to which the child involves me as another dimension of interpretation. This will vary considerably and is itself a diagnostic tool for understanding the level of object relations of the child. We can expect the autistic child to remain aloof and to treat the examiner as another object in the room, probably ignoring the diagnostician except as needed to overcome some obstacle in the environment. Psychotic children are more clingy, giving one the feeling that they desire merger with one. The highly idiosyncratic play they engage in may involve fantasy, which may or may not include the examiner and blur the boundaries between child and examiner. The disorganization of the psychosis will express itself in all behavior, including language and thought.

The largest group that we see in our clinic includes the borderline and narcissistic character disorders, most of them expressed in symptoms of conduct disturbance, behavior problems at home and at school, and learning failures. The more severely borderline ones relate with a combination of closeness and distance, splitting into bad and good objects and self. They also may be very clingy and in need of reassurance from the examiner. Language and thought will vary from intactness to disorganization, as will the play, and there may be a metaphoric quality to the play.

The narcissistic children relate overly quickly in the sessions and may want immediate gratification and materialistic evidence of the examiner's interest and admiration of their products or themselves. The quick relatedness is suggestive of interchangeability of objects without reciprocity, except as a need to be liked or to ingratiate. Play is for need gratification, not necessarily communication, and pleasure is the goal. These children may express aggressive need systems very quickly, along with fears of loss and abandonment and separation anxiety. They are less likely to be conflicted over expressions of aggression or to show anxiety in relationship to the expression of aggression. Some of these children come to the session with less ability to use the diagnostician as a need-gratifying object. Because of lack of trust and confidence in the environment, they relate to the examiner as to others, with hostility and oppositionality.

The neurotic child, however, appears the most similar to our usual understanding of the presentation of unconscious conflict, with the usual array of defensive and symbolic communications. The object relationship is more reciprocal and related to appropriate distance to a "new friend."

Sequence and Process

The interplay of the various aspects and levels of interpretation are studied throughout the play session, in the sequence and process. It is of interest to note which objects are touched and in what order, and which objects lead to which. The general rhythm of this sequence is of importance in telling us where there is tension and anxiety, pointing to a central issue. The psychosexual level of the objects and the themes surrounding the use of the objects may be further revealing. Seemingly accidental actions or circumstances can lead to an understanding of a central issue: a toy drops or breaks, or there are "not enough" pieces, leading to disruption. Inhibition then can mean conflict or incapacity. Then again, a sequence can be finished because it has said it all. The difference needs to be recognized.

OBSERVATION AND RECORDING

In all diagnostic work with children, the basic observational data are the play interactions, so first and foremost the diagnostician must be a good observer. I encourage my students to take complete process notes during a diagnostic session. This means that the diagnostician jots down physical actions and sequences while they are occurring and frequently while they are actually participating in the play. If there is verbalization, then these interactions are recorded in terms of "he said, I said." Some shorthand can be used so that the material may be reconstructed in full later. As we can see, this becomes most important to the understanding of sequence and process.

"FIRST PRESENTATION"

I consider the first contact with the child for the first projective play session to be the "first presentation." I assume that the child comes in pain, however the session has been explained to her. It is expected that she will communicate her central conflicts and issues in some graphic manner through the play and the interaction with the examiner in this first session. Experience and the literature establish that this first session need not be an hour in length. At least two sessions of shorter duration will yield the greatest amount of information. The session needs to be long enough so that not all the time is spent in exploratory and organizational play. However, looking back to the first session, my experience often has demonstrated that most of the diagnostic clues were in this first session. Subsequent sessions are elaborations on the theme.

How does one look for the themes of this first session? The clues may be found in (1) the interplay between the organizational aspect of the play and use of space, (2) the relationship between choice of material and level of conflict, and (3) the communicative value of content themes. These are considered in the context of the relationship with the diagnostician. It is also important that one not neglect an isolated nonverbal message during the play, such as the choice of a symbol, the squeezing of the nose on a toy, or any isolated nonverbal behavior that breaks through the repressive barrier. There are two important aspects to play understood in this manner: the symbolic communications and the varying levels of conscious and unconscious meanings of the behaviors. There is a repetition compulsion to reproduce behaviors and materials that relate to central issues and conflicts. The value of the second session is that one can validate hunches derived from the first session and that these derivatives will be repeated in some form. Also, any change in object relatedness may be noted.

CASE EXAMPLE OF A "FIRST PRESENTATION"

J. is a six-year-old boy who was brought for evaluation because, according to his parents, "he doesn't listen, he thinks of something else to answer, he has no attention span." They also complained that he was beginning to punch children, both little and big kids, not in anger, but saying he was going to beat them up. His parents had been divorced three years previously, and J. was living with his mother and recently had been spending weekends with his father and stepmother. There was an impending separation from his mother, while she went to settle in another state.

Observations

The following observations come directly from the on-the-spot notes made in the first presentation of this case.

> Takes out tinker toys. Says he is going to make a car. "I don't know what I can make. I don't think I can make a car." Puts wheels on and then takes apart. Makes spokes in round tinker toy. "A star." "I'll see what else I can make. Maybe I can make a space ship. I have a lot of things here." Shows me. "I'm almost done. Is that good?" (Very good) "Supposed to be an airplane" and whirls it. "Now I can make a fan. What are these things for?" Figures out they stick in the end. "I can make a guy, a duck? The head, the feet, the eye . . ." Gets up out of seat to do the rest (see Figure 13.1).
>
> "This is supposed to be a bird." (Part of top falls off, he goes to get it.) (What kind of bird?) "An eagle." (Why an eagle?) "Because it's pretty." Adds top. (What's that part?) "A propellor." Takes apart. "I'll make a car. I think I know how. I did these things before." Tries to make car but there are not enough parts. "A mouth and a tail, a dog. I can't make anything else." (Maybe you'll find something else to play with.) "I'll play with something

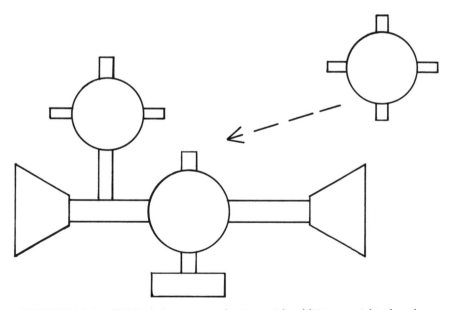

FIGURE 13.1 Child's tinker toy production, with addition on right placed on top and called a "propellor."

else." Puts things away. Takes crocodile puppet and Jill puppet and Beanie (fuzzy brown animal). Opens and closes crocodile's mouth on left hand and Jill on right hand. Puts box away. Opens each puppet's mouth and touches Beanie. He has them kiss. Then he has crocodile eat Jill. Then he has Jill pet Beanie. He moves Jill back and forth, laughs. "I'm done with that trick. Wasn't that good?" (Yes.) Puts away puppets in box. "Where'd you get this clown? I like working with puppets. I'd like to get a whole sack of them, that's what I feel like doing."

Takes turtle puzzle and tries to put it together. "Good turtle." "I know a couple of songs." Takes guitar. "I think I can, it goes like this." We sing Old MacDonald together, Mary had a little lamb, sings about Bugs Bunny. "Little rabbit named Bugs Bunny. Good?" Puts big guitar away and takes toy guitar. Takes small tub of toys. "A boy, a mom, a car." Takes each doll out. "A policeman." Takes boy. "Baby." Puts away black dolls, "daughter, father, mother, brother, sister, and sister and brother. Good?" "That looks like my mother." (Puts away.) "Doesn't it look a little like my mother? She really has brown hair." Picks up Frankenstein and puts back. "What is he supposed to be?" (About another puppet.) (Pepito.) Takes puppet out. The strings are tangled; while I fix them, he goes to the airplane and puts it down when I ask him for help. "Let's see what he looks like." "Looks like Mickey Mouse." Works puppet. (Very good, you've got him working.) He asks where Dad is and talks about coming next Saturday. I explain that we will first decide whether he needs to come back. He says, "It's fun here."

Interpretation of Play Session

J. demonstrates good ability to put together the Tinker Toys, and language and thought seem to be intact, as do his general cognitive abilities. (This was confirmed by the previous intelligence and projective testing with the Rorschach and Thematic Apperception Test.)

A review of the play process shows an interplay between demonstrating abilities and requesting frequent reassurance from the diagnostician that he is doing well ("Is that good?"). The choice of objects that he decides to make begin with a phallic-level car and culminate in the large structure seen in Figure 13.1. He calls it a bird, and when queried by the examiner, says it is an eagle because it's pretty. Meanwhile the top falls off, he adds it to the top again, and calls it a propellor. The production shifts, the eagle becomes a plane. I deflected his production with my question about what kind of bird it was, and this very sensitive child, upset by the toy falling apart (castration-level fear), shifted his designation to something inanimate and even stronger than an eagle. (I was to see this shift in response to felt criticism in subsequent play sessions.) At this point, he also takes the production apart and decides to go back to making a car, in a sense going back in the session to where he began. He desultorily thinks of making a dog when he decides there are not enough parts for the car, and then he gives up, easily frustrated and easily feeling criticism. "There's not enough . . ." (acceptance, affection).

The next sequence seems then to play out his response to felt criticism and frustration. He takes some puppets, and one is a crocodile whose mouth he opens and closes, signifying oral rage. Each puppet's mouth is opened, and then he touches the fuzzy animal, Beanie, and has them kiss. Aggression is followed by expression of dependency needs, and an affectionate making-up response. He does and undoes. He has the crocodile eat Jill, and Jill pets Beanie. The sequence is repeated. He moves Jill back and forth, and laughs, "I'm done with that trick." He has indeed told us of his conflict over angry feelings and fear of loss of dependency supplies if he does not kiss and make up. And he asks the diagnostician, "Wasn't that good?" requiring her approval. When approval is given, he focuses on what he calls a clown (denigrating because he still feels low in self-esteem, possibly related to the aggressive behavior), and tells of his neediness: "I'd like a whole sack of them, that's what I feel like doing."

J. then returns to demonstrating his abilities and mastery by doing the turtle puzzle and playing the guitar. He takes the dolls out of a small tub of toys and focuses initially on two: the policeman (representing control of impulse) and the baby (representing his regressive wishes for dependency supplies). He then tells us his central preoccupation related to these dependency needs. The doll looks like his mother. But next he picks up Frankenstein and puts him back. Does Frankenstein represent his rage at mother for unmet dependency needs, and his fear of loss of her while she goes to another state? Subsequent sessions have dealt with his denial and his underlying concern about this separation from his mother.

The next sequence has him playing with Pepito (he plays with the powerful airplane while I untangle the puppet's strings), and he asks about his Dad. He wants to return. "It's fun here." He has revealed a great deal about himself. The level of conflict appears to be phallic–oedipal, with a regression-fixation to the oral level, that is, oral rage at unmet dependency needs. There is low self-esteem, leading to his feeling easily frustrated when he meets challenge or feels criticized. Rage is handled by doing and undoing, and reaction formation and seeking of approval characterize his relationship with the diagnostician.

CONCLUSION

Play has much importance for childhood. All aspects of play interpretation—symbolic communication, wish fulfillment, mastery of reality and/or repetition compulsion—combine to create our understanding of a child's play production. Recent efforts at establishing more experimental reliability and validity confirmation have been successful. I have found, however, that the capacity to understand play communications from children is derived not from universal rules of thumb but from the diagnostician's integration of developmental theory with personality theory and frequent exposure to play productions and interactions with children.

REFERENCES

Aoki, S. (1981). The retest reliability of the Sand Play Technique: II. *British Journal of Projective Psychology and Personality Study, 26,* 25-33.

Axline, V. (1947). *Play therapy.* New York: Houghton Mifflin.

Beiser, H. (1976). Play equipment. In C. Schaeffer (Ed.), *Therapeutic use of child's play* (pp. 423-435). New York: Jason Aronson.

Buhler, C., & Kelley, G. (1941). *The world test: Manual of directions.* (Private publication.)

Erikson, E. H. (1964). Clinical observation of play disruption in young children In M. R. Haworth (Ed.), *Child Psychotherapy* (pp. 264-277). New York: Basic Books.

Esman, A. H. (1983). Psychoanalytic play therapy. In C. E. Schaeffer & K. J. O'Connor (Eds.), *Handbook of play therapy* (pp. 11-21). New York: John Wiley.

Field, T., DeStefano, L., & Koweler III, J. H. (1982). Fantasy play of toddlers and preschoolers. *Developmental Psychology, 18,* 503-508.

Freud, A. (1947). *The psychoanalytical treatment of children.* London: Imago Publishing.

Gondor, L. H. (1964). Use of fantasy communications in child psychotherapy. In M. R. Haworth (Ed.), *Child psychotherapy* (pp. 374-383). New York: Basic Books.

Klein, M. (1948). *Contributions to psychoanalysis.* London: Hogarth.

Klein, M. (1964). The psychoanalytic play technique. In M. R. Haworth (Ed.), *Child psychotherapy* (pp. 277-287). New York: Basic Books.

Krall, V. (1953). Personality characteristics of accident-repeating children. *Journal of Abnormal and Social Psychology, 48,* 99-107.

Lerner, E., & Murphy, L. B. (Eds.). (1941). Methods for the study of personality in young children. *Monographs of the Society for Research in Child Development, 6*(4), 1-289.

Lowe, M., & Costello, H. (1976). *Manual for the Symbolic Play Test.* Windsor, England: NFER.

Lowenfeld, M. (1970). *The Lowenfeld Technique.* Oxford, England: Pergamon Press.

Mahler, M. (1967). *The psychological birth of the human infant.* New York: Basic Books.

McLoyd, V. C. (1983). The effects of structure of play objects on the pretend play of low-income preschool children. *Child Development, 54,* 626-635.

Murphy, L. B. (1956). *Personality in young children* (Vol. 1). *Methods for the study of personality in young children.* New York: Basic Books.

Phillips, R. (1945). Doll play as a function of the realism of the materials and the length of the experimental session. *Child Development, 16,* 123-143.

Piaget, J. (1962). *Play, dreams and imitation in childhood.* New York: Norton.

Pintler, M. H. (1945). Doll play as a function of experimenter–child interaction and initial organization of materials. *Child Development, 16,* 145–166.

Pulaski, M. A. (1976). Play symbolism in cognitive development. In C. E. Schaefer (Ed.), *Therapeutic use of child's play* (pp. 27–43). New York: Jason Aronson.

Robinson, E. F. (1946). Doll play as a function of the doll family constellation. *Child Development, 17,* 99–119.

Sarnoff, C. (1976). *Latency.* New York: Jason Aronson.

Sears, P. S. (1951). Doll play aggression in normal young children: Influence of sex, age, sibling status, father's absence. *Psychological Monographs, 65,* No. 6 (Whole No. 323).

Sears, R. R. (1947). Influence of methodological factors on doll play performance. *Child Development, 18,* 190–197.

Sears, R. R., Pintler, M. H., & Sears, P. S. (1946). Effect of father separation on pre-school children's doll play aggression. *Child Development, 17,* 219–243.

Sjolund, M. (1981). Play-diagnosis and therapy in Sweden: The Erica Method. *Journal of Clinical Psychology, 37,* 322–325.

Udwin, O., & Yule, W. (1982). Validational data on Lowe and Costello's Symbolic Play Test. *Child: Care, Health and Development, 8,* 361–366.

14
Hand Test Interpretation for Children and Adolescents

Edwin E. Wagner

The Hand Test is a projective technique consisting of 10 cards approximately 3″ × 5″ in size. The first nine cards portray rough outline drawings of hands in different positions, while the last card is blank. The subject is asked to "tell what the hand could be doing," and, when the last card is reached, she is asked to "imagine a hand and tell me what it might be doing." Responses are recorded verbatim and scored on a special answer booklet, according to prescribed procedures. The technique is applicable across most of the lifespan and has been used successfully with the aged (Panek, Wagner, & Kennedy-Zwergel, 1983) but embodies the following special advantages for assessing younger people:

1. Reading ability is not required.
2. Both the stimuli and instructions are simple.
3. Hands are familiar to any subject old enough to verbalize a response.
4. Complexity of personality is not necessary to producing a scorable response, and even subjects with fewer psychological resources, such as individuals who are deaf and mentally retarded, can react in some way to the stimuli (Levine & Wagner, 1974).
5. The test assesses prototypical action tendencies (or the lack of them) that are close to the surface and hence apt to be expressed in behavior. In most cases, children referred for psychological assessment do not seek such help due to subjective discomfort but, rather, are referred for evalua-

tion because of observable behavioral difficulties. Hence, the Hand Test often can come close to reflecting those characteristics that bear directly on the presenting problem.

6. Antisocial behavior frequently brings juveniles to the attention of authorities. From its inception, the Hand Test has proven useful for predicting overt, aggressive behavior (Bricklin, Piotrowski, & Wagner, 1962).

7. The Hand Test can be administered in a relatively short time (about 10 minutes) and does not try the patience or exceed the attention span of children.

8. The short administration period also permits the Hand Test to be used when necessary as a screening device.

9. Rapport is easily established with children, many of whom regard the test as a game.

10. Scoring and interpretation are straightforward. Most psychologists at the M.A. level can become proficient in using the Hand Test after reasonable study and application; hence it can be used routinely by school psychologists.

11. Because of its brevity and known measurement qualities, the test can be accommodated in any basic assessment battery and integrated into a standard diagnostic appraisal.

CAVEATS

Although the Hand Test seems almost ideally suited for use with children, it is, of course, far from being a perfect assessment instrument and has certain drawbacks and limitations.

First, the test should not be administered to preschoolers. Basic rules of interpretation hold true for children aged six or over. Below that age, the relationships among the various scoring categories are radically altered and interpretation becomes hazardous. Furthermore, no dependable norms exist for prekindergarten-age children.

Second, the test is deceptively easy to administer and score, and this simplicity can carry over into interpretation, resulting in undesirably superficial evaluations. The Hand Test is a projective technique, and there is much to be gleaned of a clinical, nonscorable nature that can be overlooked by the psychologist bent on a quick appraisal who may be prone to ignoring qualitative nuances and idiosyncratic clues. For maximum results, interpretation must go beyond "cookbook" exegesis based only on scores and ratios. Experience, sedulousness, and clinical intuition are required for a well-rounded appraisal.

Third, as mentioned previously, the instrument reflects prototypal attitudes and action tendencies that are close to the efferent system and apt to be manifested in behavior; that is, it measures an individual's "façade" (Wagner, 1971, 1978; Wagner & Wagner, 1981). This is a circumscribed view of personality and does not encompass other important features such as imaginal resources and emotional strength. Hence, the Hand Test cannot be expected to yield a full clinical picture of a child or adolescent's personality and, preferably, should be used in conjunction with case history, interview impression, complementary test data, and other evaluative procedures.

NORMS, RELIABILITY, AND VALIDITY

Reliability and validity for the Hand Test have been reviewed extensively in the new Hand Test manual (Wagner, 1983), and Bodden (1984) has noted that, "On balance the validity data seem to indicate that the Hand Test stacks up well against other commonly used projective techniques such as the Rorschach, TAT, or Holtzman" (p. 320).

Since most of the Hand Test findings for adults are generalizable to protocols of children and adolescents, the technical information reported in the two Hand Test manuals provides a data base for evaluating the reliability and validity of the instrument. In addition, the original Hand Test manual, thanks to the contributions of many psychologists working with children and adolescents, contained assorted norms on a total of 1,758 youngsters, including the following groups: seven sets of normal American children assembled from various parts of the country; normal high-school students; three sets of juvenile delinquents; neurologically handicapped children; dyslexic children; students referred to school psychologists for evaluation; boys from an Australian technical high school; boys from a Japanese junior high school; Guamanian elementary-school students; and Guamanian high-school students. While these groups fall short of comprising idealized national samples, there are sufficient data available to establish reasonable normative estimations of age and sex expectations, at least for American children.

The bulk of reliability research has been conducted with adults, but there is one Hand Test study directly involving adolescents. McGiboney and Carter (1982) found significant test–retest correlations on 23 out of 24 Hand Test variables over a three-week interval in examining acting-out adolescents. Correlations varied from .21 to .91, comparing favorably with those reported by Panek and Stoner (1979) and Stoner and Lundquist (1980) and suggesting similar reliabilities for younger and older subjects.

While meaningful age and sex trends can be deduced from extant normative data, two studies have catalogued specifically some of these differences. Stoner (1978), investigating sex differences for second graders, discovered that significantly more ACT, ENV, DES, WITH, PATH, AOS, and R were given by boys. Girls evinced longer AIRT and H-L times and also were higher on EXH and FAIL. Nace (1983), comparing 12- and 13-year-olds, found that the former were significantly higher on ACT and ENV, while the latter showed more DIR, WITH, and FAIL.

Most of the Hand Test literature on children and adolescents focuses on acting-out behavior. Selg (1965) found a significant relationship between the Hand Test AOS and teachers' ratings of aggressiveness in children. Campos (1968) reported a higher AOS for children as compared to adults and suggested that this index can discriminate between aggressive and nonaggressive children as well as assaultive and nonassaultive delinquents. King (1975), working with black male adolescents, determined that aggressive subjects produced more withdrawal responses than nonaggressive subjects. Oswald and Loftus (1967) found that the following variables differentiated normal from delinquent children: AFF, AGG, DES, FAIL, R, AOS. Hoover (1977) reported a large number of relationships between Hand Test variables and overt behavior for children referred for various emotional and behavioral problems, but Breidenbaugh, Brazovich, and Matheson (1974) cautioned that the AOS was not a stable measure for a group of emotionally disturbed children.

A number of Hand Test studies were concerned specifically with delinquency. Wetsel, Shapiro, and Wagner (1967) found that the AOS and AGG significantly differentiated between recidivist and nonrecidivist delinquents in the predicted direction, and Wagner and Hawkins (1964) showed that the AOS could separate assaultive from nonassaultive delinquents with a 78-percent hit rate. Azcarate and Gutierrez (1969) attempted to relate Hand Test indices to institutional adjustment for incarcerated male juvenile delinquents. Using amount of time spent in an isolation unit as the criterion, they were able to achieve 82-percent accuracy by combining the AOS and MAL scores.

One study has been conducted with adolescents in an attempt to verify the Hand Test as a façade indicator. McGiboney, Carter, and Jones (1984) reported a large number of correlations between the Hand Test and the High School Personality Questionnaire and interpreted the overlap as representing similar façade self-characteristics.

BASIC SCORING AND INTERPRETATION

Detailed instructions on scoring and interpretation are presented in the two Hand Test manuals (Wagner, 1962, 1983). To summarize, the test measures basic, prototypal action tendencies. These behavioral proclivities are divided into four major categories, depending on whether the response involves relationships with people (Interpersonal, INT) or inanimate objects (Environmental, ENV); reflects difficulty in dealing with interpersonal or environmental interactions (Maladjustive, MAL); or denotes an inability to establish meaningful reality contacts (Withdrawal, WITH). These four categories are subdivided further into the 15 basic Hand Test quantitative scores, as shown in Table 14.1. Each Hand Test response receives one of these quantitative scores, which then are added together in various combinations to yield the following summary scores:

1. AFF, DEP, COM, EXH, DIR, and AGG are summed to produce INT. Normally, INT should constitute from 50 percent to 60 percent of all Hand Test responses.
2. ACQ, ACT, and PAS added together yield ENV, which makes up an average of about 40 percent of normal records.
3. TEN, CRIP, and FEAR are totaled to arrive at MAL. These are "neurotic" indicators and are undesirable, although one or two MAL's can be tolerated if compensated for by other positive features in a protocol.
4. FAIL, DES, and BIZ together make up WITH. These are more serious indices of psychopathology and would not be expected in a normal record.
5. The sum of all the individual scores except FAIL yields the total number of responses, R, which is an approximate index of psychological energy as it is invested in behavior. R's below 10 and above 30 are definitely pathological. The average R for adolescents and adults is around 14. For young children, the average R is closer to 10 or 11.
6. The initial reaction time (IRT) is the time elapsed between the presentation of the card and the first scorable response. All IRT's are added together and then divided by 10 (or less if any cards are failed) to obtain the Average Initial Reaction Time (AIRT). This indicates how long it takes, overall, to react to impinging stimuli. As benchmarks, an AIRT under five seconds is regarded as impulsive, and an AIRT over 20 seconds indicates too much of a delay in responding, usually due to emotional "shock" or intellectual weakness.
7. The H-L score is the difference between the highest and lowest IRT's. An H-L over 20 seconds also suggests some kind of "shock"; that is, for whatever reason (intellectual, emotional, behavioral), the subject has encountered difficulty in evincing a response to at least one card.
8. A Pathology (PATH) score is determined by adding MAL to a doubled WITH score. PATH is an approximate index of psychopathology. PATH scores between three and five should be viewed with concern; when PATH exceeds five, disturbances of a serious nature can be suspected.

Table 14.1   The Fifteen Basic Hand Test Quantitative Scores, with Examples and Behavioral Implications

Score	Example	Behavioral Implication
Affection, AFF	"Shaking hands with someone."	Warm, positive interpersonal relations.
Dependency, DEP	"Requesting help."	Subservient interpersonal relations.
Communication, COM	"Signaling O.K."	Interpersonal relations involving informational exchanges.
Exhibition, EXH	"Showing how pretty the hand is."	Interpersonal relations seeking attention and approbation.
Direction, DIR	"Ordering a child to bed."	Interpersonal relations involving domination and control.
Aggression, AGG	"Hitting someone."	Interpersonal relations characterized by hostility and negative affect.
Acquisition, ACQ	"Reaching for a can on the shelf."	Effort is involved in attaining an environmental goal.
Activity, ACT	"Moving a box."	Constructive environmental accomplishment.
Passivity, PAS	"Resting on an armchair."	An inactive relationship to the environment.
Tension, TEN	"Hand is clenched nervously."	Maladjustment resulting from strained or blocked action tendencies.
Crippled, CRIP	"A broken hand."	Maladjustment stemming from inferiority feelings.
Fear, FEAR	"Afraid it's gonna get hit."	Maladjustment due to anticipated psychological harm.
Description, DES	"Just held sideways."	Superficial and impoverished reality contact.
Failure, FAIL	(No response to a card)	Absence of an appropriate behavioral tendency.
Bizarre, BIZ	"It's a laughing skull."	Hallucinatory perceptions and/or delusional thinking.

9. The disposition of psychological energy, as it is manifested in behavior, is summarized by the Experience Ratio, ER, which juxtaposes INT, ENV, MAL, and WITH in that order. For the well-adjusted adolescent, the ER might look something like $8:6:0:0$. For younger children, a $6:4:0:0$ configuration might be more typical.

10. An Acting-Out Ratio, AOR, is computed by adding together AFF, DEP, and COM and comparing that sum to the sum of AGG plus DIR. For research purposes, an AOS (Acting-Out Score) using this formula also can be derived: $(AFF + DEP + COM) - (DIR + AGG)$. Essentially, this ratio (score) gives some idea of whether positive or negative interpersonal action tendencies predominate; thus it is an indicator of possible antisocial behavior. For normal adults, the AOR should lean toward the positive side $(AFF + DEP + COM)$ or should at least be balanced.

QUALITATIVE (PARENTHESIZED) SCORING

There is a large number of qualitative signs that can be used to enhance the meaning of a quantitative score and help develop the personality picture. These "additional" or qualitative scores are usually parenthesized and placed alongside the primary quantitative score. The following are the most common qualitative signs:

1. Ambivalent (AMB) indicates a guardedness or hesitancy in expressing an action tendency and is evidenced in statements such as, "Could be fighting, but I'm not sure the thumb would be in that position."
2. Automatic phraseology (AUT) consists of pet phrases or comments usually preceding or following a response to a number of cards such as, "I've never seen a hand like that." It can be notated by underlining the phrase wherever it occurs and represents a stereotyped effort to produce structure, often associated with an organic brain syndrome.
3. Cylindrical (CYL) is scored when the hand is seen in contact with a round, elongated object as in "Holding a baton." It has a psychosexual connotation and is seldom observed in prepubescent children.
4. Denial (DEN) entails an abrogation of a response such as, "Couldn't be shaking hands because it's a left hand." It implies a stronger disavowal of an action tendency than (AMB).
5. Emotion (EMO) involves the projection of intense affect into a percept, for example, "Just hit a home run, and he's real happy!"
6. Gross (GRO) indicates raw, unsocialized action tendencies, as in, "Smashing somebody over the head with a brick."

7. Hiding (HID) suggests disingeniousness and a masking of underlying purposes, which can be detected in responses such as, "She's got something behind her back she won't let you see."

8. Immature (IM) is scored for relationships with animals or younger human beings, for example, "A mother is reaching down to pick up her baby." The immaturity implied by such percepts must be gauged in relation to the age of the subject.

9. Impotent (IMP) reflects an admitted inability to deal with the stimulus, such as, "I'm just not smart enough to figure this one out," and is encountered most often with mental retardates and organic brain syndrome cases.

10. Inanimate (INA) is scored when the hand is seen representationally as in a picture or statue, for example, "Like that hand you see on those signs on the turnpike saying stop." The lifelessness implies action tendencies that are imaginal and less likely to be actualized in behavior.

11. Movement (MOV) represents undirected activity that releases excess energy randomly and is sometimes found in children who are classroom behavior problems. An example of MOV would be, "That hand is jumping up and down."

12. Oral (ORA) is associated with an oral-dependent orientation and involves the intake of food, water, alcohol, or drugs; for example, "Eating a candy bar." It is more common in children than adolescents and adults.

13. Perplexity (PER) involves expressions of puzzlement and consternation over the difficulty of the stimuli, as in, "That's hard to figure out because the thumb is in the wrong place, I think." PER reflects cognitive difficulties, and the interpretation is similar to IMP.

14. Sensual (SEN) stresses tactual contact, for example, "Crunching fall leaves between the fingers," and is given by individuals who enjoy hedonistic experiences.

15. Sexual (SEX) is scored for a blatant sexual act such as, "Feelin' a girl's ass," and denotes sexual preoccupation, usually pathological. SEX would not be expected at all in children's records.

16. Originals (O) are well-perceived but unusual responses; accordingly, they suggest uniqueness and novelty in the personality. Some experience with the Hand Test is necessary in order to recognize a genuine O.

17. Repetition (RPT) is scored when a response is given more than once on the same protocol. It can be notated by placing a check mark in the scoring column each time the response is repeated. Repetitions indicate either a fixation on the attitudes and action tendencies being projected or stereotypy and psychological constriction often associated with mental retardation and/or organicity.

OTHER INTERPRETIVE PROCEDURES

As with any projective technique, Hand Test interpretation is not confined to the scores. Other important tactics of interpretation are:

1. Verbs versus nouns. Generally, forceful verbs such as "lifting" carry greater behavioral implication than nouns or adjectives such as in the statement, "A left hand that could be in a lifting position."
2. Sequence analysis. How early a category appears in a record and the alternations, rhythms, and sequencing of responses can provide clues to the availability of and interactions among behavioral tendencies.
3. Idiosyncratic responses. Some responses are unique and provide special insights into the subject's personality, as when a child abandoned by his parents says, "That's a crippled hand. Nobody would want to shake it because it's sick."
4. Shocks and card pull. Each card has a tendency to elicit certain feelings and actions. For example, card VI often has an aggressive connotation because it is drawn as a fist. Therefore, time delays, difficulties in responding, and other verbal or behavioral peculiarities associated with a particular card can be termed a "shock" and attributed to the association(s) evoked by the stimulus, provided due care is exercised to avoid overinterpretation.

AGE DIFFERENCES AND
HAND TEST INTERPRETATION

If a child is of school age, the basic rules of Hand Test interpretation can be relied upon, provided provisions are made for the following age-related trends:

1. Productivity, as reflected in the total number of responses (R), varies with age. Around age seven, R averages 10 or 11 and climbs steadily until it reaches a mean of approximately 14 in the teens. Then R holds constant up to the mid-fifties, when it falls off again, dropping to 9 or 10 in extreme old age.
2. The younger the child, all other things being equal, the shorter, simpler, and more straightforward the response.
3. As might be expected, the tone of child and adolescent records reflects their experiences, interests, and developmental level. This is especially evident in the qualitative scores where, for example, an IM would

be natural for an eight-year-old, while a SEX would be totally unacceptable and pathological.

4. Intelligence interacts with developmental level so that the complexity of a protocol will vary with both age and IQ.

USING THE SCORING BOOKLET

The four-page Hand Test scoring booklet is a convenient aid for recording and scoring Hand Test responses as a precursor to interpretation. Page one provides space for identification data, page two is reserved for a verbatim transcript of the actual responses, page three summarizes all the quantitative and qualitative scores as both absolute numbers and percentages, and page four is used for notating card shocks.

We will use the case of "Alice Brown," which follows, to illustrate the use of the scoring booklet and also to show how the Hand Test can provide an individualized personality appraisal. Figures 14.1, 14.2, 14.3, and 14.4 represent the four pages of Alice Brown's Hand Test scoring booklet.

Alice was an eight-year-old girl who was referred for psychological testing mainly as a precautionary measure. Her older brother was seriously disturbed, and the parents were understandably concerned about the psychological health of their other two offspring. Alice was doing well academically in the second grade, and she was not a behavior problem. She was, however, beset by frequent colds and a skin allergy, and her mother described Alice as whiny, dependent, and at odds with her younger sister.

Alice was a well-kept, pretty girl whose conversational ability was excellent for a second-grader. She seemed interested in doing well and worked carefully and intently at all tasks. She was well-oriented and more interpersonally skilled than most children her age. Her FSWISC IQ was 123.

To begin with, in looking at her scores, serious emotional disturbance can be ruled out. The WITH score is zero and, while she does show two TEN's, the negative import of the MAL score is somewhat mitigated by her response productivity; a MAL of two is less worrisome in a protocol with 21 responses than one with 10.

Her overall energy level is above average (R = 21), and her capacity for constructive environmental accomplishment is quite satisfactory (ACT = 6). The high INT, the variety of interpersonal approaches in her behavioral repertoire, and the positive weighting of the AOS suggest that she is sensitive to people and able to relate to them in an affective and flexible manner.

FIGURE 14.1   Hand Test Scoring Booklet, page one.

THE HAND TEST
Scoring Booklet
Edwin E. Wagner, Ph.D. and Howard M. Knoff, Ph.D.

Published by

WESTERN PSYCHOLOGICAL SERVICES
PUBLISHERS AND DISTRIBUTORS
12031 WILSHIRE BOULEVARD
LOS ANGELES, CALIFORNIA 90025

A DIVISION OF MANSON WESTERN CORPORATION

Name: *Alice Brown*   Sex: *F*   Race: *W*

Address: *123 Holly Lane, Middletown, OH*   Phone: *555-4444*

ADULT	CHILD
Marital Status: _____	School Name: *Jefferson Elementary*
Occupation: _____	Grade: *Second*
Highest Grade Completed: _____	Teacher Name: *Mrs. Lovelace*

Date Tested: *1983* *7* *15*
                   year   month   day

Birthdate: *1975* *6* *4*
                 year   month   day

Age at Time of Testing: *8* *1* *11*
                                year month day

Referred by: *Parents*

Reason for Referral: *Precautionary – older brother is schizophrenic.*

Qualitative Administrative Observations: *Enjoyed the test. Speaks distinctly. Conversational level is excellent for a second grader. Very cooperative.*

Case History and Diagnostic Data: *Earning good grades in school. Not a behavior problem but described as "whiny", dependent, and at odds with her younger sister. Has frequent colds and a skin allergy*

Examiner Name: *E²W*

FIGURE 14.2   Hand Test Scoring Booklet, page two.

Card Number and Position	Initial Response Time	Position (e.g., >, <, ∧, ∨)	Examinee Response	Scoring Major	Scoring Qualitative
I	4"	∧	Saying stop. (Look like anything else?) Hmm... Might be uh... gonna catch something like this (demonstrates). Grab it	DIR / ACT	
II	3"	∧	Looks like it's going to push something like a chair. Scratching (Q) Itch. Petting something. (Q) Dog.	ACT / TEN / AFF	(SEN) / (IM)
III	4"	∧	It's sayin', "Go and do something." Or maybe, "Look at that over there." Or, "You and I can go some place."	DIR / COM / COM	
IV	2"	∧	This looks like he's gonna shake. And uh... like he's gonna take hold of his bike.	AFF / ACT	
V	6"	∧	He's goin' like this (demonstrates). (Q) Reachin' up for something... sneaking it. Arm around a lamb. (Q) Take care of it. Pet it.	ACQ / AFF	(AGG) / (IM)
VI	2"	∧	This picture looks like he's just caught a fly. Killed it. Showing it like "I killed a fly." and gonna punch somebody.	AGG / AGG	(IM) / (EXH)
VII	4"	∧	Um.... like stopping something. (Q) Toy car... doesn't want it to go off the edge. And doing her nails. One's red.	ACT / EXH	(IM)
VIII	1"	∧	Gonna pick up a little bug. And he's got an itch in his finger. And he's gonna pick up something... paper.	ACT / TEN / ACT	(IM) / ✓
IX	5"	∨	(Q) Looks like... uh... he's waving like this. (demonstrates) And... uh... that's all.	COM	
X (Blank Card)	9"	∧	Uh... Going like this. (demonstrates) Somebody gave 'em candy and he's just about to put one piece in his mouth	DEP	(ORA)

FIGURE 14.3   Hand Test Scoring Booklet, page three.

SCORING SUMMARY

Category	Frequency	% of Response	Example (Refer to the Hand Test Manual for additional examples.)
MAJOR CATEGORIES			
Affection (AFF)	3	14	"Shaking hands," "Comforting hand of a nurse"
Dependence (DEP)	1	4	"Asking for a hand-out," "Saluting your leader"
Communication (COM)	3	14	"Discussing a topic," "Talking with your hands"
Exhibition (EXH)	1	4	"Showing off her ring," "A minstrel man—dancing"
Direction (DIR)	2	10	"Giving an order," "Leading an orchestra"
Aggression (AGG)	2	10	"Punching somebody in the nose," "Trying to scare someone"
Σ Interpersonal (INT)	12	57	
Acquisition (ACQ)	1	4	"Reaching for something up on a shelf," "Trying to catch a ball"
Active (ACT)	6	29	"He's lifting some boxes," "Throwing a ball"
Passive (PAS)	0	0	"Person's sound asleep," "Hand folded on lap resting"
Σ Environmental (ENV)	7	33	
Tension (TEN)	2	10	"Looks very strained," "A fist clenched in anger"
Crippled (CRIP)	0	0	"Hand's been injured," "All beat up"
Fear (FEAR)	0	0	"Running for his life," "Trembling . . . it's frightened by something"
Σ Maladjustive (MAL)	2	10	
Description (DES)	0	0	"Just a left hand," "Firm hand . . . nothing special"
Failure (FAIL)	0	0	No scorable response given to a particular card.
Bizarre (BIZ) (Projects a response of unusual or idiosyncratic morbidity or "sees" something other than hand)	0	0	"A black bug," "Death's head . . . "
Σ Withdrawal (WITH)	0	0	

ER = Σ INT: Σ ENV: Σ MAL: Σ WITH = 12 : 7 : 2 : 0   R = 21   H-L = 8

AOR = (AFF + DEP + COM) : (DIR + AGG) = 7 : 4   AIRT = 4.1   PATH = 2

QUALITATIVE CATEGORIES

Category	Frequency	% of Response	Example
Ambivalent (AMB)			"Looks like he's hitting someone but there's not too much force to it"
Automatic Phrase (AUT) (Automatic phrasiology; underline response)			"Well, what could that be?"
Cylindrical (CYL)			"Has something long and round in his hand like a pipe"
Denial (DEN)			"Would be shaking hands except that's the wrong hand"
Emotion (EMO)			"He's just bursting with joy to see his friend again"
Gross (GRO)			"Smashing a dude over the head with a rock"
Hiding (HID)			"Covering a card with the palm so you can't see it"
Immature (IM)	4	19	"Taking a little boy's hand to walk with him"
Impotent (IMP) (Expresses inability to deal with card)			"I just can't figure it out"
Inanimate (INA)			"Like the hand of a statue I saw"
Movement (MOV)			"Waving his hand for no reason"
Oral (ORA)	1	4	"Drinking a glass of water"
Perplexity (PER) (Expresses puzzlement)			"This really is a tough one to figure out"
Sensual (SEN)	1	4	"Likes the feel of clay on his hands"
Sexual (SEX)			"Feeling a woman's breast"
Original (O)			Rare and well-seen responses; only experienced examiners should score this.
Repetition (RPT)			Repeats same or similar response; designate with a checkmark in scoring column.

FIGURE 14.4 Hand Test Scoring Booklet, page four.

QUALITATIVE ANALYSIS OF HAND TEST RESPONSES

Some of the Hand Test cards tend to elicit predictable responses and/or response categories. This expected response pattern, or "card pull," should be considered in the qualitative analysis of the Hand Test. The following is a summary of expected card pull for each stimulus card:

Card I: Represents initial reactions to new situations. Pull is toward DIR, COM, and AFF.

Card II: Pull is toward an ACT or an ACQ response. Any neurotic shock is apt to be manifested first on this card.

Card III: Tends to elicit COM, DIR, and ACT responses. This is an easy card in general and a failure may be indicative of severe deterioration.

Card IV: No strong pull. Responses may reflect more unique and individualistic traits. Usually seen as a masculine hand and may be a "father card."

Card V: Environmental pull. Possible neurotic shock and/or attitudes toward passivity.

Card VI: Attitudes toward aggression. AGG and ACT responses predominate.

Card VII: No strong pull. Percept is sometimes a reaction to the aggression suggested by Card VI.

Card VIII: Pull toward ACT. One of the easier cards.

Card IX: Psychosexual implications. However, be cautious not to overinterpret response since this is one of the more difficult cards.

Card X: No strong pull. Probably the most difficult card to respond to. Tends to reflect imaginal capacity and/or conception of one's future life role.

Responses which depart from the expected card pull or which are particularly unusual may represent "card shock." Analysis of card shock often contributes to the identification of major psychological themes or tendencies. Card shock may also be detected by reaction times that differ significantly from the AIRT or by overt behavioral reactions to individual cards (e.g., physical rejection, negative comments about the card, excessive rotation). Mild card shock is indicated for a specific card by placing a single checkmark in the appropriate space provided below; two checkmarks are used to indicate severe card shock.

Source: E. E. Wagner and H. M. Knoff, *The Hand Test Scoring Booklet.* Copyright 1969, 1981 by Western Psychological Services. Not to be reproduced in whole or in part without written permission of Western Psychological Services. All rights reserved. Reproduced here by permission of the publisher, Western Psychological Services, 12031 Wilshire Blvd., Los Angeles, CA, 90025.

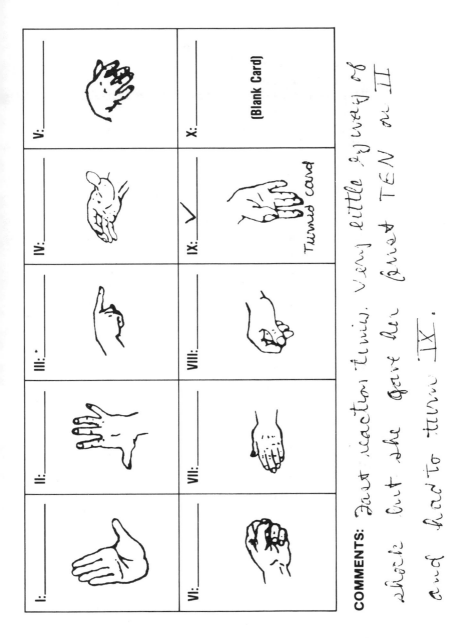

| I: ___ | II: ___ | III: ___ | IV: ___ | V: ___ |
| VI: ___ | VII: ___ | VIII: ___ | IX: ___
 Turned card | X: ___
 [Blank Card] |

COMMENTS: Fair reaction time. Very little guessing on shock but she gave her first TEN on II and had to turn IX.

293

On the opposite side of the ledger, Alice is somewhat impulsive (AIRT = 4.1); her response to card X, which often elicits attitudes toward the future, is oral-dependent; and she gives two similar TEN responses having to do with an itch. Judging from her IQ and the intactness of the remainder of the record, the repetition of the TEN does not suggest neurological impairment but, rather, a bothersome psychological fixation. The itch represents her skin allergy on an overt level, but she is probably also projecting underlying tension that manifests itself as a psychosomatic reaction. The TEN first appears on card II; empirically, it has been found that neurotic problems usually are elicited at this juncture.

There are a number of other interesting features in Alice's Hand Test record. She gives a lot of IM's that, although not unusual for her age, indicate that, despite her intelligence and apparent sophistication, she is still very much a little girl. The one ACQ is "sneaky" and suggests that she is not above using underhanded methods for getting her way. She seems unusually sensitized to the sex of the hand and, in fact, perceives many of them as being masculine. Some Hand Test users notate this tendency by scoring (MASC) or (FEM) in the qualitative column, and it is interpreted as denoting a cognizance of and sensitivity to social discriminations between the sexes. There may be a slight qualitative shock to card IX, but interpretation of this should be withheld pending input and verification from other test data.

Other subtleties of Alice's record could be discussed, but this overview should suffice to reinforce the point that, despite its brevity, the Hand Test is capable of providing a good deal of information that is personalized as well as diagnostic.

PROFILES OF DIAGNOSTIC TYPES

Hand Test records can be as individualized as the people who give them. However, for clinical purposes, it should be acknowledged that there are common diagnostic "types," that is, protocols with certain communalities that often come to the psychologist's attention. The remainder of this chapter will be devoted to a presentation of some of the more frequently occurring syndromes of childhood and adolescence, with their associated Hand Test signs and patterns.

The Neurological Profile

A common childhood syndrome is the neurologically damaged child. The case of "Charles" is a blatant illustration of how brain impairment manifests itself on the Hand Test.

Charles was an eight-year-old boy who was getting "U"s in school. His work was sloppy, he bothered the other children, and he created a general nuisance in class. Case history revealed that Charles was born prematurely with an underdeveloped eye muscle and missing vertebrae. At age two he had a serious case of croup with convulsions. On the basis of psychological testing, the child was referred to a pediatric neurologist where the organic diagnosis was confirmed.

Charles' Hand Test, which is shown in Table 14.2, is classically organic, with low R, failures, and unembellished descriptions. Qualitatively, he shows impotence, perplexity, and a content repetition—"petting a kitty" (cards V and X). The random movement on card I and the fast reaction times betoken irascible acting-out behavior. The pattern is flagrant and replete with organic signs. With more moderate neurological impairment, the picture would not be as stark. Note that, despite the extreme improverishment, there are no signs of psychotic thinking. Charles' behavioral repertoire is deficient, and he has little control over his actions, but he is not schizophrenic.

The Schizophrenic Profile

This 12-year-old boy, "Edward," was a psychiatrically diagnosed case of childhood schizophrenia. In his Hand Test protocol, shown in Table 14.3, he displayed overt symptomatology, including delusions, hallucinations, word salad, and association gaps. The five BIZ responses on the Hand Test are a sure sign of psychosis. Note also the five AGG responses, which are highly unusual and in this case suggest a lack of appreciation of socially acceptable behavior and the existence of potentially dangerous action tendencies. As with most childhood schizophrenics, he also evinced some neurological signs, including two repetitions, automatic phrasing ("little like"), and a need to demonstrate his answers with his own hands. The idiosyncratic flights of fancy whereby he transmuted the hands into jet planes, a gliding squirrel, and a movie screen are typically schizophrenic. As a rule, brain-damaged cases view the Hand Test cards as concrete but difficult tasks with "right" and "wrong" answers, whereas fulminating schizophrenics merely use the cards as catalysts for educing private fancies.

The Mild Neurological Profile

Most neurologically impaired children and adolescents who are referred for a differential diagnosis do not produce such clear-cut profiles as Charles' (see Table 14.2). Cases that are moderate to mild in severity generally give fewer neurological signs, and sometimes a definitive diagnosis cannot be made with the Hand Test alone. The diagnostician's task

Table 14.2 Hand Test Scores Showing Neurological Impairment

I	4″	Waving. Opening its hand. (Anything else?) No.	COM (MOV)
II	(13″)	Uh . . . I don't know. (Guess?) No.	FAIL
III	1″	Pointing. (Q) 'Cause other fingers are closed, right? (Q) Am I right? (Q) No person, just pointing.	ACT? (PERP)
IV	3″	To grab something. (Q) Oh, I don't know.	ACQ (IMP)
V	7″	Petting a cat or a dog.	AFF (IM)
VI	3″	Closing up your hand. (Q) I don't know why. (Laughs.)	DES (IMP)
VII	16″	Hmm. . . . I don't know. . . . A guess? Just hand like this. Don't know why.	DES (IMP)
VIII	1″	Holding something little. Like a diamond.	ACT
IX	(2″)	I don't know. Can't guess.	FAIL (IMP)
X	6″	Oh, petting . . . to a kitty.	AFF (IM) ✓

AFF = 2	ACQ = 1	MAL = 0	DES = 2	R = 8	(IM) = 2
COM = 1	ACT = 2		FAIL = 2	AIRT = 5.1	(IMP) = 4
INT = 3	ENV = 3		WITH = 4	H-L = 15	(MOV) = 1
				PATH = 8	(PERP) = 1
				ER = 3:3:0:4	(RPT) = 1
				AOR = 3:0	

then involves (1) ferreting out possible organic indicators and (2) seeking out confirmatory data.

"Mary," a 14-year-old girl, seemed at first blush to be a puzzling case. The school psychologist reported a FSWISC IQ of 111, but, despite above-average intelligence, she was doing failing work in school. She was described as a "loner" who was rejected by her fellow students because her overtures of friendship were quickly followed by hostility. The referring school psychologist characterized her as "an unhappy, nervous girl who daydreams a lot and wants to become an archeologist." Mary was supposedly overly attached to a deceased father. She currently was living with her mother and grandparents. She had been seen previously at a child guidance clinic, where her emotional problems had been attributed to her mother for not providing enough love and attention. The mother, who had to work to support the family, was understandably upset at having the blame laid at her doorstep, claiming that she did her best to care for Mary and make her happy.

Medical history revealed that Mary was sick for about 10 months as a child and was temporarily paralyzed. At the time, it was thought that she might have contracted polio. Interestingly, her facial expression was masklike and her posture and gait rigid. On the basis of psychological testing, a neurological problem was suspected, and a subsequent referral to a neurologist corroborated the diagnosis. In addition, the neurologist indicated that Mary's supposed bout with polio was, in all probability, encephalitis.

Mary's Hand Test results are shown in Table 14.4. The indices of organicity were as follows:

1. There were six AGG, which is practically unheard of in a female. These AGG were obviously a result of impaired emotional controls brought about by the encephalitis. Her labile affect (4 AFF, 6 AGG) was

Table 14.3 Hand Test Scores Showing Schizophrenic Profile

I	6″	(E) Just doing judo (D).[a] (Anything else?) No.	AGG
II	13″	Hmm. . . . Pretending it's a butterfly. (Q) No.	DES (BIZ) (EXH)?
III	3″	Little like a gun (D). Tricks in his pocket. (Pretends hand is a gun.) (Q) Shoot someone.	AGG (HID) (EXH)
IV	10″	Catching a butterfly. (Q) Kill it.	AGG (IM)
V	35″	Hmm. . . . Don't know. . . . (Guess?) I don't think . . . maybe a jet plane . . . motor's getting off . . . gliding down (D).	BIZ
VI	10″	This is a fist like to fight (D).	AGG
VII	3″	Little like more judo (D).	AGG
VIII	18″	Little like a gliding squirrel (D).	BIZ
IX	16″	Little like a rocket taking off—fire by the fingers.	BIZ
X	8″	[Looks at hand.] Movie maybe . . . starting to show the movie maybe.	BIZ

AGG = 5	ENV = 0	MAL = 0	DES = 1	R = 10	(HID) = 1
INT = 5			BIZ = 4	AIRT = 12.2	(IM) = 1
			WITH = 5	H-L = 32	(RPT) = 2
				PATH = 10	
				ER = 5:0:0:5	
				AOR = 0:5	

[a](D) indicates that subject demonstrates.

Table 14.4 Hand Test Scores Showing Mild Neurological Impairment

I	5″	Stopping someone. (Anything else?) Push someone. Slap someone.	DIR AGG AGG
II	4″	Grabbing for something. (Q) In a hurry—grab books. Could be stroking a dog or cat. That's it.	ACT AFF (IM) (SEN)
III	3″	Pointing out something. (Q) A house, a car. Running a finger down the page of a book.	COM ACT
IV	12″	Could be stroking a dog's head. Slapping somebody.	AFF (IM)✓ (SEN) AGG✓
V	18″	Hand resting on something. Be stroking something.	PAS ACT (SEN)✓
VI	12″	Trying to hit somebody. Pounding on a desk. Holding reins.	AGG DIR (TEN) ACT
VII	30″	Patting a dog on the head. Stroking an animal.	AFF (IM) (SEN)✓ AFF (IM) SEN)✓
VIII	4″	Snapping fingers. (Q) Forgot something. Holding reins.	TEN ACT✓
IX	36″	Trying to tell somebody to stop. Strike at somebody.	COM (DIR) AGG
X	19″	Pulling a trigger. (Q) On a gun.	AGG (GRO)

AFF = 4	ACT = 5	TEN = 1	WITH = 0	R = 21	(GRO) = 1
COM = 2	PAS = 1	MAL = 1		AIRT = 14.3	(IM) = 4
DIR = 2	ENV = 6			H-L = 33	(RPT) = 6
AGG = 6				PATH = 1	(SEN) = 5
INT = 14				ER = 14:6:1:0 AOR = 6:8	

undoubtedly responsible for keeping her classmates at a distance. Note also that one of her AGG was a GRO—a very rare response for a 14-year-old girl and indicative of psychopathology, despite the low PATH score.

2. There were two sets of repetitions, one involving stroking and patting animals, the other "holding reins" (probably related to her fondness for horses).

3. There was a large number of immature AFF responses that not only were repetitious but also suggest developmentally primitive affect brought about by her neurological problem.

The classic neurological indices—low R, FAIL, and DES—were not evidenced in Mary's protocol. Nonetheless, to the perspicacious diagnostician, there would be ample reason to suspect an organic brain syndrome.

The Neurotic Profile

"George," a 13-year-old boy, was ostensibly referred for vocational guidance. He was interested in the priesthood, and his parents were wondering whether he was suited for the profession. However, after test data indicated neurotic difficulties of serious proportions, considering his age, the boy and his mother admitted during a conference to more personal reasons for requesting a psychological evaluation. As it turned out, George was liked by his teachers but was unpopular with his peers. He "didn't get along" and felt that he "didn't belong." In desperation, he wrote a letter to his parents declaring that he was "queer" and plaintively pleading for help. Fortunately, the Hand Test, which had been used for personality screening, prompted further testing and brought the problem to light.

The protocol (see Table 14.5), although short, is unmistakably neurotic. George gives five MAL's, constituting 50 percent of his total productivity, and his resources have been so severely strained that he has little capacity left for environmental accomplishment (ACT = 0). Even his interpersonal relationships are circumscribed (INT = 4), and he seems to be barely holding together. With only 10 responses, compensatory assets are at low ebb.

The sexual shock is transparent on card IX, which often elicits psychosexual associations. He requires 54 seconds to muster a response, resulting in an H-L score of 50. Then he turns the card and, after a struggle, has to fall back on his first response to card I, "saying stop." His response to card X is also of interest inasmuch as it confirms George's pathetic plight and preoccupation with his own problems. Some Hand Test scorers would append the parenthesized score (PERS) to the TEN for card X, to indicate the personalization and self-concern inherent in the response.

George eventually was diagnosed as an Overanxious Disorder of Adolescence and placed into long-term psychotherapy.

The Suicidal Profile

Unfortunately, there is no *one* profile that can be used to anticipate suicide attempts in childhood and adolescence. Instead, there is a variety of configurations that might lead the diagnostician to infer that suicide is

Table 14.5   Hand Test Scores Showing a Neurotic Profile

I	6″	Saying stop. (Anything else?) Don't think so.	DIR
II	19″	Got cut on something. He's in pain.	CRIP (TEN)
III	2″	Giving a direction. (Q) Like an order.	DIR
IV	12″	Ready to grab something. (Q) Anything. (Q) Reaching	ACQ
V	16″	Shows deadness. No life in it.	CRIP
VI	5″	Holding his grip. Trying to control his anger. (Emulates.)	TEN
VII	4″	Ready to shake hands with another person.	AFF
VIII	6″	Just got done snapping his fingers. (Q) Nervous.	TEN
IX	54″	I don't know. . . . **6** kinda funny . . . **V**∗ . . . This guy looks like he's saying stop too. . . . but I don't know . . .	DIR (AMB)✓
X	10″	Scratching. (Q) My head. (Q) Thinking . . . got a problem . . .	TEN

AFF = 1	ACQ = 1	TEN = 3	WITH = 0	R = 10	RPT = 1
DIR = 3	ENV = 1	CRIP = 2		AIRT = 13.4	
INT = 4		MAL = 5		H-L = 50	
				PATH = 5	
				ER = 4:1:5:0	
				AOR = 1:3	

∗ **6** = Card turned over and over.
V = Card upside down.

at least a possibility. "Kathy's" protocol, shown in Table 14.6, is a good example. She was an 18-year-old high-school senior, and her case illustrates how one might reason deductively from a personality analysis to obtain suicidal implications.

Kathy, after acquiescing to sex, found herself subsequently rejected and rebuffed by her boyfriend. She then rushed into the school psychologist's office, distraught to the point of frenzy, where she was tested and counseled. Arrangements were made for additional counseling, but the following day she attempted suicide by trying to jump off a high bridge.

The table shows two major shocks, to cards IX and X, the former implying loss of control and perhaps dissociation in the sexual sphere, the latter further developing the theme with the suggestion of inferiority and ineptitude: ". . . just learned how . . . looked silly until she learned." The CYL in this case has a clear sexual connotation, and the fact that the trauma persists from card IX, the "sex" card, to X, the "future" card, suggests that, at the time of testing, the sexual experience followed by the termination of her romance were uppermost in her mind.

Kathy's AOR is unbalanced toward hostility, and she produced four IM's plus the semi-exhibitionistic response on card X. The flavor is hysterical, and it can be conjectured that the suicide attempt was an

Table 14.6 Hand Test Scores Implying Suicidal Possibilities

I	5″	Uh . . . like a policeman—hand up—stop. (Anything else?) No.	DIR
II	13″	Someone just holding hand up for something. (Q) Maybe little kid in class holding hand up but really straining, fingers apart. (Q) Tense.	TEN (DEP) (IM)
III	3″	Person pointing to something. Giving directions. Or signs: "One Flight Up."	COM COM (INAN)
IV	4″	Looks like someone hitting, spanking a little kid. Could be swimming too. Cupped like that.	AGG (IM) ACT
V	5″	Looks like little kid reaching . . . on top of table; can't see where he's feeling.	ACQ (IM)
VI	5″	A fist. Somebody gonna . . . in a fist fight. Or banging fist on table for order.	AGG DIR (AGG)
VII	13″	Uh . . . maybe extending to shake hands.	AFF
VIII	11″	Picking up some little thing on the table.	ACT
IX	(27″)	Don't know what . . . like that? (Emulates.) (Guess?) I don't know . . .	FAIL
X	25″	(Laughs.) No, I can't think of anything. You mean different? Grasping. (Q) Like a baton. My sister just learned how. She looked silly until she learned.	(EXH) ACT (CYL) (IM)

AFF = 1	ACQ = 1	TEN = 1	FAIL = 1	R = 12
COM = 2	ACT = 3	MAL = 1	WITH = 1	AIRT = 9.1
DIR = 2	ENV = 4			H-L = 24
AGG = 2				PATH = 3
INT = 7				ER = 7:4:1:1
				AOR = 3:4

impetuous, angry, attention-getting reaction arising from a basically immature, neurotic, and sexually conflicted young woman.

The Antisocial Profile

Antisocial behavior is certainly one of the common causes of adolescent referral. The following case is a typical example. "Ivan," a 16-year-old boy, was a completely self-centered, exhibitionistic (note Hand Test EXH) young man who had successfully manipulated parents, teachers, and juvenile authorities until the point was reached where his peccadillos could no longer be tolerated. In school he was constantly in trouble for truancy, stealing cars, and sexual escapades and was earning failing grades.

Psychopaths, because they have no guilt, produce little or no MAL. Most are hostile and therefore their AOR's tend to be imbalanced in favor of DIR and AGG. R is usually low, with responses short and superficial. Often psychopaths toss off hostile remarks such as, "A hand tellin' somebody to 'flake off.'" They can fail cards associated with areas in which they act out, and they often show problems with dependency fulfillment and/or masculinity.

Ivan's record, shown in Table 14.7, includes just about all of the common signs of the antisocial personality disorder. Of special interest is his response to card VII, where his proclivities for manipulating and "conning" others are beautifully projected. Note also the FAIL on card IX, which is undoubtedly tied in with his sexual acting-out and masculinity problems, and the absence of ACT, which is not surprising in view of his failing grades in school.

Most people with personality disorders live behind façades; therefore, the Hand Test can come close to revealing major aspects of their personalities. In many cases, however, the content and quality of the responses take on major diagnostic import, since, with personality disorders, the PATH score and the ER ratio can be normal.

CONCLUSION

Despite its simplicity, the Hand Test can yield material fraught with diagnostic significance. As can be gathered from a perusal of the seven preceding records, there are interpretive nuances that cannot be reduced to formalized scoring; therefore, in order to obtain optimum results, experience and diligence are necessary. A superficial approach to Hand Test analysis can lead to shallow and even erroneous conclusions, in which case, "The fault, dear Brutus, is not in our stars, but in ourselves."

Table 14.7 Hand Test Scores Showing an Antisocial Personality Disorder

I	9″	Hmm . . . telling someone to stop. (Anything else?) Making a sugges-tion.	DIR COM (DIR)
II	13″	Looks like it's reaching out for some-thing. (Q) Knew you would ask. (Laughs.) Something larger than his hand . . . like a basketball . . .	ACQ
III	11″	Someone's right hand pointing a direction for someone.	COM
IV	3″	Ready to hit somebody.	AGG
V	5″	This hand is sleeping. At rest.	PAS
VI	5″	A fist . . . getting ready to fight.	AGG
VII	7″	Patting someone on the back . . . like trying to get them to do what you want.	DIR (AFF)
VIII	6″	Snapping fingers. (Q) Music.	EXH
IX	(22″)	Couldn't tell you. (Guess?) No, I don't see anything.	FAIL
X	3″	A hand tellin' somebody to "flake off."	DIR (AGG)

COM = 2	PAS = 1	MAL = 0	FAIL = 1	R = 10
EXH = 1	ACQ = 1		WITH = 1	AIRT = 6.9
DIR = 3	ENV = 2			H-L = 10
AGG = 2				PATH = 2
INT = 8				ER = 8:2:1:0
				AOR = 2:5

REFERENCES

Azcarate, E., & Gutierrez, M. (1969). Differentiation of institutional adjustment of juvenile delinquents with the Hand Test. *Journal of Clinical Psychology, 25,* 200–202.

Bodden, J. L. (1984). The Hand Test. In D. J. Keyser & R. C. Sweetland (Eds.), *Test critiques* (Vol. 1) (pp. 315–321). Kansas City, MO: Test Corporation of America.

Breidenbaugh, B., Brazovich, R., & Matheson, L. (1974). The Hand Test and other aggression indicators in emotionally disturbed children. *Journal of Personality Assessment, 38,* 332–334.

Bricklin, B., Piotrowski, A. A., & Wagner, E. E. (1962). The Hand Test: With special reference to the prediction of overt aggressive behavior. In M. Harrower (Ed.), *American lecture series in psychology.* Springfield, IL: Charles C Thomas.

Campos, L. P. (1968). Other projective techniques. In A. I. Rabin (Ed.), *Projective techniques in personality assessment: A modern introduction.* New York: Springer.

Hoover, T. O. (1977). Relationships among Hand Test variables and behavioral ratings of children. *Dissertation Abstracts International, 37,* 2509B. (University Microfilms No. 76-24,406.)

King, G. T. (1975). A comparison of Hand Test responses of aggressive and nonaggressive black adolescents. *Dissertation Abstracts International, 34,* 1736A. (University Microfilms No. 73-23,947.)

Levine, E. S., & Wagner, E. E. (1974). Personality patterns of deaf persons: An interpretation based on research with the Hand Test [Monograph supplement]. *Perceptual and Motor Skills, 39,* 1167–1236.

McGiboney, G. W., & Carter, C. (1982). Test–retest reliability of the Hand Test with acting-out adolescent subjects. *Perceptual and Motor Skills, 55,* 723–726.

McGiboney, G. W., Carter, C., & Jones, W. (1984). Hand Test and the High School Personality Questionnaire: Structural analysis. *Perceptual and Motor Skills, 58,* 287–290.

Nace, R. B. (1983). Sex versus age differences in adolescents' responses to the Hand Test. *Perceptual and Motor Skills, 57,* 1110.

Oswald, O., & Loftus, P. T. (1967). A normative and comparative study of the Hand Test with normal and delinquent children. *Journal of Projective Techniques and Personality Assessment, 31,* 62–68.

Panek, P. E., & Stoner, S. (1979). Test–retest reliability of the Hand Test with normal subjects. *Journal of Personality Assessment, 43,* 135–137.

Panek, P. E., Wagner, E. E., & Kennedy-Zwergel, K. (1983). A review of projective test findings with older adults. *Journal of Personality Assessment, 47,* 562–582.

Selg, H. (1965). Der Hand-Test als indikator for offen aggressives verhalten bei kindern. *Diagnostica, 4,* 153–158.

Stoner, S. (1978). Sex differences in responses of children to the Hand Test. *Perceptual and Motor Skills, 46,* 759–762.

Stoner, S., & Lundquist, T. (1980). Test–retest reliability of the Hand Test with older adults. *Perceptual and Motor Skills, 50,* 217–218.

Wagner, E. E. (1962). *Hand Test: Manual for administration, scoring and interpretation.* Los Angeles: Western Psychological Services.

Wagner, E. E. (1971). Structural analysis: A theory of personality based on projective techniques. *Journal of Personality Assessment, 35,* 422–435.

Wagner, E. E. (1978). Diagnostic applications of the Hand Test. In Benjamin B. Wolman (Ed.), *Clinical diagnosis of mental disorders: A handbook* (pp. 393–443). New York: Plenum Press.

Wagner, E. E. (1983). *The Hand Test manual* (Rev. ed.). Los Angeles: Western Psychological Services.

Wagner, E. E., & Hawkins, R. (1964). Differentiation of assaultive delinquents with the Hand Test. *Journal of Projective Techniques and Personality Assessment, 28,* 363–365.

Wagner, E. E., & Wagner, C. F. (1981). *The interpretation of projective test data: Theoretical and practical guidelines.* Springfield, IL: Charles C Thomas.

Wetsel, H., Shapiro, R. J., & Wagner, E. E. (1967). Prediction of recidivism among juvenile delinquents with the Hand Test. *Journal of Projective Techniques and Personality Assessment, 31,* 69–72.

15
Miscellaneous Projective Techniques

Albert I. Rabin
Stuart L. Doneson

Several additional techniques will be discussed briefly in this chapter. The first two methods are described in greater detail elsewhere (Rabin & Haworth, 1960). These are the Rosenzweig Picture Frustration Study (Rosenzweig, 1960) and the Blacky Pictures (Blum, 1948), both of which have been employed extensively over the years in a number of research projects as well as in various clinical settings.

Some newcomers also are included in the present context. Early memories have been used diagnostically and therapeutically for a long time; however, the employment of early memories as a standard diagnostic method with adolescents and children, buttressed by systematic research findings, is a relatively recent development. Additional experience with this method is needed before it becomes a full-fledged instrument in the clinician's armamentarium.

The Paired Hands Test and the School Apperception Method round out the miscellany of the present chapter. These two methods are somewhat more circumscribed in their purpose, for they are designed to assess relatively specific aspects of the child's personality and interaction. As will be seen, the former test has generated a fair amount of research with different populations, adding to its construct validity.

THE ROSENZWEIG PICTURE FRUSTRATION (P-F) STUDY

Some 50 years ago Saul Rosenzweig published a brief paper on "Types of Reaction to Frustration" (1934). A part of the classic *Explorations in Personality* (Murray, 1938) also contains a section on "The Experimental

Measurement of Types of Reaction to Frustration," by the same author. Out of these theoretical considerations and empirical findings emerged the Rosenzweig Picture Frustration (P-F) Study in the 1940s. The several forms of this projective method have been in use ever since, in research and clinical settings. A more detailed discussion of the historical background of the P-F study may be found elsewhere (Rosenzweig, 1960).

The children's form of the Rosenzweig P-F Study was first published in 1948 and has been used by researchers and clinicians ever since. It is intended for children from ages 4 to 13. The materials consist of 24 cartoonlike pictures portraying frustration situations involving two persons. One of the pictured individuals on the left of the item is shown saying something (words printed in a balloon) that frustrates or describes the frustration of the other. The other person is drawn with a blank balloon above his head, which the subject is expected to fill. Subjects are encouraged to fill in with the very first words that occur to them that the individual would respond with in that particular situation. Naturally, with younger children the administration is entirely oral, with the examiner reading the material in the balloon and recording the response. Beginning with age nine years, the oral administration may be unnecessary.

Rosenzweig (1960) describes the picture selection process as follows:

> Care was taken to include a sampling of the range of needs frustrated more or less often in the life of the average child, e.g., the needs for approval, freedom, nurture, etc. as well as the various formal types of frustration, i.e., privation, deprivation and conflict. While in every instance, it was the child who was represented as frustrated, in approximately half of the items the individual inflicting the frustration or otherwise associated with it was likewise a child, while in the other half he was an adult. (p. 152)

Thus, the eight-page examination blank is a "game" for the children. The first-page instructions are read by the child or are read to her, depending on her educational development. Playing the game involves recording the "first-thought" responses to the frustrating messages. A trial demonstration precedes the actual testing. Complete details are given in the manual.

Aggression, broadly defined, is the reaction to frustration. Responses to the situations portrayed in the cartoons of this method are classified as to the *direction* and *type* of aggression. The three directions or targets of aggression are *extrapunitive* (aggression turned outward), *intrapunitive* (aggression directed inward, toward the self), and *impunitive* (when the expression of aggression is avoided altogether). Blaming others, self, and no one for the conditions of the frustration corresponds to the three categories or directions of aggression.

In addition, responses also are evaluated as to *type of aggression*. Here aggression is not synonymous with hostility but considered more broadly as activity and assertion. Thus, the type of aggression called *obstacle dominance* refers to the sort of response that "indicates only a persevera- tion at or insistence upon the presence of the obstacle." The *ego-defense* refers to either ego blame or its inviolacy; and the *need-persistence* type involves, somehow or other, the gratification of some need.

The nine *factors* on which the scoring for this test is based result from a combination of the three directions and types of aggression just de- tailed.

As indicated earlier, the Rosenzweig P-F Study has been used widely in clinical as well as research contexts. Hundreds of studies of the method, both the adult and children's forms, in several cultural settings and several languages, have been reported (Rosenzweig & Rosenzweig, 1975). In recent years, a spate of publications on the reliability of the P-F (Rosenzweig, Ludwig & Adelman, 1975) and of the children's form in particular (Rosenzweig, 1978), and of the construct validity of the method (Rosenzweig & Adelman, 1977) have appeared. It is one of the most studied "narrow-band" techniques available.

THE BLACKY PICTURES

The first publication of this method was titled "A Study of the Psychoan- alytic Study of Psychosexual Development" (Blum, 1949), which clearly indicates the purpose of this technique, designed to study the level of psychosexual development of the person, according to the stages specified by Sigmund Freud.

The first card of the test introduces cartoonlike drawings of a family of dogs: Papa, Mama, Blacky, and Tippy. The suggested instructions for children are as follows:

> I've got some cartoons to show you, like you see in the funny papers, and what I'd like you to do is make up a story about each one. Here are the characters who will be in these cartoons [show frontpiece]. Here [pointing] is Papa, Mama, Tippy, and the son, Blacky. Now for each picture I'd like you to tell me as much as you can about what's happening and what they are thinking and feeling. (Blum, 1949)

The next 11 cartoons constitute the test proper. The following are brief descriptions of the cartoons and the psychosexual dimensions they are designed to assess:

1. Shows Blacky in front of mother's nipple (oral eroticism).
2. Shows Blacky with mother's collar in his mouth (oral sadism).
3. Presents a series of four small "houses" with the name of one of the characters on each. Blacky is "relieving" himself between Papa's and Mama's houses (anal sadism).
4. Blacky, near a bush, is watching Papa and Mama make love (oedipal intensity).
5. Blacky is licking himself (masturbation guilt).
6. Tippy is shown blindfolded, and a knife is about to cut off his tail. Blacky is watching (castration anxiety).
7. Blacky has his paw raised, as if reprimanding a small toy dog in front of him (positive identification).
8. Papa and Mama are "making much" over Tippy, who is seated between them. Blacky is watching (sibling rivalry).
9. Blacky is crouching and an apparition of an admonishing angel dog is before him (guilt feelings).
10. Blacky is sleeping and a fatherlike dog appears in his dream (ego-ideal).
11. Blacky is sleeping and a motherlike dog appears in his dream (love object).

The Blacky pictures are usually administered individually, although group administration, especially for research purposes, has been utilized. In addition to the stories told to each cartoon, a structured inquiry is proposed in the manual (Blum, 1950). Further refinements, including results of factor analyses, are included in a later publication (Blum, 1962). Indeed, a fair amount of research has been reported with this technique. It has been and is being utilized clinically, primarily in psychoanalytic settings.

EARLY MEMORIES

Early memories (EM's) , by virtue of their uniqueness, specificity, and universality, appear to have the qualities required of an ideal vehicle for the study and assessment of personality. This was not lost on such early explorers of human psychology as Freud, Adler, and Stanley Hall. Indeed the theoretical implications of EM's have been elaborated in striking and divergent ways. Freud studied "screen memories" as compromise formations between unconscious wish and defense, to be deciphered into their latent elements via the process of free association. In sharp contrast, Adler focused on the manifest content of EM's as reflecting the individual's basic attitudes or lifestyle (Bruhn & Last, 1982). Likewise, the clinical utility of EM's—at least for adults—has been widely appreciated (Ansbacher, 1953; Bruhn, 1981). Harder to find, and of more recent vintage, is the empirical and quantitative exploration and articulation of this domain, especially as it pertains to the earliest memories of children. Most of this research has been derived from an ego-psychological/object-relations view that "the themes that bind together the *dramatis personae* of a person's early memories define nuclear relationship patterns that are likely to recur repetitively in a wide range of other life situations. They protrude projectively into the structure and content of his early memories, just as they protrude repetitively into his evolving relations with the significant persons in his life" (Mayman, 1968, p. 304).

Early empirical studies of EM's were focused largely on developing coding schemes for tapping relevant psychological variables. The work of Langs and his associates (Langs, 1965 a, b; Langs, Rothenberg, Fishman, & Reisner, 1960; Levy, 1965), and Mayman (1968) are concerned primarily with delineating the content and formal categories of the data. Coding schemes based on an Eriksonian model (Levy, 1965), on ego psychology (Langs et al., 1960), and on stages of object relationship and libidinal development (Mayman, 1968) were developed and employed with some success. However, none of these scoring systems has achieved anything like general agreement in the field. Indeed, more recent research has shied away from comprehensive TAT and Rorschach scoring systems in favor of those specific to the problem and populations studied (Bruhn & Schiffman, 1982). Frequently used variables include (1) presence or absence of other people, (2) degree of interaction, (3) activity versus passivity of child in memories, (4) pleasantness versus unpleasantness of memories, (5) relationship paradigms, and (6) trauma (illness, damage, conflict).

It is interesting to note that there is still variability in the instructional set given to the subjects on the various EM studies. In some, subjects are asked for their earliest memory (Langs et al., 1960; Levy, 1965); in others, the earliest and next earliest memories are requested (Last & Bruhn, 1983). One representative example of instructions states, "I want you to think back when you were a very small child. Can you tell me the very first thing you remember happening, not something that someone told about, but something you are sure happened? Try to give me as many details as you can remember" (Bruhn & Davidow, 1983). Further details are elicited by requesting the subject's age at the time, location, number and identity of other people in memory, and the affective tone of the memory. Monahan (1983) has attempted to codify the testing procedure by requesting a set of five early memories: (1) earliest, (2) earliest of mother, (3) earliest of father, (4) birthday, and (5) school. After each memory, an inquiry essentially identical to that of Bruhn's (1981) is employed.

Reliability and Validity

Interrater reliability commonly has been found by tabulating the percentage of agreement among previously trained raters (usually two or three) on each category or subcategory of the rating scheme. Thus one study required 54 separate ratings for three judges, with percentage of agreement ranging from 50 percent to 100 percent and averaging 77 percent (Langs et al., 1960). More recent studies tend to employ fewer categories, generally selected from those found highly reliable in previously published studies, which has resulted in interrater reliability scores averaging over 90 percent (e.g., Last & Bruhn, 1983; Monahan, 1983).

No systematic study of the temporal reliability of Early Memories was found. While there is clinical and theoretical reason to think that EM's can and do change for the same subject over time—for example, after psychotherapy—the extent of this change has not been documented in the literature (cf. Langs et al., 1960; Mosak, 1958).

Until quite recently, the data for most of the studies of Early Memories—both clinical and experimental—have come from the EM's of adult subjects. Bruhn (1981) argues that this neglect has been largely the result of an Adlerian preconception that the memories of children lack diagnostic signficance because, unlike adults' selective recall, children are thought to have complete access to their past experiences. In spite of this bias against children, a body of research on children's EM's has begun to appear utilizing subjects ranging from 5 to 16 years of age (Hedvig, 1965).

In a sense, the majority of studies of EM's have been validity studies, in that they have been designed to show that EM data are related to and predictive of a wide range of normal and pathological personality features. Langs and his associates (Langs, Rothenberg, Fishman, & Reisner, 1960), utilizing a scoring system for manifest content of EM's produced by 20 hospitalized women (10 diagnosed as paranoid schizophrenic and 10 as hysterical character disorders), found a number of significant differences between the two groups as far as the interrelated/solitary dimensions were concerned, with the hysterics' EM's being more action oriented and more involved with others. In a later research, Langs (1965a) also demonstrated that EM data are predictive of a large number of personality variables that are independently obtained using clinical interviews, Rorschach, TAT, Wechsler-Belleveu, and autobiographical data. The work of Levy (1965) and Mosak (1958) provides clinical documentation in the form of detailed psychological reports confirming personality profiles based on coded EM's.

Focusing specifically on a detailed clinical case study, Bruhn (1981) documents the way in which the EM's of a nine-year-old white girl highlight unresolved psychological issues of loss and deprivation, a hostile-dependent relationship with her mother, and depression. In the same study he presents a summary of pilot data based on a sample of 20 children aged 5 to 11 years who were intensively evaluated at a child guidance clinic. He found that EM's frequently encapsulate the child's major dynamics and concerns. Yet in 30 percent of these cases, the EM's did not provide clinically useful data. He found that children of dull intelligence and nonintrospective children tended not to produce EM's. Moreover, the EM's produced by children in the five- to eight-year-old group were of much more variable use than those produced by children who were at least nine years old. This is attributed to difficulties with the time concept "earliest."

Illustrative Research Applications

While theoretical and methodological issues have accounted for much of the published work in the area of children's earliest memories, there has been an increase in quantitative research in recent years. As in the study of adult EM's virtually all of these studies have focused on differentiating clinical groups based on EM data.

Bruhn and Davidow (1983) investigated EM's from 15 delinquent and 18 non-delinquent control subjects, all middle-class males, 15 to 17 years of age, equated for verbal IQ. The EM's were given to three clinicians to sort independently into delinquent and nondelinquent groups. In addition, three judges were trained to use an EM scoring system containing five codes: (1) injury, (2) rulebreaking, (3) self versus others, (4) mastery, and (5) victimization. Not only did the coding system successfully identify 80 percent of the delinquents and 100 percent of the nondelinquents, but the prediction rates obtained by the trained judges also were significantly greater than those achieved by the three clinicians. The researchers argue that EM data are useful in revealing the presuppositions and expectations that influence views of self, other, and world. In this instance, delinquents' EM's reveal expectations of victimization and of parental help in rescuing them from the consequences of rulebreaking.

Last and Bruhn (1983) examined the early memories of 94 boys, aged 8 through 11, in order (1) to determine whether EM data covary with degree of adjustment and (2) to identify which EM aspects best discriminate adjustment groups. Using a brief scoring system derived from earlier studies, dubbed the Early Memory Scoring System (EMSS), the researchers coded for (1) characters, (2) setting, (3) sensory-motor aspect, (4) relation to reality, (5) object relations, (6) thematic content, (7) affect, (8) damage aspect, and (9) memory age. Using the EMSS, two "naive raters" obtained 92.6-percent interjudge reliability and were able to discriminate well-adjusted, mildly maladjusted, and severely maladjusted groups as determined by the Behavior Problem Scale of the Child Behavior Checklist. The EM aspects that best discriminated between groups tended to be what the researchers call "structural" and not "content" categories, that is, relation to reality, object relations, and perceptions of self. The only content variable that discriminated among the groups was the presence of caretaking relatives.

In a very different setting, Monahan (1983) compared responses of 59 hospitalized suicidal and nonsuicidal children and adolescents in order to determine if there were differences in ratings of functions and object relations within EM's. The EM's were rated for three groups of subjects: (1) "talkers," or those who made verbal threats to end their lives; (2) "attempters," or those who acted intentionally to end their lives; and (3) nonsuicidal controls. The EM's were rated on a number of variables in order to test the hypotheses that attempters are more disturbed than talkers and that suicidal children are more alienated, negative, and active than nonsuicidal controls. While none of these specific hypotheses was borne out in the data, significant findings did emerge. For example, "talkers" had substantially more pleasant memories, portrayed their fathers as more caring, and represented people less often as injured or ill, thus suggesting a higher level of object relations than the other group. Moreover, "attempters," contrary to expectation, represented themselves as with another person, suggesting that they are not alienated or unconnected to important objects.

THE PAIRED HANDS TEST

The experience and conception of the self—the self-concept—has been the subject of psychological inquiry even before it became the shibboleth of a generation. In an "age of narcissism" the preoccupation with "self" tends to eclipse interest in the "other," both theoretically and practically. In spite of this imbalance of attention, self and other appear to be dialectically linked concepts, with specific kinds of self-experiences entailing specifically different experiences of the other. While it is not difficult to find theoretical support (Hegel, Fairbairn, Jacobsen) and clinical support (Rogers, Sullivan, Kernberg, Klein) for this position, experimental and empirical evidence bearing on the relation between self-concept and others-concept has been harder to find.

In an effort to rectify this situation, a research program focusing explicitly on the others-concept has been under way for well over a decade (Zucker & Jordan, 1968). Conceptualized as paralleling the self-concept, the others-concept has been defined as a "person's general expectancies or perceptions about other people along a positive–negative continuum" (Barnett & Zucker, 1977). Zucker and his colleagues suggest that the others-concept is a basic variable in such socially relevant problems as moral development, friendship, and cooperative or social behaviors. Moreover, they have employed the Paired Hands Test (Zucker & Jordan, 1968), an adaptation of the Hand Test (Wagner, 1962), as a method for the experimental exploration of the others-concept.

In its more recent incarnations, the Paired Hands Test (PHT) is viewed as a projective technique for accurately measuring "relatively deep levels of personality" (Barnett & Zucker, 1977). In particular, the test samples a child's reactions to dyadic interactions and, by inference, assesses whether her perceptions or expectations of others tend to be positive, negative, neutral, or inconsistent. The PHT consists of 20 slides, each showing one black and one white hand, engaged in some form of interaction. A set of five multiple-choice terms describing what the hands might be doing accompanies each slide (Galluzzi, Kirby & Zucker, 1980). Subjects must select which item best describes their impression of the hands. Earlier versions of the PHT employed an open-ended response format that subsequently was coded for friendliness, hostility, or neutrality (Zucker & Jordan, 1968).

Well over 2,000 children ranging from fourth grade to twelfth grade have participated in a variety of studies of the others-concept as measured by the PHT. Early versions of the test that employed an open-ended response format achieved an interscorer reliability coefficient of .90 based on an N of 31. Test–retest reliability was found to be .75 for this group of 31 children and .66 for a related group of 26 schoolchildren (Zucker & Jordan, 1968).

Several studies have reported data supporting the validity of the HTP. Children obtaining high positive scores on the HTP were judged to be friendlier and more popular by their peers, with girls scoring even higher than boys. Moreover, high-scoring students in a class for the emotionally handicapped were judged by student observers to be more affable, pleasant, and friendly than low-scoring students. In another study, behavioral data were reported showing that children with relatively high others-concepts interact more positively in small, unsupervised groups than children having relatively low others-concepts (Barnett & Zucker, 1977). These differences were more likely to show up when tasks were more challenging and unstructured rather than mechanical and routinized.

More recent studies have begun to explore some of the more subtle personality and moral dimensions implicit in the others-concept. In a study designed to investigate the relationship between moral reasoning and the perceptions of others, 244 students in grades 7 through 12 were administered the Defining Issues Test of moral reasoning and the Paired Hands Test Secondary Form, which measures the others-concepts of secondary-level students (Whiteman, Zucker & Grimley, 1978). Although the data for 20 percent of the subjects could not be used for various reasons, the results showed a consistent relationship between a student's level of moral reasoning and the others-concept. Thus, students who reached the higher stages of moral development had more positive others-concepts than those at lower stages of moral development. Furthermore, students at the antiestablishment stage had especially low others-concepts. Scores on the PHT accounted for .036 of the variance in moral reasoning scores ($p = .01$), while I.Q. accounted for .099. age .103, and socioeconomic status .001 of the variance.

A series of studies has attempted to relate children's self- and others-concepts to a number of school-related variables. One study found that children with high self- and others-concepts are better adjusted than those with low scores on these dimensions (Galuzzi & Zucker, 1977). A later study (Galluzzi et al., 1980) found low correlations between children's self- and others-concepts (personality variables) and their perception of the classroom environment (situation variables) along the dimension of involvement, affiliation, teacher support, friction, and satisfaction. A reanalysis of the data assigning children to high, medium, and low self- and others-concept groups resulted in differences among the groups on the five environment perception scales, with low-scoring children differing from teacher's as well as high-scoring children's perceptions of the classroom. These findings suggest that personality variables interact with, and may override, situation variables in the perception of the environment.

The ease of administration, the standardized scoring for individuals and groups, the appealing nature of the stimulus material, and the impressive validity data all suggest that the PHT deserves wider attention from researcher and clinician alike. In addition, it attempts to measure a theoretical construct—the others-concept—that has broad-ranging social implications. It also has conceptual implications that are waiting to be elucidated. Indeed, the most obvious shortcoming of the research on the others-concept is that it remains theoretically underdeveloped, both in terms of its grounding in or links to established bodies of psychological theory and the related question of how it covaries with different kinds of self-concepts.

More significant from the clinical point of view is that the PHT claims to provide an in-depth look at personality. While Barnett and Zucker are aware of the difference between surface and depth evaluations, as well as between defended (socially desirable) and undefended responses, it is not clear how these different levels can be derived, or distinguished, from the

PHT data. For example, does the others-concept represent a subject's public or private view? Is it conscious or unconscious? It would be illuminating to see a study of the interdigitation of PHT data with object representations derived from the TAT, Rorschach, and Early Memories tests and from dreams, as a way of demonstrating that the PHT's claims to measure depth match its more manifest surface virtues.

THE SCHOOL APPERCEPTION METHOD

The School Apperception Method (SAM) is a picture-story projective technique devised by Solomon and Starr (1968). Where most apperceptive methods deal with a broad range of dynamic personality concerns, SAM's exclusive emphasis is upon presenting school situations. The authors describe the technique as follows:

> The SAM consists of twenty-two drawings depicting children and school personnel in a wide range of interactions. The selection of the scenes is based on their relevance to significant adjustment areas of school, both scholastic and emotional. Twelve of the pictures are suggested for a standard administration (1–12), while the remaining ten (1A–10A) are included as additional or alternate pictures. Children portrayed in the SAM drawings are of median elementary school age. The pictures can be used with subjects of preschool age through adolescence. (p. 1)

It is of interest to note that five of the alternate or additional pictures are concerned with issues of racial integration and, according to the authors, may be suitable for administration to children in racially integrated schools in order to explore attitudes toward minority groups. Generally, the most important point made about this particular method is that it is primarily a *school*-focused technique and as such may be most useful to school psychologists. The manual suggests a number of areas of analysis that may be undertaken on the basis of the interpretation of SAM stories, which are obtained with the usual instructions employed with thematic methods. Such analysis includes:

1. Formal qualities, including reaction time, length and complexity of stories, manner of handling the cards, and so forth.
2. Attitudes toward the teacher and other authorities. How is the teacher viewed? What are the child's reactions to authority, generally?
3. Attitudes toward schoolmates.
4. Attitudes toward academic activity.

5. Aggression. How is anger handled? Is there physical and verbal aggression?
6. Frustration. What kind of situations cause frustration, and how is it handled?
7. Anxiety and defense mechanisms.
8. Home and school relationship. Parents' involvement with school and the relationships between home and school values.
9. Punishment. How is punishment conceived? What are the child's reactions to it?

The manual (Solomon & Starr, 1968) presents a series of illustrative cases in which the clinical usefulness of SAM is demonstrated. To date, however, published research with the method or normative data at different age levels are unavailable.

REFERENCES

Adler, A. (1937). Significance of early recollections. *International Journal of Individual Psychology, 3*, 283–287.

Ansbacher, H. L. (1953). Purcell's "memory and psychological security" and Adlerian theory. *Journal of Abnormal and Social Psychology, 48*, 596–597.

Barnett, D. W., & Zucker, K. B. (1977). Validating a measure of children's others-concept through population and behavior variables. *Journal of Personality Assessment, 41*(2), 131–143.

Blum, G. S. (1949). A study of the psychoanalytic theory of psychosexual development. *Genetic Psychology Monographs, 39*, 3–99.

Blum, G. S. (1950). *The Blacky pictures: Manual of instructions.* New York: Psychological Corporation.

Blum, G. S. (1962). A guide for research use of the Blacky pictures. *Journal of Projection Techniques, 26*, 329.

Bruhn, A. R. (1981). Children's earliest memories: Their use in clinical practice. *Journal of Personality Assessment, 45*, 258–262.

Bruhn, A. R., & Davidow, S. (1983). Earliest memories and the dynamics of delinquency. *Journal of Personality Assessment, 47*, 476–482.

Bruhn, A. R., & Last, J. (1982). Earliest childhood memories: Four theoretical perspectives. *Journal of Personality Assessment, 46*, 119–127.

Bruhn, A. R., & Schiffman, H. (1982). Invalid assumptions and methodological difficulties in early memory research. *Journal of Personality Assessment, 46*, 265–267.

Galluzi, E. G., Kirby, E. A., & Zucker, K. B. (1980). Students' and teachers' perceptions of classroom environment and self- and others-concepts. *Psychological Reports, 66*, 747–753.

Galluzi, E. G., & Zucker, K. B. (1977). Level of adjustment and the self- and others-concept. *Psychology in the Schools, 14*(1), 104–108.

Hedvig, E. B. (1965). Children's early recollections as a basis for diagnosis. *Journal of Individual Psychology, 21,* 187–188.

Langs, R. (1965a). Earliest memories and personality. *Archives of General Psychiatry, 12,* 379.

Langs, R. (1965b). First memories and characterologic diagnosis. *Journal of Nervous and Mental Diseases, 141,* 318–320.

Langs, R. J., Rothenberg, M. B., Fishman, J. R., & Reisner, M. F. (1960). A method for clinical and theoretical study of the earliest memory. *Archives of General Psychiatry, 3,* 523–534.

Last, J., & Bruhn, A. R. (1983). The psychodiagnostic value of children's earliest memories. *Journal of Personality Assessment, 47,* 592–603.

Levy, J. (1965). Early memories: Theoretical aspects and application. *Journal of Personality Assessment, 29,* 281–291.

Mayman, M. (1968). Early memories and character structure. *Journal of Projective Techniques and Personality Assessment, 32,* 303–316.

Monahan, R. T. (1983). Suicidal children's and adolescent's responses to early memories test. *Journal of Personality Assessment, 47,* 258–264.

Mosak, H. H. (1958). Early recollections as a projective technique. *Journal of Projective Techniques and Personality Assessment, 22,* 302–311.

Murray, H. A. (1938). *Explorations in personality.* New York: Oxford University Press.

Rabin, A. I., & Haworth, M. R. (Eds.) (1960). *Projective techniques with children.* New York: Grune & Stratton.

Rosenzweig, S. (1934). Types of reaction to frustration: An heuristic classification. *Journal of Abnormal and Social Psychology, 29,* 298–300.

Rosenzweig, S. (1960). The Rosenzweig Picture-Frustration Study, children's form. In A. I. Rabin & M. R. Haworth (Eds.), *Projective techniques with children* (pp. 149–176). New York: Grune & Stratton.

Rosenzweig, S. (1978). An investigation of the reliability of the Rosenzweig Picture-Frustration Study (P-F), children's form. *Journal of Personality Assessment, 42*(5), 483–488.

Rosenzweig, S., & Adelman, S. (1977). Construct validity of the Rosenzweig Picture-Frustration Study. *Journal of Personality Assessment, 41*(6), 578–588.

Rosenzweig, S., Ludwig, D. J., & Adelman, S. (1975). Retest reliability of the Rosenzweig Picture-Frustration Study and similar semiprojective techniques. *Journal of Personality Assessment, 39*(1), 3–12.

Rosenzweig, S., & Rosenzweig, L. (1976). Guide to research on the Rosenzweig Picture-Frustration (P-F) Study, 1934–1974. *Journal of Personality Assessment, 40*(6), 599–606.

Solomon, I. L., & Starr, B. D. (1968). *School Apperception Method: SAM.* New York: Springer.

Wagner, E. E. (1962). *Hand test: Manual for administration, scoring and interpretation.* Los Angeles, CA: Western Psychological Services.

Whiteman, J. L., Zucker, K. B., & Grimley, L. K. (1978). Moral judgment and the others-concept. *Psychological Reports, 42,* 283–289.

Zucker, K. B., & Barnett, O. W. (1977). *The Paired Hands Test manual.* Dallas: McCarron-Dial Systems.

Zucker, K. B., & Jordan, D. C. (1968). The Paired Hands Test: A technique for measuring friendliness. *Journal of Projective Techniques and Personality Assessment, 32,* 522–529.

VI
Clinical
Application

16
Projective Techniques with Children in the Clinic Setting

Janice Levine
Richard Levine

Projective techniques have become respected, widely utilized psychodiagnostic tools in clinics that serve children. Typically, projective testing is employed to garner specific levels of diagnostic information which then is integrated with other forms of data to comprise the broadest possible view of psychological functioning. In their applications to both children and adults, projective techniques are designed to provide insights into the subject's personality dynamics and to eventuate in a diagnosis that will lead to relevant and efficacious treatment recommendations. The use and interpretation of projective and other psychodiagnostic techniques with children diverge from that of adults inasmuch as the examiner must place particular emphasis on a child's developmental level, degree of emotional and social maturity, and relative fluidity of ego boundaries (Abt & Bellak, 1950).

Within the clinic setting it is incumbent upon psychologists to acknowledge and accommodate to the particularities in using projective techniques as applied clinical instruments, in contrast to research modalities. Clinic conditions and exigencies impede severely the potential to create a controlled environment that is more conducive to the requisite manipulation of variables in research endeavors. Moreover, while research data may provide normative standards that can serve as a useful backdrop to applied clinical work, the use of projective testing in clinical applications demands an appreciation of the idiosyncratic features of each individual and her overall life circumstances, in order to be maximally germane and effective. The clinical practitioner, unlike the researcher, is usually constrained to adduce pertinent diagnostic data within a very limited time frame. This task is rendered all the more complex by the reality that children are transiting a period of life during which their respective personalities are fluid and evolving. In the clinic setting psychologists lack opportunities to carry out longitudinal studies of children through the use of projective and other techniques. Decisions that may influence profoundly the course of childrens' lives are made quickly. Projective tests can be inordinately helpful in this context, insofar as they provide a rich source of data from which personality dynamics can be understood and treatment recommendations advanced.

As a rule, the researcher is engaged in a quest for understanding that centers on types of productions at various specific developmental levels or ages. The clinical practitioner, in contrast, is called upon to understand a particular individual in depth. Children pose particular challenges in this regard. Specifically, there are common variations in the depth and tempo of development at any given moment in a child's life, and a child's proclivity is to react intensely to elements in the test situation itself. These are factors that a sensitive examiner must take into account in interpreting projective test data and other sources of information. Given that children have relatively little power to determine or change the circumstances in which they live and that they are dependent intrinsically upon their adult caretakers, the clinician who employs projective testing to reach clinical judgments is remiss if she fails to learn as much as possible about the child's environment and the important adults who shape that milieu. Projective testing of children is meaningful only to the extent that test data can be interwoven with an understanding of the child's life circumstances. This necessitates interviews with parents and anyone else who can provide a feeling for the environment to which children are compelled to adapt.

REALITY AND FANTASY ELEMENTS IN TEST MATERIAL

The projective material produced by an adult is typically regarded as a fantasy production that is interpreted to gain insight into the interplay between primary process and coping defenses (Abt & Bellak, 1950; Altman, 1960). A child's responses to projective test stimuli may be reflective of his or her *actual*, rather than fantasized, world. To illustrate, the authors have discovered firsthand that, of 50 consecutive referrals for psychological evaluations submitted to a rural midwestern mental health center in the past two years, 46 of these involved instances where there were strongly suspected or proven occurrences of physical and/or sexual abuse of children. That these experiences permeated the projective test protocols of this group of children is not surprising. Nonetheless, were these protocols to be interpreted without the availability of information concerning the abuse to which they had been subjected, the interpreter might easily mislabel, as primary process or fantasy material, terrible realities that had become integral aspects of these children's experiences.

This example drawn from clinical experience also demonstrates in a compelling manner that practitioners who use projective and other techniques in their assessments of children need a sufficient breadth of vision to be aware of cultural currents that may bear on individual cases. Today, poverty; sexual, physical, and emotional abuse of children; the high incidence of divorce; the emphasis on individualism and competitiveness; and the threat of nuclear catastrophe all combine to contribute to childhood psychopathology. In articulating this dimension of experience, it is not necessary to discount or bypass completely the relevance of drive theory in interpreting projective test data elicited from children. The point is that these data assume meaning only when they are viewed through an array of lenses rather than in a monolithic way.

This challenge requires the clinician to be cognizant of the unique theoretical biases and life experiences that he brings to projective test conditions and interpretations. An example of how theoretical orientation might intrude into interpretation of projective test data is crystallized by recent controversy within psychoanalytic circles about a cornerstone of analytic theory—the oedipal complex. Revisionists contend that Freud and many of his adherents have neglected the widespread incidence of sexual abuse of children in order to preserve intact the notion that oedipal conflicts originate in the traversing of a "built-in" psychosexual stage of development that may be universal (Miller, 1984). In the interpretation of projective and other test data, an orthodox Freudian may be less attuned to the possibility of direct or more oblique sexual abuse of children by parents. As a result, hostile, aggressive impulses and murderous fantasies that may be present in projective test protocols will be interpreted in a radically different manner, depending upon the degree to which the interpreter subscribes to the drive theory or is willing to consider carefully the possibility that violence pervades the home environment of the child who is being assessed. The following case will illustrate clinically some of the issues that have been raised.

Nicky, a 5½-year-old boy, was referred for a psychological evaluation as part of a research study, not because of symptoms indicating emotional disturbance. Nicky, whose family was of lower socioeconomic status, was raised for most of his life by his paternal great aunt. His parents, who were young and disorganized, had been unable to provide for him and had entrusted his care to this relative. While his parents drifted in and out of his life, Nicky's aunt became the one consistent caretaker upon whom he could rely. Nicky did well in school, but he was a persistent bedwetter and, according to his aunt, tended to be "undisciplined" at home.

Nicky's aunt had been afflicted with emotional problems in her youth but appeared to have gained some insight and stability through the years. She was plagued, however, by intense guilt feelings over what she perceived as her past neglect and abuse of her now-adult children. As a consequence, she seemed unable to limit them from taking advantage of her resources. Specifically, she lent them money indiscriminately, let them use her home as a crash pad, and even feared that illegal drug sales were being conducted in her living room. Nicky's aunt observed that she was inclined to allow Nicky "to get away with too much," to compensate for her harshness with her own children when she had raised them.

An interview with Nicky's father revealed him to be a disturbed young man who feared his own proclivities to become a child abuser. As a result, he carefully refrained from disciplining his son. Nicky's mother was a pathetic, helpless, and childlike individual who was able, without much probing, to acknowledge her inability to form a maternal attachment to her son.

Nicky himself presented as a slim, pale youngster who appeared to be well cared for physically and was generally friendly in his interactions with the evaluator. The evaluation procedures for Nicky included the WISC-R, CAT, Vineland Scale of Social Maturity, and a play interview in which he produced five spontaneous drawings accompanied by stories. Most of Nicky's test material indicated average intelligence and normal developmental progression. In general, the projective test results were pervaded by an abnormal preoccupation with aggression and violence that could have been suggestive of difficulty in incorporating limits and of fear of his inability to master and channel his impulses. Nicky's play was more boisterous than average. His CAT stories reflected a concern with his own weaknesses and attempts to gain protection by alliance with stronger figures. In his conversation, Nicky demonstrated an attempt to ally and identify with his father, whom he saw as both frightening and powerful (e.g., "I want to shoot little birdies like my daddy, and when I'm bigger I'm going to get a big gun like his"). Nicky's drawings of bloody conflicts between "tarantulas and bunnies" were especially troublesome. The stories that accompanied these productions revealed Nicky to be a frightened child trying to protect himself from overwhelming aggressive impulses and a concomitant tendency to identify with the aggressor (e.g., "One bunny killed off all the tarantulas who are going to eat me, and then he attacks the other bunnies with his big rabbit teeth").

To interpret Nicky's profile as reflecting his attempts to cope with his feeling that he was unable to control his impulses and that this was catalyzed by a lack of adequate discipline is only partially correct. The importance of considering the reality of Nicky's living situation, beyond the lack of discipline and structure, was compellingly validated by events in his life. While his participation in the study was continuing, the violence he portrayed in fantasy productions erupted into terrifying reality when a murder was committed in his home, replete with the blood and violence he had depicted in his drawings.

USE OF COLLATERAL INTERVIEWS

In investigating the emotional concerns of young children, it is particularly vital that the psychologist garner as much information as possible about the child and his overall living situation. This might necessitate collateral interviews with family members, as well as social workers and other professionals. In cases where the possibility of actual abuse or neglect exists, this is an essential requisite perspective that the examiner should possess in interpreting the child's projective material and in making recommendations. Children who are known or suspected victims of incest may reflect, in their projective and other responses, efforts to integrate and cope with their experiences in a variety of complicated, veiled or more obvious fashions. The examiner must be exceptionally careful in interpreting and recognizing such material, since there are as yet few research norms for reactions of children at various ages to such traumatic experiences.

In other instances, comprehensive collateral information pertaining to the child's current life situation will help to rule out premature and erroneous conclusions about the existence of serious psychopathology. Children, particularly young children, are so reactive to transient as well as focal events at home that special sensitivity is required to discriminate between reactions to temporary life circumstances and central personality trends.

To cite a clinical example, consider the four-year-old boy who gave the following story in response to card 1 of the CAT. (Prior to administration of this test, it is noteworthy that this boy had eaten all of the candy in a dish on the examiner's desk.)

> It's a mommy chicken and her baby chickies. They're having breakfast. She's giving them porridge and it's yucky. They hate it because it is bitter and they start to cry. But she says no! Cluck, cluck, cluck. The daddy is not there. The end.

This story, taken out of context, could be interpreted as revealing a young child's frustration at his experience of oral deprivation by a cruel and withholding mother who attends to her childrens' physical needs but does not give them the sustaining emotional nourishment they require. The child appears to be deserted by the father as well.

Further investigation into the circumstances of this child revealed a less disturbing situation. The week of the testing, his parents decided to limit his intake of sweets and in particular drastically reduced the customary amount of maple syrup which had formerly been poured over his morning oatmeal. In addition, the child had a strong attachment to his father, who worked long hours and often expressed genuine disappointment that he could not spend more time together with his son.

THE IMPACT OF THE TESTING SITUATION

The child's often extreme sensitivity to the test situation itself also must be taken into account. The examiner should be particularly aware of emotional responses he may evoke in the child. The establishment of a positive relationship is even more crucial with a young child than it is in carrying out diagnostic work with adults. "Blank screen" approaches are likely to frighten and alienate a child, thereby creating projective test responses whose pathological content becomes an artifact of the test environment.

The context of the test situation is of paramount importance. Many children who are referred for psychological evaluation as part of a court-ordered investigation of possible abuse or neglect sense and reflect the emotional tension that their appointment with the psychologist is causing in their families. These children often fear that they have done something wrong and that they will be punished or that their parents will be hurt and angry about what they disclose. In many cases, children are told explicitly by one or both of their parents not to reveal certain secrets, typically involving their own victimization. Younger children often will tell an examiner with whom they feel comfortable about the pressures to which they have been subjected. Sometimes these revelations emerge directly in the course of interviewing or conversation; at other times they will surface in projective test responses. It is important to recognize that many children respond to projective tests in a restricted manner because they sense the task-oriented nature of the instruments. These children often will be more relaxed and expansive in a free-play situation that they themselves can structure; under such circumstances, they frequently will engage in revealing conversation.

The examiner always should be mindful of the intrinsic powerlessness of children, both in the test situation and in the world at large. Performance pressures galvanized by parenting figures and a competitive society contribute to making task-oriented test instruments more threatening to many children than freer expressive methods such as unstructured play, puppetry, or art. In contrast, some older children are reassured by the focus imposed by more directive test methods and consequently are better able to distance themselves and their situation from the particular task. This group of children is more apt to produce test protocols that represent internal concerns.

The examiner is also responsible for always bearing in mind the uses to which her report may be put. Discussion of data among staff members within a clinic setting can be freer than analysis of information that must be sifted, simplified, focused, and translated for judges, lawyers, and parents. Since psychological evaluations of children may have profound consequences, it is critical that the psychologist attempt to discern whether projective tests and other productions are expressive of transient reactions to situational factors or more enduring personality dynamics and trends. The age of the child must be factored into the interpretive equation. It is more likely to be a sign of serious disturbance when a seven-year-old tears the arms and legs off dolls than when a four-year-old engages in the same activity. To the greatest extent possible the examiner ought to be acquainted with a broad view of normative developmental behaviors. Projective and other test results are revealing and useful only when they are examined from diverse perspectives.

Even with a grasp of developmental norms the examiner may stumble if he or she does not allow for individual variability within expected parameters. For example, the following referral was made because of a flawed understanding of developmental standards.

A boy of 3½ was brought to a clinic for psychological testing after his nursery-school teacher expressed concern to his parents that "his body image was distorted and he was beginning to have bad feelings about himself." The teacher, a layperson, reached this conclusion after viewing a self-portrait done by this boy which consisted essentially of unstructured scribbling and chaotic lines. The psychologist who had been requested to assess this child noted that he was particularly uneven in his development. Specifically, he was precocious verbally and in most fine motor skills. Socially his interaction with his classmates seemed somewhat tentative for a child his age, in that he confined himself mostly to engaging in parallel play. On the other hand, this boy watched the other children, expressed interest in them to his teacher, and openly showed disappointment if they were absent from school.

When this child had been an infant, he had experienced two febrile seizures that had left no discernible neurological damage. Although he was sturdy and strong, he had been late in sitting up and walking and was somewhat, but not markedly, awkward in large motor coordination. This child was described by his parents as having an intense temperament and forming strong attachments to family members and animals. He conveyed the impression to his parents and other adults of being strong willed (stubborn) and having a strong sense of self. On the basis of this total picture, the examiner concluded that the nursery-school teacher's assessment of this child's self-portrait was narrow and erroneous. A broader understanding of developmental norms and their variability plus a more comprehensive appreciation of this individual child contributed to correction of this misinterpretation of a single piece of "data" by a well-intentioned but poorly informed layperson.

In conclusion, the task of the psychologist as evaluator in the clinic setting is as challenging as it is intricate. The examiner must seek out and integrate as much information as possible about the children whom she is requested to evaluate. The child's total environment, developmental norms and individual variability within those norms, and the reasons that lead to the request for evaluation all must be included in tackling the challenges and intricacies of putting together a meaningful and useful assessment of a child's personality dynamics. Influences in the test situation and in the child's culture are additional factors that will affect his projective test and other productions. Children are intrinsically powerless in relation to the adults upon whom they depend for survival. The psychologist who carries out psychological evaluations of children in the clinic setting must be an active advocate of the child's interests. This advocacy role should enhance the evaluator's capacity to understand individual children and to make recommendations that will further their interests.

CASE STUDY: "LINDA"

The following case was chosen to illustrate some of the processes and problems described in this chapter. The material illustrates how the psychologist must consider and integrate a variety of different types of information into a final report.

Background Information

At the age of 13 years, two months, Linda was referred by her parents at the suggestion of the school guidance counselor. Her performance at school had taken a drastic turn downward. She was often truant. At home, Linda's behavior was becoming increasingly rebellious and "uncontrollable," according to her parents. During the past year she had become defiant toward her parents and refused to obey their rules regarding curfews and outside activities. She had run away from home numerous times, returning on her own within a day or two. Linda's parents were concerned that her new friends were "known troublemakers," and they suspected she was becoming involved in drug experimentation.

One of the most perplexing things about this case was the suddenness and lack of obvious causation with which Linda's troubles seemed to have begun. In addition to the behavior just described, Linda had recently broken friendships of long duration and withdrawn from gymnastics, an activity to which she had shown a serious commitment since age 10.

Linda came from an intact, upwardly mobile, middle-class family. She was the middle child in a sibship of three. Her sister, four years older, was a freshman at college and lived away from home. Her brother, eight years younger, was apparently doing well. According to her mother, up to the past year, Linda had been a "model child," compliant and quiet. She could amuse herself but had friends as well. She was described by her mother as a timid child who needed extra reassurance and praise and was compared somewhat unfavorably to her more adventurous older sister, who seemed to have been the parents' favorite of the two girls. Linda's insecurity had surfaced outside the family in first grade and then in grade seven, when she had difficulty coping with transitions to new schools.

Linda's mother was intelligent and well spoken but somewhat constricted. Her appearance was fashionably conventional. She had quit college to marry Linda's father, an insurance executive. She appeared depressed but attributed this to "worry over Linda." She described the atmosphere at home as "positive" and denied any conflict between herself and her husband. Her tone and posture relaxed noticeably when she described "her baby," the youngest child of the family, a little boy of five.

According to Linda's mother, her husband was a hard-working, ambitious person who, of necessity, spent much time away from home. She said the larger share of responsibility for raising the children fell to her, although, when he was home, her husband's authority went foremost. Appearances, in his line of work, were important, and Linda's mother said she had to expend a great deal of energy entertaining her husband's clients. She maintained that she was "not resentful" of this, because it helped enable the family to maintain a comfortable standard of life.

The procedures used to evaluate Linda were a clinical interview, the Rorschach, and the Thematic Apperception Test.

Interview Results

Linda was an attractive, well-spoken girl who took the tasks of the evaluation seriously, despite her expressions of boredom and impatience with their length. She expressed bewilderment at her situation and said she could not understand why she had started to "mess up." She said she did not feel depressed but, rather, "antsy and impatient most of the time." She was angry with her parents and school authorities for what she interpreted as their lack of sympathy and inability to help her behave. She was keenly aware of her failure to live up to parental expectations and told the examiner she hated herself for this.

In contrast to her mother, Linda described her family home as having been cold and unsupportive. She described a competitive relationship with her older sister in which she "always loses," a father who was "the big boss" despite his lack of concern with daily family affairs, and a mother who was constantly "put down" by her husband. Linda dwelt at length on her concerns with her parents' poor marital relationship, particularly identifying with her mother's position. She resented both her mother's passivity in this regard ("She should tell him where to get off") and her father's lack of affection and respect for her mother. She speculated on whether he "had a girl friend on the side." The theme of unhappiness in love was mirrored by her recent rejection by her first serious boyfriend. However, the one enthusiasm and future goal Linda expressed was a desire to get married and have a family. Like her mother, Linda expressed the most warmth toward her little brother.

During the interview, Linda described her difficulty expressing her emotions in words. She described "things" going around in her head and tension building to the point of "explosion." It was at these times when Linda ran away. She acknowledged, when asked specifically, that she sometimes thought of suicide at these times, as a means to escape the intense internal pressure. She admitted experimenting with drugs, given or sold to her by her new friends, to blot out this psychic pain. Unfortunately, Linda could not connect this pressure with external events, other than hating school, an explanation she described as "ridiculous."

Rorschach Results

Linda's productivity was low. She referred to the blots after she had seen the first four as "dark," but interestingly did not associate directly to the shading (Y) on any particular percept. She was realistically aware that some of her responses were of poor form quality, but insisted in a mildly belligerent manner that "that's still what I see, so you might as well write it down." The individual associations, response scorings, and summary are shown in Table 16.1. The scoring method used is Beck's (Beck, Beck, Levitt, & Molish, 1961).

Thematic Apperception Test Results

A sample of Linda's TAT responses is reproduced in the following paragraphs.

Table 16.1   Linda's Rorschach Test Results

I.	3″	1. D F + A	Hornet
		2. W F + A	Spider
II.	2″	3. WSF − Ad	Cat's face
III.	23″	4. WSF − Ad	Spider head
IV.	3″	5. WFV + H	Tall man or monster
V.	2″	6. W F + A P	Bat
VI.	5″	7. D FT + Ad	Giraffe
		8. D F + AHbP	Bearskin rug
VII.	6″	9. W M + HRc	Dancing
		10. W MFT H P	Angels
VIII.	3″	11. W F + A P	Bears
IX.	6″	12. Ws F + Tr	Spaceship
X.	4″	13. Ds F − Ad	Animal face
		14. D F + A	Two insects fighting

W = 9	M = 1	H = 3	F+ % = 70
D = 5	MFT = 1	A = 6	A % = 71
R = 14	FT = 1	Ad = 4	P # = 4
	FV = 1	Tr = 1	S # = 4
EB = 2:0	F+ = 7	R = 14	S % = 28
EA = 2	F− = 3		T/1R = 5.7
	R = 14		

Card 1.   Don't know . . . I think he's just given up . . . started to learn, but he just can't concentrate so he just gave up on it. . . . Maybe he'll end up doing it though. Do I have to do all of them?

Card 3GF.   She got in a fight with her husband and he left. She tried to call him back but he wouldn't come [sigh]. . . . I think he'll come back, but maybe she won't take him back.

Card 6GF.   He's mean, and he caught her doing something she wasn't supposed to. He'll probably hit her and leave. Then he'll probably come back and they'll get back together, but she'll hate him.

Card 7GF.   I think they got in a fight, but now they're talking about it, but I think they'll go on having more fights. I don't know what will happen in the end. She'll probably grow up to be a mean, rotten kid. (Laughs.)

Card 9GF.   Is this water? She's reflecting in the water and seeing what she really is, and she'll change herself to be a better person.

Card 12BG.   Someone went and killed themselves. That's about all I can say about it; got fed up I guess.

Card 13MF.   I think she was a hooker. He went out and got drunk and went to bed with her. Now he's realized what he did and feels really bad. He'll go back to his wife and confess. I think their marriage will get better, and they'll be closer because he confessed.

Card 14. I think he's in prison for something he didn't do and his cellmate is sick. He'll break out, but when they catch him they'll put him back. Later they'll find out he didn't do it. His friend will get better and everything will go forward for them.

Interpretation and Synthesis

The results of the Rorschach, despite the limited number of responses, furnished evidence of Linda's defensive style and personality structure. The TAT gave more specific information regarding her conflicts. None of the material gathered in the interview or test material contradicted the examiner's hypothesis that Linda's reactions to conditions at home precipitated her troubled behavior. A joint interview with her parents, conducted after the testing was completed but before the report was written, added further confirmation to this view. Some excerpts from the report follow.

Linda is a girl of above average intellectual potential who is not functioning up to capacity because of emotional problems. . . . Linda's defensive style is similar to that of a child several years younger than her thirteen years. Instead of depression being expressed or felt as sadness, it is discharged in activity and general irritability. Linda tends to be impulsive and often reacts too quickly when she feels under pressure. Repression and denial are also hallmarks of her reactive style. She blocks out useful information and then is left to make faulty interpretations based on inadequate information. Therefore, she often exhibits poor judgment. Her reasoning shows no sign of thought disorder, however. She is too constricted now to allow herself to recognize and express many emotions consciously, and therefore she may seem inappropriately unaffected by circumstances.

Linda is preoccupied with difficulties in male–female relationships. Anger, rejection, and love lost permeate her TAT stories. She has a low opinion of herself and is often pessimistic about her possibilities for the future. On an unconscious level, Linda views herself and her concerns as unimportant to anyone. There is some indication that she suffers from a more basic feeling of being unloved and longs for the security and protection of emotional nourishment. She is stubborn and strong willed, however.

Clinical interview data support the conclusion that Linda's disruptive behavior is depressive in nature. She is excessively preoccupied with what she perceives as her parents' bad marriage. She identifies with her mother as a passive recipient of pain, but rebels against this quality in herself. At the same time, she is pessimistic of her ability to win the struggle.

Linda's conscious thoughts of suicide as a solution to her misery are a concern. These thoughts and her TAT association that "someone went and killed themselves," in combination with her anger, masked depression, impulsivity, and poor judgment, suggest the possibility that Linda might act out in suicidal gestures. These results do not indicate that she is actively suicidal at this time, however.

Disposition and Follow-up

Outpatient psychotherapy that focused on the family rather than on Linda as the "identified patient" was recommended to the family. The parents were willing to provide treatment for Linda but refused involvement in it themselves. Linda participated in individual psychotherapy once weekly for a period of approximately two years. Her general behavior improved along with her self-esteem and overall outlook. During the first year after the evaluation, Linda's parents separated and eventually divorced. Linda's mother entered psychotherapy and returned to college, and the relationship between the two improved.

SUMMARY

The task of the psychologist evaluating children in the clinic is both challenging in its complexity and exciting in its potential for positively influencing the course of events in the lives of the children being examined. This chapter has attempted to delineate the complexity of the task in hopes of alerting the examiner to the pitfalls and possibilities of the practical application of projective testing of children.

Because the focus of clinical evaluation is on the individual, rather than on the establishment of normative data, the examiner must integrate a host of information, based on research, with the peculiarities of one person. The particular characteristics of one child, which always vary in some way from the norms, must be appreciated for a full understanding of that child's functioning in her world. Often the examiner's intuition will be crucial in integrating this totality and making recommendations.

The examiner must be aware that, although projective techniques typically elicit fantasy material in adult subjects, children's productions might be veiled descriptions of their actual situations. Besides reflecting reality, their productions will show their attempts at interpreting and coping with this reality. For this reason, much effort should be expended in gathering auxiliary information. The psychologist also must be sensitive to the child's reaction to the test situation and mindful of his own impact on the child.

In addition, the examiner must be ever mindful of the intrinsically powerless position of children in relation to the adults who determine the basic parameters of their life situations. The examiner must be prepared to assume an advocacy position in relation to the child's interests. This is especially important in cases of suspected abuse or custody disputes.

When the psychologist is cognizant of all these factors and skillful in approach, the ability to provide a meaningful report describing the personality dynamics and functioning of a particular child can make a valuable contribution to the treatment of the individual child as well as to the field of the clinical practice of psychology.

REFERENCES

Abt, L., & Bellak, L. (Eds.). (1950). *Projective psychology*. New York: Knopf.

Altman, C. (1960). Projective techniques in the clinic setting. In A. I. Rabin & M. R. Haworth (Eds.), *Projective techniques with children*. New York: Grune & Stratton.

Beck, S. J., Beck, A. G., Levitt, E. E., & Molish, H. B. (1961). *Rorschach's Test* (Vol 1). *Basic processes*. New York: Grune & Stratton.

Miller, A. (1984). *Thou shalt not be aware*. New York: Farrar, Straus, & Giroux.

17
The Challenge of the Clinical Use of Projective Methods: A Case Demonstration

Hagit Benziman

For more than two decades, psychotherapy (with all of its ramifications and variations) has maintained a place of prominence, remaining on the top of the list of functions of the clinical psychologist while diagnostic testing has taken a back seat (Rabin & Hayes, 1978). Because of the lures of psychotherapy, most clinical psychologists do not find diagnostic testing a professionally satisfying activity.

The aim of this chapter is to illustrate the clinical role of the tester and to show—by a case demonstration (taken from Benziman, 1982)—that diagnostic testing is not only important and useful but also challenging and exciting for clinical psychologists. We will demonstrate only a partial test battery, but we will try to analyze it in the fullest possible detail. The case will be described as if the tester were thinking aloud, thus enabling the reader to follow the tester's thinking process step by step.

CASE BACKGROUND

Tamar, referred for psychological testing by her homeroom teacher, is a 10-year-old pupil in the fifth grade who, since entering school, has suffered from learning difficulties and is considered deviant and disturbed. According to her teacher, Tamar is weak in all the school subjects, displays no interest in the material taught, lacks concentration, and often is seen deeply immersed in daydreams and cut off from the world around her. Socially, as well, she does not integrate. She appears very eager to be involved in the society of children but has not succeeded. Her classmates tend to keep distant from her, reject her, or even to annoy her. Physically, Tamar is a very thin girl, weak, pale, and rundown. "All her functioning," said her teacher, "seemed void of any will to live, lacking in vitality. We, the teachers, feel that we are witnessing the girl wasting away."

Tamar's father, to whom she was very attached, died two years prior to her referral for examination. According to the teacher's report, Tamar's condition has deteriorated since her father's death, although her general condition previously had been on a low level.

Her teacher has no doubts concerning Tamar's intellect, believing she is an intelligent child. "Her learning difficulties," she stated, "result from deep emotional problems rather than from poor intellectual abilities."

The teacher has sought to help Tamar, to find a way to get through to her and a way to understand the meaning of her distress, so that she can arrest her "wasting away" and restore her "will to live" and her vitality. The efforts of the teachers at school to arouse her, encourage her, draw her close to them, and to help her, especially in her studies, all have been in vain.

ADMINISTRATION OF TESTS

Tamar entered the room, but before entering into the rigid and structured framework of the psychological testing, I started a conversation with her. I wanted to "warm up" the atmosphere and to dispel the sense of strangeness and tension of being confronted with an unfamiliar professional. I knew that there was no way to extinguish the anxiety and the defense mechanisms evoked by the testing situation (Schafer, 1954), but I felt that it was my duty to reduce them. This was my duty not only due to humanistic considerations, but due to some very practical reasons as well: I wanted to get a valid impression of Tamar's optimal functioning and therefore I had to enable her to relax. I also knew that this was for her the first acquaintance with a psychologist and therefore wanted her to be positively impressed.

Tamar was able to talk about herself easily, to describe her difficulties, her fears, and her distress. Her words flowed on, one story leading to another, with little or no need for me to encourage her to talk or to ask her questions. She seemed to cry out for an attentive ear. She spoke of being sad, often feeling lonely and bored. She felt that no one else cared what happened to her; that no one paid attention to her or loved her. Tamar expressed her apprehensions that her mother would remarry and described recurring haunting nightmares.

In the course of her talk, she mentioned how much she liked to draw. She said that sometimes, following a quarrel with her mother, she would go into her room, draw by herself, and calm down. In school, also, she occasionally remained during recesses and after classes to draw on the blackboard. Even in my room, she went spontaneously to draw on the blackboard. She drew a heart and inside it a flower. On her own initiative she composed a story about the drawing. On the blackboard, alongside the drawing of the heart, she wrote "True Story" and then, "Once upon a time there was someone and he had an illness." Tamar erased the first sentence of her story immediately after it was written. She began her story anew: "Once upon a time there was someone and she had an illness in which she would steal all the time. One time the police caught her. . . ."

Here, Tamar paused for a moment in her writing. She returned to the title and changed the name of the story from "True Story" to "Make-believe Story" and then continued, ". . . but the police didn't do anything to her. One time she invited the police to her father and then she killed him and he died. The end."

I paid attention to each detail. As a tester I have to use a multitest battery (Rapaport, Gill, & Schafer, 1968) and multisense awareness. I have to be a sensitive seismograph in order to sharpen my observation and to broaden the sample upon which I base my acquaintance with the subject. The erasure of the first sentence in the story, the pausing for a moment in her writing, the change of the story's name—all these details were very important and served later as very meaningful sources of information about Tamar's inner world.

After spontaneously drawing and telling the story of her picture, I asked Tamar to make additional drawings of a man or a woman, a boy or a girl, and to accompany them with stories. This Draw a Person test is one part of the regular test battery (Machover, 1949). In this case I decided to start the testing procedure with this test because it was a logical and natural continuation of Tamar's previous activity. By doing this, I enabled her to pass into the stage of formal testing without any anxiety and confusion. Tamar's drawings are shown in Figure 17.1.

First, Tamar drew a figure in trousers. "That's a man," she said. Immediately afterward she drew a stork standing on a branch of a tree, accompanying the drawing with the verbal description, "This is a stork." Underneath it, without commenting, she drew another stork. I did not say a word and did not try to draw Tamar's attention to her departure from the original instructions. Of her own initiative, Tamar returned to the original instructions and, after drawing the two storks, said, "Now

FIGURE 17.1   Tamar's Draw-a-Person Test.

I'll draw a woman." In the lower part of the sheet of paper she added the figure of a woman.

Tamar accompanied the drawing of the man with the following story:

> He decides to find himself a wife. He gets angry and does not find a wife. In the end he went to the train station and saw a girl and wanted to start up with her, and she also liked him and also wanted to start up with him. Then he said, "Come, I'll invite you to a cafe," and he paid for her and said to her, "Maybe you'll come to sleep at my place?" He did everything she wanted and was her boyfriend. And the following night they went to a movie and she was afraid, so she said to him, "Come, let's go to a cafe because I don't want to. This is not a nice movie." And he said, "O.K.!" They went to a cafe and drank. They stayed until midnight and they decided that they need to go to a discotheque, and he went with her because he promised to do all she wanted

and he told her that he was tired. Then she said, "It's not worth leaving. It's better at the discotheque because we have nothing to do at home." That's it.

About the drawing of the woman, Tamar told the following story:

> The woman always thought that she was proud and that nobody loved her. Her parents didn't love her, and she remained alone. Then one time she was riding on the train and a young man came to sit next to her and he began to start up with her. She didn't want that and said, "I'm proud and nobody loves me so I don't want you to start up with me." Then suddenly he said to her, "Come, I'll invite you to a cafe," and she said, "I don't want to. Everybody thinks I'm proud. I simply want to return home. If you'll buy me a house or a palace then I'll go out with you." Then he said to her, "O.K." He started to work and work until he earned more than $2,000. He had a lot of money and bought her a palace and she was his girlfriend. But she didn't love him and was unfaithful to him. Then one time they decided to get married because she saw that he bought her a palace and was very attentive to her, and they got married and she was happy and that's it.

After hearing her stories about her drawings, I asked Tamar to tell stories in response to the pictures of the TAT (Henry, 1956; Rapaport et al., 1968). She responded willingly, her stories streaming forth, necessitating little encouragement, prodding, or asking of leading questions.

In response to picture 1 (a picture of a boy sitting beside a violin), she told the following story:

> A boy went into his room and saw a present on the table. He began to think about it. To think. Until he decided to do something. He went. He threw it somewhere where no one would see. Then his parents said to him, "Where is the present we brought you?" He said to them, "I threw it out." That's it. [Tamar thereby concluded her story, but in order to reveal a little more I went on to ask, "Why did he throw out the present?"] Because he thought it was a bomb; he felt that it was a bomb. He saw a clock.

This was Tamar's story in response to the first of the TAT pictures. It then was necessary for me to decide which additional pictures should be presented to her. Customarily, I do not use the full set of test pictures, especially when dealing with children for whom long periods of concentration are difficult. In each case I decide which pictures to administer to the person being tested according to which pictures are likely to motivate her to relate to subjects that are still unclear to me and not completely understood. While sitting with Tamar, looking at her drawings and listening to her stories, I was continuously occupied with forming hypotheses. I concluded that Tamar had revealed the web of her emotions toward the male figure in previous tests, but as yet her feelings toward the mother figure had not been expressed. I therefore chose to show her specifically those pictures presenting contact between women.

Picture 18GF (a picture of two women that usually leads to stories of mother–daughter relationships or the relations between two sisters) aroused in Tamar the following story:

> Oh, here is a witch. She wanted to kill this girl because she had a boyfriend and she began to be jealous. She hated her so much that she wanted to murder her. Then her boyfriend decided to kill the old woman. He said to her, "Come, let's wash your hair." He heated up water and burned her head. Her brain exploded. Afterward they lived alone without the witch.

Picture 7GF presents a situation between mother and daughter where the daughter holds something resembling a doll or a baby. Tamar told the following story in response to this picture:

> Her mother had a baby, and the girl held the brother in her arms. The girl loved him very much. And one time the mother decided that the girl was bothering the baby, and she wasn't bothering him. And the mother wanted to hide the baby, and she put him in a crate on the river. Then she hid him and the girl didn't go to school, and was weaker than everybody, and began to wear things that were not pretty, and she told her mother that so long as she didn't return the baby she wouldn't be a good girl. Then once she went outside and saw a baby in the river and called to him. He remained in the crate. He was a year, a year and a half, old. She ran away with the baby and the mother found out that the baby was gone. She wanted to kill herself and began to cry over the missing baby. She went to the police and chased after the girl. They didn't find the girl and thought she killed herself together with the baby in the pool. Then they emptied the pool and didn't find her. In the end they found her killed and the baby killed. No, no, not killed. He was crying . . ."

INTERPRETATION OF DATA

Tamar did not want to leave at the end of the session. "Don't want to go home," she said, "I like being here. I want to sleep here." Her attempts to cling to me, to somebody she had just met, and her desire to find in the new and unfamiliar place a substitute home, were heartrending. I had the impression that her whole being cried for warmth and contact. What are the reasons for these feelings of lack of warmth and love? Tamar herself related her sadness to the fact that she missed her deceased father. This is a very extreme mourning reaction. It has lasted too long and its effects are out of proportion in comparison to normal mourning reactions. What is hidden behind this reaction? What did her father mean to her and what was her mother's reaction to the father's death? Tamar expressed her apprehensions that her mother would remarry, but I checked with her mother the factual basis for these apprehensions and she revealed that she entertains no thoughts of forming a new tie with a man. Since her husband's death she is absorbed in herself and maintains relations only with members of her family. Tamar's apprehensions, like her extreme grief, derive from her inner world. I am trying to reveal this inner world by analyzing her tests.

The Heart with the Flower

Had Tamar not told her story, I would not have attributed great significance to her drawing on the blackboard. I would have assumed that this was merely a drawing typical of 10-year-old girls who, preoccupied by the subject of romance, express their wishes and fantasies in the drawing of hearts. However, Tamar's story is a different story. In relation to a heart and flower drawing, in relation to the subject of love, Tamar embarked on a true/imaginary story unique to her. There seems to be no connection between her story and the story she told. However, there is no doubt that, in her inner world, in her thoughts and fantasies, they are related, for she herself linked the story to her drawing. This, therefore, is the story of Tamar's love, a love that is bound to a male person who "had an illness." Tamar did not continue the story she wanted to tell. It is as if she severed the thoughts about this same person and instead began a new story in which the sick person is not male but female and does not have a physical illness. "She had an illness in which she would steal all the time," a sort of unrestrained craving. This same "someone" in Tamar's story was not, in reality, sick but bad, guilty and deserving of punishment, "and one time the police caught her."

The turnabout that Tamar made in her story from the sick male "someone" to the bad female who steals and who is deserving of punishment is not incidental. Thought follows thought, one association follows another. That is the way of fantasies, memories, stories. They are created as a chain in which each link is connected to those preceding it and those following it. The picture of the heart aroused in Tamar the thought of a male "someone who had an illness," and that "sick someone" inspired the story of the bad female who stole and deserved punishment. It seems plausible to say that Tamar expressed in her drawing and in her story a bond of love for a sick man toward whom she feels bad and guilty. At this stage I can already hypothesize that her story reveals the complexity of her emotions toward her father, who became ill and died. This hypothesis is confirmed as the story continues and Tamar tells that the male "someone" is a father and the female "someone" is none other than his daughter, who is guilty of her father's death: "One time she invited the police to her father and then she killed him and he died." Tamar herself seemed frightened to face these thoughts and tried not to attribute them to herself. The moment she began talking directly of a father and daughter, she changed the title of the story to "Make-believe Story." It is as if she wanted to say that it is just a story, far removed, a fabrication with no basis in reality.

Draw-a-Person

It is imperative that I follow the events from their beginning. Tamar first drew a man. I tend to assume that this is a hint that she is closer to the male figure than to the female. According to normative data it is more natural and expected for a girl of 10 to draw a female figure of about her own age (Machover, 1949). However, the male figure that Tamar drew is not just close to her. This is a figure in which central facial features are missing and whose balance is upset—a weak, defective figure who seems about to fall. Is it possible that Tamar was simply careless in the drawing, slighted it, and did not put any effort into the task? No. It does not seem reasonable that Tamar would be careless specifically in drawing this picture. It was the first of her drawings. She had not yet tired of her task; neither had she expressed in words or behavior any reservations about fulfilling the assignment; and afterward she continued to pay careful attention to the drawings and even added, on her own initiative, drawings she was not asked to do.

The meaning of the "carelessness" was not a general carelessness but rather was linked to the specific subject she drew—to the specific drawing of a man. Perhaps the male figure was not drawn adequately because it was her first drawing? Maybe at the beginning of her task Tamar felt self-conscious and was afraid she would not perform well. This supposition is also unacceptable, since, in fact, the drawing of the man was not Tamar's first drawing. Preceding this drawing was the drawing of the heart with the flower inside it. When she was asked to draw a human figure, it was a logical continuation of her previous activity. Tamar did not even perceive that she was passing into a stage in which psychological tests were being administered, and therefore it is hard to suppose that she was overcome by anxiety and confusion.

Obviously, there is no place to claim that the lack of details and the lack of stability that characterize the man in Tamar's drawing are typical of her manner of drawing in general, for, included in her other drawings, drawn on the very same sheet of paper, is a detailed face of a woman including a nose, mouth, and cheeks. She is drawn standing in a stable position. The two storks, as well, are standing upright. The deformity and fragility, therefore, specifically characterize the male figure. My conclusion is, therefore, that in this drawing Tamar expressed her feelings toward the male figure: She is close to him, her thoughts are initially focused upon him, yet he is perceived by her as defective and detached, or possibly arouses in her the desire to mutilate or hurt him.

I cannot determine, at this stage, whether Tamar perceives the male figure as weak and deficient or whether she harbors aggressive fantasies toward him. A person's drawing may express the way he perceives reality, but it also may express his wishes and desires concerning reality. It is up to me to determine whether Tamar perceives the male figure as weak and deformed or whether she harbors in her heart wishes to mutilate and hurt him. I shall look for additional data and impressions in order to reach a decision.

Upon completing the drawing of the man, Tamar went on to draw two storks, one after the other. I intentionally refrained from telling her that she was not following instructions. It is precisely this sliding into other drawings, to other subjects, that may be of utmost significance. Still, I don't see this as a serious phenomenon indicating dissociation from reality and immersion into fantasy. Tamar is still a child, and children occasionally tend to deviate from the strict outline of the prescribed framework. Futhermore, after drawing the storks, Tamar, on her own initiative, returned to the instructions of the test and added the drawing of a woman. However, these additional drawings came solely from an internal motive, from Tamar's private and unique world. They most likely reveal deep underlying emotions. Why, then, did she draw the two storks? How did it occur to her to draw them, and what do they represent?

The storks were drawn following the drawing of the man, and so they probably are related to it. My first supposition was that Tamar felt that the drawing of the man was defective and not very successful, and that she, therefore, tried to demonstrate her drawing abilities with a different picture in which she had more practice. However, I rejected this possibility when she drew another stork. The second drawing of a stork is, without question, less advanced than the first. Had Tamar intended to prove her drawing abilities and amend the impression she created in her drawing of the man, she certainly would not have drawn the second stork.

I therefore turn to another hypothesis, another explanation for the drawing of the storks. I tend to assume that Tamar's need to draw them arose due to their hidden content. After drawing the male figure, there arose in Tamar the need to draw a female figure, represented by a stork. (Tamar's native language is Hebrew, a language in which a stork is strongly associated with a female figure.) After drawing a figure of a deformed man, about to fall, there arose in her the need to draw a figure of her own sex, a surrogate to a drawing of herself, and this figure turns her beak toward herself as if about to peck at herself, as if to hurt herself. I can hypothesize, therefore, that the man's deformity aroused in Tamar guilt feelings creating the need to turn her aggression inward, on herself. In the guise of the stork about to peck at herself, Tamar expressed her feeling that she deserves punishment for deforming the figure of the man. This hypothesis is upheld when examining the second drawing of the stork. Tamar was not contented with the drawing of the stork turning its beak upon itself. She developed this subject further in the second drawing, where the stork does indeed hurt itself and the figure is seen as being cut off, deformed, and fractured.

This analysis of the meaning of the drawing of the stork enables me to answer the question I asked myself earlier: Does the drawing of the man express the male figure as it is perceived in Tamar's eyes, or does it express her aggressive wishes toward the man and thus the ensuing guilt and punishment? Two different and independent cases have led to identical hypotheses, and now I can feel confident of my interpretation.

It has become clear that Tamar feels guilty and deserving of punishment for having injured the male figure, for having caused her father's death. Yet why does she carry such feelings within her? Children are unable to distinguish clearly between fantasy and reality. They attribute real power to their words, emotions, imaginations, and desires. It is as if life and death are placed in the hands of the tongue and the wishes of the heart. A common mental phenomenon is the existence of deep guilt feelings resulting from fantasies and wishes that have had no expression in reality. I find it plausible that Tamar harbored certain aggressive wishes toward her father. It is also possible that she felt guilty and deserving of punishment for harboring these wishes. When her father became ill and died, these feelings were greatly aggravated. Reality seemed to prove to her that her wishes held real power. Her anger and her aggressive wishes toward her father were fulfilled and in her mind were the true cause of his death.

I know that these statements are unobjective. I have deviated from a precise analysis of Tamar's tests and, without any concrete evidence, have reached conclusions concerning the inner workings of her mind. I seem to resemble the archeologist who, having exposed the foundations of an ancient building, reconstructs the whole building using not the stones found at the excavation but other stones. I am aware of the fact that the foundations of the building were derived from the analysis of Tamar's tests, but additional bricks came from another source. But sometimes in the process of interpretation it is necessary to use this method, filling in the missing layers of bricks ourselves. I do not fill in these empty spaces haphazardly. I note that Tamar presents the male figure as deformed and then feels guilt and a need to punish herself. Upon learning of her father's death, I allow myself to fill in the gaps with this other brick not directly discovered in Tamar's tests.

There is one more point I have to check within myself: To what extent was my analysis influenced by information previously obtained? I already knew of the death two years earlier of Tamar's father, to whom she had been extremely attached. I also knew that since the death of her father, Tamar's condition had deteriorated. Was I not biased in my analysis? Had I not interpreted Tamar's drawings in the light of what I knew about her? Would I have arrived at the very same conclusions had I not known these facts?

I do my utmost to understand a person's character on the basis of an unbiased impression of her and of her test analysis, and Tamar is no exception. If I have succeeded in being honest with myself, then even my analysis of Tamar's tests thus far have not been prejudiced by prior information. Tamar's inner world could harbor aggressive intentions concerning her father and their ensuing guilt feelings even if he had not died. Only after having analyzed her drawings and stories, only after having learned what occurred in her mind, did I try to link these to the facts of her life.

After drawing the storks, Tamar drew a woman. Judging by this drawing, she sees the female figure as being more stable than the male, stronger than him and even more aggressive. Tamar drew the woman in an upright, sturdy posture and detailed her drawing with accentuated fingers and sharpened fingernails. The woman is even perceived as emphasizing her beauty and femininity: she smiles, her cheeks are high-lighted, and her curly hairstyle is particularly elaborate.

Another question comes to mind at the sight of Tamar's drawing of a woman. Tamar took great efforts in her drawing, detailing each and every curl, yet why did she omit such important and essential features as the pupils of the eyes? This woman's hair is styled, but her eyes are empty. The vacant eyes in the figures of both the man and the woman hint at the difficulties Tamar has in forming social relationships (Machover, 1949). It is as if she avoids looking into people's eyes. It is as if they avoid her, avoid relating to her or leveling their gaze at her. She herself drew a pupil in the stork's eye but left the humans void of expression. A person's eyes are her windows to the world. Through them she acquaints herself with the happenings around her, and with them she expresses her innermost feelings. The eyes are the contact, the silent tie between people and between person and environment. It is this contact that Tamar avoids in her drawings.

It is hard not to be amazed by the significance of this story. Is the storyteller really a 10-year-old girl? Are these her fantasies—of nightlife, a world of cafes, discotheques, temptations, courting, and sexual relations? I would expect to hear this from girls of 16 or 17, but what do they have in common with Tamar?

Were Tamar exceptionally well developed, a girl who matured early both physically and sexually, I could have attributed these imaginings to her physical development and the awakening of her sexual drives. However, Tamar is a slight girl, looking approximately eight years old.

Had Tamar grown up in circumstances in which she was exposed to stimulations of the kind she raised in her story, I would have attributed her words to the traumatic experiences she had assimilated. However, she grew up in a sheltered, conservative, middle-class family; moreover, as previously stated, following the death of her father, her mother refrained from social encounters and entertainment outside of the home and family.

Tamar's preoccupation with the world of nightlife, with the lifestyle of cafes and discotheques and with the constellation of courtships and sexual relations, does not spring, therefore, from a natural physical awakening, nor is it a product of her environment. A certain mental state led her to a preoccupation with these fantasies.

If we pay close attention to Tamar's story, we certainly will hear that the voices emerging from it are not only the voices of sexual drives. They are voices of the desire for contact, of searching for pleasures and joys. It is as if, looming in the background, is a sense of profound loneliness, a feeling of emptiness and deficiency. The man in the story is a man who searches; a man who says, "Maybe you'll come to sleep at my place," a lonely person searching for a living soul. And the young woman is a sort of street person who can be found at a train station, a place we associate with a search for ways or crossroads. That same young woman has no address or home of her own, and, even when she is afraid of the movie or of the man who keeps asking to take her to his home, she does not leave. It is hard to avoid the thought that this young woman, in reality, personifies Tamar herself and her profound feeling of loneliness. She is not willing to abandon the man she found in the street because "he did all she wanted and was her boyfriend" and later "promised to do all she wanted." This, it seems, reflects her desire to find someone who will love her, fulfill her desires, and bring her happiness.

These feelings are not new. The young woman responding to a strange man and clinging to him are like Tamar clinging to me and asking to remain in my room. "Don't want to go home," she said, "I like being here. I want to sleep here." In her talk with me Tamar spoke openly of her sadness, of her feelings that no one loves her. When she drew people, she drew them void of expression. This hunger for warmth and for contact is not a thing to be taken lightly. It affects everything Tamar does—her behavior, her drawings, her stories—and it is obviously very powerful.

However, I have not yet exhausted all that lies hidden behind her story. I have to remember that Tamar's wish for warmth and love was not translated into a story of a boy searching for a mother or a story of a man searching for a home. Her desires were translated into a story of a man searching for a young woman or a young woman searching for a man. In her imagination she sees the source of warmth and support precisely in the male figure and in male–female relationships. These fantasies concerning the relationships between man and woman, the relationships between herself and any man, probably express Tamar's latent desires. She was asked to tell a story about a man, and, without any external provocation, she immediately bound him to a lonely young woman who, according to my interpretation, was none other than Tamar herself.

Time and time again there was evidence of Tamar's tendency to search for intimacy with a man through a deep and complex emotional involvement. The story accompanying the drawing of the man revealed yet another aspect of Tamar's feelings toward the male figure: her desires for physical affinity and for sexual relations with him. "He . . saw a girl and wanted to start up with her, and she also liked him and also wanted to start up with him." Yet, as Tamar's love for the male figure is not unequivocal and includes aggressive intentions toward him, so her desire for sexual relations with him is also not unequivocal. With it are fears of, and aversions toward, such relations. The young woman in her story who submits to the man's temptings seems suddenly frightened of active intimacy with him. At the beginning of the story all the initiative is placed in the hands of the man: He went to the train station; he wanted to start up with her; and he said, "Maybe you'll come to sleep at my place." And yet, at precisely the moment when the relationship seems to reach a climax the initiative passes into the hands of the young woman: "and he did all that she wanted," and so forth.

Tamar seemed suddenly to become frightened of yielding to temptation, of giving in to sexual desires, of a passive submission to a man and to her own desires. Perhaps then she turned the man into one who is passive, weak, and dragged along, while the young woman became the initiator, the active one, the one who dominated and overrode his wishes. "He went with her because he had promised to do all she wanted," and, when he told her that he was tired, she said, "It's not worth leaving. It's better at the discotheque because we have nothing to do at home."

Here, again, emerges an undertone of aggressiveness toward the man and a desire to silence him. Here the meaning of this aggressiveness also becomes more apparent: It is precisely her intense lust and sexual desire for him that have increased her anxiety regarding intimacy and thus aroused her aggressiveness.

Tamar's feelings toward the male figure seem clearer to me now. I may describe them as a sort of chain of emotional events, a chain whose first link is love, attraction, and sexual desire. This is followed by fears and apprehensions of these desires, which in turn generate aggressive intentions toward the man. The last link in the chain reflects her guilt feelings and the need of self-punishment in response to the aggressive wishes. On the basis of our previous observations and deductions as well as inferences from Tamar's own words, it seems reasonable to me that this emotional entanglement reflects none other than the essence of her feelings toward her father.

Tamar remained consistent. Her story about the drawing of the woman is like a repetition and a continuation of her previous story. However, I need not pass over it hastily simply because it is repetitious. It is precisely in these repetitions on the same motif that additional elaborations occasionally surface, presenting new emphasis worthy of consideration. Two motifs were overemphasized in Tamar's second story: the need to disavow her sexual desires and avoid becoming too close to a man, and the sense of loneliness.

In regard to Tamar's apprehension in the face of sexuality, she did not, in this case, permit herself to express even a trace of desire for physical contact with a man. In her former story she did attribute the woman with a will "to start up with" the man, but the fright that overcame her afterward and the tendency to disavow these desires continously increased until, in her second story, she denied them again and again, as if to say, "This drive does not exist within me." It is possible to discern from her words an attitude of moral values stating that physical intimacy with a man is a bad, forbidden deed. She has the woman say, "I'm proud." Although it is not clear whether she uses this word correctly, there is no doubt that it contains for her the connotation of reservation, modesty, and the maintenance of boundaries and distance. It does not seem incidental that Tamar repeated this phrase three times. She needed to say these words over and over again, because she herself did not believe them to be convincing, because she herself was not convinced of their truth. She seemed to try by these repetitions to still the voice of her sexual drives.

The voices of loneliness also were overemphasized in her story about the woman. If in her male-figure story it was possible through deduction to discern her sense of deficiency and loneliness, here she expressed them in a straightforward and unequivocal manner: "Nobody loved" the woman in the story. "Her parents didn't love her, and she remained alone." This is not a woman at all. This is a homeless girl, lacking parental love, who is searching for support and warmth. "I simply want to return home," she says to the man she meets. Yet suddenly, she seems to remember that she has no place to return to, that she is not loved in her own home, and so she asks him, a strange man, to serve as a substitute home for her. "If you'll buy me a house or a palace then I'll go out with you." It is specifically a palace that she needs. She is not satisfied with a modest house, since the lack of primary, basic, parental love leaves her hungry and deficient, needing more and more.

It has become increasingly apparent that Tamar suffers from severe emotional deprivation. The voices that burst forth from her throat are like those of a homeless, orphaned girl raised in institutions. Her parents' physical presence was not sustained in her mind as being beneficial, warm, or accepting. Her primary relations with them did not provide her with a loved child's feeling of security, but rather with a sense of inadequacy, loss, and lovelessness. These are not problems that can be dismissed easily. They envelop her whole being, influencing her sense of self, her perception of the world, and her contacts with her environment. They also arouse within me a great deal of concern for her fate if she does not receive immediate help. This hunger for love may drive her again and again to search for love substitutes—to vagrancy, addiction, or prostitution.

Tamar's Story for TAT Card 1

The story began, "A boy went into his room and saw a present on the table." If I had tried to guess the continuation to this opening sentence, I probably would have thought that the boy would be curious or surprised. I certainly would have told of the boy's joy, of his impatience to discover what the present contained or from whom it came, for a present is a gesture of good will, of attention paid, and is pleasant to receive. However, Tamar continued her story differently. The boy in her story did not rejoice in the present. He was shocked, alarmed, perplexed, and, in the end, he went "and threw it somewhere."

Tamar did not explain, at this stage, why the boy threw out the present, yet even without an offer of an explanation, I can conclude that she spoke in her story of a boy with an impaired relationship with his parents. He was unwilling to receive their present, perhaps being suspicious of them and not trusting the integrity of their intentions and the nature of their generosity. Perhaps he was angry at them and by throwing out their present intended to insult them: I'll have none of your honey and none of your sting.

Upon being asked the meaning of the act, Tamar answered that the boy thought it was a bomb. This boy was so suspicious of his parents, was so lacking in trust for their feelings toward him, that he was capable of believing that they cunningly would present him with a gift containing explosives. He saw his parents as enemies who wished to annihilate him.

Tamar's thoughts concerning the relationship between the boy and his parents serve as added verification of my previous observations. I had found that her primary relations with her parents did not provide her with a sense of security as a loved daughter, but rather with a feeling of inadequacy, loss, and lovelessness. Her latest story added yet another dimension. She perceived her parents not only as neglecting and unloving, but also as hateful, aggressive, cunning, and dangerous.

I have to take into consideration the reality of Tamar's life. Tamar lived in Jerusalem at a time when bombs were occasionally discovered and the public was called upon to be alert to the presence of suspicious objects. Therefore, it is conceivable that the bomb that was introduced into her story was borrowed from real-life situations that justifiably aroused her anxiety. Indeed, it does seem plausible to me that the idea of the bomb was derived from the reality of her life; however, this does explain why she spoke of throwing away the present, even before she mentioned the bomb.

The boy in the story throws away the present without accounting to himself the precise reasons for this action; it suffices that if the present was given to him by his parents it was something that should be thrown away. Thus, even without the subsequent addition of the bomb theme, it is possible to conclude that, hidden behind Tamar's story, is a distrust of the integrity of the parents' intentions. Moreover, even if her concern about bombs is taken from real life, only if she were actually suspicious of her parents and attributed to them malicious intentions toward her would she translate the call for greater alertness in the street to a call for greater alertness toward her parents and the occurrences in her own home.

Furthermore, this particular TAT picture, a picture of a boy with a violin, usually elicits stories that deal with achievement, motivation, the will to succeed, or the struggle to overcome hardships (Henry, 1956; Rapaport et al., 1968). None of these themes appeared in Tamar's story, for how could her mind be free to relate to issues of learning, achievement, and success when she lacked such basic items as warmth and love?

Tamar's Story for TAT Card 18GF

The aggressiveness erupting in this story is not incidental; it is not merely a figment of Tamar's imagination. The woman whose face can be seen clearly is usually perceived as a strong figure, dominating or bad. The interaction between the women in this picture usually inspires stories of antagonistic relationships (Henry, 1956; Rapaport et al., 1968). Nevertheless, Tamar's story deviated from conventional responses to this picture. The magnitude of aggressiveness that arose in her story was, without a doubt, much more extreme and exaggerated than expected. The force of the aggression and its causes came from Tamar's own inner world.

The stronger woman appeared in her story as a witch—a stereotype of that which is evil, black, and frightening. She hated the girl and because of her jealousy wanted to destroy her. The girl's aggression toward the witch was also very forceful and unrestrained. With a great deal of pleasure and in cruel detail, Tamar told how the old woman was murdered: "He heated up water and burned her head. Her brain exploded." Tamar's feelings toward the female figure and the relations between women as expressed in this story are those of envy, hate, and destructive aggressiveness.

Whom do these two women in her story represent? It may be assumed that the girl in the story represents Tamar herself, for she was designated by Tamar "a girl," despite the fact that in the stimulus picture she appears as a woman. By describing her as a girl it is as if Tamar brought her close to herself. As the story continued, I sensed that Tamar identified with her, desired her welfare, and fought her battles.

The witch, envious of the girl, hating her, and plotting to remove her from the world, was of another, older generation. She was somehow involved in the girl's life, observed her movements, and was part of her environment. Only after they killed her were they "alone without the witch." These "identifying details" about the witch suggest the hypothesis that this is none other than Tamar's representation of the mother figure. Tamar sees her mother as a rival for the male figure, as jealous of her, and hating her so much that she wishes to remove her from the world.

It cannot be assumed, of course, that this rivalry between Tamar and her mother over the male figure does in fact exist. It is not even possible to assume that Tamar encountered, in any form whatsoever, a hostile attitude on her mother's part toward a young man she loved, for the subject in question is not an adolescent girl who forms romantic ties with young men, as Tamar is only 10 years old. It is possible, therefore, to hypothesize that the male figure that appears in her story is the only significant male figure who exists in the world of a 10-year-old girl, the figure of her father. He is the object of her desires, and it is over the exclusiveness of his intimacy that she struggles with her mother.

Tamar's father was not alive at the time she told this story, but stories often express past impressions and relics of experiences, and the web of relationships and feelings that have been stamped into a person's mind become a part of her. In this story, Tamar expressed a familiar conflict in the minds of four- and five-year-old girls, namely, the awakening of the sexual drive toward the father, rivalry with the mother for exclusive intimacy with him, and aggressive intentions toward the mother. However, the forcefulness of her expressed aggressiveness greatly exceeds the expected, and had her emotional development been normal, this oedipal conflict would have subsided or would have been resolved long ago.

Actually, certain indications of this web of relations could be found in

Tamar's former tests, especially the flower inside the heart, which was related to the father figure or the wish for intimacy with the male figure who appeared in her stories accompanying the drawings. However, these indications are partial: I have not yet ascertained the mother's place in the family network, or Tamar's feelings toward her.

Tamar's Story for TAT Card 7GF

Tamar did not use the picture in front of her as a framework for the story. It served as a stimulus from which she went on into a story of her own. She did not describe what was happening in the picture, but rather what it aroused within her in relation to the portrayed figures of the mother, daughter, and baby. While the content of the previous picture could provoke a story of hostile relations, this picture contained no such provocation. Nonetheless, Tamar once more created a full drama of hostile relations, struggles, and rivalry between mother and daughter which provides positive support to my hypothesis concerning Tamar's feelings toward her mother.

The focus of the struggle between mother and daughter is the baby. Both loved him: the mother who feared for him and tried to protect him from all evil and "the girl who loved him very much." Each one used force and cunning in her struggle for exclusive relations with him; the mother hiding the baby from the girl, and the girl running away with him. In the picture itself these three figures appear together, close to one another, but Tamar seems unable to build a story on this shared presence. In her world this situation is only momentary and cannot continue, due to the fierce rivalry between the mother and her daughter. "This one says he's mine and that one says he's mine. . . ."

In one way, the parallel between this story and Tamar's previous story is self-evident: Two people, a mother and her daughter, struggle over one male figure. Yet, is the parallel really so clear? In her response to the first picture, the struggle between two women was over a young man, while in this story they struggle over a baby. Is the love of a woman for a man really comparable to the love of a mother for her son? Is it possible to interchange the women's struggle over a man with their struggle over a small baby?

It is indeed true that the bone of contention between the two women is not exactly the same in both stories. However, while searching for a person's personality traits, for similar motifs that are threaded through his stories and tests, one has to distinguish between what is significant and what is not. The very same theme may be expressed in various ways and forms. One must try to identify the theme that is hidden beneath changing external masks. It appears to me that the difference between

Tamar's two stories is only superficial, a difference of plot details. The underlying theme, with its web of relations and emotions, is identical in both stories. In both, Tamar spoke of women separated by age (an old woman and a girl; mother and daughter) who, despite the difference in their ages, contend over the same love object. This love object is the source of their envy, hatred, and fierce aggressiveness toward each other.

I interpreted Tamar's story in response to picture 18GF as an expression of her inner struggle with her mother over her father, and I interpret similarly her story about picture 7GF. In one picture the father assumed the form of a boyfriend and in the other the form of a baby.

In order to be stringent with myself, I have to ask myself another question: Had I heard only Tamar's story about picture 7GF, would I have reached these same conclusions? Is not my analysis influenced by what I heard from her previously, from her response to the preceding picture (18GF)? Had I not heard Tamar's story about picture 18GF, I still would have been cognizant of the hostility between her and her mother, of the struggle and fierce aggressiveness between them, yet it is doubtful that I would have interpreted her desire for intimacy and possessiveness over the baby as an expression of a desire for intimacy with the husband–father figure. This interpretation certainly is influenced by Tamar's first story; however, there is nothing wrong with this. It is for this reason that I usually administer a complete battery of tests to a person, presenting him with a variety of tasks. By utilizing such a battery of tests I may note the presence of indicators in one or more of the tests that may call attention to more subtle indicators that I might otherwise overlook (Rapaport et al., 1968). The aggressiveness of the girl in Tamar's story is worthy of greater consideration. The girl fights her battle and struggles with her mother, but her aggressiveness, in the end, is not directed only toward her mother. She also directs her aggressiveness toward her love object, toward the baby itself. While, in the end, Tamar said that the baby was "not killed," thoughts of killing the baby emerged in her story: "They . . . thought she killed herself together with the baby in the pool. . . . They found her killed and the baby killed." These thoughts certainly reflect latent wishes within her. Besides a fierce love there also arises within her a fierce aggressiveness. So great was her love and her unwillingness to relinquish the common love object to her mother that she was willing to kill it, as long as it would not belong to her mother.

These aggressive fantasies toward her love object already had been expressed in Tamar's former drawings and her stories of the drawings. I previously described Tamar's feelings toward him as a kind of chain of emotional events: love—lust—fright—anger—remorse. Now, after hearing Tamar's later stories, after witnessing her struggle with her mother, it seems to me that her aggressive wishes toward her father are not just the product of fears and apprehensions over her sexual longings for him, but also a result of an unrestrained jealousy of her mother.

The last link in the chain reflects her guilt feelings and the need for self-punishment in response to her aggressive wishes, and this is confirmed in Tamar's story about the baby. Her aggressiveness is directed toward herself: In the end of the story "they found her killed and the baby . . . no, not killed." In the end, Tamar punished herself, the girl in the story, and allowed the mother to win the battle, leaving the live baby to her. In her fantasy it seems that at the last moment Tamar altered the facts. She cannot alter them in reality. Her father is dead, thus realizing her wishes to take him away from her mother. Unable to bring her father back to life, she lives with her heavy guilt for what she feels she did to her father and mother.

DIAGNOSIS AND TREATMENT

The teacher who referred Tamar for psychological testing wanted to understand the meaning of Tamar's distress and why she seemed "void of all will to live, lacking vitality, and wasting away." Systematically and slowly I traced each of Tamar's footsteps, trying to understand the workings of her mind and the meaning of her distress.

Tamar's distress, I discovered, is weighty and of long standing. Its origin lies not in the death of her father but much earlier. It is not surprising that, even upon entering school, Tamar had learning difficulties and was considered deviant and problematic. From infancy she had not felt warm and loving maternal attention. She did not internalize the sense of security that comes from being rejoiced in and loved. Her childhood experiences left her with an image of an abandoning and neglecting mother; a mother who is bad and full of hatred; a jealous mother, cunning and cruel toward her daughter. Throughout her whole being, Tamar carried within her a sense of emptiness and deprivation, a sense of profound loneliness.

Her father was like a ray of light in her world. To him she directed her hunger for warmth, support, and love; and to him were directed her emerging desires and sexual fantasies. However, as a result of these wishes, Tamar was thrown into a fierce and complex emotional maelstrom: extreme hostility toward her mother and wishes to eliminate her in order to remain alone beside her father; hostility toward her father, her love object, for being her mother's husband; fears of the mother's retribution; fear of her own desires and of her father who is the source of that temptation; and aggressive intentions toward the father and guilt feelings for the existence of these aggressive intentions.

Her father's death increased and complicated Tamar's distress. The person who was near and dear to her disappeared from her world, and her sense of loneliness and yearning for love intensified within her as if she were left homeless and without redress. Following her father's death, her feelings of guilt over her aggressive intentions toward him also intensified. She saw herself as responsible for his death, guilty for what she had done to him and to her mother, and deserving of punishment.

It is no wonder, then, that the teacher's efforts to help Tamar were in vain. Her problems were too deep and complex. In her condition, the teacher's help was like offering a straw to a drowning man. Tamar was in urgent need of psychotherapy. She needed a relationship with a steady, stable, and accepting figure; a relationship through which her profound feeling of loneliness would be relieved and her attitude toward herself and the vision of her world would change. She needed a figure who would enable her to work through her feelings and experiences toward her father and mother, who would help her to rid herself of the guilt feelings she carried within herself and relieve her of her inner need for self-destruction and self-punishment.

Without this type of therapy, Tamar would continue to "waste away" and even degenerate to a hopeless lifestyle containing the elements of a search for love substitutes and degradation and self-destruction.

In a conversation with Tamar's mother one could sense that she had never been conscious of her daughter's needs and problems. For long periods, from the time Tamar was a year old, the mother had worked and was absent for long hours from the home while Tamar suffered from neglect and lack of attention. The father, owing to his work, also was absent from the home for long periods. "She was a daddy's girl," said the mother of Tamar. "He was very attached to her. When she used to wake up at night and find it difficult to fall asleep, I would scream and get angry, but he used to say, 'I'll bring her in to sleep with me.' She always used to run to her father and say, 'Look what Mother does to me.' She was his loved one. Too attached. . . ."

These events are like crumbs of information that anchor the workings of Tamar's mind to the reality of her life. Memories, experiences, and fantasies that emerged during her therapy served to confirm all that was discovered in the tests. At the beginning of the therapeutic relationship, Tamar, directly and indirectly, expressed her desire for a home and for warmth. She could not be content with the limited framework of two weekly hours of therapy. She asked the therapist to be her mother. During this time, she expressed in play and in words her fantasies of a bad witch–mother and her complex feelings toward her father, who took the form of a figure called "Dadu" who lay in wait for her in the streets, threatening to kidnap and do "something" to her. The psychologist who treated

Tamar observed and deciphered these expressions and also responded to
and interpreted them, helping her to understand, work through, and free
herself of these emotions.

CONCLUSION

There is no doubt that the diagnosis was of great aid in understanding
Tamar's problems, suggesting psychotherapy and directing the psycho-
therapist in the treatment given. The process of diagnosing Tamar, like
any process of psychological diagnosis, involved very complex psychological work. It was no less challenging than therapeutic work.

REFERENCES

Benziman, H. (1982). *Out of the maze: Pathways to psychological diagnosis.* (In
    Hebrew). Tel Aviv: Dvir.
Goodenough, F. L. (1975, orig. 1929). *Measurement of intelligence by drawings.*
    New York: Arno Press.
Henry, W. E. (1956). *The analysis of fantasy: Semantic apperception technique in
    the study of personality.* New York: John Wiley.
Machover, K. A. (1949). *Personality projection in the drawing of the human
    figure: A method of personality investigation.* Springfield, IL: Charles C
    Thomas.
Rabin, A. I., & Hayes, D. L. (1978). Concerning the rationale of diagnostic testing.
    In B. Wolman (Ed.), *Clinical diagnosis of mental disorder* (pp. 579-600). New
    York: Plenum Press.
Rapaport, D., Gill, M., & Schafer, R. (1968). *Diagnostic psychological testing*
    (rev. ed.). New York: International Universities Press.
Schafer, R. (1954). *Psychoanalytic interpretation in Rorschach testing.* New York:
    Grune & Stratton.

Subject Index

Author Index

Italicized numbers indicate pages on which references appear.